Essays in Thankfulness for Peter Barnes

Standing *for* Orthodoxy

The Historical Endeavour in the Service of God's People

Brett Lee-Price
Editor

Tulip Publishing
Lansvale, New South Wales, Australia

Standing for Orthodoxy: The Historical Endeavour in the Service of God's People: Essays in Thankfulness for Peter Barnes

Published by Tulip Publishing
PO Box 3150
Lansvale, NSW, Australia 2166

Cover Design and Interior Formatting by 100Covers.

HARDCOVER ISBN: 978-1-922584-13-7
DIGITAL ISBN: 978-1-922584-14-4

Contents

Foreword

Iain. H. Murray

It was a little over forty years ago, in 1979, that I first met the friend who is the occasion of this book. On a first visit to New South Wales, it meant much to be welcomed by the circle of men whose purpose was the renewal of the Presbyterian Church in the power of the word of God and the truths of the Westminster Confession. While the circle had a shared commitment to the literature of the older evangelicalism, the average age was on the younger side, with Peter Barnes, just finishing training for the gospel ministry, among the youngest. Even so, he was the one who was often asked to write upon subjects that arose from time to time.

Since then, we have done a number of things together, from cricket practice in the yard of the manse at Nambucca Heads to sharing in speaking at the same conferences and, in later years, to having been among his hearers on Sunday evenings at Revesby Presbyterian Church. Yet, living ten thousand miles apart for most of these forty years, our chief contact has been in correspondence and reading one another in print. It has been a treasured friendship, deepening with the years and from which I have gained much. All I can do here is to mention features of our friend's life that point to the meaning of a faithful ministry.

It is a ministry that has exemplified what the Puritans called 'practical divinity'. By this, they meant that biblical beliefs and truths are given to us for practice: the practice of living God-wards, loving Him with heart, soul, and mind, and our neighbours as ourselves. A true pastor is not addicted to ideas and detached study; although he needs time alone, his overriding interest is with Christ and his people. The objective is to be useful in a dying world. 'Do you love me?' Christ asks, then 'Feed my sheep' (John 2:16). Life is too short for a pastor to teach his people anything that is not 'for the edifying of the body of Christ'.

So, it is a misreading of the Bible and of history where a genuine 'reformed' pastor is mistaken for an intellectual or an academic. Peter Barnes belongs to the succession of ministers whose ambitions were exemplified by John Dod. On being encouraged at Cambridge as professor of theology at the University of Cambridge to lecture students in Latin, he replied that his choice was to stay where he was and preach to his people in plain English. This was not to disparage knowledge or the instructors of students. An important part of Peter Barnes' life includes lecturing on church history at Christ's College, Sydney, but that is not the chief part. The call to be a pastor and preacher among his people had the uppermost claim. If college ever comes before church and the lecture hall before the pulpit, there is something wrong.

The love the Holy Spirit gives, which precedes practice and usefulness, is always marked by sympathy for people. Christ, anointed by the Spirit, was moved with compassion at the sight of the multitude. The breadth of Peter's interest in people has been present since his early years among Pacific islanders in Vanuatu, as well as his current concern for Muslims in Australia. The ethical issues that prompted him to write on such subjects as education and abortion are another aspect of the same breadth.

The desire for usefulness can bring with it a temptation that may destroy usefulness. The minister needs 'a good report of those that are without', but if a line is crossed which leads to coveting popularity and to having 'all men speak well of you', the long-term effect is akin to building houses on sand. This has been illustrated in recent history. The decline of the church in the English-speaking world came with the introduction of the idea that Christianity would lose its position in the world unless she recognised that influence comes from being in harmony with the spirit of the age. When 'the newest is the truest' is the maxim upheld by current scholars and celebrities, opposition may seem futile. Sometimes, facts may seem to bear that out, and those left to maintain the finality of divine revelation are few. But in the end, truth belonging only to a remnant will prevail. I say, in the end, for in the meantime, it may require faithfulness unto death to withstand a popular tide.

The witness of Peter Barnes has gone around the English-speaking world in his books, editorials and articles. In times when it is more comfortable to stay quiet, he has repeatedly registered protests, his title, *Open Your Mouth for the Dumb,* being only one of the convincing instances. What he has movingly written on Dietrich Bonhoeffer and Paul Schneider—who refused to bow with a majority—reflects a measure of his own experience. 'When Christ calls a man,' wrote Bonhoeffer, 'he bids him come and die'.[1]

Christians are not judges of their own usefulness, and a higher motive is needed to keep gospel ministers from being swayed by considerations of success and popularity. All need grace to remain God-centred and faithful to his word. Trust in the Lord, delight in the Lord, knowing that his 'lovingkindness is better than life'—these are the first and the last lessons in practical divinity. We thank God for the grace our friend and his wife have been given as the guides of others. Let us continue to pray for his ministry, the awakening our generation so sorely needs, and for young men and women who will live the old Presbyterian watchword of glorifying God and enjoying him forever!

Iain H. Murray,
Edinburgh, May 5, 2021

[1] Dietrich Bonhoeffer, *The Cost of Discipleship* (New York, NY: Touchstone, 1995), 89; Also see Peter Barnes, *Lamp Unto My Feet: How God has Used His Word through the Ages* (Christian Focus, 2013), chapters 94–97. If there is a more compelling introduction to Christian history, I do not know it.

Editor's Preface

Brett Lee-Price

Without desiring to venture into a hagiography,. it is difficult to contemplate an individual who has had as much impact on Reformed Christendom in Australia in the last forty years as Peter Barnes. An astute and committed Presbyterian, Peter's work and influence stretch well beyond the structure of Presbyterianism and the geographical boundaries of Australia, as indicated by the range of contributors in this volume.

Peter's life of service has been one of tireless dedication to the Church and theological education. He has served in diverse roles: from the mission field in Vanuatu to rural ministry along the Nambucca River in northern New South Wales. Peter's steadfast commitment to the gospel and his sharp theological mind have left a lasting impact in each of these contexts. Whether as a pastor, a teacher, a historian, a mentor, or a friend, Peter's guiding principle has always been to contend earnestly for the faith once delivered to the saints.

Perhaps one of Peter's most enduring contributions is his work as a historian, undergirded by a deep desire to serve the people of God. He has never viewed history as an end but as a tool to illuminate the present and guide the Church forward. Subsequently, his prolific writings have spanned topics from the early church to contemporary theological issues. His biography of Athanasius, *Athanasius: His Life and Impact,* perfectly illustrates this approach. In this work, Peter does not merely recount the story of the 4th-century bishop's defence of Trinitarian orthodoxy; he brings Athanasius' life and theology to bear on contemporary issues, showing the ongoing relevance of historical theology for the modern Church. This volume and many others demonstrate Peter's deep conviction that history when rightly understood, is indispensable for the health and vitality of God's people.

This same concern has been evident in Peter's teaching and his broader involvement in Reformed theological education. As an adjunct lecturer at Christ College in Sydney, where he has taught Church History for four decades, Peter has been instrumental in training a generation of pastors and church leaders. His former students, many of whom are now in ministry themselves, often speak of his profound impact on their understanding of history and theology and their personal formation in the faith. His passion for history and its applicability for the church today also fuelled his ThD research, which focused on the rise of liberal evangelicalism in the Presbyterian Church of New South Wales between 1865 and 1915. This work is emblematic of his career-long endeavour: to resist theological drift and maintain the Church's adherence to historical, biblical orthodoxy. His analysis of this period has been invaluable in understanding the shifts within Australian Protestantism and has warned subsequent generations about the dangers of theological liberalism.

Alongside his academic and pastoral work, Peter has been a prolific writer and editor. As the editor of the *Australian Presbyterian* magazine, he has shaped much of the theological discourse within Australian Presbyterianism over the last several decades. His editorials, articles, and reviews have guided, challenged, and encouraged readers across Australia as he challenges them to remain faithful to their Reformed heritage. Having written extensively on topics ranging from Reformation theology to contemporary church issues, Peter's firm commitment to the authority of Scripture and the centrality of the gospel is evident. However, his influence is not confined to Australia; it extends to the broader Reformed world. His works are distributed internationally, and his reputation as a scholar and pastor has garnered him invitations to speak and teach in numerous contexts beyond Australia.

It could not go without saying that Peter has also been a steadfast advocate for the unborn. As president of *Evangelicals for Life,* he has passionately defended the sanctity of life from conception, urging Christians to be a voice for the voiceless, a theme echoed in his booklet *Abortion: Open Your Mouth for the Dumb.* His work with *Hope House* further reflects his commitment to providing theological and practical support to women facing unplanned pregnancies. Through these efforts, Peter has mobilised Australian Christians to uphold the dignity of human life and stand against the dehumanising practices of abortion while also caring for the deep emotional and spiritual pain that women often experience.

This volume, *Standing for Orthodoxy: The Historical Endeavour in the Service of God's* People, brings together essays from scholars, pastors, and church leaders who share a common admiration for Peter's work. Peter's ministry has personally touched each contributor, whether as a student, a fellow pastor, or a reader of his books. The essays in this volume cover a diverse range of topics—church history, theology, pastoral care, and more—all areas in which Peter has made significant contributions.

As we look back on Peter's life and ministry, it becomes clear that his impact on the Church has been immense. Whether through his pastoral work, academic contributions, or involvement in theological education, Peter has been a steadfast defender of Reformed orthodoxy. He has resisted the tide of theological liberalism, always pointing the Church back to its biblical and historical foundations. His work has not only strengthened the Presbyterian Church in Australia but has also had a considerable impact on other Reformed traditions, least of all the burgeoning Reformed Baptist movement, which has significantly benefited from his scholarship, pastoral wisdom, and friendship.

This volume is a testament to Peter's enduring legacy, which will undoubtedly continue to shape Reformed Christendom in Australia and beyond for many years to come. Long planned but slowly executed, this volume was initially intended to have been released at a point which then became the global pandemic that impacted the world between 2020 and 2021. Nevertheless, the delay has allowed us to take a broader view of Peter's life and ministry, with his retirement from the ministry at Revesby Presbyterian Church in 2022 and the conclusion of his tenure as Moderator-General of the Presbyterian Church of Australia, a role he held from 2019 to 2023.

It is appropriate to close this preface by reflecting on Peter's humility and his consistent refusal to seek recognition or accolades for his work. Those who know him well will attest to his aversion to the spotlight. Yet, it is precisely this humility that has made him such an effective pastor, teacher, and scholar. Peter's life has been one of quiet, faithful service to Christ and His Church, and it is fitting that this volume is dedicated to him—not to elevate Peter Barnes, the man, but to honour the God whom he has faithfully served.

It would equally be remiss not to recognise the indispensable support of Peter's wife, Lyn. Her steadfast love and encouragement have been foundational to Peter's work. Much of what he achieved would have been possible without her unwavering partnership. Together, their shared devotion to Christ and His Church has borne much fruit, and it is fitting to acknowledge Lyn alongside Peter in this dedication.

In the end, however, this festschrift is not just a tribute to Peter Barnes but to the work of God in and through his life. We pray that this volume will serve as a fitting reflection of Peter's lifelong commitment to the Church and the gospel and that it will encourage others to follow in his footsteps as faithful servants of Christ.

Brett Lee-Price,

Sydney, November 14, 2024

Peter Barnes: A Biography

Graham Barnes

I am grateful to be able to write this chapter on Peter Barnes's life. I am his second oldest child, Graham, and we are six siblings in total.

Several years ago, I saw a quote from Richard Gregory, one-time editor of the scientific magazine *Nature.* He said, 'My grandfather preached the gospel of Christ, my father the gospel of socialism. I preach the gospel of science.' In some ways it reminds me of Dad's family, only the order is different. I have heard that Dad's grandfather was a union man with explicit political opinions. Dad's father was a scientist; a chemical engineer. Dad was a historian and teacher; he then became a Christian, a pastor, and a preacher of the gospel of Jesus Christ. He would wholeheartedly agree with Martyn Lloyd-Jones, 'I gave up nothing; I received everything. I count it the highest honour that God can confer on any man to call him to be a herald of the gospel.'[1] A pastor has been given the highest honour:

'...publish abroad his wonderful name;
the name all-victorious of Jesus extol;
his kingdom is glorious and rules over all.'

Yet, even before the honour of proclaiming Christ, there is the joy of being a Christian and belonging to Christ Jesus, my Lord and Saviour.

Based on my knowledge, below is a short background of Dad's life.

---

[1] Iain H. Murray, *David Martyn Lloyd-jones: The First Forty Years, 1899–1939* (Edinburgh: Banner of Truth Trust, 1982), 150.

Early Life

Dad was born in Bega in 1953. His early years were primarily spent in the Western Sydney suburb of Merrylands before his family moved to the beaches of Cronulla while he was still reasonably young. Dad said that his family was on the fringe of the local Presbyterian Church; however, the gospel was sadly weak, if at all. Ten-minute pep talks were the standard for preaching. As a teenager, Dad began reading the bible but struggled to understand it, and the minister was little to no help.

Dad went to Caringbah High School and after leaving school, he studied history at Sydney University, including an Honours year. He said his lecturers fell into two categories: those with Marxist leanings and 'the others'. The difference was that those with Marxist leanings saw purpose and reason in history, while 'the others' were empty. At this time, he started to realise that there must be a third way. After graduation, he became a teacher and liked teaching *Animal Farm* by George Orwell. Several years later, Dad received a letter from a former Year 9 student who in school had announced that he was a communist and was particularly obnoxious. The letter announced that he had gone to a church and found Christ.

The Beginnings of God's Grace

Dad and Mum met at Sydney University and were married in 1976 in Kingsgrove Catholic Church. Mum was a primary school teacher and they initially lived in Kingsgrove above the chocolate factory that Mum's family owned. Around this time, Dad thought he would improve his teaching if he studied some church history, so he enrolled in the Bachelor of Divinity course at Sydney University. It was theologically liberal. The resurrection of Jesus Christ was anything but historical and meaningful. Dad mentioned that he could only think of a single lecturer, and a part-time lecturer at that, who he thought believed the Bible.

Yet, God, in His goodness, used this situation to bring Dad to Himself. He once said that he always saw atheism as intellectually—and morally—deadening. He saw, too, the foolishness of liberal theology. At the same time, he began attending Hurstville Presbyterian Church, where Graham Miller was pastor. It was there that he said he heard true preaching for the first time, and it was heaven to him.

Dad is well known for his many books and messy study. Around this time, he once had to buy a car part to repair their car, but he passed a bookshop on the way to the wreckers. He never quite made it to the wreckers, but he did return home with a few new books. In God's grace, it was the Book of Romans and Augustine of Hippo that particularly impacted upon him.

I remember him once saying that until this time, he thought the church was simply another kind of club, only it was a club for people who were a little religiously minded. The church was nothing more than that. But all that changed when he came to faith in Christ Jesus. He realised that the church is God's people, redeemed and chosen, washed clean, coming to worship Him. He now realised the Divine foundations of the church.

Later, Mum said that this was a particularly difficult time for them in their marriage, because Dad was now a Christian and she wasn't. This situation continued for almost a year and then Mum too was converted, suprisingly, at a Catholic retreat.

Vanuatu

Having become a Christian, Dad tried to switch to Moore College, just down the road from Sydney University, but they wouldn't recognise the subjects he had studied as part of the Bachelor of Divinity at Sydney University. And so he continued at Sydney University and was ordained a Presbyterian minister at Como Presbyterian Church.

At one point Mum and Dad considered moving to Tamworth, NSW, but in the end, and I'm sure it was with the encouragement of Graham Miller, they went to Vanuatu instead. Vanuatu was called the New Hebrides up until that time. From 1980 to 1983, Dad taught Church History at the Presbyterian Bible College in Vanuatu on the island of Santo. He later completed research on John Geddie, one of the early Presbyterian missionaries to the New Hebrides. My older brother and I were born during this time. Dad has always had a well-deserved reputation for being useless with anything practical. But he is adamant that he built a chook house door in Vanuatu that somehow survived a cyclone.

Nambucca

In 1983, Mum and Dad moved to Macksville on the NSW mid-north coast, and from that time until the end of 1999, Dad pastored Nambucca River Presbyterian Church. This included helping to establish the Nambucca Valley Christian Community School. Dad's view on Christian schooling is that it doesn't replace Christian parents—theirs is the God-given, covenant task of raising their children to know the Lord—but it is to be an extension of the home. It was during these years that Dad wrote a musical for *The Lion, the Witch and the Wardrobe,* which the school performed.

In the mid-1990s, the NSW government outlawed the use of corporal punishment at schools. Dad and the school dug their heels in. The Proverbs speak about the rod of correction and a Christian school should have the right to discipline the children in its care as the parents see fit. Ultimately, the school was threatened with fines and closure and had to give in to continue operating.

Dad played squash and tennis when we were growing up. He had a reputation for not leaving anything on the court. He also followed rugby league and always supported the underdog.

Since the mid-1980s, Dad has taught Church History at the Presbyterian Theological Centre in Burwood, Sydney, now called Christ College. He used to catch the bus down to Sydney and back, 8 hours in each direction, in order to lecture. He once was so tired that he fell asleep giving the lecture! Yet, he has always been a pastor first and a lecturer second. He would never dare separate the task of lecturing from the call to pastor. He completed a ThD entitled *Living in a Halfway House: The Rise of Liberal Evangelicalism in the Presbyterian Church of NSW between 1865 and 1915.*

Revesby

At the start of 2000, Mum and Dad moved to Revesby Presbyterian Church in the southwest suburbs of Sydney. Dad has been involved in many things. He helped set up *Evangelicals for Life* and has supported other pro-life causes. He continued to teach church history at the Presbyterian College in Burwood. He preached each Lord's Day, morning and evening. In the local community, Dad has maintained friendships with several Muslim men, which has led to good conversations and opportunities to point them to Jesus, the Son of God. Yet, apart from worship on the Lord's Day, I think that the highlight of his week was teaching Scripture at the local Primary schools, including a class of children with severe disabilities. He would sing Christian songs to them week by week. However, there was one week where one of the students had died and although the other students in the class couldn't express it verbally, they all felt the loss of their classmate. There was sadness about the class, and Dad said it was one of the most moving times he had known. He sang *Jesus loves me this I know* to them. The following week, he had the same class, but in the course of the lesson, one student vomited, chaos ensued, and another student, who happened to be blind, groping around on the floor, found Dad's leg and bit him. Unperturbed, Dad continued playing the guitar.

Dad has a unique musicality and ability to write lyrics for every occasion. Recently, having given Mum three bags of manure for the garden as a Mother's Day present, he then went on to pen what Mum called a 'romantic serenade';

For Mother's Day, here's something unique,
Of which you may be reluctant to speak,
Some give flowers or a bottle of wine,
And in their own way, I suppose that is fine.
But you have something of which you can boast,
To show other mothers that you are the most,
Others have speeches and songs to be sung,
But you have for your garden, three bags of dung!

Dad's only comment was, 'Sung right, it can bring tears to one's eyes.'

In 2019, he was elected Moderator of the Presbyterian Church of Australia, preaching on Isaiah's vision of the valley of dry bones coming to life (Ezekiel 37).

In 2022, Dad finished, after 22 years, as pastor at Revesby Presbyterian Church. However, the year had also been a sad and difficult year, with the death of their granddaughter, Emily, aged 5 years old, from a brain tumour. Dad said, 'Nothing has hurt as this hurt and continues to hurt.' It is our hope in the Lord that sustains us.

Conclusion

The following are a few thoughts and observations on Dad, in particular his theological convictions and understanding of things. He would be much better at writing this than I am, but nonetheless, I hope these are accurate enough:

- **Reformed, evangelical, conviction:** God's grace must be electing grace in order for it to be truly gracious. Yet, a baby must learn to crawl before it can walk, and the first step is to know repentance, faith, and Christ as Lord before we go on to the great truths of predestination and God's providence.
- **A little deviation in truth, is a terrible thing:** We are to contend earnestly for the faith once and for all delivered to the saints (Jude 3). Dad would agree with J. Gresham Machen's statement, 'One wobbly evangelical often does more harm to the cause of the gospel and leads more of Christ's little ones astray than a dozen Modernists.'[2] A pastor tackles every issue in light of the Scriptures and following much prayer. We are to bring the Word of God to all people, whatever their background, seeking that God will work through His Word by His Spirit. Dad has persevered in bringing God's Word moment by moment and has not grown weary of doing good.
- **Sanctification takes time, and so we must be patient:** God's word is to form every conviction, yet we are to be loving

[2] J. Gresham Machen, 'Notes on Biblical Exposition,' Christianity Today 3:4 (1932), 12.

and gentle with people. God will complete the good work that has begun within us.

We don't often write down prayers to God, but it would be the best way to finish this introduction to Dad's life by praying for him;

Gracious God and Heavenly Father,

The heavens declare Your glory and You have made us in Your image to know You. Your Kingdom will never end and Your Word is true in every generation. Lord, renew our strength today in You, give us a new song of praise to You for You are our Great God. We thank You that You spoke and brought into being all of creation.

Father, forgive our stubbornness and our sinful, stiff-necked natures towards You. Our sinfulness runs deeper than we know.

We thank You for our Saviour's death on the cross and the perfect atonement He paid for His people. Thank You that He is now risen to life, never to die again and that life has meaning and purpose because He is alive.

Thank you that the Holy Spirit brings life to dead bones and blows like the wind through a field, bringing life. Thank You for Your grace in bringing Dad and Mum to faith in Christ Jesus.

We thank You that Dad can properly say with Paul and every other believer, 'I count everything as loss because of the surpassing worth of knowing Christ Jesus my Lord.'

We thank You for the example of faithful believers who have gone before us. Now, especially, we thank You for Dad's many hours of study, work and labouring over Your Word that he has done in order to know You and to feed Your people.

We thank You for his many hours of prayer—wrestling in prayer—for people and situations. Thank You that Dad has not trifled with truth and that he has sought to make best use of the time that You have given him.

We thank You that You have given him a mind, mouth and skill to praise You.

We thank You that the gospel that we believe transforms us and conforms us more and more into Your image.

We thank You for the people whom have helped to sharpen Dad—elders pastors and other believers. Thank You, above all, for Mum.

In the years ahead, please give Dad a double portion of Your wisdom and a sharper knowledge of You. Grow his love for You and trust in You.

Fit him for every battle that is ahead. Fit him too, with a sense of heaven and let that encourage and strengthen him.

Fill him again and again with Your Spirit. Let him know more and more Your glory. To pray as John did about Jesus, 'He must increase, and I must decrease.' To grow in the grace and knowledge of our Lord and Saviour Jesus Christ.

And now to the King Eternal, immortal, invisible, the only God—Father, Son and Spirit—the True and Living God—be all honour and glory and praise, now and forever. In our Saviour's Name we pray, Amen.

Part 1
The Outworking in Pastoral Theology

One

Keeping the Faith in Pastoral Care

David A. Burke

Introduction

In 1911, Dean Inge cautioned that 'if you marry the spirit of your own generation you will be a widow in the next.'[1] This is a warning to be wary of embracing the fads of the moment. An historical perspective enables us to see today's fads more clearly and then to refer to the Scriptures and the great tradition of the church (in the best sense of that term) to evaluate those fads through the lens of Scripture.

This is certainly true when it comes to pastoral care. The nature of pastoral care, its foundational assumptions, and its methods have varied over time and have sometimes become hostage to the fads of the day. By bringing an historical lens to pastoral care, we gain perspective on the fads of our day and can test and reform them in keeping with the faith once for all delivered to the saints. The past has much to teach the present when it comes to pastoral caregiving.

This chapter lays biblical and theological foundations, sketches the present scene in pastoral care, considers some historical examples, and draws some conclusions. It demonstrates that historical perspectives are useful in informing pastoral care and pushing back against both the present captivity of pastoral care by the social sciences and the reduction of pastoral care to discipleship (as narrowly conceived).

The following is used as a working definition of pastoral care and is discussed later: *Pastoral care is an intentional activity designed to address the holistic needs of people in ways that promote their growth into and in Christ.*

[1] 'If You Marry the Spirit of Your Own Generation You Will Be a Widow in the Next,' *Quote Investigator*, 16 February 2019, accessed 12 May 2020, https://quoteinvestigator.com/2019/02/16/spirit/

The Lord Is My Shepherd

Any understanding of the work of pastoral care should be set in the foundational context of the Lord's care for His people and his delegation of their care to his appointed leaders. Shepherd imagery is key to this.

The representation of God as Shepherd is widespread in the scriptures, hence the dying Jacob who testified of 'the God who has been my shepherd all my life long to this day' (Gen. 48:15).[2] At the other end of the scriptures, Peter speaks of Christ as the 'chief Shepherd' who will confer the crown of glory at his appearing (1 Pet. 5:4) and Revelation speaks of the Lamb who 'will be their shepherd' (Rev. 7:17). Timothy Laniak shows how the identification of the Lord as Shepherd is fundamental to his self-revelation and to leadership among his people.[3]

Psalm 23 speaks of the Lord as the Shepherd who feeds his people (Psalm 23:2), who leads them both in this life and into eternity (Psalm 23:3b, 5–6), and who cares for them in multiple ways (Psalm 23: 3a, 4). His shepherding is of such sufficiency that nothing is needed beyond it: 'The Lord is my shepherd; I shall not want' (Psalm 23:1). Here is a foundation of biblical pastoral care—it rests on, and points to, the Lord as the one whose care is sufficient for his people's needs.

The revelation of Jesus as the Good, Great, and Chief Shepherd (John 10:14; Heb. 13:20; 1 Pet. 5:4) brings this biblical theme to its climax. He is the Shepherd in whom the sufficiency of the Lord's care for his people comes to its fullest and final revelation.

The long-standing description of the threefold offices of Christ as Prophet, Priest and King can be related to his identity as Shepherd.[4] In

---

[2] Unless otherwise noted, biblical quotations in this chapter are from the ESV.

[3] Timothy Laniak, *Shepherds After My Own Heart: Pastoral Traditions and Leadership in the Bible*, New Studies in Biblical Theology (Downers Grove, IL: IVP Academic, 2006)

[4] See John Calvin, *The Institutes of the Christian Religion*, ed. John T. McNeill and trans. Ford Lewis Battles (Philadelphia, PA: Westminster Press, 1960), Vol. 2.Ch. 15, for the classic Reformed statement of the threefold offices. Also see the following: Westminster Larger Catechism, Questions 23–26; Wayne Grudem, *Systematic Theology: An Introduction to Biblical Doctrine* (Grand Rapids, MI: Zondervan, 1994), chapter 29; Michael Horton, *The Christian Faith: A Systematic Theology for Pilgrims on the Way* (Grand Rapids, MI: Zondervan Academic, 2011), Ch. 15. This view of the threefold offices may be foreshadowed by the fourth-century church historian Eusebius of Caesarea who refers to

his prophetic role, he is the Shepherd who feeds his people with his Word of revelation. As Priest, he is the Shepherd who brings the Father's mercy, both in the temporal sense of feeding, healing, and suchlike and in the redemptive role of his atonement. As King, he is the Shepherd who ushers in the Father's kingdom and who is the Way or Door through which his people enter it. As the Shepherd-King, he is the *way*; as the Shepherd-Prophet, he is the *truth*; and as the Shepherd-Priest, he is the *life* (John 14:6).

Church Leaders—Undershepherds of the Lord Who Cares for His People

Scripture applies the shepherd imagery of the Lord to the leaders of his people. This is true for the Old Testament[5] (e.g., Psalm 78:70–72; Ezek. 34). It is also explicitly stated for leaders of the New Testament church.[6]

Thus, Paul urged the Ephesian elders to 'Pay careful attention to yourselves and to all the flock, of which the Holy Spirit has made you overseers, to care for the church of God' (Acts 20:28).[7] Shepherd imagery also appears in the next verse as Paul speaks of fierce wolves coming among the flock (Acts 20:29). In his letter to Ephesus, he refers to the offices given to the church by its ascended Lord, including 'the shepherds and teachers' (Eph. 4:11).[8]

The Apostle Peter, who had received more than a small portion of the Lord's shepherding care, wrote to his 'fellow elders' urging them to 'shepherd the flock of God that is among you' (1 Pet. 5:1–2) and then connects their faithful labours to the reward that the 'chief Shepherd'

'Christ . . . who is the only high priest of all, and the only king of every creature, and the Father's only supreme prophet of prophets' (Eusebius of Caesarea, 'Ecclesiastical History,' in *Nicene and Post-Nicene Fathers, Second Series,* ed. Philip Schaff (Grand Rapids, MI: Eerdmans, 1982), 1:86).

[5] Laniak, *Shepherds After* My Own Heart, chapters 4–9.

[6] Tim Witmer builds on Laniak's work in a detailed and practical discussion of how the shepherding functions work out in the daily life of the church (Timothy Z. Witmer, *The Shepherd Leader: Achieving Effective Shepherding in Your Church* (Phillipsburg, NJ: P & R Publishing, 2010).

[7] 'Care' (ESV) is a translation of ποιμαίνειν, 'to shepherd.'

[8] The debate as to whether 'shepherds and teachers' are one office or two separate ones is outside the scope of present concern.

will give them (1 Pet. 5:4). In calling them his 'fellow elders' he links his apostolic office and a shared identity and function as shepherds to the office of elder.

We can, therefore, trace a direct line from the Lord's shepherding of his people to the identity and functions of church leaders, ranging from the function of apostles to that of elders. As shepherds, these leaders are to follow the Lord's example by feeding his people with his Word, leading them in his kingdom ways, and caring for them as an extension of his mercy.[9] As undershepherds, they are to do all this on his behalf, under his rule, and for his glory. As Tidball summarises: 'God the shepherd defines the relationship and function of the pastor to his flock.'[10]

Of course, it must be said, and repeated, that there is a uniqueness about Jesus' shepherding role as Prophet, Priest and King that is not shared with church leaders. He is *the* full and final revelation of God. Leaders with word ministries are but witnesses and preacher-teachers of that revelation. He is *the* Priest who makes the one-for-all, once-and-for-all atoning sacrifice of which Christian ministries of care are but a shadow. And he is *the* King and Lord over the church of whom church leaders are only delegates. Our ministries of word, care, and rule arise from, depend on, and reflect his roles without in any way replacing them or standing in their stead.

The ministry of pastoral care nests within this discussion of the biblical shepherd's role. It is a key aspect of church life and a key responsibility of church leaders. As leaders exercise pastoral care, they enter the Lord's work of shepherding his people. *Christian* pastoral care will always be grounded in the Lord's shepherding care for his people and in his Word. To neglect pastoral care is to neglect a key part of the shepherd's calling. Likewise, if we detach the nature, means, and

---

[9] Edmund Clowney presents a developed discussion of how these three functions manifest in the structures of the church within a three-fold view of office(Edmund Clowney, *The Church,* Contours of Christian Theology (Downers Grove, IL: IVP Academic, 1995), Ch. 14). I question his separation of the three functions of feed, lead, and care to pastors, elders, and deacons respectively and prefer to see these functions as interlocked and as distinct emphases of each of the three offices.

[10] Derek Tidball, *Skilful Shepherds: An Introduction to Pastoral Theology* (Grand Rapids, MI: Zondervan, 1986), 33.

ends of pastoral care from the Lord and his Word, it ceases to be *Christian* pastoral care. Such neglect and detachment have both happened in church history and are dangers in the contemporary scene.

Pastoral Care in Contemporary Perspective

Consider these three pastors.

- *Pastor Henry* made pastoral care a high diary priority, often at cost to working on his sermons. If someone were sick, Henry would be at the bedside with a soothing presence, whatever the hour. He would ask who needed to be phoned and what needed attending to. Likewise, in his welcome visits to the list of shut-ins in the churches he led, people were glad when he dropped by with a listening ear and a calming presence. He and his wife occasionally had lost souls stay over in their house, and Henry was ready with a helping hand to anyone who knocked on his door. He saw pastoral care as helping to meet everyday needs in the name of Christ.
- *Pastor John* became interested in counselling while at theological college. After graduation, he took some courses in psychology and counselling at a nearby university and brought them into his pastoral ministry. His focus was therapeutic, and he became skillful at diagnosing mental and emotional disorders and then selecting from a suite of contemporary approaches to address them. In time, he left pastoral ministry to serve in a chaplaincy role with an agency operated by a church that took pride in using the best of the world's wisdom to help people.
- *Pastor Dan* had watched Henry's ministry and dismissed it as a 'well-meant but pointless presence.' As for John, Dan respected his profession of faith but saw him as essentially a secular worker who had lost sight of the gospel. Dan's focus was on gospel discipleship. He organised the church's small groups to be focused on Bible study with sharply personal applications and deep accountability. Group leaders were encouraged to ask how people were going but not to be dis-

> tracted by being caught up in meeting everyday needs. Dan held that, if you helped people grow in Christ, their everyday problems would be a means of personal growth, and he held that their ability to cope with them was a measure of their growth.

These people are, of course, fictional caricatures—*perhaps*. Put together, they represent three contemporary trends in pastoral care in an approximate chronological order.

Pastor Henry's approach has a loving warmth to it, and none of the things he was doing were bad. Rather, there was lot of good in them. His problem was a reduction of pastoral care to mercy ministries focused largely on physical and emotional needs. In short, he was acting as a deacon rather than as a shepherd (Acts 6:1–3).

Pastor John is more problematic. At its worst, his approach represents a Babylonian captivity of pastoral care. His focus is on emotional and mental needs, and his source material is the social sciences rather than the means of grace. His pastoral care menu is largely reduced to psychological therapies with the occasional garnish of a biblical text. He sees people mostly in their mental and emotional identities, into which he merges spiritual matters. Because this is such a common issue in contemporary pastoral care, it is discussed further below.

Pastor Dan represents something of a reaction against both Henry and John. His whole ministry is devoted to presenting people mature in Christ as he helps them grow from fickle spiritual infancy to spiritual adulthood, as represented by likeness to Christ, through the means of grace. Giving attention to everyday needs was never an important end for him, at least not in and of itself, but rather, it was an instrumental opportunity for spiritual growth. There is much good in Dan's approach, especially as compared with Henry and John, but the balance does not seem to be quite right. He has reduced pastoral care to discipleship and sees people somewhat as disembodied souls whose physical, mental, and emotional needs are of lesser significance than their growth in Christ.

Above, I mentioned the Babylonian captivity of pastoral care to the social sciences. Hence Tidball who notes both the post-WWII shift from a focus on pastoral theology as the application of doctrine to a focus on praxis, on the one hand, and the psychological captivity of pastoral care, on the other.[11] Hurding comments on the dominance of secular psychologies and a failure of theological nerve in the present phase of pastoral care, along with the varied Christian responses to this captivity.[12] Purves calls for a return to classical tradition as he observes and bemoans how the contemporary North American pastoral care movement revolves around psychological categories regarding human experience and symbolic interpretations of God where the focus is on questions of meaning , truth, and self-actualisation rather than the re-alisation of God.[13] Lauterbach sees this reliance on the social sciences as coming from a loss of confidence in Scripture, along with the other old sources, and a shift to social sciences for insights into pastoral work such that 'pastors now seek to mimic the esteemed professions of the manager and the therapist.'[14] Several of these writers link the psychological shift in pastoral care to a change in broader pastoral theology from rooting pastoral identity and function in relationships with God and people to rooting pastoral identity and function in techniques and management.[15]

Clebsch and Jaekle represent a push-back against this critique by Purves and Lauterbach. Clebsch and Jaekle claim that 'pastoral care has always utilised current psychologies and produces no unique psychology of its own.' And again: 'In most of the historical epochs of pastoring, nonchurch agencies have devised the theoretical psychologies that pastors employed in their work.'[16] That may be so, but the psychologies historically 'current' did tend to be formed on a biblical and theological base—they may not have come from within the church

---

[11] T. J. Tidball, 'Practical and Pastoral Theology,' in *New Dictionary of Christian Ethics and Pastoral Theology*, eds. David J. Atkinson, et al. (Downers Grove, IL: IVP Academic, 1995), 42–43.

[12] R. F. Hurding, 'Pastoral Care, Counselling, and Psychotherapy,' in *New Dictionary of Christian Ethics and Pastoral Theology*, eds. David J. Atkinson, et al. (Downers Grove, IL: IVP Academic, 80–81.

[13] Andrew Purves, *Pastoral Theology in the Classical Tradition* (Louisville, KY: Westminster John Knox, 2001), 2.

[14] M. Lauterbach, 'Physicians of the Soul' (D. Min diss., Trinity Evangelical Divinity School, 1998, 7–8.

[15] Lauterbach, M. 'Physicians of the Soul,' 6–10.

[16] Clebsch, W. A. and C. R. Jaekle, *Pastoral Care in Historical Perspective: an Essay With Exhibits* (Hoboken, NJ: Prentice-Hall, 1964), 69, 76.

but were developed within a broader Christian intellectual tradition. Note, however, that Clebsch and Jaekle wrote in 1964, before the worst of the captivity to the social sciences was evident, and that they also concede both that pastoral care is presently in transition with 'confusion as to the nature, purpose, and functions of pastoral care,' and that it is marked by 'willingness to experiment with new methods, modes, and techniques.'[17] The source of the confusion that they note may be close at hand!

To observe and lament this Babylonian captivity is not to dismiss the social sciences from having *any* place in helping with understanding and caring for the needs of people. Thus A. A. Hodge comments that 'the book of revelation and the book of nature are both from God' and again 'that the Scripture was not designed either to prevent or to take the place of a scientific understanding of all existing phenomena.'[18] The problem is not in *some* use of the social sciences in pastoral care (for example, to help describe and analyse what is happening in a particular situation) but when social sciences displace Scripture and theology and become a new canon.[19] At that point pastoral care is apt to become people-centred and dedicated to temporal wellness rather than being set in the larger canvas of God and eternal realities. It also ceases to be distinctly *Christian* pastoral care.

The dangers here are twofold. The greater present danger in pastoral care is that which was just mentioned—the replacement of biblical and theological foundations with an essentially anthropocentric approach that is not recognisably Christian. The opposite danger is the refusal to admit any insights from the book of God's world into pastoral care. This latter danger often involves a confusion between the

---

[17] William. A. Clebsch and Charles. R. Jaekle, *Pastoral Care in Historical Perspective* (Lanham, MD: Jason Aronson, Inc., 1975), 76.

[18] A. A. Hodge, *The Confession of Faith: a Handbook of Christian Doctrine* (Philadelphia, PA: Presbyterian Board of Education, 1869; reprint, Edinburgh, Banner of Truth, 1978), 83. These are Hodge's comments on the two books with respect to the biblical teaching on creation and the controversy that erupted just ten years earlier with the publication of Charles Darwin's *The Origin of the Species*. Although they pertain to that specific controversy, his words also make a useful point about wider Christian epistemology.

[19] Thus Lauterbach, who is most critical of the psychological captivity of pastoral care, notes: 'While these have contributions to make to modern soul care, they must not be allowed to become its core.' (M. Lauterbach, 'Physicians of the Soul,' 8).

sufficiency and exhaustiveness of scripture, such that the Bible alone is seen to provide all that is needed at the level of fine detail in understanding and helping people.[20] The latter view is apt to result in the abuse of scripture as its texts are forced into applications that are nonsensical in light of the original context, as well as to confuse the sufficiency and exhaustiveness of scripture. More work is yet needed on this topic!

The late Jay Adams (who died as this chapter was drafted) represented a push-back against the dominance of Christian counselling[21] by psychology in his nouthetic approach, as expressed in his writings and as developed in the Christian Counselling and Educational Foundation (CCEF).[22] While his approach has been critiqued as an example of causal reductionism in his reaction against the dominance of psychology, Adams represents a welcome attempt to recover a consistent biblical and theological approach to counselling.[23]

---

[20] In a recent discussion, a young ministry worker opined that psychology had nothing to add to the Bible in caring for people. The Christian mental health professionals in the room disagreed, as did the theologically trained discussion chair.

[21] In my view, Christian counselling and pastoral care should not be equated, although they do overlap. Christian counselling is a specialised activity with specialised skills and a therapeutic focus. Pastoral caregiving is a broader ministry field focusing on care and discipleship and is best understood through the biblical language of shepherding.

[22] See Jay Adams, *Competent to Counsel* (Grand Rapids, MI: Zondervan, 1986); Jay Adams, *The Christian Counsellor's Manual* (Grand Rapids, MI: Zondervan, 1986); and *A Theology of Christian Counselling* (Grand Rapids, MI: Zondervan, 1986). CCEF can be found athttps://www.ccef.org/

[23] In more recent years CCEF has interacted more positively with social and medical sciences under the leadership of John Bettler and David Powlison (also recently deceased). The following links will help track these developments: Justin Taylor, 'David Powlison (1949–2019),' The Gospel Coalition, 7 June 2019,https://www.thegospelcoalition.org/blogs/justin-taylor/david-powlison-1949–2019/;https://www.ccef.org/wp-content/uploads/2018/08/25-Years-of-Biblical-Counseling-An-Interview-with-Jay-Adams-and-John-Bettler.pdf; Kevin Carson, 'In Memory of Dr. Jay E. Adams: From the Third Generation,' *Kevin Carson: Wisdom for Life in Christ Together*, 15 November 2020,https://kevincarson.com/2020/11/15/in-memory-of-dr-jay-e-adams-from-the-third-generation/.

Escaping the Present Captivity with a Backwards Glance

An historical perspective can help us escape the above captivity. Some of the same writers who observe the dominance of the social sciences in contemporary pastoral care also comment on the lack of historical perspective, which has reached the point of a contemporary amnesia. To cite Purves again:

> The great pastors were theologians, and the great theologians were pastors ...

and

> The classical pastoral writers, in other words, deconstruct our theological subjectivity and its concomitant pastoral subjectivity by insisting on the capacity of Christian doctrine to really talk about God truthfully and the need to guide the souls of the people accordingly.[24]

Lauterbach speaks of how a balanced historical perspective can help avoid the danger of 'an immersion and adaptation to modernity with its endless quest for being up to date.'[25]

The older traditions of pastoral care tended to be shaped by the Bible and theology and were fundamentally theocentric rather than anthropocentric and worked on an eternal horizon rather than a purely temporal one. Of course, these traditions differed, depending on which theological outlook served as their foundation, but they did share a common theocentric foundation. Purves identifies elements that do not constitute a singular classical tradition in pastoral care, but which do give common threads: rootedness in Scripture, a salvific focus, the complexities of the pastoral role, and the awareness of God at work in and through people's lives.[26]

Attention to these older traditions is a corrective to the present Babylonian captivity of pastoral care. It pulls discussion back to the biblical tradition as we seek to answer the leading questions of who does what, to whom, why, and how in pastoral care. As Lauterbach

---

[24] Purves, *Pastoral Theology*, 2, 3.

[25] Lauterbach, 'Physicians of the Soul,' 15.

[26] Purves, *Pastoral Theology*, 8.

says: 'We have much to learn from our ancestors in the practice of spiritual attentiveness. Utilising their mature reflections forms a filter for evaluating modern insights in ministry.'[27]

Contemporary pastoral care can hardly be a clone-like reproduction of past patterns, but it can draw on them as it escapes its present Babylonian captivity. As Lauterbach again remarks, the goal of a backwards glance is not 'an obscurantist revival of neo-Puritanism, repeating old phrases and styles without regard for context ... the goal of exhuming ancestral pastoral culture is not to revive togas and sandals.'[28]

Pastors Henry, John, and Dan can all benefit from a backwards glance, as church history helps us consider matters such as the definition, means, and goals of pastoral care.

A good example of such a useful backwards glance is available in a recent work discussing pastoral care in situations of anxiety and depression. A retrospective and recent collaboration between Richard Baxter (a 16th-century Puritan pastor who is discussed below), J. I. Packer (a 20th-century theologian), and Michael Lundy (a 20th-century Christian psychiatrist) provides a balanced and practical guide that rests on strong Christian foundations for the benefit of pastoral caregivers. [29]

The Definition of Pastoral Care

This definition of pastoral care was given earlier: *Pastoral care is an intentional activity designed to address the immediate and deeper needs of people in ways that promote their growth into and in Christ.*

Each part of that definition is important. Pastoral care is addressed to *holistic needs*, for we were made as organically interconnected creatures with hearts, souls, minds, and bodies. Any of these aspects can become disordered in a fallen world, and a disorder in one aspect can

---

[27] Lauterbach, 'Physicians of the Soul,' 13.

[28] Lauterbach, 'Physicians of the Soul,' 15.

[29] Lundy, Michael S., *Depression, Anxiety and the Christian Life: Practical Wisdom from Richard Baxter* (Wheaton, IL: Crossway, 2018).

affect all the others. For example, Psalm 32:3–5 provides an example of how unconfessed sin can affect the physical body.

Note also the word *addressed* in the definition. Helpers cannot solve all needs, and the role of pastoral care is often to help devise the best way to manage a situation. For example, many notables from church history went to places like infirmaries and jails which were otherwise overlooked.[30] They could not always remove a need but they could help address it. That is why the sixteenth-century Christian William Perkins started visiting Cambridge prison soon after his conversion. He met a convicted man who knew enough of matters eternal to fear the judgement following his imminent death. Perkins could not deliver him from the gallows but could so apply the gospel to him that he went to his death with much comfort as he saw heaven opened to receive his soul.[31]

This example from William Perkins illustrates another part of the above definition. The convicted criminal was in anxious dread of judgement. Perkins did not dally to explore the man's feelings ('What colour reflects your mood today?') or to offer meaningless platitudes ('Don't worry; your troubles will soon be over') but rather led him to the gates of hell and then to the foot of the Cross. This is a clear example of *Christian* pastoral care that not only arises from Christ but also points to Christ.

The addressing of holistic needs makes for pastoral *care*. The fact that it is done in ways 'that promote their growth into and in Christ' makes it deeply *pastoral* in ways that link to the shepherding roles discussed earlier. If either genuine care or the link to Christ is absent, it is not quite pastoral care. In this sense, pastoral care nestles somewhere in the intersection of mercy ministries and discipleship, all within the greater mission of the church to glorify the Lord by the ingathering and perfecting of his chosen people that they might glorify and enjoy him in this life and in eternity. Pastoral care helps with the needs of this life and helps prepare people for eternal life.

---

[30] For example, during the eighteenth century, John Wesley and George Whitefield had similar ministries in prisons and other marginalised places.

[31] Ian Breward, ed., *The Work of William Perkins* (Appleford, Sutton: Courtenay Press, 1969), 8.

The example of William Perkins could be multiplied many times over. The greatest of the past saints joined neither Pastor Henry (practical care without discipleship) nor Pastor John (care detached from Scripture and the gospel), nor Pastor Dan (discipleship without holistic care) but typically ministered to whole people on both temporal and eternal horizons.

Historical Perspectives on Pastoral Care

As might be expected, pastoral care has taken different shapes at different periods.

The Early Church

Clebsch and Jaekle see the period up to AD 180 as one of sustaining people amidst the crisis of early Christianity, the period 180–306 as dominated by a concern to respond to issues arising from persecution, and the post-Constantine period as one of guiding people in Christian living in the new era of peace and privilege.[32] That is, pastoral care was not delivered in a vacuum but arose from, and was addressed to, the circumstances of changing times.

The post-Constantine period gave opportunity for literary reflection on pastoral care, along with much else, as the church developed the settled institutions that eventually morphed into Roman Catholicism.[33] Writers such as Basil the Great (d.379), Gregory of Nazianzus (d.390), John Chrysostom (d. 407), and Gregory the Great (d.604) contributed to this literature, setting pastoral care within the broader work of ministry, rather than segregating it into a separate and specialised role as noted in the above review of contemporary perspectives.

John Chrysostom is worthy of note.[34] After a period of monastic life and pastoral ministry at Antioch, he became bishop (or patriarch) of Constantinople in 398, ministering there amidst controversy and

---

32 *Clebsch and Jaekle, Pastoral Care in Historical Perspective,* 13.

33 *Purves (Pastoral Theology in the Classical Tradition, 5–74) gives a helpful overview of the early pastoral tradition.*

34 A standard biography of Chrysostom is J. N. D. Kelly, *Golden Mouth: the Story of John Chrysostom—Ascetic, Preacher, Bishop* (Ithaca, NY: Cornell University Press, 1998).

conflict with church and civil leaders until his death in exile. His *Six Books on the Priesthood*[35], written as an apologia for his own behaviour in resisting the priesthood, were completed by 385 and are an important early text on ministry.[36]

Chrysostom had a high view of the priest's role as a shepherd caring for a flock or as a father who had to deal with his congregation's ignorance, biases, and boredom and as the one who brought heaven to earth.[37] Chrysostom cannot be squeezed into the identity of a Reformed pastor (his sense of priesthood counters that immediately). However, his view that pastoral care is an extension of word ministry sits well with the integrated 'feed, lead and care' model presented earlier. [38]

The great Augustine of Hippo (d. 430) is primarily thought of as a bishop, along with being a major theological writer and polemicist.[39] However, his work as a bishop was more like a modern 'senior minister' than a regional ecclesiastical overlord.[40] Pastoral instincts arose soon after his conversion and were evident in his later ministry at Hippo and the wider ministry that arose from it. Important features of his pastoral work were the way in which it drew on a deep knowledge of people (he anticipates a number of modern psychological insights) and his deep knowledge of God. Once again, the notion of pastoral care as integrated with the whole identity of a church leader and as arising from sound theology is a notable contrast to some contemporary emphases.

More can be said on pastoral care within the early church period, but the examples sketched above illustrate that it was seen as an important task of church leaders and was integrated with other aspects

---

[35] The text of these is readily available online by searching under the title or in *The Nicene and Post-Nicene Fathers of the Christian Church*, ed., Philip Schaff, vol. IX, Grand Rapids, MI: Eerdmans, 1978 (reprint), 33–83. The letters of Chrysostom (also available in the same volume) also have examples of his pastoral approach.

[36] Andrew Purves (*Pastoral Theology in the Classical Tradition*, 33–53) gives a useful introduction to Chrysostom's pastoral theology.

[37] Purves, *Pastoral Theology*, 46, 50.

[38] Purves, *Pastoral Theology*, 48–49.

[39] The old, but still well-regarded, standard biography is Peter Brown, *Augustine of Hippo: a Biography* (London: Faber & Faber, 1967 (& updated version).

[40] An introduction to Augustine as pastor is available in J.B. Bernardin, 'St. Augustine as Pastor,' in *A Companion to the Study of St Augustine*, ed. R.W. Battenhouse (Oxford: Oxford University Press, 1955), 57–89.

of ministry, and especially with word ministry, whether in preaching, letters, or one-to-one conversation. Pastoral care was applied word ministry directed towards the cure of souls as the art of arts.[41]

Transition to the Reformation

In their review of the history of pastoral care, Clebsch and Jaekle agree that the medieval period saw a largely sacramental focus but then make the astounding claim that 'the Reformation's great upheaval in doctrine and in ecclesiology never generated a corollary revolution in the cure of souls.'[42] Purves catches the mood far better in his remark that 'the reformers also understood that all dogmatic theology is inevitably pastoral theology.'[43] This latter remark sees a double-sided emphasis in the Reformers: both that the gospel of grace issues in changed pastoral approaches and that all pastoral ministry arises from sound theology. There is a real sense in which the key Reformation leaders were primarily pastoral theologians with their renewed scriptural and theological insights addressed and applied to the life of the Reformed church.

John Calvin of Geneva (d. 1564) and Richard Baxter (d. 1691) of Kidderminster are discussed below as representatives of Reformation thinking and practice on pastoral care. Calvin is important as the key shaper of Reformed approaches to ministry and Baxter as a leading example of mature pastoral practice within the post-Restoration Puritan period.

John Calvin (1509–1564)[44]

The basic outlines of Calvin's life and ministry are well known. He was born in northern France, was earmarked for the church, and started

---

[41] A view represented by Gregory of Nazianzus (Purves, *Pastoral Theology*, 17, 20).

[42] Clebsch and Jaekle, Pastoral Care in Historical Perspective, 13.

[43] Purves, *Pastoral Theology*, 6–7.

[44] Parker, T.H.L, *John Calvin* (J.M. Dent: London, 1975) and Alister E. McGrath, *A Life of John Calvin: A Study in the Shaping of Western Culture* (Oxford: Blackwell Publishers Ltd, 1990) are useful introductions to Calvin. Understanding of Calvin's pastoral approach has been greatly advanced by the publication of Scott M. Manetsch, *Calvin's Company of Pastors: Pastoral Care and the Emerging Reformed Church, 1536–1609*, Oxford Studies in Historical Theology (New York, NY: Oxford University Press, 2013).

preparations towards the Roman priesthood before switching to legal studies. By 1533 he had broken with the Roman Catholic Church and come to Reformed convictions. Fear of persecution led him to from Paris to Basle, where he wrote the first edition of his famous *Institutes* in 1536 as a handbook for the common Bible reader. In God's calling, a passing visit to Geneva in July 1536 led him to join William Farel in leading the newly Reformed church there. Late in 1538 he and Farel relocated to Strasbourg after a dispute over the powers of church discipline. While in Strasbourg he pastored a French congregation, taught in a theological school, befriended Martin Bucer, studied the early church fathers, and refined his own thinking. In 1541 he was invited back to Geneva, where he stayed until his death. From 1541–1555 he faced continued internal opposition as he sought to establish a Reformed church order. Calvin is remembered for his impact on the wider European Reformation and his continuing influence, but he was always, and first, a local church pastor.

The Influence of Martin Bucer

Mention was made of Calvin's contact with Martin Bucer in Strasbourg. Bucer was both older than Calvin and preceded Calvin in commencing a Reformed ministry. His approach to pastoral ministry was one way in which he influenced Calvin. In the year that Calvin arrived in Strasbourg, Bucer published his *On the True Care of Souls*, which is a pastoral theology designed to aid the further reformation of the church.[45]

Bucer framed pastoral work through the biblical language of shepherd (noted earlier in this chapter) within which he identified the key tasks of searching for the lost, gathering the strays, binding the wounded, strengthening the weak, and feeding and protecting the flock. Scripture was the central means of pastoral work as pastors applied the fourfold applications mentioned in 2 Tim. 3:16—teaching, reproof, correction, and training in righteousness.

Bucer thus modelled to Calvin an approach to pastoral ministry that emphasised the means of the Word, the identity of the pastor as

---

[45] Martin Bucer, *Concerning the True Care of Souls* (1538). Repr., Edinburgh: Banner of Truth, 2009. The following summary of Bucer's pastoral theology draws on Purves, Pastoral Theology in the Classical Tradition, 76–94.

shepherd, and a wide-ranging scope for pastoral caregiving. Purves comments on the danger of reductionism in Bucer such that pastoral care is identified with gospel work, but this seems to be an overstatement.[46] Rather Bucer shows a holistic care for the Lord's flock which includes evangelism, discipleship, and church discipline, but which is not bounded by them.

Calvin as Pastor

Calvin's theological views, his preaching, and his remarkable influence in his day and beyond are well documented. Until recently, his broader approach to ministry, including pastoral care, has been less well known. Manetsch has helped fill this imbalance with his seminal 2013 study.[47]

The 1541 Ordinances[48] (Revised 1561)

Calvin presented Geneva's council with a framework for reorganising and reforming local pastoral ministry when he returned in 1541.

The 1541 Ordinances provided for the four offices of pastors, doctors, elders, and deacons to lead the various functions of the church.

What nowadays is broadly called pastoral care was a responsibility shared across pastors, elders and deacons:

> The duty of pastors
>
> Pastors are sometimes named in the Bible as overseers, elders, and ministers. Their work is to proclaim the Word of God; to teach, admonish,

---

[46] Purves, *Pastoral Theology*, 94.

[47] Scott M. Manetsch, *Calvin's Company of Pastors: Pastoral Care and the Emerging Reformed Church, 1536–1609*, Oxford Studies in Historical Theology (New York, NY: Oxford University Press, 2013).

[48] A copy of the 1541 Ordinances is available in J.F. Bergier and R. M. Kingdon, *Registres de la Compagnie des pasteurs de Geneve au temps de Calvin*, 2 vols. (n. p., 1962–4), Registres I, pp. 1–13. The translated version is J.F. Bergier and R.M. Kingdon, *Jean Calvin, trans.* G.R. Potter and M. Greengrass (London: Edward Arnold, 1983),. http://individual.utoronto.ca/mmilner/history2p91/primary/eccleord.htm.

> exhort, and reprove publicly and privately; to administer the sacraments; and, with the elders or their deputies, to issue fraternal warnings.
>
> ...
>
> Here follows the third order, or elders
>
> Their duty is to supervise every person's conduct. In friendly fashion they should warn backsliders and those of disorderly life. After that, where necessary, they should report to the Company [of pastors] who will arrange for fraternal correction.
>
> ...
>
> The fourth order of ecclesiastical government, namely, the deacons
>
> There have always been two kinds of these in the early church. One has to receive, distribute, and care for the goods of the poor (i.e. daily alms as well as possessions, rents and pensions); the other has to tend and look after the sick and administer the allowances to the poor as is customary.

This distribution of duties shows a holistic responsibility for the care of God's people (as do the following provisions with respect to a hospital and beggars).

Calvin's provision for the diaconate shows that pastoral care for the bodily identity of people mattered and overlaps with mercy ministry. Note also how his description of the role of pastors and elders develops. It includes, but is more than, building people up in the knowledge of God. There is a particular concern to apply that knowledge in the giving of 'warnings' and in supervising people's lives. This is the old notion of the cure (or care) of souls seen in the early church.

As would be expected in a Reformed church, the regular means of grace are central to the care of souls as pastors 'proclaim ... teach, admonish ... exhort and reprove publicly and privately, [and]... administer the sacraments.'

The Ordinances Incarnated

It is one thing to have a good structure for pastoral care, but it is another thing to implement it. By the mid-1540s Calvin had established the Company of Pastors (henceforth Company). It was essentially a weekly

(Friday) staff meeting of the city and rural pastoral staff, along with some theological teachers and teaching staff. [49] Along with the Consistory, to which elders were added, the Company gave a platform for regular, comprehensive, and personalised oversight of church leaders and members. It was the engine room of pastoral care.

Alongside public worship with its preaching, prayers, and sacraments, pastoral care was also given through the ministry of visitation. This is consistent with the above-quoted duty of pastors 'to proclaim the Word of God, to teach, admonish, exhort, and reprove publicly and privately' (underlining mine).

Calvin realised that pastors needed to know people individually to care for them and give personal applications of Scripture. In 1550 pastors were given permission to visit every Genevan household quarterly, which was later made an annual visit in the 1561 revision of the Ordinances.[50] In addition to this required annual visitation, household visitations were made under circumstances of poverty, bereavement, and illness, alongside hospital and prison visits.[51] Visitations typically examined people's understanding of the faith and participation in the means of grace and applied Scripture to address household issues and problems. They are an example of pastoral care that was personalised, Bible driven, and applied in holistic care.

Stepping Back

There is much for contemporary church leaders to take from Genevan pastoral care, even if they are not seeking simply to replicate it, a practice Lauterbach warns against.[52]

Genevan pastoral care could stray into an overzealous inquisitiveness and micromanagement of human lives, as Calvin's libertine opponents and later writers claim, and these dangers should be heeded.[53]

---

[49] Manetsch, *Calvin's Company of Pastors*, 28.

[50] Manetsch, *Calvin's Company of Pastors*, 281.

[51] Manetsch, *Calvin's Company of Pastors*, 283–84.

[52] See footnote 27 and the accompanying in-text remarks.

[53] His attempt to replace taverns with dry cafes where refreshments came with a side dish of prayer and Bible readings was unsuccessful and soon ended!

Despite these issues, Calvin's emphasis on pastoral care as Bible driven, holistic, and personalised through the public and private use of the means of grace speaks into some imbalances of the contemporary scene in pastoral care. His emphasis on pastoral visitation creates a link to the somewhat different figure of Richard Baxter, to whom we now turn.

Richard Baxter (1615–1691)[54]

Richard Baxter is one of the later seventeenth-century English Puritans who ministered from the pre-revolutionary era and then through the Commonwealth and the Stuart restoration of 1660 before his final days after the 1687 Declaration of Indulgence. His ministry started in the national Anglican Church, but he broke with episcopacy and is most identified with the Independents.

A Halfway Man?

In many respects Baxter dwelt in a halfway house. He was a man who sought peace, unity, and cooperation across the then-current ecclesiastical divides. Theologically, through major works such as his 1681 *Methodus Theologiæ Christianæ* and the 1673 *Christian Directory,* he sought to reconcile Calvinist, Arminian, and Roman Catholic views on the doctrines of grace. As might be expected, this left no one satisfied and started down a path that led to later deviancies.[55] With respect to polity, he sought to bypass differences between the prevailing parties of Presbyterians, Anglicans, and Independents and find common ground for shared work in local and wider ministry, even proposing a broadly inclusive national church. Again, this was not greeted with universal acclaim.

---

[54] Baxter wrote an autobiography (Richard Baxter, *The Autobiography of Richard Baxter* [London, Dent; Totowa, N.J.: Rowman & Littlefield, 1974] and is introduced by J. I. Packer in his introduction to the Banner edition of *The Reformed Pastor* (Edinburgh: Banner of Truth, 1974) and reprints.

[55] See J.I. Packer's introduction to Richard Baxter, *The Reformed Pastor,* 1655 ed. (Edinburgh: Banner of Truth, 1974) and reprints, 9–10. On this note, see also Packer's comment on page 14 that the word 'Reformed' in the book's title refers not so much to Reformed Calvinistic theology as to reformed or renewed ministry practice.

Baxter was an outlier to the Puritan movement, and some may question his place there.[56] However, his brief involvement with the parliamentary army, his rejection of episcopacy (despite being offered a bishopric), and his sufferings in the Stuart restoration justify his inclusion there on an historical basis.

Baxter the Pastor

Whatever the halfway house of his theology and churchmanship, Baxter excelled as a pastor. In April 1641, when he was just twenty-six, he was elected to minister at Kidderminster (near Birmingham). Aside from the interruptions of his war service, he served there with great effect until the post-Restoration Anglican hegemony saw him barred from preaching.

As a pastor, Baxter was pre-eminently a preacher and teacher who showed a deep knowledge of people, an ability to discern their deeper states, and an ability to minister to them from the Scriptures. The heart of his ministry lay in devoted preaching, visitation, catechetical instruction, counselling, literature distribution, and his own writings.

There is presently a renewed appreciation of Baxter's pastoral method, which featured extensive, regular, and purposeful home visitations as a complement to his public ministry. [57] Baxter visited his people in their homes as family units. He asked pointed questions. He listened. He taught the catechism. He discussed recent sermons. He counselled. He prayed.

Despite the difference of contexts, there is much for modern pastors to appropriate here, in a day when the pastoral focus is often on ministry programs or dependent on people going to their pastor in his space. Perhaps we cannot go from house to house as Baxter and the apostles did (e.g. Acts 5:42), but there is much to be learned from visiting people in or near their workplaces or homes. Doing this shows people that we value them and their daily activities and gives opportunity to see more of who they really are. Again, Baxter's intentionality

---

[56] J. I. Packer discusses the question of Baxter's Puritan identity in his introduction to Michael S. Lundy, *Depression, Anxiety and the Christian Life: Practical Wisdom from Richard Baxter* (Wheaton, IL: Crossway, 2018), 18.

[57] For example, see the contributions of Belli and Miller listed in the bibliography.

in conversations is a role model in our day of distracted busyness. Can we follow his example and prepare patterns of strategic questions and comments, or suggest topics of conversation, that enable precious pastoral time to be well used? [58]

The Reformed Pastor

Baxter sought to pastor beyond his own congregation at Kidderminster. He became involved in the Worcestershire Association, which held a weekly meeting of regional pastors. Baxter had been asked to speak on his program of pastoral visitation, based on Acts 20:28, but was ill on the appointed day. The illness was providential, for it resulted in him writing *The Reformed Pastor* to explain and commend his approach.[59]

This frequently reprinted work is gold as a guide in pastoral caregiving. Consistent with a modern emphasis on care of the caregiver and mindful of the importance of example, Baxter begins by urging pastors to 'the oversight of ourselves' and discusses why and how this should be done. The majority of the book discusses the nature, motives, manner, and means of caring for the flock. The tone is warm and pastoral. Baxter shows deep insights into people and anticipates many more recent therapeutic approaches. The discussion is detailed. And always, the great concern is to grow people in Christ and to help prepare them to face their Judge with gospel confidence and consolation.

The Reformed Pastor moves beyond its circumstances of origin and style of expression to give timeless advice in pastoral care. Along with Augustine's *Confessions* and Calvin's *Institutes*, it deserves a 'must read' place for those entering ministry.

[58] I recall a church small group leader who hosted lunches of five or six people in the financial district of Singapore where they all worked. The 40–50-minute conversation over food avoided idle chatter and went straight to issues of how they were going in their Christian life and how their faith played out in the workplace. This is a great example of modern 'visitation,' which combines the effectiveness of intentionality with efficient use of time.

[59] Richard Baxter, *The Reformed Pastor* (1655; reprint, Edinburgh: Banner of Truth, 1974)

Conclusion – Letters to the Pastors

Looking back on historical perspectives

John wrote that Jesus did more than could be recorded, and John added that he chose what he wrote so that people could know who Jesus was and believe (John 20:30–31; 21:25). Likewise, the writer of Hebrews drew on stories from the vast 'cloud of witnesses' as an encouragement to ongoing faith (Heb. 11:32; 12:1). In similar manner, the stories of past figures who have much to teach about the conduct of pastoral care could be multiplied many times beyond the handful covered in this chapter. However, perhaps the point is made through these examples: the past has much to teach and to help keep us from becoming a widow in our own day, to apply Dean Inge's quip from the beginning of the chapter.

The above brief historical survey has illustrated key themes that arose from the earlier and equally brief biblical and theological survey.

- Pastoral care is an important task for church leaders as an extension of the ministry of the divine Shepherd who feeds, leads, and cares for his people
- Pastoral care overlaps with mercy ministries and discipleship activities but is distinct from them
- Pastoral care addresses the entire human being – both our created and redeemed identities
- Pastoral care is not to be conducted apart from biblical and theological truth, but rather is to arise from and be conditioned by it.

In light of this, what can we say to Pastors Henry, John, and Dan, who were introduced earlier? Here are some examples of possible letters:

- *Dear Henry,*

  It's good to be in touch again – you are my father in ministry. I admire the way you put yourself out to serve the people of God in such practical ways. When I was your student intern, I learned a lot about being there for people in moments of need, asking questions, and listening to people. At first, I found it a distraction to be sent to the shut-ins to listen to their stories yet again, drive them to medical appointments, and pick up groceries for them. However, over time I came to appreciate your words that every person we meet is needy and broken in some way; that God made us heart, soul, mind, and body; and that pastoral care is directed to all that.

You recently spoke of attending some conferences that gave you a sharper focus on the old truths of the faith. I'm so glad you went, and I can hear a change in your website sermons (yes, I listen in from time to time). Here's my encouragement and recommendation to you – that this sharper focus on the old truths makes the move from your preaching into your pastoral care. You are good at 'reading' people. I encourage you to work at speaking gospel truths into their needs and situations. How can you address their situation and needs in ways that help them grow in Christ? Don't give up your loving, practical care for people (I still have much to learn from you there) but do go the next step in loving care and take them to Christ.

Your habit of visiting every person in your church on a regular basis is a good model for younger men like me who have moved from the old 101s of pastoral care and forgotten that the apostles went from house to house. I've ordered a copy of Richard Baxter's 'The Reformed Pastor' that I am sending your way. Baxter, like John Calvin, was great in house-to-house visits and is a big help on how to move beyond superficialities to engage with the souls of people.

I look forward to seeing you soon and to chatting about the Baxter book!

- *Dear John,*

  G'day mate!

  It was so good to see you at the EU reunion the other week. Those were great days when we were both young and stupid as newbies in the faith but were newbies who turned up to the lunchtime Christian talks when people from the local theological college taught us Bible and theology.

Congratulations on your recent PhD in clinical psychology and appointment as clinical director at St. Thomas' counselling ministry – you have certainly moved a long way from the struggling students that we both were back in those days.

I'm glad to see Christian people going out to harvest and apply insights from the book of God's world. Do you remember that EU talk from that Christian philosopher who told us that what mattered was not where a truth was found, but that it passed muster when measured against the gold standard of Scripture? We both reacted against it, but I think we have matured since then. We both know that we can only know God as he reveals himself in the Bible, but that there is much to be learned about the world, including about how people function, from observing the world. We read the world as it appears to us, but we must read it through the frame of God and his Word.

I looked up your thesis recently. I'll confess to being a bit surprised at where you went in your discussion of human identity, human needs, and the matching therapies. I reckon you have missed the nub of the matter. In my view, our core identity is as beings created by, and for, God, and our deepest need arises from our rejection of that identity in favour of an I-world that is anthropocentric in a reductionist way. If our basic identity lies with God and our deepest need arises from rejecting that, it's pretty clear that no therapy that cuts God out of the picture and refuses to reckon with sin can usefully address our deepest needs.

On that theme, have you read Augustine's Confessions? He displays remarkable insight into human motivations and states, yet his discussion of them is grounded in biblical and theological insights. Perhaps that's a paper for you to write one day: 'A Reappropriation of Augustine's Anthropology in Pastoral Care'?

Anyway, I'll see you at the Assembly meeting next month – we really are a bunch of grey-haired dinosaurs.

- *Hi Dan,*

  It was good to see you at the bookshop yesterday – it's so important to keep refreshing ourselves in ministry. As you are discovering, ministry is such hard work, and we are like Paul's frail jars of clay (I think of polystyrene coffee cups). We need the fresh air of good books.

  Thanks also for sending through your recent policy paper and action plan for revitalising small groups. It's a great resource that will help upskill me as we look at our local situation.

  I notice your clear statement that small groups serve the church's mission of presenting every person mature in Christ. Three cheers for that sharp gospel edge. However, I was a little troubled when I read this: 'Every small group meeting should include a time when members are asked how they are going. However, this should not dominate the group meeting or distract from our discipleship goals.'

  I wonder if you are overreacting against old imbalances. For sure, it's a problem if small groups become sessions where people only share their life needs, offer advice to one another, and pray. And I agree that in every one-on-one pastoral situation, we should be asking how we can help this person grow in Christ. But I wonder if there's a bit more space for engaging with and caring for people in their everyday situations and working through that caregiving to help them grow in Christ.

  In saying this, I'm mindful of Jesus, who fed and helped people in the everyday business of life, but who always did so with a kingdom horizon nearby. And I'm thinking of people like William Perkins, John Wesley, George Whitfield, and Thomas Chalmers, who embraced the both/and nature of care and discipleship rather than making them an either/or.

  Just a thought to talk about another day. Coffee at the usual next week?

Like Henry, John, and Dan, we are all prone to reflect our context and the trends of our time in pastoral care. Perspectives drawn from the best of the great tradition of past centuries can help redress our balances and take us back to pastoral care that reflects the Heavenly Shepherd, his Son, and his Word.

Two

Preaching Christ in Early Reformation Bern[1]

John McClean

The Acts of the Synod of Bern of 1532 are obscure, at least in the English-speaking world.[2] The few writers who have examined them have focused on the relation of church and magistrate or sacramental debates.[3] Yet their central concern is gospel ministry and its theological foundations and they offer a fascinating early reformed approach to this theme.

The Most Significant Forgotten City of the Reformation

Bruening comments that 'Bern is the most significant forgotten city of the reformation' since it came to play a key role in supporting the Reformation across Switzerland.[4]

'Thriving, ambitious, aggressive' Bern was a dominant city in the Swiss federation during the 15th and early 16th centuries.[5] Its patrician

---

[1] It is a delight to offer this essay in honour of Rev. Dr. Peter Barnes and his faithful and fruitful ministry. He has been a great encouragement to me, and to many in the Presbyterian Church of Australia and beyond. Among many other blessings, the Lord has used Peter to remind us of the relevance of our Christian heritage, especially from the Reformation. I hope this essay does something similar, encouraging gospel ministry from a little known Reformation document.

[2] The Acts are found in James T. Dennison, Jr. *Reformed Confessions of the 16th and 17th Centuries in English Translation: 1523–1693* 4 Vols (Grand Rapids, MI: Reformation Heritage, 2008–2014), 1:227–276, references are given to relevant chapters in the text.

[3] See Michael .W. Bruening, *Calvinism's First Battleground: Conflict and Reform in the Pays de Vaud* (Dordrecht: Springer, 2006), 67–71.

[4] Bruening, 61. For instance, Bernese military action effectively bought the Reformation to Geneva in 1536; in 1538 Bern commissioned Guillaume Farel (1489–1565) to promote reform in the surrounding cities, including Geneva and the support of the Bernese authorities was crucial to Calvin's ministry.

[5] See Clive H. Church, Randolph C. Head, *A Concise History of Switzerland* (Cambridge:

leadership was relatively independent of the church hierarchy. The city itself, sitting on the Aare river, straddled the territories of the bishops of Basel and Sion and the dioceses of Constance and Lausanne also had oversight of parts of Bernese territories. This overlap of episcopal territories with no resident bishop allowed the city council considerable freedom to direct church matters. The Church of St Vincent was a virtual cathedral and the provost, appointed by the council, had episcopal powers.[6]

Berchtold Haller (c.1492–1536), a school friend of Philipp Melanchthon (1497–1560), became preacher at St Vincent's in 1515 and in time became a canon and the people's priest. He was a reformist preacher even before he developed links with Zwingli from 1521. In 1522 local clergy complained about the provocative preaching of Georg Brunner who publicly identified the pope as the antichrist. Without reference to church hierarchy, the city council organised a disputation and endorsed Brunner's preaching.[7] The following year another reforming cleric, Sebastian Meyer (1465–1545), clashed with a Dominican priest. The council backed Meyer, and directed that the clergy of Bern should only preach from the Scriptures.[8]

The Council was determined to retain control of church matters and did not move quickly to any fuller adoption of Reformation. It may have hoped to pursue a 'Catholic reform'. A July 1523 edict condemned the teachings of Luther but required clergy to preach 'nothing other than the gospel and God's teaching'. A similar edict in November 1524 lacked the prohibition on Luther's teachings. In April 1525 the Council affirmed the city's loyalty to Roman Catholic worship and seven sacraments but allowed the circulation of Luther's writings on Scripture.

Cambridge University Press, 2013), 40–72 for a summary of the growth of the confederacy and Bern's leading role. On the Reformation in Bern seee E. G. Rupp, 'The Reformation in Zurich, Strassburg and Geneva' in *The New Cambridge Modern History*, ed. G. R. Elton (Cambridge: Cambridge University Press, 1990) 2:111; Martin Sallmann, 'The Reformation in Bern,' in *A Companion to the Swiss Reformation*, ed. E. Campi and A. Nelson Burnett (Leiden/Boston: Brill, 2016), 126–28.

[6] Sallmann, 'The Reformation in Bern,' 132.

[7] Kaspar von Greyerz, 'The Reformation in German-Speaking Switzerland', *A Companion to the Reformation World*, ed. R. P. Hsia (Oxford: Blackwell, 2004), 90.

[8] Bruce Gordon, *The Swiss Reformation*, (Manchester: Manchester University Press, 2008), 102.

In 1525 Bern, along with most of the Swiss cities, sent representatives to the Baden disputation where Johann von Eck (1486 –1543) was the polemicist for Rome. In Zwingli's absence, the evangelical position was presented by Johannes Oecolampadius (1482–1531).[9] Eck was victorious and the resolutions declared Zwingli and Luther heretics. Bern did not declare for either side.[10] The Catholic territories pressured the Bernese but refused them access to the records of the disputation. This strained the relation of Bern with the Catholic cities.[11]

The city remained neutral for another three years, keeping connection with the Catholic cantons without cutting ties with Zurich. Catholic worship continued with preaching from Scripture alone. Clergy and others were able to promote reformation ideas. Through this period Zwingli's influence grew in the city, especially in the religious houses, yet the population in the extensive rural areas remained committed to traditional religion.[12]

Under pressure for reform, the Council called a disputation for January 1528. It sought to have all four territorial bishops attend though none did, nor did any of the Catholic territories send representatives. Haller and Franz Kolb (1465–1535) drafted the theses for the disputation and were supported by a large contingent from Zurich including Zwingli, Oecolampadius, Martin Bucer (1491–1551) and Wolfgang Capito (1478–1541).[13] The opposition, while not incompetent, had no speakers of great reputation.[14] The Reformed position of the Theses was approved by the attending clergy 235 votes to 46.

The Word of God is the key theme of the 1528 Theses. The opening thesis states that 'the holy catholic church, whose sole head is Christ, has been begotten from the Word of God, in which also it continues,

---

[9] I.D. Backus, *The disputations of Baden, 1526 and Berne, 1528: neutralizing the early church* (Princeton: PTS, 1993), 1–78.

[10] Gordon, *The Swiss Reformation,* 70.

[11] Sallmann, 'The Reformation in Bern,' 143.

[12] Gordon, *The Swiss Reformation,* 102–4.

[13] Jan Rohls, *Reformed Confessions: Theology from Zurich to Barmen,* trans. John Hoffmeyer. (Louisville: Westminster John Knox Press, 1998), 11.

[14] Dennison, *Reformed Confessions,* 1:40; Euan Cameron, *The European Reformation* (Oxford: Clarendon Press, 1991), 238; Martin Greschat, *Martin Bucer: A Reformer and His Time Edition* (Louisville, KY: Westminster John Knox Press, 2004), 78–79.

nor does it listen to the voice of any stranger'.[15] The Word is dynamic—creating the Church—as well as authoritative in contrast to human traditions.

The Theses present a full view of salvation in Christ—'Christ alone is our wisdom, righteousness, redemption, and satisfaction for the sins of the whole world,' and warn that presenting any other source of salvation or satisfaction for sin denies Christ (Thesis 2). Correspondingly, Christ is the only Mediator and Advocate and the Bernese renounce any other who are 'beyond the bounds of this world [and] above the foundation of the Word of God' i.e. saints and angels (Thesis 3).

The rest of the Theses develop the twin focus on the Word and Christ. The identity of the Word and Scripture is explicit in Thesis 8 which refers to 'the Word of God comprehended in the books of the Old and New Testament'. On the basis of the authority of Scripture they reject the doctrine of transubstantiation, the sacrifice of the Mass, purgatory and the worship of images (Theses 4,5,7,8). They finish by allowing clerical marriage, since any prohibition is contrary to Scripture, and condemning clerical immorality on the basis of Scripture (Theses 9,10).

The Bern Reformation in Crisis

Bern joined a movement which was far from secure. In 1529 Zurich and its allies in the *Christliches Burgrecht* declared war against the Catholic cantons, though a concordat was negotiated and the First Battle of Kappel saw no direct military action from either side. Zurich, encouraged by Zwingli, imposed harsh sanctions on the Catholic cantons, stopping supplies of food. Finally, in 1531, the Catholic forces moved against Zurich and defeated it in the Second Battle of Kappel, during which Zwingli was killed. Bern contributed no forces for the initial battle. Bern sent reinforcements only after Zurich's defeat, and the Catholic army overpowered the combined force. Zurich and its allies sued for peace.

These events made Bern's political and military situation precarious and amplified internal tensions. While the Catholic forces did not

[15] Dennison, *Reformed Confessions*, 1:41.

attempt to reverse the Reformation in the cities, they held a far stronger position. Not only was Zwingli gone, but Oecolampadius, his presumed successor died in Basel, and Haller was too sick to preach in Bern. Zwingli's colleague Kaspar Megander (Grossmann) (1495–1545), a pastor and professor of theology in Bern, fiercely denounced the city's failure to provide intial military support for Zurich and urged his hearers to renew the battle against the Catholic forces.[16] The city's preachers were sharply divided about this and Megander was suspended from office. Meanwhile, residents in Bern's rural districts complained about the imposition of reform, especially by 'foreign' ministers with their bellicose preaching.[17]

The Council called the Synod to deal with this crisis. Capito was in the city at the time, touring the Swiss cities from Strasbourg on the recommendation of Bucer. When he discovered that the Synod would be held, he asked to be present. The Bern authorities not only granted him access but co-opted him to lead the process. He prepared the material for the Synod and chaired the sessions. He had to mediate between feuding preachers, including conciliating Megander and Haller, and re-establish trust between the magistrates and the preachers.[18]

Capito's irenicism was satisfied in this case. The clergy discovered a real unity, which deeply moved them.[19] When the council added its preface it was extravagant in its thankfulness for the 'faithful admonition' the clergy had given to one another and announced its approval of the Acts as 'godly and edifying' and happily confirmed and ratified them.[20] The pastors and the council embraced the articles and committed themselves to following their regulations.

The Acts and the Reformation of Ministry

The resolutions clarified the role of the council and clergy in religious matters. This was a major concern of the synod and is addressed in the

[16] Gordon, *The Swiss Reformation*, 138.

[17] Sallmann, 'The Reformation in Bern,' 155.

[18] James M. Kittelson, *Wolfgang Capito: From Humanist to Reformer* (Leiden: Brill, 1975), 151, 191.

[19] Dennison, *Reformed Confessions*, 1: 226.

[20] Dennison, *Reformed Confessions*, 1: 229.

preface (entitled 'The mission and warrant of the temporal magistrate concerning the worship of God, with an exhortation to the honourable government of Bern'). The magistrates were to regulate external arrangements including worship and government of the church, including suppression of heresy. However, they were not called to try to enforce faith: 'no magistrate should compel the conscience, or command and forbid with respect to anything more than what is outward, lest good consciences should be burdened and the Holy Spirit constrained. Jesus Christ our Lord, to whom God has given all authority and the power of the Holy Spirit, is alone the Lord of the conscience'.[21]

The Acts are framed as resolutions of the clergy of Bern, so we should read them as both an expression of Capito's theology and also of the shared views of the clergy. They address a series of practical concerns about ministry, including what and how to preach, the place and administration of the sacraments, their relationship with the magistrate, training children, visitation, sermon preparation and the lives of the clergy.

Preaching, a key element in the crisis, is the most prominent concern. The Reformation, which had led to the *Kappelerkriege* was a preaching movement. Yet, the preaching had failed to produce in Bern the personal and social transformation for which the Reformers hoped. Instead, it had become the focus of criticism and council discipline and the preachers were at odds with each other. Consequently, almost half of the 44 chapters of the Acts directly address the task of preaching.

Preaching the Law and the Old Testament

Several times the Acts return to the question of preaching on the law and the Old Testament, reflecting a major concern in late medieval and early reformation pastoral practice. Late medieval Germany had seen a resurgence of preaching on biblical law, largely traced to the influence of Gabriel Biel (1420–1495). Biel considered that law served both to prepare sinners to receive God's grace by directing them to do what was in them and to come to the sacrament of penance, and also then directed their love for God enabled by grace. As a devoted pastor, Biel

[21] Dennison, *Reformed Confessions*, 1: 231–232.

laboured to preach God's law. Oberman summaries the content of his sermons in two phrases from the New Testament announcing the curse and the blessing of the law—*arbour non faciens bonum fructum excidetur* ('a tree that does not produce good fruit shall be cut down' Luke 3:9) and *si vis ad vitam ingredi serva mandata* ('if you wish to enter life, keep the commandments' Matt. 19:17). [22]

Biel's friend and student Johannes Geiler (1445–1510) was for thirty-two years the people's priest in Strasbourg. In his ministry the sermon particularly had the role of proclaiming God's demand on people to bring them to the altar to find grace, but also to train the citizens to form a godly society.[23] In both these tasks biblical law played a key role. Geiler was an immensely popular and widely published preacher, and since Capito settled in Strasbourg only thirteen years after his death, the Reformer must have been aware of this preaching tradition.

Martin Luther (1483–1546) developed his theology in reaction to Biel.[24] He held that the law had a preparatory role in salvation, but one which was quite different to Biel and the legal preachers. Luther emphasised the 'theological' use of the law to convict of sin. For him, Romans 3:20 was decisive: 'through the law we become conscious of our sin'. Wengert explains that for Luther this meant that the law produces an existential awareness of God's wrath toward sin. In contrast the gospel reveals to sinners the Saviour they need: 'the law thunders and threatens: the gospel consoles, heals, and comforts'.[25] Beyond this use of the Law, Luther has little place for it in the Christian life. He considered that the Christian kept the law by (or from) faith, but hardly

---

[22] Heiko A. Oberman, *The Harvest of Medieval Theology* (Grand Rapids: Eerdman, 1967), 22–23.

[23] David C. Steinmetz, *Reformers in the Wings: From Geiler Von Kaysersberg to Theodore Beza*. 2nd ed. (Oxford: Oxford University Press, 2001), 12.; R. Voltmer,. 'Political Preaching and a Design of Urban Reform: Johannes Geiler of Kaysersberg and Strasbourg.' *Franciscan Studies* 71 (2013): 71–88.

[24] Matthew Barrett, 'Can This Bird Fly? Repositioning the Genesis of the Reformation on Martin Luther's Early Polemic against Gabriel Biel's Covenantal, Voluntarist Doctrine of Justification' *SBJT* 21.4 (2017): 61–101.

[25] Timothy J. Wengert. 'Martin Luther' in *The Decalogue through the centuries: from the Hebrew Scriptures to Benedict XVI*, ed. Jeffrey P. Greenman and Timothy Larsen (Lousiville, KY: Westminster John Knox, 2012), 99.

needed the law to direct in that—'Christians have no need of the law or of rule books to tell them what to do. A good tree bears good fruit automatically. One does not need to read a botany book to an apple tree to save it from possible confusion in the spring. The law is irrelevant for Christian ethics. The only demand laid on Christians is the demand of love'.[26]

Melanchthon, also in Wittenburg, developed a different view. He held to the theological use of the law, but also stressed the moral use of the law. His view was that 'the law is binding on believers as well as unbelievers'.[27] Having been justified by faith Christians were to live in obedience to the law.

This view brought Melanchthon into sharp disagreement with Johans Agricola (1494 –1566), another enthusiastic Wittenburg reformer. The first round of this dispute took place in 1527/28 in the course of the preparation for the reformation visitation to the churches of Saxony. The visitation was urgently needed in light of the Peasants War (1524–25) and general confusion in social life generated by the Lutheran Reformation. Melanchthon came to the conclusion that the Reformation message had been misunderstood to offer a false 'evangelical freedom' which was, in fact, anarchic antinomianism. He prescribed the application of the preaching of the law both for conversion, as a first penance, and also for ongoing repentance, a second penance. Agricola vigorously protested what seemed to him to be a return to the legalism of Rome. His view was that 'repentance should come forth from faith in the gospel of forgiveness, without use of the law'.[28] The disagreement involved a series of writings, culminating in the Torgau conference of November 1527, at which Luther negotiated (or enforced) a compromise. The issues would erupt again in 1536, but already it was public, and formed something of the background to the Bern Articles.

Although Capito was from the Wittenberg circle, Zwingli had been the major influence on Bern. The 'affair of the sausages' at the start of the Reformation in Zurich in 1522 sprang from Zwingli's teaching about freedom from the Lenten fast. His sermon in response made it

[26] Steinmetz, *Reformers in the Wings*, 52

[27] Steinmetz, *Reformers in the Wings*, 54

[28] Herman A. Speelman, 'Melanchthon's innovative contribution on penance in 1527: a corrective addendum to Luther?' *WTJ* 81 (2019): 49–70

clear that not only had the church no right to impose extra food laws, but that the Old Testament food laws were abrogated for believers. He argues that 'although certain foods are forbidden in the Old Testament, they are on the contrary made free in the New'. He takes Luke 16:15–16 to teach that 'the law and the prophets were only a symbol or have lasted only to John' and that the ceremonial and civil law are now 'superseded'. He considered that the continued observation of ceremonial law is highly esteemed by humans but is 'abominable' to God (Luke 16:15).[29]

In some very early writings Zwingli viewed the role of the law in a way similar to Luther's 'theological use'. Sinners cannot keep the law, and Christ gives the law to show this and drive them to Christ. Soon, however he developed his typical emphasis that the gospel and faith in Christ comes first in the Christian life. Faith, then, is 'the foundation on which the law is built'. He related law and gospel closely since the gospel is 'everything ... God has made known to us through his own Son' including Christ's commands which are embraced by faith.[30] Christ frees believers from the condemnation of the law and satisfies God's righteousness. He releases them from subsequent despair and fear, shows them how they are to live for God and is at work by his Spirit teaching them to love. If faith were perfect, there would be no need for the instruction of the law. Since many have weak faith, the instruction of the law is necessary: 'from the law the faithful and elect learn the will of God'.[31]

These debates about the place of the law and the Old Testament are an important context, for the Acts address the task of preaching. Given Capito's work as a Hebraist such questions naturally drew his attention.

---

[29] Huldreich Zwingli, 'Von Erkiesen und Freiheit der Speisen (Regarding the Choice and Freedom of Foods)' in *The Latin Works and The Correspondence of Huldreich Zwingli: Together with Selections from His German Works*. ed. S. M. Jackson, and trans. H. Preble, W. Lichtenstein, and L. A. McLouth (New York/London: Knickerbocker, 1912), Vol. 1:77.

[30] Zwingli, *Works*, 7:263.18–265.24.

[31] W. P. Stephens, *Zwingli: An Introduction to His Thought* (Oxford: Oxford University, 1992), 71–72; Zwingli, *Works*, 4:63.31–45; G. W. Bromiley, ed. Zwingli and Bullinger (Louisville, KY: Westminster John Knox Press, 2006), 273.

God Known in Christ

The Acts open with the re-dedication of the ministers to their vocation—'first of all, we as ministers and preachers, more than anyone else, ought to be, and ought to be called, the ambassadors of Christ, servants of the Spirit, and stewards of the mysteries of God' (ch 1). From this starting point the Acts address the need for pure doctrine and the nature of a teaching ministry which is truly a stewardship of the mysteries of God.

The theology of the Acts develops from the second chapter which makes the striking claim that sound doctrine is found only in 'the unique and eternal Word of God, and the kindness and good will which the Father has manifested to us through Christ'. The allusions to John 1 make it clear that the 'Word of God' here is Christ. This is more explicit in the following sentence: 'this doctrine is nothing else than Christ Jesus Himself', and Christ is described as the One crucified and raised 'to procure the righteousness by which we are justified' (ch 2). So then, Christ and his gospel are the test for all doctrine. Just as the Son was sent by the Father, taught only what he heard from his Father and served him faithfully, so the Christian minister is to serve Christ and preach him.

The next chapter develops this theme in a rich formulation which presents a compact statement of the Triune work of revelation and redemption.

> The Father speaks to us still today by His Son, who through the Holy Spirit dwells in our hearts. God the Lord also reconciles us to Himself by His Son. In the Son we perceive the acts of God and His fatherly heart towards us. Through this understanding and experience of Christ, the believer thrives and grows daily, carried forward by daily exhortation (ch 3).

It follows that preaching must present Christ and fails if it speaks of God 'in the manner of the pagans'. The preacher is to declare 'this God as known in the face of Christ, who is the brightness of His glory, His very truth, image and sign'. Without the message of Christ, people become increasingly wicked and become like the heathen 'who have heard and spoken a great deal of empty talk about a God known naturally, but who have perceived nothing of their gracious Father in heaven' (ch 4). The danger lies not merely in methodological or epistemological shortcomings of natural theology, but in the fact that it fails to point to God's grace expressed in Christ and so does not transform the hearer.

Chapter 5 then offers a subtle account of revelation in Christ, and its relation to Old Testament revelation. Again, the burden of the chapter is to call for preachers to present Christ and not to speak of God apart from him. Echoing Hebrews 1, the Acts state that 'God constantly declares Himself in His acts and made Himself plainly known by sundry traits and signs'. This might seem to set up a contrast with revelation in Christ but turns out to be an argument in support of the Christological view. The chapter offers a summary of God's acts and signs through the Old Testament, from the tree of life to three items which in the Mosaic covenant are called by the name of the Lord—the ark, the temple and the city of Jerusalem. These are each proleptic revelations of Christ in which God was certainly revealed, albeit obscurely. In contrast 'today the true Christian knows Him with clarity, certainty, and without mistake, through the Lord Jesus Christ' though contemporary Jews refuse to come to Christ. So, while Old Testament revelation was revelation for its era, it is only revelation for Christians in its fulfilment in Christ. There is 'a new symbol and sign in which God appears, in that He has reconciled the world to Himself in Christ'. This is supported by a reference to a prophecy in Jeremiah 3:16–17 that the ark will be transcended ('it shall not come to mind or be remembered or missed; it shall not be made again') when Jerusalem itself will become the throne of God. This is viewed as a prophecy of Christ developed with an allusion to Gal. 4:26 'Jerusalem above is free'. The view of the Acts is that a Christian reading of the Old Testament must be in light of Christ and must lead to Christ.

This assertion of revelation of Christ leads to the conclusion that sermons should 'be entirely about and from Christ'—'all servants of God and preachers of the kingdom of Christ should diligently proclaim this one Lord Christ Jesus, the knowledge of whom excels all things' (ch 6). This does not mean that a preacher simply repeats a formula such as 'Jesus Christ is Saviour', rather Christian preaching consists of the gospel which turns people to God and transforms them. Christian preaching, following Jesus's teaching of the apostles (Luke 24) and the preaching of Acts, should begin with the death and resurrection of Christ and include his ascension and the gift of the Spirit and on that basis declare repentance and forgiveness in his name (ch 7). Even the events of Christ's birth and life should be understood in light of the cross and resurrection—Christ obeyed the Father in his life in preparation to be the Saviour, and his works are signs of the inner healing and life he brings by the Spirit.

The position of the Acts is that true faith comes from hearing the message of Christ and this work of the Spirit leads to genuine repentance—'the Spirit of Christ increasingly manifests and brings to light the secret sin and hidden corruption of the heart, daily consuming it and daily refining it as a fire does the silver, to purify from the refuse and filth of sins' (ch 14). The Acts condemn preachers who use the law (at least to Gentiles) to expose sin and move hearers to repentance. This practice 'is darkening the principal mystery and the glory of Christ' which is that the Holy Spirit was given to Jews, under the law; but also to Gentiles apart from the law (ch 16). The thought is that it is Christ who gives the Spirit who brings repentance. If we insist that the law is necessary for repentance, we obscure the gift of the Spirit from Christ. So the prophetic calls of the Old Testament to repentance need to be 'heard with Christian ears'. The repentance for which they call springs from knowing Christ and his gospel, not from the law (ch 17).

This view of the place of Christ and the Spirit in revelation has implications for assurance. The Acts states that ministers should encourage hearers to examine themselves to determine if they are elect, which to say they should consider if they truly know Christ. The key to knowing this is an inner experience, for true conversion is 'renewal of the heart, to become an inward, spiritual and heavenly man, who is without sin insofar as he is born of God'. Through Christ's death 'one acquires an acquaintance with sin and true repentance', 'through His exaltation, forgiveness of sin becomes known'. So the spiritual realities of true repentance and true faith, which are personal and inner experiences are the product and sign of a genuine encounter with Christ (ch 18).

The Place of the Law

The Acts move from the commitment to evangelical preaching to address the question of the place of the law in preaching. They present a position remarkably close to that of Agricola, arguing that the law is neither the key means to convict sinners of their need for Christ nor to lead to repentance and holy living. Like Zwingli and Agricola, the Acts state that God's love revealed in Christ's death exposes the horror of sin (ch 8): 'it is evident how much mischief and accursedness lies in our hearts, which may be cleansed and healed only through so costly a sin offering and the sprinkling of the blood of God'. That is, 'it is simply through Christ, rather than by the law, that the Gentiles have been shown their sin and the reconciliation'. There is no need for 'a backward glance at Moses' (ch 9). So, the ministers commit to following Paul's method of preaching to the Gentiles: 'exposing sin by reference to Christ rather than by the law and proclaiming grace and forgiveness of sin by starting from Christ and as known through Christ' (ch 13).

According to the Acts, the Christian stands in a different relationship to the law of Moses than did an Old Testament Jew—'the believing Gentile does not need a legal schoolmaster, for he has already attained the freedom of sonship'. Even Christian Jews kept the law 'voluntarily, and without the law's constraint', for the sake of their fellows. Gentiles 'should discover grace in Christ without the law' (ch 12), so ministers should preach Christ and expose sin in the light of the gospel.

While the Acts side with Agricola against the medieval, Lutheran and Zwinglian use of the law this seems not to be a doctrinaire position—despite the condemnation of the use of the law to address sin. Later the Acts recognise that Moses and the law may have a role in showing the need for salvation: 'in the two commandments which make reference to God and the neighbour, Moses teaches what is deficient in us respecting integrity towards God and our neighbour' (ch 23). We will also see below that they retain a place for the Ten Commandments in catechising children. The Acts are primarily concerned to shape pastoral practice rather than to establish a precise doctrinal position about the role of the law, nevertheless there is a tension between statements which reject preaching the law to sinners and those which allow it.

The Uses of Scripture

Later sections in the Acts turn to more general questions of the place of the Scriptures, especially the Old Testament, in Christian preaching. It is not difficult to imagine that the Acts could be understood in a spiritualist way so that there was no need for any means in the Christian life. Since the Christian is to follow Christ, not Moses and the prophets, it might seem that there is no need for the Old Testament Scriptures or even for any Scriptures. If Christians have Christ and the Spirit, what else do they need?

The discussion of chapter 19 has shown that the sacraments are 'external means' by which 'Christ is presented to believers, he being present in the Holy Spirit, filling and imbuing the heart'. The same point is now made about the Scriptures using 2 Timothy 3:14–16 to show that faith in Christ comes from Scripture and is not, at all, opposed to Scripture as a God-given means: 'the apostle would have Timothy to continue in faith towards Christ, and in the use of Scripture' (ch 23).

The chapter enumerates five ways in which Scripture can be used. Following the theology already established and the text from 2 Timothy, the primary use of Scripture is to make readers and listeners wise for salvation in Christ. Beyond this Scripture is also provides 'doctrine', by which the Acts mean an 'acquaintance with the fruits, gifts, and graces which flow from the cross' rather than the basic articles of the faith. The section then considers 'promises about temporal things' such as Old Testament promises for land and military victory (e.g. Dt 28:1–14). These should be primarily interpreted with a 'spiritual sense' in reference to Christ, though they then allow for a 'temporal sense when once the Spirit of Christ has fulfilled the higher function among us'. Presumably, this refers to eschatological fulfillment. The Acts explain that this approach is to avoid treating promises 'beside and outside of Christ' and even offer the counter-example of Thomas Müntzer (c.1489–1525) who falsely assured peasants they would be protected from cannon fire. The conclusion is that 'we, the servants of the Spirit, should interpret all things spiritually, as in Christ they are all spiritual and true'.

The third use of Scripture is to correct errors. The Acts explain this on the basis of a realistic view of the Christian life. Faith brings 'some measure of knowledge', yet Christians are also 'full of darkness and ignorance' and need correction. Preachers oppose error by 'explaining Scripture according to the analogy of a faith in Christ' not as a 'dead letter'. Finally, Scripture serves for correction and instruction in righteousness through the historical narratives and figures who demonstrate virtues and vices.

The chapter closes with guidance for preachers in their 'reproofs'—these last three uses of Scripture. First, they should make sure that what they decry as unjust truly is so before God. Presumably, what is in view here was the pre-Reformation preaching which condemned people for failing to keep church ceremonies. To pronounce God's judgement on an action which is not, in fact, sin makes the preacher a false prophet, liable to punishment. Second, 'prophetic reproof should be muted and softened in our Christian hearts by the Spirit of Christ', so preaching against sin is done with the sweetness of love. Following the approach of this chapter allows preachers to use a passage of Scripture properly, even if they do not see how it points to Christ. The chapter closes with a final encouragement to preachers to 'faithfully execute our commission to preach Christ'.

This important chapter on the place and use of Scripture maintains the Christological focus of the Acts, yet the other uses of Scripture are described in a somewhat *ad hoc* way. The possibility of using Scripture, especially the Old Testament, for spiritual benefit without finding its foundation in Christ again seems in some tension with the Christocentric emphasis.

The Practice of Preaching

Later chapters address practical aspects of preaching and preaching ministry. Chapter 24 considers how the preacher should address the corruptions of the 'papal church'. Preaching should first present Christ, it is not simply about the corruptions of the church. Yet this is an area which should be addressed to settle the consciences of the poor, who may not understand the need for the changes of the Reformation. The correction is not to be done 'all in one sermon'—presumably that would be overwhelming and ineffective. Rather, the preacher should deal with various faults as appropriate, and should have a plan to do this systematically.

The chapter offers a model of how a minister could preach on the statement that 'Christ is the head of the church, and he is the saviour of his body.' (Eph. 5:23). The sermon would 'present Christ', explaining that the living and true Christ saves, sanctifies and rules his people, inwardly, by his Holy Spirit 'without the mediation of any creature'. This positive gospel truth then provides the basis to critique papal claims to be a mediating representative of Christ. This claim denies that Christ is present to his church, connected as the head to its members, infusing the body with life and power by his Spirit.

The Acts deal with the tone of the preaching on the basis of their Christological view of revelation. Preaching should deal with sin in an evangelical manner, exhorting people to go to Christ and find the fruits of righteousness in him. In that context, the preacher should warn not only about 'outward sin and gross vice ... but also the secret, hidden and spiritual dishonesty of the flesh' such as self-confidence, hypocrisy, spiritual pride and selfishness. Preaching against sin should not spring from 'human passion' and a fighting spirit but from the gospel with a true love for the people. This calls for 'temperate and upright speech be employed, which will serve to edify and not to destroy the weak' (ch 25).

Preaching should focus on those who are present and should correct them and their sins. The task of the preacher is not to preach against people from another city or those (and especially those) in Catholic cities who are spiritually dead, but are not served by denunciation from the pulpits of Bern. Capito explains this with a striking analogy: 'it is as if one were to carry a dead person to be bathed, and leave the chimneysweep blackened in his soot and filth. This latter has need of the bath, but attention is not given to his need. The other, that is the corpse, has no use for a bath, except to prevent his stinking sooner because of the hot weather.' (ch 26).

Given the importance of Scripture, ministers have duty to read them 'industriously' (ch 37). They should confer with each other about their understanding of the Scripture, working with their ministerial colleagues to grow in their knowledge of Christ (ch 38). Sermon preparation requires meditation on Scripture, not merely consulting other sermons and commentaries. This study of the Scriptures is for the sake of the congregation, not so the preacher may display his 'ingenuity or profound spirit'. The Acts do not provide detailed hermeneutical or homiletical instruction, rather they express confidence in the spiritual effectiveness of the Scriptures themselves under the work of the Spirit:

'The truth itself is in the heart, and the love of God issues prescriptions' (ch 39). Ministers may read 'worldly books' (e.g. histories) and may mention them in a sermon, but these do not improve the heart or help the congregation spiritually. Rather, 'all doctrine, admonition, reproof, and correction should come from the Spirit of Christ and divine Scripture' (ch 40).

Preachers and Magistrates

The Acts had to deal with the relationship of the preachers to the civil authorities. The minister is to preach simply and boldly on the basis of the Scriptures. The authority of preaching does not depend on the authority of the magistrates as some preachers have implied. 'Faith considers God alone, and comes from the living Word of God and the illumination of the heart, and does not depend on your excellencies or any human judgement' (ch 27). The alternative error is for the preacher to cast his role as the critic of the authorities, railing against decisions of the council. This style of preaching is often a way to build a following among the common people. (The Acts note that often these preachers are bold in their attacks on the magistrate in their absence but fawning if the authorities are present). The advice is to largely avoid political issues: 'It does not pertain to a servant of Christ that he should subjugate to himself the country's subjects or the magistrates, or that he should put himself forward as something' (ch 28). This is not to say that the magistrates are not subject to the word of God, so the Acts appeal to magistrates to bear with preaching which criticises them (ch 30). Finally, beyond the chief goal of exhorting people to inner sincerity (ch 31)—preaching should also address outer things including obedience to the magistrate in 'Christian discipline and morals' (ch 32).

Catechetical Ministry

When the Acts address education for children in Chapter 35 they illustrate the implication of the doctrine of revelation. As was traditional, children should be taught the Apostles Creed, the Lord's Prayer, and the Ten Commandments, which together are 'the Bible of novices and children'.[32] The Creed is foundational since it teaches 'about God and Christ' and so shows 'how grace and life will commence, grow and reach perfection'. The Lord's Prayer is the way in which someone turns to Christ in faith and receives his grace. The Ten Commandments, while traditional in catechism sit uncomfortably in this curriculum given the earlier assertion that Gentiles 'should discover grace in Christ without the law' (ch 12). The later article concedes that teaching the Ten Commandments is 'an external exercise'—they do not bring grace to the heart. Instead, they humble the flesh and make it conscious of its sin and have to be 'understood by beginning from Christ' in order for knowledge of sin to be profitable.

The Acts: Nascent Reformed Theology

The Acts of the Synod of Bern is an early Reformed confession. In following decades, the movement refined its view on several topics in the Acts, expressing its theology with greater precision and clarifying the connections and distinctions. These developments in Reformed theology display maturation of insights implicit in the Acts, they do not offer radical correction of the Acts.

For instance, the Acts recognise that the Old Testament presents God's grace and looks forward to Christ—'God at all times was declared, though it was with obscurity, by means of various works of grace and definite acts or signs. Today the true Christian knows Him with clarity, certainty, and without mistake, through the Lord Jesus Christ' (ch 5). By 1539 Calvin gave the classic comprehensive formulation of the relationship between the Testaments: 'The covenant made with all the patriarchs is so much like ours in substance and reality that the two are actually one and the same. Yet they differ in the mode of dispensation'.[33]

The *French Confession* (1559) expresses a similar view to the Acts about the relation of the law to Christians asserting that 'all the types

---

[32] For a discussion of the traditional use of Creed, Prayer and Commandments in catechism see Gordon A. Jensen, 'Shaping Piety through Catechetical Structures: The Importance of Order.' *Reformation & Renaissance Review* 10.2 (August 2008): 223–46.

[33] John Calvin, *Institutes of the Christian Religion*, J.T. McNeill, ed., F.L. Battles, trans. (Louisville, KY: Westminster John Knox Press, 2011), 2.10.1, 429.

of the law ended when Christ came in the flesh' though with more clarity the Confession adds that 'the substance and truth of them abides always in His person, who fulfilled them' (Art XXIII).[34] The 1561 *Belgic Confession* presents the more precise position that 'the ceremonies and symbols of the law ceased at the coming of Christ, and that all the shadows are accomplished… yet the truth and substance of them remain with us in Jesus Christ', and 'we still use the testimonies taken out of the law and the prophets to confirm us in the doctrine of the gospel, and to regulate our life in all honourableness to the glory of God, according to His will' (Art XXV).[35]

The Heidelberg Catechism (1563) offers a more mature account of the place of the Ten Commandments in the Christian life applied to external actions and also to the inner life of the Christian. While not even the holiest person can keep the Commandments fully, the Christian earnestly begins to keep all the Commandments. God requires obedience to the Ten Commandments for two reasons so 'we may learn more and more to know our sinful nature … and so the more earnestly seek forgiveness of sins and righteousness in Christ' and so that we will ask for the work of the Spirit 'that we be renewed more and more after the image of God, until we attain the goal of perfection after this life' (Q 114, 115). [36]

Although later decades would refine theological insights, few later documents rival the Acts for a vibrant insight into the great Reformational insight that God reveals himself and redeems his people in Christ. The Acts recognise that all genuine Christian doctrine is grounded in the gospel. True Christian teaching declares 'the kindness and good will which the Father has manifested to us through Christ … who was crucified for our sins, and was raised from the dead to procure the righteousness by which we are justified' (ch 2). This is the brilliant insight that guides the whole document.

From this insight the Acts offer the key hermeneutical principle that all Scripture must be interpreted in light of Christ and his gospel. Every aspect of both Testaments points to Christ. They provide multiple

---

[34] Dennison, *Reformed Confessions*, 2:148.

[35] Dennison, *Reformed Confessions*, 2:438.

[36] Dennison, *Reformed Confessions*, 2:796.

examples of how the Old Testament looks forward to Christ and how his birth and life anticipate his death and resurrection. It may take interpreters time to find these connections, so the Acts offer secondary strategies when the preacher has not been able to find Christ. These too are guided by gospel insights to enable the preacher to continue to preach Christ.

The theological and hermeneutical insights serve the pastoral directions which dominate the Acts. Preachers are to proclaim Christ as the revelation of God and the Saviour of sinners. Sermons are not to be about political concerns but about Christ. The pulpit is not the place for the preacher to attack the magistrates nor to fawn to them. The errors of Rome need to be corrected in light of the gospel, showing that Christ is the present and sufficient saviour and mediator. This gospel will grant hearers forgiveness and also train them in righteous living. The answer to the crisis in Bern was for preachers to attend faithfully to their vocation as messengers of the crucified and risen Christ.

Three

The Importance of Confessional Sufficiency

Carl R. Trueman

Sufficiency: Scriptural and Confessional

Protestants are typically very familiar with the concept of the sufficiency of Scripture. It is true that it has been construed in slightly different ways by different Protestant traditions. Anglicans and Lutherans see Scripture as normative for doctrine but allow that matters of ecclesiology, worship, and aesthetics are not prescriptively covered by Scripture and that the church has some freedom in these matters. The Reformed tradition follows a stricter line, as exemplified in the regulative principle. But the different traditions are agreed on the essential point, that Scripture, and not some independent, ecclesiastically mediated, stream of tradition is to be normative for doctrinal declarations and dogmatic formulations. It is theologically very important.

In this essay, I want to suggest that a principle of similar ecclesiological significance is that of the sufficiency of subordinate confessional standards. Clearly, they do not have the same significance. That is, confessions are 'normed norms' and Scripture is the 'norming norm'. And yet a failure to grasp the importance of confessional sufficiency can lead to problematic and counterproductive situations in the life of the church.

What I denote by the term *confessional sufficiency* is as much a part of the ecclesiastical imagination or culture as it is a self-conscious principle of action. It is the idea that as the church faces new challenges, whether at the level of life in the local congregation or at the more general level of the wider culture, her instinct is to address such using the established tool available, i.e., the confessional standards, without either adding to or revising such. As I noted, this is as much an attitude, or a function of how we imagine the church to be, as it is a principle of operation. We as church members need to see it as a desirable thing in order to commend it through our practice.

The Pressure on Confessional Sufficiency

The church's confessional standards serve a number of purposes. They provide a doctrinal standard for office bearers, allowing them to be held accountable both by each other and by congregants. They give a transparent public summary of the church's position on key elements of the Christian faith. They set forth an aspirational norm for the doctrinal education of laypeople. In short, they are the immediate and most convenient source of the church's public teaching and thus an obvious place to look for guidance of the church in whatever context she finds herself.

Now, it is a truism that we today live in an era of great change and flux. This takes numerous related forms. Two obvious examples are morality and technology. In the moral sphere, questions of sexual *morality* have morphed into questions of sexual *identity*, presenting the church with a situation where her traditional teaching on the former now renders her vulnerable not simply to the perennial accusation of prudery in denying the legitimacy of certain patterns of behaviour, but also of immorality in denying the legitimacy of certain notions of identity. To reject homosexual behaviour is today not simply to disapprove of particular acts, but to reject how certain people think of themselves at the deepest level.

In the technological sphere, human beings demonstrate an amazing and ongoing ability to manipulate nature and overcome significant natural barriers. One example of pressing importance for many Christians is that of artificial reproduction. Where once a couple who were prevented from conceiving a child by some quirk of nature, now that same couple might well be able to have a child through fertility treatment or in vitro fertilisation or surrogacy.

These two examples are useful because they present the challenge of change in distinct forms. In the first, that of sexual morality, the challenge is not simply the church's teaching on behaviour; it is also a deeper challenge to the concept of identity. In the second, the challenge is to what we might call the hierarchy of goods: the desire for a child is a good thing; but is it such a basic good that any means will justify the end? And if not, how can we relate it to other goods in a manner which allows for truly faithful and Christian guidance on such?

These are just two of the most obvious examples of the ways in which Western society had changed dramatically in the last fifty years and, with the rapidity of changes in the technological sphere, the continued status of flux throughout society is likely to continue apace for the foreseeable future. And in such a context, the question of the contemporary sufficiency of a confessional statement is appropriate and important. To focus on the Presbyterian tradition, it is surely legitimate to ask if a document written in the seventeenth century in a culture so different to our own can be truly adequate for the needs of English-speaking Christians today, let alone those from cultures which do not even share the same Anglophone roots.

One obvious answer to this is that we should abandon the Westminster Confession and redraft a completely new document of more relevance to today. Such a radical move would have the advantage of being a contemporary document, framed in the language of our day, and (at least in theory) tailored towards addressing the most urgent matters the church faces in a pertinent and accessible manner. The problem—and, for me, a fatal problem—would be that such a document would be in danger of losing that continuity with the past which is of the very essence of historic Christianity. Paul's mandate to Timothy in 2 Timothy 1:13, that he follow the form of sound words, and his appeals to 'the traditions' in 1 Corinthians 11:2 and 2 Thessalonians 2:15 both speak to this. It is also obvious that a message rooted in historical actions and their unchanging significance, as is the gospel of Jesus Christ, should possess a historical continuity of content which requires any confessional production by the church to take into account that which has gone before. In common parlance, the gospel cannot and need not be reinvented for the present age of technological innovation any more than the wheel. In short, wholesale confessional replacement is neither necessary nor wise for the church.

A second answer is that the Confession should be revised or supplemented to take account of new challenges posed to the church. This is a more plausible option precisely because it affirms the historical continuity of the church's testimony even as it takes account of current changes and challenges. Thus, one could envisage additional paragraphs or chapters which cover the relevant topics—say, something on same-sex marriage or gender or in vitro fertilisation.

While I would not argue that such an approach is intrinsically wrong, as I am prepared to do with the first suggestion, I believe this approach is unwise, for a number of reasons.

The first reason it is unwise is the ecumenical implications that supplementation brings in its wake. The most famous example of this is, of course, the addition of the *Filioque* clause to the Nicene Creed at the Second Council of Toledo in AD 527. While the split between Eastern and Western churches did not formally take place until 1054, the revision of the Creed was a contributing cause to the schism and remains a point of contention between Western Christianity and the various branches of Eastern orthodoxy to this day.

I do not raise this example in order to address the specific point at issue in the addition of the *Filioque* but to point to the implications of any alterations to established creedal and confessional standards, particularly those done by way of addition: the documents immediately become less catholic and ecumenical in scope. Protestantism is woefully fragmented already. When even churches who share an identical confessional standard start adding to that standard, the result is likely to be the generating of yet more fractures and divisions.

Now, it is arguable that the addition of something like the *Filioque* raises this issue in a peculiarly acute from precisely because it addresses a matter of theology proper and thereby the very definition of God. To add a section on, say, same-sex marriage, does not pose quite such immediate risk, dealing as it does with what we might argue are implications of the Confession's teaching rather than significantly adding to the overall theological structure of Christianity. I would concede that, but then point to the fact that, if this is so (which I believe it is) then the need for such an addition is moot. If it is merely making explicit what is implicit in the Confession, then why add to the Confession?

A second reason against such revision is the question of burdening consciences. The more documents to which a minister needs to subscribe, or the more additions made to the Confession, the more his conscience is burdened and bound. Now, there is nothing intrinsically wrong with such a notion. The whole idea of confessional subscription is predicated upon such binding. As a minister, I have willingly taken vows to uphold the teaching of the Confession, vows that I was not required to take simply as a Christian believer. Should I now deny the Confession's teaching at any point, I am rightly liable to prosecution and discipline by the courts of the church.

So why do I find that the idea of adding material to the Confession raises the issue of the burdening and binding of the conscience in a problematic form? It is this: it is not the principle of the matter considered in the abstract, but the practical precedent which such additions set. Once one has allowed for an addition to the Confession, the question of how and where to stop becomes acute. If one adds a clause on same-sex marriage, should one add a clause on racism, for example? While some may respond 'Of course!', the problem is that, sooner or later, an issue is going to come to the fore on which Christians legitimately disagree. Numerous examples come to mind: healthcare, welfare, even racism itself, given that its very definition is now a matter of real contention in Christian circles. In short, additions to the Confession might not only have ecumenical implications for relations with other churches; they might even provide cause for tension and even formal division within a single denomination.

Twice over the last decade I have been invited to sign (non-ecclesiastical) statements about issues in our contemporary world. One expressed revulsion at child abuse, the other asserted heterosexuality as the norm for human beings. In the first case, my refusal to sign led to correspondence with people who wondered if I did not care about abused children, in the second with those wondering if I had changed my opinion on homosexuality. I will discuss my response below. Now, while neither case was an instance of a group intentionally adding documents to ecclesiastical subscription, it is worth noting that these reactions were interesting precisely because new statements, additional to the Confession and non-ecclesiastical in nature, had somehow become tests of Christian orthodoxy. In both cases, a group to which I did not belong was using a document on which I had no formal influence to assess my biblical fidelity. Of course, this is not a case of formal addition to a confession; but it is indicative of a mentality, common among evangelical Protestants, that such documents can in effect function as such additions.

A third reason for not taking the route of adding to the Confession is that such action can end up being a form of confessional 'whack-a-mole.' Such a term might sound somewhat flippant but the danger it describes is most significant. In the game of Whack-A-Mole, the mole randomly appears at various holes on the gameboard and the player has to try to hit it on the head before it disappears. In practice, the mole is usually so fast and his appearances so random that the player lands his mallet a moment too late to actually score a point.

That is the danger with making additions to the Confession. We are creatures of time and place. More specifically, we are creatures of the time and place in which we find ourselves. And we are also creatures whose minds tend (understandably) to be preoccupied with the pressing issues of that time and place. Transgenderism, for example, is obviously an important issue for us, both politically and pastorally, in a way that it was not for our spiritual ancestors, even those of recent decades. We need to reflect on this issue in a way that they did not. Of course, our ancestors were subject to the same kind of thing in their own day: English Christians in the First World War no doubt had to wrestle with matters such as conscription and conscientious objection; American Christians in the late eighteenth century had to address the matter of colonial rebellion; French Huguenots in the sixteenth century had to confront the issue of a Roman Catholic magistracy. Every generation has its own cultural problems and pathologies.

Further, the speed at which our culture is changing makes the whack-a-mole problem a very real one. Precisely because confessions are very important documents, the process for revising or adding to them is appropriately cautious, difficult, and protracted. Instant responses to cultural challenges are thus impossible to mount in terms of confessional revisions. Therefore, by the time the process for confessional addition is completed, the likelihood is that a new clear and present danger will be present in the culture. Same-sex marriage is a good example: in the United States the Supreme Court judgement of Obergefell v. Hodges (2015) occurred at a point when transgenderism was already exploding onto the scene in the form of Bruce/Caitlyn Jenner.

This is where the corrosive nature of time is such a great help. Ironically, it is the very age of the Westminster Confession which offers one reason why it is such a useful document. Time itself is witness to the fact that the matters upon which the Confession opines have a perennial relevance. Now, this is not to say that there have not been confessional revisions, but such are interesting. In the American version, for example, the pope is no longer identified as the Antichrist in WCF 25:6, the Establishment Principle has been dropped from WCF 31:2 (though, due to an oversight it remains in the Larger Catechism 191), and the interdict on a man marrying his dead wife's sister has been removed from WCF 25:4. Time has, as it were, dissolved parts of the Confession that had more to do with the immediate context of seventeenth-century England than with the gospel of Jesus Christ. And there is a lesson there for us: we must beware of raising the most real and pressing issues of our own day to the level of the perennial problems of every age. Sin is always going to be a problem; the ways in which sin manifests itself change, often dramatically, over time. Focusing on the symptoms has its place but not generally, I would argue, at the level of confessional subscription.

And that leads me to the fourth issue I have with confessional additions: Where does it stop? Once we move in this direction, the precedent is set, and the ecclesiastical imagination becomes attuned to the idea that this is the way to handle challenges as they manifest themselves in the church and in the wider culture. At that point the whole idea of the Confession as a normative document for the transmission of a stable tradition becomes less and less plausible. It is not so much an authoritative document as an ongoing testimony to and running commentary on the various things the church has thought important at various times.

Confessional Sufficiency and Contemporary Concerns

If neither writing a new confession nor supplementing the existing one are prudent options, I would argue that what we need is a culture where the ecclesiastical imagination is informed by the notion of confessional sufficiency. By this I mean that the response to new challenges, theological and ethical, within both church and wider society should be to address them via the Confession as it now stands. This requires significant effort on the part of the church but avoids the pitfalls outlined above.

To return to my refusal to sign the statements on child abuse and homosexuality. In neither case were the groups involved attempting to add to a confessional document, but my refusal to sign was connected to my own view of the Westminster Standards' sufficiency. In short, in adhering to the Standards, I was already committed to a moral framework which precluded both child abuse and the legitimacy of same-sex marriage, even though neither are explicitly mentioned in the Confession or the Catechisms. The positive teaching on marriage in WCF 24 clearly excludes same-sex marriage, while LC 129–130 and 136 have obvious significance for anyone intending harm against children.

Same-sex marriage and child abuse are, of course, relatively simple cases to address via the Standards. But what of transgenderism? Are the Standards sufficient to address the basic issues involved in this modern cultural pathology?

First, it is useful to note the various assumptions necessary to make transgenderism plausible. It assumes a separation of sex and gender, such that one can have the body of a man and yet really be a woman. It prioritises psychology, in that one's inner convictions are fundamental and decisive for identity. And it assumes that the notion of 'man' and 'woman' are at base culturally constructed performances which have no tight connection to the physical characteristics of the body. Let us take each of these in turn.

On the first, the Confession clearly affirms the Bible's teaching of human beings as being created male and female (WCF 4.2). Then, in the chapter on marriage, it reiterates the distinction between male and female, this time linking it to marriage, the second function of which is procreation (WCF 24.1–2). The obvious assumption is that male and female are to be understood in part in terms of physical complementarity. This would seem quite sufficient for the church to reject the distinction between sex and gender and the idea that 'man' and 'woman' are socially constructed performances. In this context, however, it is worth noting that the Confession offers little in the way of further prescriptions about what behaviour should be expected from men and women. This silence allows room for the fact that concepts of masculinity and femininity do vary from time to time and place to place.

As to the prioritising of psychology in identity, WCF 6 renders confidence in apparently natural instincts and intuitions as highly problematic. That one feels something is no safe guide to reality. To be convinced that one is a woman trapped in a man's body is thus an idea which needs to be subjected to the authority of Scripture, and not immediately assumed as legitimate.

In sum, while the Standards do not address the transgender issue directly, they provide sufficient clarity on a number of biblical points that can be used as a framework for doing so. Now, this is not to say that the Standards push for a one-size-fits-all approach in all pastoral situations. But it is to say that they provide a set of guiding principles by which each situation can be understood.

Yet there are even more complicated and heart-wrenching challenges than transgenderism—for example, the question of artificial reproduction where the moral issues are far more complicated and cross-pressured. On the issue of homosexuality, the desire for sexual union with someone of the same sex is obviously sinful as it stands outside the bounds of sexual activity as prescribed by the Bible and summarised in the Standards. Transgenderism is perhaps trickier in that the rebellion involved is in one sense of a different kind to that of homosexuality, in that it does not necessarily involve illegitimate sexual desire; but in another sense, it is very similar, in its rejection of the authority of the body. It too desires something that is wrong. By contrast, the infertile couple seeking treatment so that they might have a child desires something good—to give life and to give their love to another. They want their marriage to do what marriage is biblically intended for: the creation of new life. And yet does the good intention justify any means by which it might be achieved?

This is too complicated an area to resolve in a brief essay, but we can at least make a start at pointing to a number of principles in the Standards which should guide our thinking.

First, part of the spirit of our technological age is the assumption that because something can be done, it should be done. While this should not need to be stated, the spirit of the age has a habit of shaping all of our intuitions and so the first thing we need to remember in addressing a matter such as artificial reproduction is that the technology is not its own justification, but that it needs to be set within a larger moral framework. And that is a clear implication of WCF 19. That Adam and Eve could sin, and that we can continue so to do, is no justification for us acting in such a manner. The universe has a moral structure which is not defined by what we *can* do, but instead determines what we *should* do.

Second, the Larger Catechism's teaching on the Sixth Commandment makes it clear that the taking of life is illegitimate with the exceptions of public justice, war, and self-defence (LC 136). This would seem to make any approach to reproduction which involves the creation of what we might call 'surplus embryos' illegitimate for a Christian.

Third—and here we enter somewhat trickier territory—there is the question of how the process of artificial reproduction turns the gift of life into a commodity. Several things come into play here. First, the doctrine of creation indicates that life is a gift of God. This is the implication of WCF 4. There is also a distinction between the creation of children and the production of anything else. Procreation is one of the purposes of marriage, WCF 24.2. The production of nothing else—not the growing of crops, nor the making of a piece of pottery nor the writing of a computer code—is subject to the same restriction of origin. The creation of life has a unique moral status and a unique moral context. Reproduction is part of what marital union is intended for; marriage is not simply one possible way of producing children.

Now, none of this is to say that discussion of artificial reproduction is foreclosed in all of its forms by the WCF, but it is to indicate that some basic elements of that necessary discussion are contained therein. The challenge may be a new one, post-dating the Westminster Assembly by over three centuries, but this does not mean that the Confession has nothing to say or that the church needs to supplement it with more chapters. And it may be an issue that vanishes in the future, depending on the state of medical technology, and so (unlike, for example, the doctrine of the Trinity or human depravity) lacks the perennial relevance to merit status as an item worthy of confessional definition. Yet the Confession nonetheless speaks, if indirectly, to it.

Conclusion

Same-sex marriage, child abuse, transgenderism, and artificial reproduction are merely four of the more obvious examples of where modern culture is putting pressure on the church in its roles both as witness of the truth to the wider world and as the mother of her people. In a very real sense three of these are also new and unprecedented challenges. In an age already inclined to dismiss history and tradition and to root authority in innovation and technique, the temptation to supplement or even sideline confessional documents is very strong. And yet that temptation must be resisted for ecumenical and theological reasons. If church unity is important to us, and if we take seriously the Bible's teaching about the unchanging nature of God's truth and the consequent importance of its faithful transmission from generation to generation, then we need to cultivate an attitude which takes confessional sufficiency seriously.

This is not to say that confessional revision or supplementation is by definition wrong. But it is to argue that the default position should always be to strive to use the confessions we have to address the issues of our day. It is, one might say, a matter of church culture or imagination which leads us to assume confessional sufficiency. Of course, as Presbyterians we can and should avail ourselves of our ability to authorise study committees whose task is to show how the teaching of Scripture, summarised in the Confessions, applies to the complex and urgent needs of any given hour. Such documents are vital to the life of a healthy denomination. But let us be very, very hesitant to alter or supplement our confessions.

Four

Functional Deism: The Challenges in the Pew

Noel K. Weeks

As I preach in various churches and as I talk to people from various churches, I hear a frequent complaint: 'We are not being encouraged and edified by biblical teaching, but we are constantly being told that our duty and role is to be evangelists.'

A little questioning reveals that the complaint centres around the paradox felt by congregations, where they feel that they are not fed by teaching on the glories and power of Christ, but feel that they are being expected to be proclaimers of those very realities. To be fair it is possible that the expectation is more that they be 'publicisers' of church programs, but they themselves are feeling unenthused about what the church is giving them.

In writing this in a volume dedicated to Peter Barnes, I am not suggesting that Peter shares this problem. Rather I hope that, as somebody committed to the health of the church universal, he will welcome exploration of this issue.

I do not know of anybody else who has written on this phenomenon, who might have historical knowledge, which I lack. Hence much of this essay will consist of postulated cultural and theological background. The direction I am examining has become so universal, in certain quarters, that there has not been a need felt to explain and justify, or if that has been done, it has been done in terms of the desired objective, ignoring the fact that the route chosen to meet the objective needs explanation. What 'everybody' does, but 'nobody' feels the need to explain, is hard to analyse. If I suggest the wrong causes, I hope it will inspire an 'insider' to give a better explanation.

What Does the Bible Say?

The paradox of the whole issue is that the concentration on creating evangelists, rather than edifying the saints, stands in marked contrast to what we find in the documents of the New Testament church. It is very hard to find anything in the New Testament epistles that could be interpreted as urging the believers to get out and evangelise. The one such command is addressed to the church planter, Timothy (2 Tim. 4:5). Conversely, the building up of the congregation in truth and conduct is universally present in the epistles. Since the described trend is most concentrated in churches that would see themselves as being 'evangelical', the discrepancy needs explanation.

Ignoring the New Testament data on the church has historical precedent. However, that had been a response to a political situation where monarchs and ruling oligarchies found it easier to control the church through appointed bishops. Political necessity was justified under the doctrine that the NT church form was not meant to be a model.[1] However, historically, evangelical episcopal churches were as anxious as anybody to build up the people of God in Christ, and in some cases put all others to shame in that respect.

Thus, while a conviction of the non-exemplary nature of the NT church may have contributed to the present situation, it cannot be the only factor. I am going to suggest that there are two other significant interacting factors, one theological and one cultural. The cultural factor is well documented and explored. It is the fact that Deism is the atmosphere in which most formal theology and much of ecclesiastical practice operates in our culture.

Deism

Deism may be considered from different perspectives. It is the theology that complemented the Enlightenment, or The Age of Reason. True, or classical, Deism reflected a search for a more lenient religious practice than that which characterised the two sides, Protestant and Catholic, which fought devastating wars of religion in the wake of the

[1] It is not strictly part of this topic, but it seems to me that Paul thought differently. See 1 Cor. 11:1,16, 23; 14:32,36; 1 Tim. 3:14.

Reformation. Some of its inspiration comes from classical stoicism. It found that position by giving a theological form to the physical theory which came out of early modern science. The world was seen as having been constituted by God to operate in conformity to a set of physical laws. Since these laws were perfect, as coming from a perfect God, there was no need for God to intervene in the world after the initial creation. To believe in ongoing divine activity could even be stigmatised as lack of belief in the effectiveness of divine law.[2] God was thus excluded from the world by his own law. In this emphasis it reflects the desire of the unbeliever to be as far away from God as possible.

Parallel to this set of physical laws was a set of perfect moral laws, also of divine origin. However, the doctrine of the exclusion of God meant that these laws could not be seen as an act of revelation. They were postulated to be innate in man as he was created. Thus there is no notion of a Fall in this theology, but yet something was needed to explain the sorry state of the present world. A simple Protestant history of the church was taken, secularised and universalised. Whereas Protestantism saw a fall from the gospel simplicity of the church because of a priestly take over of the Ancient Church, Deism postulated that the simple, original, ethical religion of all mankind had been perverted due to a sacerdotal takeover of religion. If there was conflict in the world, then the 'priests' were to blame. Protestant clergy, since they historically believed something different to this Deist theology, also fell into the category of evil 'priests'.

Several basic features were removed from Christian theology by the doctrine that God was excluded from the world by his own law. Jesus could not be God. The Bible could not be inspired by God. There could be no regeneration of the sinner, or 'new birth'. Since denial of the real sinfulness of man went along with this theology, these losses were not viewed as significant.

The consequence was decline and decimation of the church. As so often happens, while there were those who thought that espousing the

---

[2] There is a thorough exploration of the consequences of Deism and its development into evolutionary theory in J.C. Greene, *The Death of Adam: Evolution and Its Impact on Western Thought* (Ames, IA: Iowa State University, 1959). For examples of the argument that for God to play a continuing role in the creation disparaged his law and thus God see p. 22.

views of the world would make the church popular, it did not work in the past, nor does it in the present.

A Crucial Consequence

As explorations in the physical sciences continued, there came a growing realisation of the complexities of physical matter. Basic atomic theory developed and with it a study of forces. Hence the 'understanding' of the original state of creation changed. It came to be seen as a creation of a world in a primordial state. An illustrative example was the discussion of the original state of the universe: Was a completed Earth the original state, or did the Earth develop from a more primordial state? The logic of Deist thinking, where there is a desire to make God more distant, made the original state more and more unformed. A consequence of this logic was that life was not part of the original creation but rather a later development. Additionally, the physical laws, which influenced Deism, were understood as laws of mechanics and therefore the logic of the system required that life be understandable in mechanical terms.

The reverse consequence was that if life had come into being and had no mechanical explanation, then God would have had to intervene to create it. If he did, then Deist theory was in ruins. Hence the drive to find a natural explanation of the origin of life, 'natural' in these terms meaning conceivable in mechanical terms without divine intervention. That is, the central modern intellectual framework must collapse without a theory of biological evolution.

Original Deism had postulated an innate moral consciousness within every human. As exploration led to the discovery of more 'primitive' societies, with very different ethics, and as the direction of thinking was more towards creation in rude and primordial states, that thesis became more implausible. Yet revealed divine law had disappeared with the rejection of revelation. Without an ethical structure, moral and civil law has no foundation. The logic of Deism was already threatening the basis of civil society.

Consequently, in what is called the 'Scottish Enlightenment', proponents, especially Adam Smith, set out to create a basis for law and the operation of society from factors internal to society and its development. Smith thought as a developmentalist long before biological evolution was generally accepted. In his scheme, man began as hunter-gatherers, developed to nomadic herders, then to farmers and finally to commercial society.[3] Each development brought with it a development in the law of property. Nomadic hunters have no possessions besides a few personal weapons and utensils. Since they have no fixed abode, they have no law of real estate. Nomadic herders have property in their herds but not in land. Hence law is a natural development of the state of societies since nomads have no land ownership.[4]

Smith applied a similar approach to the dynamics of commercial life. He observed that specialisation within the manufacturing process led to efficiency.[5] He argued that if producers were left without interference, their natural desire for profit would lead merchants to try to undercut each other in price and thus the public would profit by reduced costs.[6] Thus competition between producers had a beneficial effect. The less efficient and competitive might be driven out of business but the result would be public good.

There are crucial Deist ways of thinking underlying these arguments. Deists saw a perfect world as a world in which God did not interfere. The benefit of non-interference is now being carried over to thinking about the state. Commercial life and society will operate best when the logic of the process is left to work of itself and the state does

---

[3] Smith was not alone in proposing a four-stage theory of human development. For others see A. Kuper, *The Reinvention of Primitive Society: Transformations of a Myth*, 2nd ed. (Abingdon: Routledge, 2005), 30; R.L. Meek, 'Smith, Turgot, and the 'Four Stages' Theory,' *History of Political Economy* 3 (1971), 9–27.

[4] It is intriguing that in the Mabo (1992) discussion, that is the exploration of the injustice that white settlers to Australia took no notice of the fact that they were depriving the original inhabitants of their land, there was a lack of reference to the legal 'basis' on which the white settlement acted. Is that because Smith's theories were so integral to the modern attempt to operate without God, that they could not be exposed to criticism—even belated criticism? Could it also be that Smith's thought was seen as a pinnacle of academic wisdom and we are reluctant to face the fact that respectable academic wisdom results in practical misery?

[5] Adam Smith, *An Inquiry into the Nature and Causes of the Wealth of Nations* (London, W. Straman and T. Cadeli, 1776), 1:1.

[6] Smith, *Wealth of Nations*, 1:2.; H.D. Kurz, 'Adam Smith on Markets, Competition and Violations of Natural Liberty,' *Cambridge Journal of Economics* 40 (2016), 615–38.

not interfere. Even what might be seen as bad, namely human desire for profit, serves a greater good.

The obvious objection to this non-involvement of the state is that it allows opportunity for criminal elements. In his *Theory of Moral Sentiments*[7] Smith developed a moral theory in terms of things intrinsic to men. The crucial element in this theory is 'sympathy'. We develop our moral system by awareness of the moral sentiments of those around us. Their disapproval of our actions creates shame in us. Thus there is a remedy within the system without outside interference.[8] Of course there is an unstated and unexamined premise here. It is that those around us, that is, humanity as a whole, have good moral instincts. For if people are not basically good, the exclusion of God's justice from the world, coupled with a tendency of the system to make the state inactive, must lead to moral chaos. The goodness of man is a necessity for a Deist system. Whenever a shifting to an inactive God occurs in theology or ethics, a belief in human goodness must accompany it.

I have wandered into the commercial side of Deist theory for a specific reason. Smith's theory made competition something that sometimes had sad consequences in inefficient, insufficiently entrepreneurial, companies going out of business, but the result was the greater good. The struggle of competition is good and leads to progress. That logic was applied to competition between races[9] and then became the 'solution' to the problem that life raised for Deism. Darwin's 'survival of the fittest' is simply Smith's economic theory applied to animals.

[7] Originally published 1759.

[8] Smith's thought and the way it has influenced later society is a classic example of a system that is wrong in principle, but sometimes practically right, but for the wrong reason, and therefore a disaster in operation. His defence of free trade and commerce rests on the wrong foundation but often succeeds temporarily better than socialism because socialism involves the diversion of the state from its primary, God given responsibility, of administering justice. Capitalism, founded on Smith, likewise fails because the Deist logic of Smith tells it that sin is not a real problem and the internal dynamics of society and commerce will take care of it. A history of Australian Liberal governments shows many examples of efforts to free commerce that led to the downfall of governments because there was indifference to the exploitation of those efforts by evil men.

[9] Hence it was argued that as an inferior race Australian Aborigines were doomed to die out and nothing could be done about it. Note this was being said before Darwin published: J. Harris, *One Blood* (Sutherland, NSW: Albatross, 1990), 124, 343.

Darwin needed a theory of evolution that worked mechanically without divine intervention. Survival of the fittest gave him that. He also needed a theory or an explanation of the shape of nature, with its division into distinct types. The biologists with whom he had to contend, such as Georges Cuvier and Richard Owen, were by no means modern creationists. They were aware of the huge gaps that separated birds from mammals, shells from worms, plants from animals. So they postulated independent creation of these major groups. 'Survival of the fittest' might explain how these groups came to exist but it would not explain why, here and now, we do not see forms intermediate between these major groups. Darwin found his solution in the way H. Milne-Edwards, a French zoologist, had applied the economic principle of specialisation, or the division of labour, to zoology. Milne-Edwards was clear that his theory was based upon political economy, but Darwin omitted to mention that.[10] In Darwin's treatment an animal with an advantageous tendency to specialisation would be favoured by the principle of the survival of the fittest and produce more progeny than the less specialised. Hence the less specialised would die out, leaving the observed gaps between major biological groups.[11]

Thus we see thinking, developed to solve a Deist need in one area, applied to solving a Deist dilemma in another area. When we understand that, we understand the crucial weakness of Darwin's theory and all its recent variants. Smith's theory of competition was developed in terms of humans capable of rational thought and of developing new inventions and models.[12] As mentioned above, in this theory, competition was seen as inherently good and progressive. However it was then applied to the animal kingdom, where there are no entrepreneurs

---

[10] If other scientists were aware that ideas were coming from political economy, why was that not pointed out against Darwin? The reason must be because Adam Smith's ideas had become common sense wisdom. To see it, one had to disagree with Smith. One person who saw that Darwin was dependent upon English social and economic thought was Karl Marx, who nevertheless welcomed Darwin as a promoter of atheism: D.J. Depew & B.H. Webster, *Darwinism Evolving* (Cambridge, MA: MIT Press, 1995), 105.

[11] S.S. Schweber, 'Darwin and the Political Economists: Divergence of Character,' *Journel of the History of Biology* 13 (1980), 195–289.

[12] James Watt, the inventor of the steam engine, was part of Smith's circle. Smith stressed the importance of invention for economic growth.

made in the image of God.[13] What then gives the progressive, new impulse to biological evolution? Specialisation can certainly be observed in particular biological groups. However in terms of modern genetic theory, what is happening is the selection of certain genetic compositions from the wider range present within that population. Darwin's theory requires that it keep on happening. Continued inventions can happen in human industrial life because of the unique human brain. Diminished concentrations of genetic diversity in animals are not going to produce even greater genetic possibilities in the future.[14]

Yet we must be aware that the present doctrine of evolution could collapse and metamorphose into a doctrine equally favourable to Deism, as long as that Deism is not so based on mechanical images. Darwinianism is being held to because, at present, the whole attempt to remove God from our world goes down if it goes down. There are signs in the wind of an alternate model. Anybody who takes an interest in the history of science knows how such an alternate can take over.[15] Besides the inability of random events to produce viable organisms, there are two crucial weaknesses with current theory. One has been known for a long time, the other has arisen out of more recent research.[16] Major biological groups are characterised by group-defining features that are standard for the group though developed in slightly different forms. An example is the limbs of mammals. Whether adapted for swimming in the dugong, burrowing in the mole, running in the horse, or flying in the bat, there is a basic skeletal form. Feathers in birds are another

---

[13] Competition and thus selection in nature was recognised before Darwin and by a naturalist that Darwin read. However it was seen as a conservative principle. If one assumes animals are well adapted to their environments, then a variation is less likely to be suited to the environment and likely to be eliminated by natural selection. What Darwin did was to change thinking about the relation of animal and environment: L.C. Eiseley & A. Grote, 'Charles Darwin, Edward Blyth, and the Theory of Natural Selection,' *Proc. Amer. Phil. Soc.* 103 (1959), 101.

[14] There is the possibility that some of the older genetic complex may remain and be selected for if the circumstances change. Thus domestic animals that go feral tend to return to their original pre-domestication 'wild type'. It was because of this fact that Wallace rejected Darwin's arguments from animal and plant breeding.

[15] Thomas Kuhn, *The Structure of Scientific Revolutions* (Chicago: University of Chicago, 1962).

[16] For a popular description see Michael Denton, *Evolution: Still a Theory in Crisis* (Seattle: Discovery Institute, 2106).

example, as are flowers in angiosperms. If Darwinianism is true and the body plan of an organism is a response to the influence of the environment, why would we see, for example, fins and wings develop in some mammals but the basic plan remain unaltered? An alternate plan, more adapted to swimming or flying is surely possible.

Furthermore, if we postulate some earlier evolutionary process that led to this basic, later preserved plan, where is the evidence for this process of development in the fossil record? The failure of intermediary forms leading to the basic plan is part of the 'gaps' in the record. To add to the problem, it is very difficult to conjecture the series of intermediary forms leading to the fixed plan, each of which, under Darwinian doctrine, have to be superior in function to the previous form and capable of surviving. What are the intermediary stages in the development of the feather, remembering that a feather is useless without the body structure and metabolism for flight?[17] Basic body plans, whose origin and persistence cannot be explained by Darwinism, are a biological fact. Furthermore Darwin was correct about the need for specialisation. Yet Darwinism took over the supposed generalised ancestors of the specialised forms as the evolutionary precursors of the later specialised form. Thus the supposed forefather of rats, bats, dugongs, whales and so on was claimed to be a mammal without speciality. Yet just as it is hard to make a living as a man without a trade, so it is hard for a non-specialised animal to survive. The 'missing links' between major animal groups are missing because they contradict one of Darwin's basic insights.

A second problem arises from embryology, or the study of the development of the young of the species. Many crucial developments in structure do not arise from genetic control but from a reaction to the stage of development reached under genetic control. Real examples are very complex, so allow me to set up a hypothetical illustration. Two proteins form, each under genetic control. They then interact to produce a structure that is different to either and essential for the organism. Darwinian evolution must operate by giving a greater chance of survival, and hence progeny, to an organism with a particular gene. Yet here an interaction of genes is essential. How can 'blind', 'chance',

[17] For refutation of the attempt to derive feathers from reptilian scales see Denton, *Evolution: Still a Theory in Crisis*, 170–80.

evolution know to preference genes, which, only in combination, lead to the required form? What makes the two proteins interact to produce the needed structure? There are many examples of this problem and they are far more complex than this illustration, making development by Darwinian evolution even more unbelievable.[18] Connected to this problem is the fact that the genetic template for an organism is extremely complex. Random change in it produces chaos, not evolutionary developments.[19]

Michael Denton and others are moving towards a different model. It is the idea that reality is inherently structure building. Order, in the sense of biological order, arises spontaneously out of the inherent character of reality. This model is anathema to a Darwinian, because Darwinism reflects the physical-mechanical thinking of the Enlightenment. However the Enlightenment model has been challenged. Romanticism was a reaction against the impersonalism of the Enlightenment.[20] The realisation of the existence of a 'Goldilocks Zone'[21] and the difficulty of finding other planets in the same zone has made the existence of our Earth an enigma. How, apart from an act of God, can we explain life here on Earth? Where Denton and others are going is towards an intrinsic tendency to life and structure in the very depths of Nature. Obviously that idea can be put in Deist terms and many promoters of it before the triumph of Darwinism were Deists. As Darwinism

---

[18] For examples see Denton, *Evolution: Still a Theory in Crisis*, 130–224.

[19] For a significant interchange between evolutionists see Marcel P. Schützenberger, 'Algorithms and the Neo-Darwinian Theory of Evolution' in *Mathematical Challenges to the Neo-Darwinian Interpretation of Evolution* ed. P.S. Moorhead & M.M. Kaplan (Philadelphia: Wistar Institute, 1967), 73–75. The recorded discussion after the lecture is fascinating because of the unwillingness of some of the evolutionary biologists present to accept that one cannot subject a complex coded system, such as the genotype, to random change without producing chaos. C.H. Waddington retorts that asking for an alternate model to the criticised Neo-Darwinian model is an argument for special creation. In other words Neo-Darwinianism must be right because without it we are back to special creation. The same basic objection to evolutionary theory is presented in M.J. Behe, *Darwin's Black Box* (New York: Touchstone, 1996). The general response of the scientific establishment to ban any discussion of 'Intelligent Design', shows that they have no answer.

[20] See 'Goethe and the Idea of Scientific Truth' in Erich Heller, *The Disinherited Mind* (Cambridge: Bowes & Bowes, 1952)

[21] This refers to the fact that life on a planet is possible only in a zone that is 'just right', such as not too hot, not too cold and so on.

fails and as we are in a culture averse, for right and wrong reasons, to the hard mechanicalism and impersonalism of the Enlightenment, the door may open for a 'scientific revolution' which will promote a theory of intrinsic organisation in Nature leading to structured life. My concern is that it would still be a Deist model and thus bring with it the same problems the church is currently facing.

I come back to the basic point that biological evolution was crucial or the whole Deist scheme would collapse. Therefore when a mechanism was 'found' it was seized enthusiastically. Since a totally inactive god is little different to no god, Deism progressed to Atheism. Atheism needs evolution just as much as Deism did. To accept evolution in any form, including 'theistic evolution', is to accept the principle behind Deism, namely an inactive, distant god.

A Second Consequence

The dominance of mechanical theory in the shaping of Deism means that everything is conceptualised as matter in motion, operating according to definite laws. That means that in theory the motion of any large body can be understood as a product of the forces that have impinged upon it. If it can be so understood, then its motions can be predicted if one knows all the impacting forces. If that is so, then we can say that it is determined by the forces acting upon it.

Apply that to a human. We must be totally determined by the forces acting upon us. If that is not the case, then once again Deism is threatened. While nobody seriously proposes that he could write all the equations that describe all the internal and external motions of a human, such understanding was held to be a theoretical possibility. Of course when we talk of forces acting upon a human we are not talking of simple physical forces such as cannon balls and solar rays. However it can be postulated that complex social and psychological pressures are ultimately resolvable into simpler physical forces. It follows therefore that while we think we are engaging in free creativity, we are actually controlled by outside forces. Since the forces of any one age have similarities, the human products of any particular age are likely to be the same as each other, and to contrast with the products of another age.

I have already noted that Deism denies divine revelation. What then is the Bible? It must be the product of the particular forces operating at the time the Bible was written. Hence it, or any human product from a past age, can have no enduring validity. Theoretically the same should apply to any human product of the present age. However an idea of progress, without any rational validity, leads to present thought being seen as superior to the past. The fact that future ages will see it as ignorant and superstitious is ignored. Postmodernism has acknowledged that implication of the whole system of thought, and with it the collapse of any certainty. However the movement I am discussing wants certainty of some form, so it is closer to modernism.

A Dilemma

It follows that if Christianity is to have any chance of attracting modern populations it must shed things that have come from the past. Anything which makes it seem old- fashioned must go. It must conform to the 'norms' of the modern age. We see this logic worked out in churches that are generally characterised as theologically Liberal. Their declining numbers show the reality that few will go out of their way to join a church that offers nothing more than what the outside world offers. Intellectually Deism leads to Atheism; ecclesiastically it leads to death.

What does that mean for an evangelical church? It could mean a rejection of Deism and all its implications. However Deism and consequent Atheism is part of the intellectual and cultural air that we breathe. To reject it totally will make us very different to those around us. Indeed, we are already being told by the opinion shapers that we are strange and irrelevant.

There have been periods of rejection of Deism. The Great Awakening, with its emphasis on the 'New Birth', was attacking one the principal consequences of Deism, that is the impossibility of regeneration by the Holy Spirit. The more recent battle over the inspiration of the Bible is also part of an evangelical rejection of Deism. Those positions also isolate us.

Is there a mediating position that will make us seem less peculiar? My thesis is that theological attempts at mediating positions lead to the ecclesiastical practices with which I started.

Acting as if Deism is True

While not formally espousing Deism, much of the evangelical church in Australia acts as if God is not active in the world. I do not mean to appear to lampoon, but 'theistic evolution' seems to say that everything happened just as the atheist says, with the same mechanisms and processes, but God was active in that process. This leads to questions for explication. Does it mean, as the older Deists said, that everything happened because of the outworking and impact of the forces God put in the stuff that originally formed the universe? If that is the case, we have pure original Deism and we should accept the consequence that Jesus is not God, and so on. Alternatively, does it mean that God was 'active' in the process of the creation and development of life, but his activity would have been undiscernible to even a divine intelligence, because physical processes totally explain what happened? The only difference of that from original Deism is that it postulates an 'active' God who does nothing. That is surely just a variant on Deism. Or does it mean that at some crucial point God intervened to create what would not have happened otherwise? If that is what is being said, what is that crucial point and how do we know when that point is?

Often that crucial point is stated to be the creation of man. However there are evolutionary theories, having no weaker basis than general evolutionary theories, that 'explain' the origin of man. A purely religious rejection of these theories of the origin of man lands Christians in the same situation as rejection of Darwinian theory as a whole. Actually it lands them in a worse situation because the case against Darwinism in all its forms can be mounted scientifically, particularly given the growing knowledge of the complexity of living organisms.[22] If evangelicalism refuses to take on broader Darwinism it lands itself in an impossible intellectual situation. The logic of the compromise must roll on. As the historicity of Adam is rejected, so the doctrine of

---

[22] It is no accident that the 'Creationist' movement is largely a movement of scientifically trained people. Evolution is a theological necessity for Deists and Atheists. Only fear of the collapse of the modern synthesis keeps it in place. However the church leadership is heavily biased towards people trained in the humanities, who have a false reverence of 'science'. One of my reasons for the excursion into Adam Smith is to show that if we understood intellectual history, not just science, we would have a better understanding of the situation.

the Fall lapses and with it the doctrine of the sinfulness of man and the significance of the substitutionary death of Jesus. Already there are movements afoot, supposedly within 'evangelicalism', to totally recast evangelical theology without Adam, and with redemption through Christ totally reshaped. Those evangelicals who say they are too busy 'preaching the gospel' to consider the issue of evolution are allowing the foundations of their 'gospel' to be undermined.

Generally these vital questions about theistic evolution are not asked, or when asked they are brushed aside without answer. Thus there is acceptance of a Deistic way of looking at the world and that perception must influence other parts of our thought. Others who might not accept evolution accept the implications for ecclesiology of an inactive God, without examining the roots. How do we know that God is active in the regeneration of the sinner, if he is not active in the creation of physical life? Certainly we may assert that God is active in regeneration but that is mere assertion.

Let us go to another consequence. I have made the point that the Deist model makes human action a result of impinging forces. That must influence the way we see the writing of the Bible and the way we interpret the Bible. Further the Deist model sees an evolution in human society from primitive to more civilised forms. Since the 'primitive' societies known from historical times are animist or polytheist, it is assumed that monotheism is a late evolutionary development. That means that the religion of ancient Israel must have polytheistic roots and that also, looking carefully, we should see the origins of biblical forms and ideas in polytheistic societies.[23] Hence much of OT studies are devoted to finding such assumed precursors. Given that polytheists and monotheists ultimately must have had shared forebears, and given that polytheists and monotheists lived in the same world and were sometimes speaking the same language or were recipients of the same literary tradition, similarities are bound to exist. What characterises studies that effectively assume Deism is that they see similarities as proof of derivation of the Bible from pagan roots, rather than exploring alternate explanations.[24]

---

[23] For an attempt at a biblical alternative see my 'The Completed Creation and Its Implications.' *Mid-America Journal of Theology* 28 (2017), 109–33.

[24] A good example of somebody, who claims to be an evangelical, but pursues the

A variant of the same assumption is the belief that the Bible, especially where it disagrees with prevailing modern approaches, is simply reflecting the ideas of its time and in that respect is irrelevant for our time. If the premise is true, everything the Bible says should be irrelevant. What one sees happening is that the sphere of irrelevant material grows. For, example, some 'evangelicals' gladly abandon what the Bible teaches on gender roles but want to hold to a doctrine of substitutionary atonement. They are perplexed when their own arguments for irrelevance are turned against them. Commonly the supposed 'background' to dispensable practices is simply bad scholarship created by a circular mental process. Since the unfashionable biblical teaching 'must' have derived from the Bible's original context, scholarship naturally finds what it expects.[25]

Another variant is to take the supernatural out of the Bible. Accurate prophecy runs against Deist assumptions, hence the desire to explain prophecy away. It is asserted, even when the wording makes it improbable, that the biblical prophet was not really meaning to speak of the future. Or that what NT writers took as predictions about their own day were really speaking about something else, but taken as relevant to the present by the later author.

I began by mentioning that much of contemporary preaching acts as though the biblical emphasis on the edification of believers is irrelevant. In a way, that is consistent. If the Bible is the product of its times, and those times are different to our times, then what the Bible says is not what our times need. Thus the doctrine of the practical irrelevance of the NT church as model and example, adopted originally under political pressure, can come together with another presupposition that leads to the same practical result.

---

objective of proving that the Old Testament is essentially identical to the surrounding pagan cultures is John Walton. See my 'The Bible and the 'Universal' Ancient World, A Critique of John Walton,' *Westminster Theological Journal* 76(2016), 1–28; 'Problems with the Comparative Method in Old Testament Studies,' *Journal of the Evangelical Theological Society* 62 (2019), 287–306.

[25] For an example of making the data fit the presupposition see the chapter on the social role of women in Joachim Jeremias, *Jerusalem in the Time of Jesus*. See also a comparison with the evidence in ch. 18 of my *The Sufficiency of Scripture* (Edinburgh: Banner of Truth, 1988).

Of course this is applied inconsistently. Many precious and vital doctrines are inconsistently retained. Many times we must praise God for inconsistency. The danger is that inconsistent positions often over time tend to become dangerously consistent.

Practical or Functional Deism

If we tend to assume that God is not active in the world, how will that impact church practice? It must mean that human actions in bringing people into a church become crucial. Given the illogical combination of Deism and belief in progress already mentioned, it will also mean that church practice must avoid the appearance of being old-fashioned.

Deism rejects the doctrine that men are basically sinful. They may be misled by evil 'priests', but they are not bad at heart. For all the changes that have taken place since the age of classic Deism, including the shift to dominant Atheism, denial of human sinfulness remains as a persistent belief. Some atheists may delight to take the church head-on, but the agnostic or functionally atheist mass prefers not to enter debate where conscience-stirring issues of right and wrong arise. It is easier to say that the church is out of date and old-fashioned. In accepting that opinion we accept that the alienation of the masses from the church is a cultural and not a spiritual issue.[26] To be fair it also has to be said that sometimes the church, by connecting indifferent aspects of culture such as clothing and speech styles[27] with spirituality, has aided that false impression. However the crucial issue is whether man's alienation from the truth is cultural or spiritual.

The so-called 'Worship Wars' often come down to this simple issue. If we believe that the main obstacle the church has to overcome is cultural alienation, then we will go out of our way to remove things which distinguish the church from present practice. Of course at this point blessed inconsistency enters. To remove everything that does not agree with present fashion would mean to remove the gospel. Yet one can preserve a sort of gospel, while ignoring the NT teaching about

[26] Making the issue 'cultural' goes with rejection of sin as the basic human problem.

[27] Please note, I do not say that all questions of dress or speech are indifferent. I suggest only that there are some cases where we cling to styles that are culturally shaped. However these crucial distinctions are not the subject here.

personal change and holiness. It will not be a consistent gospel. It will leave believers feeling deeply frustrated because they know there must be more, but the church leadership is afraid to go into that 'more' because it will conflict with the culture.

The consequence is both superficial analysis of the present culture and separation of the church from its heritage. The intellectualism that accompanied the Enlightenment was barren and soul destroying. The Romanticism that arose in reaction has degenerated into feeling without reason. Contemporary culture is left trying to be jolly while being unhappy, and watching frothy TV so as to avoid worrying thoughts. The church in trying to be like the culture becomes frothy and empty. Yet it is afraid that being serious will look old-fashioned and will scare people. The church, because of its superficial analysis, cannot address the deep malaise and distress of modern life. Those who are most keen to be culturally relevant are often the worst analysts of culture.

The church has resources for addressing this situation, in its heritage. Primarily that heritage is the Bible. Yet as we have seen, a combination of factors has led to avoidance of those parts of Scripture that speak most clearly to the misery that sin brings into practical life. To use the great example, the Psalms, because they foreshadow the rejection and suffering of Jesus and the consequent suffering of his disciples, have been the great solace for the suffering believer through the ages. But who would be so foolish as to sing Psalms today? They are sombre. They are real. They cannot out-jolly the TV.

The same applies to the great heritage of devotional and theological literature and hymns. Congregations have split over the doctrine that that no early hymns may be used. Of course there are good modern hymns that should be sung, but many, which are being chosen purely because they are contemporary, are poetically and theologically poor and difficult to sing.[28] There are two objections against hymns written

[28] Part of the conformity to the present culture has been the development of church services on the model of popular concerts, involving professional standard singers. These singers, with the appropriate level of musical accompaniment, are able to sing compositions that are musically challenging. Congregations modelling on them struggle to sing such performance composition. There is a difference between performance music and participation music. By not thinking through the distinction some congregations are killing congregational singing.

more than a century ago. One is their date. The second is they are not upbeat and frothy. Perhaps we have listened too much to the objections?

The second area where the practical implications of functional Deism emerge is in the approach to evangelism. The issue is not evangelism in itself. If we believe that only God can change the heart and that God is active in our world, we pray for conversions and we preach the Word. It is no accident that churches blessed with bringing people to Christ tend to be churches with a culture of prayer. Often God blesses such churches with people who have particular gifts in the area of evangelism. For contrary to common modern practice the Scripture does not say that everybody has to be an evangelist.[29] It talks rather of a variety of Holy Spirit bestowed abilities.[30] If we doubt the present activity of God, we must look for alternate strategies. Hence we decide what abilities are needed, apparently only evangelists, and set out to create them ourselves. Where God is looked to provide gifts through his Spirit, and the NT practice of building the congregation up in godliness is followed, the lives of members often create evangelistic opportunities for them.

Yet the peculiar practice which aims to create guilty consciences in members, if they are not specialist evangelists, cannot be understood without looking at other theological and cultural dynamics.

Four-Point Calvinism

Romans 8:29, 30 are crucial verses because they map out a path from foreknowledge, to predestination, to calling, to justification and final glorification. The assertion that foreknowledge is only God's knowledge of the fact that some would believe goes against the logic of the passage which follows from the control by God of all things (verse 28). It also contradicts Ephesians 1 and other passages. These verses describe

---

[29] John McIntosh traces its popularity to *Dwight L. Moody: Anglican Evangelicalism in Sydney 1897 to 1953* (Eugene, OR: Wipf & Stock, 2018), 79. Given Moody's Arminian theology that would fit. McIntosh also notes its popularity amongst Moore College graduates in 1996. For a similar emphasis in the Billy Graham crusades see Ruth Lukabyo, 'The 1959 Billy Graham Crusade in Sydney as a Youth Revival,' *Lucas* Series 2, No,13 (2019), 66. Yet this doctrine and practice was not very pronounced until the last decade or so. What has changed?

[30] Rom. 12:6–8; 1 Cor. 12:4–11, 27–30; Eph. 4:11; 1 Pet. 4:10,11.

an unbreakable chain that stretches from God's original purpose to the conformity of the believer to Christ, which is also called glorification.

It is probably common knowledge that Arminians object to this unbreakable sequence on the ground that it does not give room for human free will. In this objection they show a superficial understanding of the depth of human sin and of the inability of man to change and believe without the work of God's Spirit. These objections were explored and rejected by the Synod of Dordt.[31]

Practically what the Arminian position does, even when it gives some role for divine grace, is to break the chain. Generally, between calling and justification a gap has to be introduced for where human decision is determinative. The unbroken chain assures the believers that God will persevere with us until he achieves his purpose of making us like Christ. The great discouragement for the Christian is his continuing sin. Just as the power of a gracious God is the encouragement to the sinner facing damnation, so the power and determination of the gracious God is the encouragement for the failing Christian. However the Arminian has cut the chain at a crucial point and proclaimed that it now depends on man. Something that depends on man is a duty to be done. Put another way, it is law. People who supposedly believe in sovereign grace can present the Christian life as a discouraging sequence of duties, but they are going against the logic of their own belief. The reality is that the God who commands also enables. Sure, after our conversion we add some feeble effort, but sanctification is still a work of God's free grace. When Arminian preaching on the Christian life degenerates into a list of things we must do, they are being consistent with their theology. Arminianism in the doctrine of salvation leads logically to legalism in the doctrine of the Christian life.

Four-Point Calvinism is a strange animal. As usually explained, it says that it agrees with the other heads of doctrine expounded by the Synod of Dordt, such as total depravity and irresistible grace. It has a problem only with the idea that the effectiveness of the death of Christ is limited to covering the sins of the elect, rather than covering the sins of all mankind. It says that Christ died to take the punishment for the

---

[31] W. Robert Godfrey, *Saving the Reformation: The Pastoral Theology of the Canons of Dordt* (Sanford, FL: Reformation Trust, 2019).

sins of all mankind but that his death is *effective* only for those who believe.

This may appear to give a role for human decision, but in saying they are Four-Point Calvinists they proclaim that they agree with the other points of the Synod of Dordt. Really? Let us take total depravity. That doctrine says that all sinners are so depraved that they are incapable of believing the gospel unless the Spirit of God changes them, and God does that only to the elect. What then, on the basis of their own doctrine, is the usefulness of the universal atonement of Christ? Or take irresistible grace. It says that those renewed by the Spirit of God have no option but to believe. Where then is the choice supposed offered by a universal atonement? At best it is a mockery.[32]

The truth is that the various aspects of the salvation process are so interwoven in biblical logic that you cannot remove one and keep the others. I fear that the attraction of Four-Point Calvinism is that one can sound like an Arminian while claiming to believe in grace. That brings me to why I am going into this topic in this context. I fear that it will bring Arminian logic into the church. As pointed out above, the Arminian cuts the chain and thus makes salvation dependent upon man, which then puts the onus of sanctification on man. It also shifts to man the onus for the success of evangelism.

---

[32] In addition it is quite unbiblical because the Bible knows nothing of making the work of grace to depend upon human free will. Long ago John Owen exhaustibly refuted the doctrine in his *The Death of Death in the Death of Christ*. Jonathan Moore argues that believers in particular redemption, such as John Owen, were willing to soften their position so as to have a united front against the threat of Arminianism. Further the Canons of Dordt and the Westminster Confession allowed a little wriggle room so that believers in English Hypothetical Universalism could subscribe: 'The Extent of the Atonement: English Hypothetical Universalism versus Particular Redemption' in M.A.G. Haykin & M. Jones ed. *Drawn into Controversie: Reformed Theological Diversity and Debates Within Seventeenth Century British Puritanism* (Göttingen: Vandenhoeck & Ruprecht, 2011), 124–161. He does not explore why allowing Christ's death to benefit all men 'in some sense' was seen as important, nor whether the Hypothetical Universalists really answered the theological and exegetical arguments of Owen. The subsequent history of English Presbyterianism raises the question of whether, if it was a tactical move, this 'softening' had a good result.

Functional Deism and Four-Point Calvinism

One cannot be a true Deist and be a Christian. Denial of the deity of Christ, of the depravity of man, of the divine inspiration of the Bible, of the necessity of conversion, and on and on, cannot coexist with true faith. Yet there may be various degrees of being influenced from the surrounding culture into not expecting God to be as active as the Bible says he is, and still be a Christian. Just as I would not accuse all Arminians of being unbelievers, so I would not reject all Four-Point Calvinists. All of us are far from being fully biblical. My concern is the practical results of Deism and Four-Point Calvinism. Both acknowledge a God active at the beginning but then the emphasis swings to human action. My suggestion is that these two are combining to produce the sad state of the church that leads to the complaints with which I began. If we cannot expect God to be active, and if our doctrine of salvation tells us that man makes the crucial decision, then the future of the church is precarious. It is all hands to the pumps to save the sinking ship. Those gifted in other ways for the edification of the saints must devalue their callings and turn into evangelists.

If the chain of grace has been cut, how are Christians to become conformed to Christ? The emphasis naturally falls upon human effort. That means law, and law kills.[33] Preachers may repeatedly harp upon the need to pray, read your Bible, love one another, and so on, but the emphasis is on human effort and that is discouraging to preacher and hearers. Besides it seems more important to get out and evangelise.

Cultural Complications

As I said before, those concerned to address the contemporary culture can be very poor analysts of that culture. One of the fads that recently swept through our culture was 'managerialism'. In some ways it is a practical outgrowth of Enlightenment thinking. There are supposed to be general laws of management, which once learned in a formal course, will equip a person to shape and turn any enterprise to prosperity. The result has been managers attempting to rule enterprises without

---

[33] When I say law kills, I am not being Antinomian. Commands without the accompanying work of the Spirit achieve only condemnation and discouragement. I am saying that these tendencies turn us away from dependence upon the Spirit.

knowledge of the intricacies of operation. Of course some will have risen through the ranks. However the example of universities illustrates the problem there. There are some academics who have a prime interest in their discipline. Some of these are also gifted administrators and under great pressure and for the sake of the institution may be induced to set aside their studies to administer. Others see the discipline as the road to power. They choose the currently popular research topics, often politically correct ones, avoid teaching because of the time it takes, and rise to commanding positions. The groans from those lower in the ranks, who suffer the burden of policies made without understanding of the realities of the tasks, are simply ignored. I hear such complaints, not just from universities, but also from a wide range of large organisations.

The church model of a leadership whose primary role is not to edify and encourage believers, but to scold the congregation for not being evangelists, is set up for being taken over by managerialists. In managerialism the manager does not have to be able to do the practical job, he just has to get others to do it. The conflict that develops in congregations as a result is neither edifying nor evangelistically profitable. If the church would just observe what is happening in the society around it, it would avoid a lot of heartache.

The Enlightenment, and consequently Deism, had a physical, mechanical, model of man. There are physical aspects of the human body, but the reduction of man to the mechanical is just wrong. Though Romanticism was misguided in many ways, it was a reaction against that error. Management of people cannot be done by rules and numbers. Managerialism introduces a dehumanising and humiliating aspect into human relations. For the church that is supposed to be characterised by love, it should be anathema.

If management can be learned and character is an irrelevant consideration, then sanctification is an irrelevant consideration for leadership in the church. We have already seen how contrary biblical teaching can be ignored. If Deism prevails, so must the rationalistic impersonalism of the Enlightenment. Biblical truth becomes impersonal doctrine. Certainly the church may organise programs, which in certain demographics will attract people. However being attracted to programs is not conversion.

A Deist inactive God goes logically with a denial of human sinfulness. It is no surprise that our present society strongly rejects the doctrine of human sin. A church trying to fit the culture downplays that offensive doctrine. However, practically the preacher is a sinner. As he preaches the power and riches of Christ's redemption, he speaks to his own soul. There is no such self-edification in a ministry of organisation. It is not surprising that the role of manager and organiser, if unaccompanied by confrontation with our own sinfulness and need of forgiveness, will tend to produce unhealthy arrogance. This is another source of tension in churches which have chosen to conform to the present culture.

Spiritual Complications

I dare to suggest that in our fight against sin and to be conformed to Christ, the knowledge of the presence, love, power and grace of God is crucial. I do not want more of man, because I am a man and a weak and sinful one. It is those realities of divine power and presence that I want to proclaim as a preacher because that is what encourages the believer, and encouraged believers make the best evangelists.

The push I am confronting is just wrong-headed. God is real. God is active. He is not standing aside letting us do everything. He may withdraw in judgement but that is something else. For the crushed, discouraged, struggling believer, he is there. And the message of that mighty presence is what gives energy to our sanctification, and the prime aspect of our sanctification is love. Church squabbles are seldom characterised by love and that applies to both parties. For people to believe that they will encourage unbelievers to come to church by dividing the congregation over hymns and music belongs to the regions of insanity.

Please let us escape the dominant cultural influences of Deism and Atheism. Let us turn in prayer to the mighty God, not neglecting the prayer that he may raise up pastors and teachers and evangelists. Let us seek his help to overcome the sins that make us such poor advertisements for the faith. God is real and active. He can and will do it.

Part 2
The Outworking in Historical Theology

Five

The Later Latin Fathers & Calvin on the Cross: Convergence or Divergence?

Andrew M. Bain

In this chapter, we will explore several points of comparison between Calvin and selected later Latin Fathers, in particular highlighting certain similarities between them. The focus will be on three patristic authors—Jerome, Ambrose, and Hilary—who are not usually seen as having a natural affinity with Protestantism, let alone Reformed Protestantism. In doing so, we will observe some surprising parallels. It should first be noted that this chapter is not seeking to establish or explore influences between particular patristic authors and Calvin. The clearer instances of direct borrowing have been well-documented for some time, and when it comes to the matter of possible allusions, indirect borrowings and influences, the potential for speculation for students of Calvin is almost endless (and likely to be without end). This is not at all to say that such an exercise is fruitless, but that here we will concentrate on a different kind of task.

Regarding the task at hand, two questions will arise for many readers at the outset. The first of these is: why engage in such an enterprise at all? From a Protestant and evangelical point of view, after all, would not a more valuable exercise be to compare what Calvin or various of the Fathers have to say in light of the teaching of Scripture itself, leaving comparisons between historical figures to boffins who are interested in history for history's sake? This might well be a more valuable exercise, but there is a good reason for looking at what Calvin has to say about an important matter alongside what the later Latin Fathers have to say. The Greek and Latin Fathers of the early Fourth Century through to mid-Fifth Century are regarded—and have almost always been regarded—as representing something of a golden age of dogmatic formulation for all major Christian traditions. Many of the minor figures of this period, as well as most major personalities, are regarded across almost the full spectrum of Christianity as having at least some valuable things to say and being useful dialogue partners. More frequently, they have been regarded as secondary or subordinate 'authorities'—people whose opinions have stood certain tests and should generally be assumed correct until disproven conclusively from Scripture. Calvin himself in his commentaries and elsewhere makes copious use of various Fathers for precisely this reason. The people Calvin addressed, particularly his Roman Catholic opponents, had a high regard for the Fathers as authorities. Thus, if we can show that what he is saying has parallels in these authors then it lends his case greater credibility, as well as something that mattered in his day more than it matters in ours—the stamp of antiquity.

Moreover, why continue to do this kind of work today? This is our second question. Our 21st Century context is quite different from Calvin's, and relatively fewer people would pay attention to the patristic authors in general now, or in a post-Enlightenment world regard the mark of antiquity as having much value along the same lines that Calvin's contemporaries did. So why should we today still be interested in similarities between Calvin and the Fathers of the Fourth and early Fifth Centuries? The answer in part is because many evangelicals, including most Reformed Protestants, believe our own theology to be directly descended from Calvin and his approach is something of a model for us: he remains today the best-known Protestant systematic theologian and one of the most-read Protestant biblical commentators. Calvin remains a central representative figure within Protestantism, and therefore is a highly useful point of reference for an exercise such as that carried out here. Add to this, the fact that in today's ecumenical environment there has been something of a resurgence in respect for and interest in the Church Fathers, as representatives of a time when Christendom was supposed to be united, and was able to come to a unified theological position on difficult matters. Therefore, demonstrating that the godfather of our own theology bears a positive relationship to key figures from this time still has great significance in the context of today's theological discussion. The later Latin Fathers might not be regarded as 'authorities' in the same sense today that most 16th Century Roman Catholics and Protestants regarded them, however they are figures who are being quoted with increasing frequency again by fashionable advocates of postmodern theology, paleo-orthodox theology, 21st Century neo-orthodox theology, post-denominational theology, and more. They are names and opinions that are credible in any context, in a way that the major figures of the Reformed tradition over the past 500 years are not. The patristic authors are also figures who were preaching and writing in a context that in some ways is more similar to our own than that of the 16th Century: a situation not only where major theological questions were up for grabs, but where Trinitarian, small 'c' catholic Christianity was only one option among several on the religious smorgasbord, even if it was the most popular option.

Jerome, Ambrose, and Hilary are particularly worth examining in an exercise such as this for a closely related reason. Drawing comparisons with and noting similarities between Augustine and Calvin (and various other Reformers) is a habit for Protestant readers that is almost as old as the Reformation itself, and understandably so given the heavy positive reliance of Luther and many of those who followed in the years after him on Augustine's thought. One does not need to read various key Reformed thinkers for very long before noticing the importance of the connection from their perspective. Warfield for example believed and argued at length that to be Calvinist is to be Augustinian and to be truly Augustinian is to be Calvinist.[1] Many have trodden the same path in the century since, James Packer being a representative example.[2] For this reason, there is value in looking not so much at Calvin and Augustine, as at Calvin and three other significant figures from the same golden age of Latin patristic theology, Ambrose, Jerome, and Hilary. Normally these three figures are not names who would be closely associated with Calvin's doctrines or theological method, particularly when it comes to matters like the practice of biblical exegesis, or the meaning of the cross and the resurrection. Hilary is a somewhat secondary figure in the context of Western theology, whose theology is usually regarded as not being as fully formed on many matters of importance compared to people like Augustine who followed a generation or so

---

[1] See particularly Benjamin B. Warfield, *Calvin and Augustine*, ed. Samuel G. Craig. (Philadelphia, PA: Presbyterian and Reformed, 1956), where Warfield argues for this as a central theme of this entire longer work.

[2] James I. Packer, *Keep in Step With the Spirit* (Grand Rapids, MI: Baker, 1984), 122–132.

after him, let alone a much later thinker like Calvin. Ambrose and Jerome, of the later Latin Fathers, have tended to be regarded by Protestants as being more 'Roman Catholic' than other figures of the Fourth Century, taking significant steps in the direction of negative medieval innovations such as the cult of Mary, veneration of the saints, relics and holy places, and deficient views of the Lord's Supper. However, if it can be shown that the theology of Calvin—the theology of people like us—has more in common with an unlikely trio such as this than is typically assumed, then we have come some way in demonstrating that the almost universally well-regarded theology of the post-Nicene Fathers has a real and positive connection with classical Protestant thought. If not just a 'usual suspect' like Augustine can be recognised as holding similar views to key Reformers, but also the supposedly proto-catholic or theologically immature like Hilary, Jerome and Ambrose more than occasionally, then it can be argued that Protestant Christianity is not as narrow and selective as has been assumed and that it has wide support from patristic catholicity. If this can be shown with reference to how the authors in question handle the critical biblical texts concerned with the centre of our faith, the death and resurrection of Christ, this is notable indeed.

The remainder of this chapter will therefore indicate where some notable areas of similarity lie between these three early Christian authors and Calvin, with reference to their commentaries on the cross and the resurrection. The sources we will concentrate on are Calvin's *Commentary on John*[3] and his *Harmony on Matthew, Mark and Luke*,[4] Ambrose's *Expositions on Luke*,[5] and Hilary and Jerome's commentaries on Matthew.[6] Although the three patristic authors are each commenting

---

[3] John Calvin, *Commentary on John*, eds D. W. Torrance & T. F. Torrance and trans. T. F. Torrance (Grand Rapids: MI: Eerdmans, 1959), Vol. 2. Hereafter: Calvin, *John.*

[4] John Calvin, *A Harmony of the Gospels Matthew, Mark and Luke*, 3 vols, eds D. W. Torrance & T. F. Torrance and trans. A. W. Morrison (Grand Rapids, MI & Carlisle: Eerdmans & Paternoster, 1995). Hereafter: Calvin, *Harmony.*

[5] Ambrose. *Expositio evangelii secundam Lucam.* Edited by Marcus Adriaen. *Corpus Christianorum Series Latina* 14 (Turnhout, Brussels, 1957). Hereafter: Ambrose, *Lucam.*

[6] Jerome. *Commentariorum in Matheum,* ed. David Hurst and Marcus Adriaen (Turnhout, Brussels, 1969). *Corpus Christianorum Series Latina* 77. Hereafter: Jerome, *Math;* Hilary. *Sur Matthieu,* 2. ed. Jean Doignon (Paris: Les Éditions du Cerf, 1979). Hereafter: Hilary, *Matt.*

on a different gospel, they also range across all four of the canonical gospels as they write, and it is therefore possible to draw appropriate comparisons.

Calvin

We begin with some observations on doctrinal themes and exegetical habits which are particularly prominent in his commentaries on the crucifixion & resurrection accounts, before correlating these with similar observations on the three selected patristic authors.

Calvin underlines the depth and seriousness of the problem of sin a number of times, for example in his comments on Matthew 27:39, 'This scene reveals how wretched a state we were in if we had no redeemer'.[7] However, particularly in his *Harmony*, this is not mentioned at every opportunity or raised in a laboured manner, but normally briefly and in passing, although often enough that the reader cannot fail to notice and remember.[8] Christ's condemnation and death were above all for our sin: for example, on John 19:12—'the evangelist so carefully examines and insists on these details, for it is very important for us to know … that it was not on his own account that he was condemned, but for our sins'.[9] These things show us, in Calvin's words, 'both the dreadful weight of His wrath against sin and the immeasurable greatness of his goodness towards us.'[10] At the cross, we learn about God's character and his will and ways towards the human race.

In Calvin's *Commentary on John*, divine providence is an ever-present theme. God's powerful superintendence governs every detail of the passion account in particular for Calvin, such as the pen of Pilate writing the notice on the Cross, the removal of Christ's garments, the piercing of Christ's side with a spear without his legs being broken.[11] Relatedly, the fulfilment of Old Testament Scripture as the clear

---

[7] Calvin, *Harmony*, 3:198.

[8] E.g. Calvin, *John*, 159–60 (on John 19:17–18), 167 (on John 19:30).

[9] Calvin, *John*, 175.

[10] Calvin, *Harmony*, 2:177–78.

[11] Calvin, *John*, 161–63, 168–70, explicitly refers to the working of God's providence in the specific events being described in the Gospels and commented on in these parts of the commentary.

outworking of the Lord's providential plan is repeatedly noted, and at some points strongly highlighted.[12]

In both his *Harmony* and his *Commentary on John*, a great deal of space is devoted to the theme of faith. Firstly, the details given in the accounts of the resurrection are highlighted: 'since the resurrection of Christ is the chief article of our faith, and without it the hope of eternal life fails, the Evangelists are the more insistent to prove it.'[13] This is how Calvin introduces, and arguably sums up, what John has to say about the resurrection. The greatest part of space devoted to the lengthy accounts of the post-resurrection experiences in John is given over to analysing what these passages teach about true faith: for example, what is the difference between faith for good as opposed to superstitious reasons, or willing 'obstinacy' as opposed to 'blind indifference,' how faith is born and develops as shown in the actions of Peter and John in going to the tomb,[14] and how Christ's dealing with Mary after the resurrection illustrates the way his calling works in bringing forth a right response of faith, little by little, yet effectively and unfailingly.[15] Calvin notes that initially John and others were lacking in faith and understanding immediately after the resurrection, and spends his account thereafter showing how Christ brought about a change from this.[16] Jesus himself is presented as devoted in everything he does to supporting the faith of his disciples and the reader—in Luke 24:41, Christ is said to take the food and eat it, not because his resurrected body needed it, but to show the disciples that they could have faith in the fact that he was risen indeed.[17] Repeatedly, Calvin makes brief remarks as he passes from verse to verse indicating that a large part of his purpose, and the purpose of the narratives, is to call for faith in the unbeliever, and edify the faith of God's people, comments such as 'this narrative can also edify our faith.'[18] He wants believers to develop in their faith in Christ, to grow in their confidence in his death for them

---

[12] E.g. Calvin, *John*, 166.

[13] Calvin, *John*, 189.

[14] Calvin, *John*, 179–180.

[15] Calvin, *John*, 182–184.

[16] Calvin, *John*, 195.

[17] Calvin, *Harmony*, 2:189.

[18] Calvin, *John*, 168 (on John 19:31). A virtually identical remark is found in his comments on John 20:30: Calvin, *John*, 198.

and the hope his resurrection affords them. He wants Christian teachers to reflect and learn more about encouraging the faith of others, such as in his comments on Christ's direction to Peter to 'feed my lambs.'[19] Calvin often notes that things that the biblical characters say and do in the passion and resurrection accounts is exemplary for later Christian readers, but in most cases, he is careful to refer these to matters central to faith and salvation, rather than more peripheral forms of 'Christian living' advice.[20]

Jerome

In handling the cross, Jerome's most evident concern is to stress the fulfilment of Old Testament prophecy in the events of the passion. However, this is not at all an indiscriminate use of typology, let alone a reflexive joining of features of the gospel narrative to Old Testament texts by means of indiscriminate allegory. In fact, he is anxious to dismiss such over-eager attempts at joining together the Testaments artificially or inappropriately. For example, in handling the reference to the 'place of the skull' in Matthew 27:33, he spends some time dismissing the view, common in his day, that Christ was crucified over the place of Adam's burial, where Adam's skull might be found.[21]

Jerome is concerned not only with the fulfilment of promises between the Old and New Testaments, but with the consistency of the Lord, his Word, and his purposes across many centuries and within the Gospels themselves. He often urges the reader to observe how various details of the passion and resurrection fulfil things that Christ has spoken of previously. He encapsulates his own emphasis here when he sums up the transition from the death of Christ to his resurrection by saying that 'he will rise and accomplish his promises'[22]—for Jerome, above all, that is what the death and resurrection of Christ shows—that Christ has come to fulfil the promises of his Father, and he himself, of a certainty, fulfils his own promises, made on earth as a man. God is

[19] Calvin, *John*, vol 2, 203–206.

[20] Calvin, *John*, 164 (on John 19:24–25), 172 (on John 1938), 182 (on John 20:16), 202 (on John 21:7) 206 (on John 21:17)

[21] Jerome, *Math.*, IV, 1656–80.

[22] Jerome, *Math.*, IV, 1943–4 (Note: all translations from Ambrose, Jerome, and Hilary are mine, unless otherwise attributed).

consistent, and Lord over history. This central emphasis of Jerome's neatly mirrors Calvin's constant awareness of providence when reading the same texts: the terminology is often different, but the same theme is prominent in both authors.

Jerome is often regarded as a dry exegete with little interest in practical application generally, let alone in his written commentaries.[23] However, not infrequently when dealing with the Cross and resurrection he pointedly comments that what is described has happened and been recorded in order to encourage and promote our faith.[24] For example, talking of the fact that a guard was placed at the tomb he says that this 'will strengthen our faith, for as much as this tomb be guarded, so much more the power of the resurrection is demonstrated.'[25] Here, the setting of the guard and the sealing of the tomb strengthens our faith by making it harder that the body might have been stolen.

At quite a few points, the actions of various followers of Jesus are regarded as positive exemplars for how Christians in later times should act in various situations, often in quite small matters. For instance, attentiveness of the women to the body of Jesus after his death, following on from their supporting his needs during his life, is seen to encourage the female family members of those in Christian ministry to support their men.[26] More generally, though, he regards the actions of various people to be positive evidence of their faith in the slain one, and a positive example for us. The believing thief on the cross next to Christ stands as an example of faith,[27] and the attentiveness of Jesus' followers to his ordeal on the Cross underlines the importance of the Christian focusing and reflecting upon the Cross.[28] Both Jerome's general stress on how these texts support faith, and his specific references to the exemplary modelling of faith-driven behaviour by actors in the biblical narrative, are emphases which are clearly echoed in Calvin.

---

[23] E.g. Hans Von Campenhausen, *The Fathers of the Latin Church,* trans. M. Hoffmann (London: A & C Black, 1964), 167; Manlio Simonetti, *Biblical Interpretation in the Early Church: An Historical Introduction to Patristic Exegesis* (Edinburgh: T&T Clark, 1994), 103.

[24] See also some similar examples at: Jerome, *Math.*, IV, 1705–11, and 1899–1900.

[25] Jerome, *Math.*, IV, 1899–900.

[26] Jerome, *Math.*, IV, 1747–56.

[27] Jerome, *Math.*, IV, 1740–5.

[28] Jerome, *Math.*, IV, 1699–71.

Ambrose

In considering Ambrose's treatment of the passion and resurrection accounts, it should be noted and acknowledged that in some respects he is obviously distinct from Calvin. This is certainly true of Ambrose's exegetical methods. Quite frequently, much more so than Hilary or Jerome as well as Calvin, Ambrose uses highly developed allegories to make his point, particularly allegories based on verbal features of the text which sometimes do not bear much relation to the real events they are connected to. In terms of content, he quite often emphasises the Cross as conquest or triumph. While one might find the occasional reference in Calvin to this theme in relation to the Cross, for Ambrose it is one of the primary ways in which he understands the cross, which can at crucial points in the narrative move attention away from other features of the atonement which Calvin and later Reformed Christians would draw from the text.

Ambrose has sometimes been regarded by Protestants as an early advocate of 'cultural Christianity', opposing the secular authorities more to assert medieval-style church influence over the state than to support authentic Christianity, and helping in the importation of pagan ideas into Christian theology. However, in contrast to this impression, when it comes to his work on Luke, Ambrose does make a good number of remarkably clear comments reinforcing vital, distinctively Christian ideas about Christ's death and resurrection, and ideas that are not too dissimilar to Calvin's.

According to Ambrose, Christ remained on the Cross, rather than giving in to the demand that he save himself and come down before his death, in order that he might 'suffer for me.'[29] Further, Christ 'suffered as our substitute.'[30] He 'died, and descended to the dead, for our sin.'[31] For Ambrose, the forgiveness of the penitent thief is declared by Christ before Jesus requests his disciple John to look after his mother, as an indication of his priorities—'he came first to save sinners'[32]—'in

[29] Ambrose, *Lucam*, X, 115–6.

[30] Ambrose, *Lucam*, X, 175.

[31] Ambrose, *Lucam*, X, 175.

[32] Ambrose, *Lucam*, X, 131. Translation from: Ambrose, *Select Works and Letters*. In *Nicene and Post-Nicene Fathers: Second Series* 10. Translated by Henry De Romestin et al. (New York: Christian Literature, 1896). Hereafter: Ambrose, *Select Works*.

my view his purpose was the aim of undertaking to redeem and accomplish deliverance from sins.'[33] The particular stress which Ambrose lays on the Cross as the means of salvation from human sin in these biblical texts reflects Calvin's like emphasis on human sin in these texts and the work which Christ was enacting on the Cross to deal with sin.

When it comes to the resurrection and the appearances that follow afterwards, Ambrose like Calvin is sensitive to the range of spiritual positions that the followers illustrate in their responses to the risen Christ. He distinguishes between doubt and stubborn unbelief, between confident faith and faith that is there, but struggling to grasp the enormity of it all. However, he errs a little in the same direction as Jerome: for Ambrose, the actions of the key disciples are typically seen to be blameless from the moment they encounter the possibility that Christ might be risen. Ambrose even goes so far as to assert that Thomas had not doubted the resurrection prior to meeting the risen Christ in person, and employs a subtle distinction: he 'doubted not the Resurrection of the Lord, but rather concerning the nature of the Resurrection'[34]. For Calvin, Christ's post-resurrection responses to his disciples are seen to be affirming of positive, believing actions and gently rebuking of those that are not responses of faith. Therefore, while Ambrose has a more optimistic perspective on the level of faith which Jesus' followers actually possess in the hours and days after his resurrection, Ambrose like Calvin is quite concerned to view the actions of the disciples in terms of what they say about faith: both the disciples' faith, and that of Christians in their own times. Likewise, Ambrose's understanding of why the post-resurrection appearances are recorded in such number and detail, particularly in John, is much the same as Calvin's, that is, so that we might be *demanded* to faithfully believe.[35]

Hilary

For Hilary, the gospel account is a theological narrative. The events attested to by the text tell a theological story—for him, this is in fact why

[33] Ambrose, *Lucam,* X, 131. Translation: Ambrose, *Select Works.*

[34] Cesare Pasini, *Ambrose of Milan: Deeds and Thought of a Bishop,* trans. by Robert L. Grant. (New York: St Pauls, 2013), 216.

[35] Ambrose, *Lucam,* X, 161. Translation: Ambrose, *Select Works.*

the events are described by the text, to point out important theological truths for God's people. However, there is nothing random or arbitrary in how Hilary proceeds in this regard; while he does sometimes skip over a verse or two, he proceeds through the text in order, dealing with the events of the account in sequence, handling most features in a straightforward way, frequently with appropriate reference to the immediate context, and with a minimal reliance on allegory. Rather than using allegory to jump to distant parts of the Scriptures, Hilary prefers typology and the fulfilment of prophecy. Unlike Augustine and many of the Greek Fathers, Hilary is in constant communion with the text before him, using it as a prompt for him to reflect on the events described and their theological significance, rather than as a jumping board for adventures in far-removed passages or pet doctrinal topics. Almost all of the brief remarks of which Hilary's commentary is made up are statements imparting theological meaning to the events at hand. Typically, he proceeds by noting an event in the account, succinctly stating the theological significance of the event, before noting another event, and continuing on in the same manner.

For Hilary, it is the theological story told by the events of the Gospel that is central to his understanding of the text. For this reason, he frequently places the historical events of the account and theological remarks closely side by side, even in the same sentence. However, it must be emphasised that Hilary does not regard the Gospel text as a framework upon which he can hang theological ideas as he pleases. His exegesis is therefore not heterogenous or impulsive.[36] Rather, he allows the text to direct which theological themes he raises at particular points. This is because he believes that the events of the Gospel narrative tell *the* story of God's working, rather than merely enabling him to tell *his* story.[37] This can be seen clearly in the example of Hilary's observation on Matthew 27:32 that 'they placed the cross of the passion on a man from Cyrene who was passing by. He who bore Christ's cross was an innocent Jew, to indicate that the faith of the Gentiles was

---

[36] *Simonetti,* 'Note sul commento a Matteo di Ilario di Poitiers.' *Vetera Christianorum* 1 (1964) 35–6, here 50 argues this with particular reference to his use of allegory.

[37] Relatedly, 'The Transfiguration in Hilary of Poitiers' Commentary on Matthew.' *Aug* 24 (1984) 395–420, here 401, argues that 'meaning is believed to be embedded in this order' (of events).

left behind and the cross and suffering was being turned to.'[38] In this example, the taking of the Cross by Simon is seen to signal a shift in the theological narrative away from the faith of the Gentiles (discussed shortly beforehand in relation to the Pilate account) to the cross. Hilary, turning to the account of the crucifixion itself, then proceeds to point out theological matters which relate directly to what Christ was doing (theologically) on the Cross.[39] By contrast, Jerome's interpretation is not rooted in the theological narrative of the account, but points away from it, towards the future nature of the Gentile Church.[40] For Hilary, the theological story is very much one where God is the director, arranging things for our benefit, and also for our learning and edification. As was the case with Jerome, this ever-present emphasis of Hilary's on God's working as the continual and omnipotent director of his story, closely mirrors Calvin's repeated stress on divine providence in reading the same texts in the Gospels.

Hilary has a strong, reflexive tendency to talk about the theological significance of events in the gospel with an orientation towards contemporary application. Hilary is clearly concerned to connect the events of the Gospel with practical matters, often through brief, straightforward remarks. Thus, in response to the guards' acceptance of money in payment for lying about the resurrection, he makes the succinct comment that 'he whose praise is in money—he is denied glory.'[41] Another example is his comment on Christ's being mistreated by the soldiers that 'he assumed all of the infirmities of our bodies.'[42] He is not interested only in how the events of the Gospel prefigure contemporary realities of a cosmic scale, such as the continuing unbelief of the Jews or the nature of the Church, but also in how they can encourage the Christian. Hilary's exegesis of the burial of Christ illustrates this further:

For according to the teaching of the apostles, the body of the Lord is placed in a new and empty [place of] rest cut out of stone, indeed

---

[38] Hilary, *Matt.*, 33.4.

[39] Hilary, *Matt.*, 33.5.

[40] Jerome, *Math.*, IV, 1655–65.

[41] Hilary, *Matt.*, 33.9.

[42] Hilary, *Matt.*, 33.3. Cf. Jarred Mercer, 'Suffering for Our Sake, Christ and Human Destiny in Hilary of Poitier's *De Trinitate*,' *JECS* 22(4) (2014), 562–3.

roughly cut, and also new and devoid of doubt before God's entry. And so that nobody besides him may enter into our hearts, the stone is rolled against the door; furthermore, in order that nothing unclean would enter into us once the knowledge of the divine author had been placed in us, nobody apart from him was carried in afterwards.[43]

Here Hilary encourages his readers by stating that the stone against the door represents God's powerful guarantee that no one apart from Christ can enter into the hearts of Christians, once Christ has entered in. He also describes the knowledge of God which enters by faith as something *placed in* believers (by God, and not something which believers create themselves), with the clear implication that it is God who has placed this knowledge in those who have faith, and that it is the power of God which works against things which are unclean or sinful from entering into the life of the Christian after faith has been born. Such a grouping of ideas concerning faith and the gracious work of God clearly would be strongly affirmed by Calvin and the Reformers as a whole.

In fact, the theme which receives the most attention in Hilary's exposition is an eminently practical one: faith. As noted above, this is also a theme of central importance for Calvin as well as Jerome (and to some extent Ambrose as well), in commenting on these same biblical texts. Hilary repeatedly stresses the faith of God's people, usually in contrast to unbelief or unfaithfulness. In so doing, he stresses that the events of the Gospel, particularly the theologically vital events of Christ's death and resurrection, are objects of faith. Sometimes he does this through a negative example:

Due to a fear that the body might be stolen, a guard was placed at the tomb which was sealed. These [actions] are testimonies to their stupidity and unbelief, since the fact that they chose to seal up his tomb shows that they recognised in advance that he would be raised from the tomb of death.[44]

---

[43] Hilary, *Matt.*, 33.8, on Matthew 27:64. By contrast, Jerome and Ambrose both simply note the reason why the stone is referred to in the narrative, and leave the reader to draw any encouragement implied by this for themselves: Ambrose, *Lucam*, 136; Jerome, *Math.*, IV, 1896–1907.

[44] Hilary, *Matt.*, 33.8.

Hilary also connects the events of the Gospel with the faith-experience of believers: 'Furthermore the invective here of the two thieves against the Passion indicates that for all who themselves believe, the Cross will be a cause of scandal.'[45] The events of the Gospel call those who witness them (and by implication those who read of them) to faith, as in the case of the sealing up of the tomb, and the positive example of Pilate's wife in Matthew 27:19, where 'in this woman there is the image of the Gentile people, who already believing calls with the faith of Christ to the unbelieving people [the Jews] among whom she lived.'[46] The penitent thief represents all of those, who are 'saved by justifying faith', who are only different to those on the left of Christ's Cross and the left of his throne by the presence of this faith. Both this emphasis on faith in general, as well as the actual content of how Hilary describes faith, is similar to how Calvin (and the Reformers in general) speak of and understand faith: faith believes in God's promises concerning Christ, faith justifies those saved, faith chases away doubt and is itself a gift of God.

Some Reflections: Calvin, the Latin Fathers, and the Cross & Resurrection Today

The three patristic figures considered here are by no means proto-Calvinists. We should not expect them to be, and it is important to not overstate the case which has been briefly outlined above. We need to acknowledge the fact that in matters of both hermeneutical form and doctrinal content, Jerome, Hilary and Ambrose differ on various points from Calvin to a greater or lesser degree. Calvin is substantially more exegetically systematic than Ambrose, more tied to the realities behind the text as opposed to the grammatical features of it than Jerome, and more cognizant of the 'human' element of the text and the characters in the Gospels than Hilary is. Calvin's explicit emphasis upon 'both the dreadful weight of His wrath against sin and the immeasurable greatness of his goodness towards us,'[47] that is, Calvin's consciousness of the way the Cross event reflected upon the character of God and his

---

[45] Hilary, *Matt.*, 33.5. Cf. Carl L. Beckwith, *Hilary of Poitiers on the Trinity: From De Fide to De Trinitate* (Oxford: Oxford University Press, 2008). 185–86.

[46] Hilary, *Matt.*, 33.1.

[47] Calvin, *John*, 226.

ways towards humanity, is not clearly paralleled in any of the patristic authors surveyed.

That said, it is notable that all the major hermeneutical and doctrinal elements identified above in Calvin's commentary on the Cross and resurrection can be found in abundance in at least two out of three of the patristic authors examined here, and sometimes in all three of them. Given these three authors are not typically held up as prefiguring a Protestant let alone a Calvinist theological perspective, this is noteworthy indeed, and indicates that some of Calvin's key themes in discussing these central elements of the faith are not idiosyncratic but worthy of attention from those of quite different theological persuasions. For example, that Calvin's well-known emphases on faith and providence are to be found in earlier figures such as Jerome, Ambrose and Hilary as well as in more likely places, suggests that these aspects of his doctrine are not the unusual products of a narrow form of Protestantism, but more widely present including in figures normally held up as leading teachers within other Christian traditions.

Turning to the 21st Century, it is appropriate to conclude with a pertinent reflection. On a number of matters highlighted above, Calvin and our three patristic authors not only share similar views but are also keen to strongly emphasise various of the themes in question. However modern evangelicalism gives some of these points far less emphasis than either Calvin or the Latin Fathers. For example, 21st Century evangelicals continue to rightly stress the theme of calling people to faith and supporting the faith of believers, although they give less attention than the authors considered to unpacking how all the details of the text call forth faith. Sadly though, the same is often not true today of Calvin's repeated stress on the theme of providence, paralleled by the confidence of all three patristic authors in the Lord's superintendence of the events in question. Outright denials of this theme are thankfully very rare in contemporary Reformed evangelicalism, but in-depth discussion and grounding of the theme in the lives of believers commonly falls well short of its near-omnipresence in Calvin, Jerome, or Hilary. On this point, these authors provide a useful reminder to us overly-confident late-moderns that the Lord is the master of our destiny and that of our world: that it is the Lord rather than our plans, programs and professionalised capabilities who works all things for the good of God's purposes and people.

Reflecting upon how frequently and reflexively these historical figures treated the biblical theme of providence, we are reminded that we should do better than the modern habit of taking divine providence as something which can be hastily noted in passing and assumed, even with respect to events such as the Cross and resurrection, the most important events in the history of the world. The same could be said regarding the related matter of fulfilment of prophecy, which is repeatedly emphasised by all the authors examined above. Our four commentators continually draw attention to this aspect of biblical revelation in order to point to the greatness of the Lord, his faithfulness to his promises down to the least detail, his patient care for his people through the ages, and as a witness to the Scriptures as a fully integrated and unitary whole. This practice which they model, and the reasons for it, remain as relevant today as they were in the Fourth or the Sixteenth Centuries. The same might be said of other points where Calvin and various unlikely bedfellows in historical theology are found to agree: we could learn and recover much of importance by paying careful attention in such cases.

Six

The Life and Vision of Abraham Kuyper[1]

Joel R. Beeke

In 1898, Benjamin B. Warfield introduced Abraham Kuyper to American readers, saying, 'Dr. Kuyper is probably today the most considerable figure in both political and ecclesiastical Holland.' Abraham Kuyper was a scholar, theologian, preacher, reformer, educator, journalist, writer, orator, politician, and statesman. He was also a devout Christian, a passionate family man, a prodigious worker, a patriot, and the leading exponent of Calvinism's world and life view.

According to Kuyper, the dominating principle of Calvinism was 'the sovereignty of the Triune God over the whole cosmos, in all its spheres and kingdoms, visible and invisible.' He spent most of his life working out the implications of that principle. 'There is not a square inch in the whole domain of our human experience over which Christ, who is Sovereign over *all,* does not cry, 'Mine!'' he wrote.

Here is a brief look at Kuyper's remarkable life and some highlights of his Calvinistic worldview.

Childhood and Education

Abraham Kuyper was born October 29, 1837, in the small fishing village of Maasluis. He was the eldest son of Henriette Huber, a teacher of Swiss descent, and Jan Frederick Kuyper, a minister in the *Hervormde Kerk* or Dutch state church. By that date, liberal modernists who had

[1] I am grateful for this opportunity to present this chapter in honor of Peter Barnes, whom I first got to know through his short but very readable and helpful articles in *The Banner of Truth*. Later on, it was my privilege to make his acquaintance more personally during one of my trips to Australia where I was also privileged to preach for him. I felt we bonded well at that time—and it didn't hurt our budding friendship that his study was in similar condition to mine!

abandoned Reformed confessional theology occupied most of the pulpits in the Netherlands and held significant posts in the universities and seminaries. Orthodox Reformed ministers and people were a minority within the state church. Abraham's father took a middle position between liberal modernism and the orthodox Reformed.

In 1841 the Kuyper family moved to Middleburg, provincial capital of Zeeland. In this historic seaport, young 'Bram' developed a strong love for the sea and yearned to be a sailor. He was homeschooled, chiefly by his mother, who taught him French. His father taught him German. Bram showed an aptitude for languages and was able to master nearly any subject.

In 1849 Bram's father took a call to Leiden. For six years Bram attended the Leiden Gymnasium, a school that prepared students for university. He delivered the valedictory address in German titled 'Ulfilas, the Bishop of the Visigoths, and his Gothic Translation of the Bible.'

In 1855 Kuyper entered the renowned University of Leiden. The school was infested with modernism. Kuyper was most influenced there by Matthias DeVries, professor of literary studies, who taught the beauty and power of good writing. Kuyper graduated in 1858, *summa cum laude*.

Following in his father's footsteps, Kuyper prepared for the ministry at Leiden in the years 1858 to 1861. The theological faculty was uniformly liberal. Church history professor, L. W. Rauwenhoff, embraced an evolutionistic view of history. Abraham Keunen, a higher critic, taught Biblical studies. Joannes Henricus Scholten, who taught systematic theology, denied the bodily resurrection of Christ. Kuyper was deeply influenced by the modernist theology of his professors. At one time, he even joined other students in applauding a professor who openly denied the bodily resurrection of Jesus Christ.

In addition, two schools of thought in the Netherlands moulded Kuyper's thinking. The Groningen School, which dominated the state church until about 1860, promoted Christian humanism based on the thinking of Erasmus, the most famous Reformation era humanist. P. Hofstede de Groot (1801–1866), foremost Groningen theologian and author of *Natural Theology*, promoted a religion of feelings. He said

Christ was to be venerated as the leader of humanity, a supreme religious teacher, and an excellent moral example. But he denied the deity of Christ and the Trinity of Persons in the Godhead. He and his colleagues at Groningen published *Truth in Love,* a journal aimed at 'cultured Christians to promote reasonable faith.'

The other influence was the Ethical School, which promoted a religion of tolerance based on the inner, ethical life of man. Ethical Theology was championed by Daniel Chantepie de la Saussaye (1818–74), a pastor in Leiden. He published *Ernst en Vrede* ('Sincerity and Peace'), a magazine that said that 'ethical' conveyed the personal kind of faith missing in orthodox Calvinism. Ethical theologians denied the doctrine of human depravity and embraced theories of the day about the origin, composition, and unreliability of the Bible. By God's grace, Kuyper never fully succumbed to modernism. But Kuyper's flirtation with liberal theology helps explain why he became such an ardent foe of modernistic thinking after his conversion to orthodox Calvinism.

Kuyper earned a doctorate in theology on September 20, 1862, after completing a dissertation comparing the ecclesiology of the Polish reformer John à Lasco with that of John Calvin. Kuyper's dissertation was significant in two ways.

The first was the extraordinary way in which Kuyper located a treasury of à Lasco's writings after a fruitless search of the holdings of major European university libraries. While Kuyper was at Leiden, the theological faculty at Groningen offered a prize for the best essay comparing the ecclesiologies of à Lasco and Calvin. The problem with this project, as Kuyper discovered, was that the majority of à Lasco's writings seemed to have disappeared. Matthias DeVries, the Leiden professor who encouraged Kuyper to write for the prize, suggested that he check some private libraries, beginning with that of De Vries's father, a clergyman in Haarlem. Kuyper was astonished to discover a treasury of à Lasco's writings. Twelve years later Kuyper described that find as 'a miracle of God' *(een wonder Gods)* given by the 'finger of God' *(vinger Gods).* Kuyper wrote the essay in Latin and obtained the prize, then developed it later for his doctoral dissertation.

The other effect of this study was that it acquainted Kuyper with the writings of John Calvin, which served him well in later years. It also raised questions in his mind about ecclesiology and church reform. Kuyper's later work as a reformer in the Dutch State Reformed Church was deeply influenced by the ecclesiology of à Lasco.

Conversion and Early Ministry

Kuyper's conversion from liberal modernism to Reformed orthodoxy and his subsequent passion for church reform were influenced by three factors. The first was God's providential leading in the discovery of the à Lasco collection.

Second was Charlotte Yonge's novel, *The Heir of Redcliffe,* which Kuyper read during a time of nervous exhaustion due to overwork. The story of a proud successful man, Philip de Morville, who is humbled, convicted Kuyper of his own sin. He later wrote: 'What I lived through in my soul in that moment I fully understood only later, yet from that hour, after that moment, I scorned what I formerly esteemed, I sought what I once dared to despise.' Nevertheless, Kuyper did not yet understand or embrace the gospel.

Third was Kuyper's experience of conversion, which happened during his contact with church members in his first pastoral charge at Beesd from 1863 to 1867. The summer after graduation, Kuyper married Johanna Schaay and moved to Beesd. The church consisted of simple villagers, some of whom had embraced modernism, as well as others who were committed Calvinists and would concede nothing to liberalism. Pietronella Baltus, a peasant woman in her thirties, confronted Kuyper about his modernistic thinking, lack of Reformed experiential preaching, and lack of saving faith in Christ. She even refused to shake the pastor's hand.

In successive conversations, this young woman told Kuyper that he was preaching false doctrine and that his soul was in danger of eternal hell. Such biblical forthrightness wedded to the spiritual practice of such parishioners convinced Kuyper that they possessed a faith in Christ that he lacked. Eventually, God used those humble yet determined parishioners to lead their pastor back to Calvin and the Reformed fathers, to the Scriptures, and to personal faith in Jesus Christ.

Preacher and Pastorates

Kuyper's preaching dramatically changed after his conversion. His sermons combined head and heart knowledge. He began attracting attention both for his oratorical skills and for how his teaching satisfied the hunger of the spiritually-minded *kleine luyden* ('little people,' or common folk) such as Pietronella Baltus. 'My life's goal was now the restoration of a church that could be our mother,' Kuyper said.

In 1867 Kuyper accepted a call to Utrecht, a church with eleven ministers and 35,000 members. During his three years in Utrecht, Kuyper became a very popular preacher. He met Groen VanPrinsterer during that time and took up the cause of the Anti-Revolutionary Party.

In 1870 Kuyper accepted a call to the Reformed Church at Amsterdam, the most influential and prestigious church in the country, consisting of 140,000 members, 136 office-bearers, 28 ministers, and 14 sanctuaries and chapels. Here Kuyper reached the height of his power as a preacher. He was able to reach both the intellectuals and the common folk, whom he loved. Children were also fascinated with his teaching. His prayers were eloquent and humble; his reading of Scripture, heartfelt. A fellow professor, Frederik L. Rutgers, said that just hearing Kuyper read Psalm 148 from the pulpit was a clearer exposition than most sermons preached on that Psalm.

But Kuyper's preaching also evoked opposition. When Kuyper preached a sermon on 'The Assurance of Election,' for example, a modernist colleague preached the following Sabbath: 'Let Anyone Who Comes with Another Gospel than that Christ Died for All Men be Accursed.' After prolonged struggle and bitter infighting, the majority of ministers and elders in Amsterdam sided with Kuyper. That did not mean that the liberals were expelled, however, for the state church was a comprehensive church, embracing all shades of belief and practice as a matter of policy.

Church Reformer

The battle lines drawn between Kuyper and the modernists in the Dutch Reformed Church eventually led to a major secession of conservatives from the state church in 1886. The breach was called the *Doleantie,* from the French word *doleance,* meaning 'grievance' or 'complaint.' Kuyper and his followers were dubbed the *Dolerenden, 'the aggrieved ones.'* In many ways the *Doleantie* was a continuation of the long-standing protest against modernism in the Dutch Reformed Church that had led to the *Afscheiding* ('Secession') of 1834. The *Dolerenden* were protesting the doctrinal tolerance and laxity (*leervrijheid,* 'liberty of doctrine') of the state church. Like the leaders of the Secession of 1834, Kuyper and others called for a return to the theology of the Reformed confessions (Belgic Confession of Faith, Heidelberg Catechism, and Canons of Dort), and the Church Order of Dort.

The Church Order of Dort, which stressed the autonomy and authority of the local congregation and its consistory or council, had been struck down by the royal decree of 1816. A change in the form of subscription, which office-bearers in the church had to sign to indicate their agreement with the Reformed confessions, raised questions about their binding character. The debate raged furiously in the nineteenth century and centred on whether the confessions were binding *because (quia)* they agree with the Word of God, or *insofar as (quatenus)* they agree with the Word of God. Liberalism was making its influence felt. By 1854 candidates for the ministry were only required to acknowledge and promise to defend 'the spirit and main points of doctrine' contained in the confessions. From 1878 on, consistories were not permitted to refuse church membership to anyone for doctrinal reasons.

The matter of church membership and the authority of local consistories to exercise church discipline had been the main impetus for the *Doleantie* of 1886. The insistence of the majority of the Amsterdam consistory on maintaining strict standards for church membership resulted in the suspension of Kuyper and four other ministers, forty-two elders, and thirty-three deacons. Two hundred congregations, with about 150,000 people, chose to leave the state church. This exodus resulted in the formation of the *Nederduits Gereformeerde Kerk (Dolerende).*

The Secession of 1834 and the Reformation movement of 1886 proceeded from similar principles. Both were committed to the doctrine set forth in the Reformed confessions and the polity of the Church Order of Dort. Both strove for a church free from the domination of the state and deviations from Reformed doctrine. Like the Secession of 1834, the *Doleantie* was strongly supported by the common people.

This tie was not only a matter of political expediency but of principle. For Kuyper, Calvinism would always be a democratic movement of the common people.

The Secession and the *Doleantie* were also alike in stressing personal piety. The Reformed experiential emphasis of the Secession is most evident in Kuyper's meditations that appeared weekly in the journal *De Heraut* ('The Herald') and later collected in volumes such as *Falling Asleep in Jesus, To be Near Unto God, As You Sit in Your House,* and *Honey from the Rock.* Many of Kuyper's followers later departed from this experiential emphasis, but that didn't negate Kuyper's evident commitment to it in his meditations.

Even so, the Kuyper-led *Doleantie* was also different from the Secession of 1834. Doctrinal differences centred on the covenant of grace. The Secession churches stressed the need for covenant children to be born again and to experience saving grace, whereas most of the *Doleantie* churches embraced Kuyper's notion of presumptive or presupposed regeneration and treated covenant children as possessors of saving grace in Christ from infancy. That naturally led to downplaying the experimental emphasis prevalent in Secession churches.

Then too, the Secession had been strictly a church reform movement. The *Doleantie* wanted more, because of Kuyper's expanded interpretation of Calvinism, sometimes called 'neo-Calvinism.' For Kuyper, Calvinism stood for a total world and life view (Dutch: *wereldbeschouwing;* German: *Weltanschauung*), not merely an ecclesiastical, confessional, or theological system. As such it was opposed to the world and life views presented by other belief systems such as paganism, Islam, Romanism, and modernism. Kuyper's goal was not only church reform but also a spiritual victory in all areas of life over the atheistic worldview of modernism.

Despite these differences, Kuyper was instrumental in merging the *Doleantie* churches with the majority of the 1834 Secession churches in 1892, giving birth to the *Gereformerde Kerken in Nederland* ('Reformed Churches in the Netherlands'). The new denomination consisted of 400 Secession churches, 300 *Doleantie* churches, and 300,000 members. Similarly in North America, the Christian Reformed Church, founded in 1857 by Secession immigrants, welcomed large numbers of *Doleantie* immigrants who crossed the Atlantic in the 1890s and later.

The merger was a tenuous one, however. Eventually people referred to the churches of the Secession as the 'A-Stream' churches, and the churches of the *Doleantie* as the 'B-Stream' churches. Frequently, ministers or people of one group refused to preach or worship in the churches of the other.

As a leader of the Anti-Revolutionary Party, Kuyper insisted that Christians draw clear battle lines against life systems of contemporary European culture, which he traced back to the French Revolution. He wrote:

> If this battle is to be fought with honour and with a hope of victory, then *principle* must be arrayed against *principle;* then it must be felt that in Modernism the vast energy of an all-embracing *life-system* assails us, then also it must be understood that we have to take our stand in a life-system of equally comprehensive and far-reaching power. And this powerful life-system is not to be invented nor formulated by ourselves, but is to be taken and applied as it presents itself in history. When thus taken, I found and confessed, and I still hold, that this manifestation of the Christian principle is given us in Calvinism. In Calvinism my heart has found rest. From Calvinism have I drawn inspiration firmly and resolutely to take my stand in the thick of this great conflict of principles.... Calvinism [is] the only decisive, lawful, and consistent defence for Protestant nations against encroaching and overwhelming Modernism.

So Kuyper taught that modernism in all of its socio-cultural manifestations must be fought in idea and principle. It was a spiritual struggle for the heart and soul of the nation, Kuyper believed, and pivotal for the very future of Western civilisation. According to Kuyper, the finest fruits of European civilisation in art, science, commerce, and industry were due to the influence of Calvinism. Calvinism was the origin and safeguard of constitutional political liberty. Only by forsaking the ideals of the French Revolution and returning to a pre-Enlightenment theonomous (but not theocratic) ideal could Western civilisation hope to survive. That was Kuyper's lifelong pursuit as a journalist, as the founder of a Calvinistic university, as the leader of a Calvinistic political party, as a member of parliament, and as prime minister of the Netherlands.

Theologian

For Kuyper, the 'dominating principle' of Calvinism, he noted, 'was not, soteriologically, justification by faith, but in the widest sense cosmologically, *the Sovereignty of the Triune God over the whole Cosmos* in all its spheres and kingdoms, visible and invisible.' This idea of the 'Sovereignty of the Triune God over the whole Cosmos' led Kuyper to three important doctrines.

1. Common grace. This doctrine is based on Kuyper's conviction that prior to and independent of the *particular grace* (Dutch: *genade*) of God expressed in redemption, there is a *universal grace* (Dutch: *gunst*) of God at work in creation and providence. This universal or common grace, which restrains sin and mitigates its consequences in human society, is the basis of Kuyper's call for Christian involvement in the general cultural, socio-political life of humanity.

The doctrine of common grace enabled Kuyper to stand against wrong views of culture held by many Christians. On the one hand, Kuyper opposed Anabaptists and pietists who shrank from cultural involvement, fearful of contamination or 'worldliness.' On the other hand, Kuyper rejected the ecclesiasticising of cultural life practiced by the Pre-Reformation papal church, seeking to bring all of life under the control of the institutional church. Cultural life, rooted in creation and common grace, has a life and a goal of its own, apart from the sphere of redemption and particular grace, Kuyper believed.

Kuyper's explanation of common grace in *Gemeene Gratie* wasn't always consistent. He was less concerned with a systematic definition of common grace than he was with its value in overcoming the cultural alienation of many orthodox Dutch Reformed people. According to S. V. Zuidema, Kuyper used the doctrine of common grace 'to stimulate, as well as to justify, truly Christian action by God's people from out of the particular grace of regeneration by the light of Holy Scripture. Common grace supplies the believer with the material for fulfilling his calling to be culturally formative and to fight the battle of the Lord in the world of culture.'

2. The Antithesis. Kuyper's view on common grace was linked with his insistence upon a radical *antithesis* between general human cultural activity and Christian cultural activity. Kuyper's doctrine of common grace is misunderstood if it is regarded simply as a call for Christians to join with all men in a human cultural project. As Kuyper wrote, 'Two *life-systems* are wrestling with one another, in mortal combat.'

Regeneration by the Holy Spirit is the theological foundation for the doctrine of the antithesis. According to Kuyper, Christianity speaks of regeneration 'which changes man in his very being, and that indeed by a change or transformation which is effected by a supernatural cause.' So, just as two kinds of people will develop two kinds of science because their conflict is not between faith (or religion) and science, but between *'two scientific systems…each having its own faith,'* so Christians and humanists promote different types of cultural activity.

Kuyper therefore devoted his life to the establishment of Calvinistic cultural institutions of many kinds, including a Calvinistic university, a Calvinistic political party, Calvinistic labor union, and numerous associations and organisations.

3. Sphere sovereignty. Kuyper was not satisfied with opposing the spirit of modernism with general Christian principles but with specifically Calvinistic principles *(gereformeerde beginselen).* Chief among these principles was the doctrine of sphere sovereignty. This theme was formulated to counter the notion of statism or state sovereignty in various areas of life. As Kuyper explained: 'In a Calvinistic sense we understand hereby, that the family, business, science, art and so forth are all social spheres which do not owe their existence to the state, and which do not derive the law of their life from the superiority of the state, but obey a high authority within their own bosom; an authority which rules, by the grace of God, just as sovereignty of the state does.'

The various spheres are autonomous in their own right. This autonomy was God-given in creation and it is to God alone that they are ultimately responsible. As Kuyper wrote: 'In this independent character a special *higher authority* is of necessity involved and this highest authority we intentionally call *sovereignty in the individual social spheres,* in order that it may be sharply and decidedly expressed that these different developments of social life have *nothing above themselves but God,* and that the State cannot intrude here, and has nothing to command in their domain.'

The doctrine of sphere sovereignty roots all authority in divine sovereignty, thus safeguarding the public order from all forms of state absolutism and providing the guarantee for civil liberty. The state has certain responsibilities to the various spheres, however. As Kuyper says: 'It possesses the threefold right and duty: 1. Whenever different spheres clash, to compel mutual regard for the boundary lines of each; 2. To defend individuals and the weak ones, in those spheres against the abuse of power of the rest, and 3. To coerce all together to bear *personal* and *financial* burdens for the maintenance of the natural unity of the State.' Only constitutional government and constitutional law can properly guarantee civil liberties and the proper autonomy of the various spheres.

The doctrine of sphere sovereignty also countered the medieval Roman Catholic notion of church sovereignty in society. God's rule over the spheres of human society is not mediated by the church but is direct and immediate, Kuyper said. Prior to and quite apart from his relation to men as redeemer, God is directly and universally related to men as their Creator, and His law is the law of their life. Kuyper distinguished between the church as *organism* (the people of God in the world) and the church as *institute,* gathered into congregations, governed by office-bearers and assemblies (consistories, classes, and synods), bound by the confessions, and regulated by the church order. Accordingly, Kuyper called for organised Christian activity in areas other than work of the institutional church. Christians were expected to respond to the needs of society, not as church members but as Christians in society, by forming Christian labor unions, Christian political parties, Christian social organisations, and institutions of Christian education.

Politician

In 1869 Kuyper got to know the secretary of the king's cabinet, Groen VanPrinsterer (1801–1876). It turned out to be a career-changing experience.

VanPrinsterer, who had a doctorate in law and in literature and was a gifted lawyer and historian, had been converted through the influence of the Reformation historian J. H. Merle d'Aubigne (1794–1872). He was also greatly influenced by men associated with religious revivals in various parts of Europe, beginning in French-speaking Switzerland after the defeat of Napoleon. That movement, known as the *Réveil,* (French for 'Awakening') countered the rationalism of the German Enlightenment *(Aufklärung).* When the *Réveil* reached the Netherlands, Willem Bilderdijk (1756–1831), a Calvinist poet, started a study group aspiring to restore the Reformed faith in the churches. One of his converts, fellow poet Isaak da Costa (1798–1860), assailed rationalists within the Dutch Reformed Church and opposed the spirit of modernity.

The Dutch *Réveil* greatly influenced Hendrik de Cock (1801–1842) and other pioneers of the 1834 Secession as well as VanPrinsterer, though they responded to the influence in different ways. VanPrinsterer described his own worldview as 'anti-revolutionary' and 'Christian historical.' VanPrinsterer was the mastermind of what would evolve into the Anti-Revolutionary Party (ARP) in the Netherlands. This party would assert Christ's lordship over public affairs and oppose the principles expressed by the French Revolution and political liberalism in general.

Kuyper cast in his lot with the ARP. In 1874, he was elected to the Second Chamber of Parliament. Since Dutch law excluded ministers of churches from membership in the Parliament, Kuyper resigned his office as pastor. Many people questioned the wisdom of Kuyper's choice. The following year Kuyper was reelected, but his term was interrupted by another nervous breakdown. He was incapacitated for fifteen months, most of which were spent in Switzerland and Italy.

When he returned to work, Kuyper thoroughly reorganised the ARP with a constitution, a statement of principles, and a well-formulated platform. Under his leadership, the ARP became the first properly organised Dutch political party, complete with a national committee, headquarters, treasury, newspapers, and an annual national convention. In 1878 Kuyper published *Ons Program* ('Our Program'), the party's political manifesto.

In time, Kuyper concluded that the only way to break the hold of the two main liberal parties in Parliament was to form a coalition with the Roman Catholics. Though the two groups were theologically opposed to each other, they did have mutual concerns about education. Their coalition defeated the liberals in the election of 1888, but lost again in 1891 and didn't regain power until 1901, when Kuyper was asked to head the new government as prime minister.

Kuyper's five-year stint as prime minister was only partially successful. A school bill was passed that gave Christian schools legal parity with government schools. Kuyper was also instrumental in ending the railway strike of 1903. Most of the ARP goals, however, were not achieved.

Kuyper's coalition was defeated in the election of 1905. Kuyper briefly served Parliament two more times but achieved little because of medical problems. In his last years Kuyper became increasingly critical of his own party. Some viewed him as a bitter old man who could not surrender his autocratic leadership nor tolerate the leadership of any who disagreed with him.

The ARP abandoned most of its principles in the twentieth century. By 1980 it merged with the Catholic People's Party to form the Christian Democratic Appeal.

Journalist and Writer

Kuyper's influence continued through five decades because of his prolific writing. That career began in 1866 with the preparation of à Lasco's works for the press. Kuyper wrote a lengthy introduction for those works. Later, he edited selected writings of Franciscus Junius (1545–1602) and Gisbertus Voetius (1589–1676), leading Dutch Reformed theologians.

In 1869 Kuyper became editor of the weekly *De Heraut*, calling 'For a Free Church and a Free School in a Free Land.' In 1872 Kuyper became editor of *De Standaard* ('The Standard'), a Christian daily newspaper and official organ of the ARP. He continued to edit both papers until he was eighty-two years old. He wrote thousands of articles, many of which were later published as books.

Kuyper was a multifaceted writer. He wrote about theology, history, philosophy, politics, and aesthetics. Some of his books were warmly devotional, such as *Nabij God te Zijn (To Be Near Unto God).* He wrote hundreds of meditations and scores of articles on practical Christianity, and allowed his *Dictaten Dogmatiek* ('Notes on Systematic Theology') to go to press unedited. He published an exposition of the Heidelberg Catechism, *E Voto Dordraceno* ('According to the Wish of Dort'), so named because the Synod of Dort had recommended the Catechism as a form of instruction for use in the churches and schools of the nation. Kuyper's greatest work was probably his *Encyclopedia of Sacred Theology* (3 vols). He also wrote three volumes on common grace *(Gemeene Gratie),* a massive volume on the Holy Spirit, and a book on Revelation. He published four volumes on eschatology, *Van de Voleinding* ('Of the Consummation') and three volumes of *Pro Rege* ('For the King').

In 1898, Kuyper delivered the Stone Lectures at Princeton University and received an honorary doctorate. The lectures set forth his Calvinistic worldview, and have often been reprinted as *Calvinism.* He wrote two large volumes on the geography, history, and cultural life of the people of the Mediterranean basin. Four volumes of his political speeches were published from 1908 to 1910. Other significant volumes include *Dat de Genade Particulier is* (newly published in English as *That Grace Is Particular). De Leer der Verbonden* ('The Doctrine of the Covenants'), *De Hedendaagsche Schrift Kritiek* ('Today's Criticism of the Bible'), and *De Engelen Gods* ('The Angels of God').

Kuyper's writings influenced thousands throughout the twentieth century. His books and articles generated praise as well as criticism. Men such as Herman Bavinck and Herman Dooyeweerd, though not uncritical of Kuyper's thinking, were greatly influenced by him. Professors Lucas Lindeboom and Maarten Noordtzij, representing the 'A-Stream' churches, felt that Kuyper's theology was not sufficiently scriptural. They believed it was too speculative and deductive, particularly his views on baptism, on justification from eternity, and on the scientific character of theology. G. C. Berkouwer wrote, 'There was doubt about his doctrine of common grace, doubts about his view of the antithesis between Christianity and other life-views, and doubts about the polemics that those views had aroused.' Many people feared that Kuyper's ideas would secularise Christianity. They said such 'Neo-Calvinism' was 'a deceptive synthesis' and that his use of secular worldviews weakened his case for the distinctiveness of the Calvinistic worldview.

Cornelius VanTil advanced Kuyper's ideas in the United States, particularly in the area of presuppositional apologetics. Francis Schaeffer also helped popularise some of Kuyper's ideas. Various Dutch Reformed denominations in North America have been greatly impacted by Kuyperianism. South Africa's Potchefstroom University for Christian Higher Education was modelled after the Free University of Amsterdam and has greatly impacted Christian education and scholarship in Africa. Today Kuyper's influence may be stronger in North America and South Africa than in the Netherlands.

In the twentieth century, Kuyper's doctrines of common grace and presumptive regeneration spun off views and practices that carried the movement well beyond what Kuyper would have approved. Though Kuyper made common grace a doctrine of importance far beyond traditional Calvinism, he would not have endorsed his successors using his doctrine of common grace to elevate social responsibilities above evangelism or to justify their conformity to worldly ideas and practices.

Kuyper's notion of presumptive regeneration led some to conclude that baptism assures salvation, or at least that covenant children should not be told that they need to be born again. Many children grew up thinking that sound doctrinal knowledge and biblical ethical conduct are sufficient for salvation without experiencing conviction of sin and conversion, or any need for self-examination with regard to the marks of grace. The net result was that, over time, Reformed experiential religion became deemed largely superfluous.

Educator

Dissatisfied with government schools and universities, Kuyper established a Christian university free from state control or influence. The Free University of Amsterdam, designed to affirm a biblical and Reformed worldview throughout its curriculum, was established on October 20, 1880. Kuyper organised it as a school operated by Christian parents and supported by the prayers and gifts of Reformed Christians.

The university began with five professors and only five students, but continued to grow, training ministers and school teachers for the *Gereformeerde Kerken*. Kuyper served as rector and professor at the Free University from 1880 to 1901.

As prime minister, Kuyper helped pass a law granting full legal standing for private universities and technical schools that were preparing students for higher education. The Free University then received state recognition of its awarded degrees.

The Free University strayed from Kuyper's teachings in the twentieth century. By 1960, many of its 12,000 students expressed little or no allegiance to the Christian faith. The institution even declared in 1971 that it had abandoned its commitment to Calvinism, though it would retain the gospel for its basis of teaching.

As a Man

Kuyper lived out his Calvinistic faith as a believer. He revelled in the life of his family with his wife, five sons, and two daughters. He faithfully conducted family worship after the evening meal, reading and explaining the Scriptures to his family and servants.

Like other believers, he struggled with losses. His 9-year-old son passed away in 1892 and his beloved wife in 1899 at the age of 58. Kuyper never remarried. He continued his heavy workload—except for periods of nervous exhaustion—to the end of his life.

Though short of stature, Kuyper's appearance was commanding. He held audiences spellbound with his uncompromising convictions and compelling oratory. Spiritually, communion with Christ sustained him throughout his long career.

Perhaps Kuyper's greatest personal flaw was his intolerance of those who disagreed with him. His tendency to act like a dictator in ecclesiastical and political matters seemed to grow with age. The last years of his life were neither happy nor fruitful.

Abraham Kuyper died on November 8, 1920, at the age of 83, after a public career of fifty-seven years. The funeral was simple, at Kuyper's request, but thousands attended, including so many deputies from Parliament that no business could be conducted that day due to a lack of a quorum. It concluded with the singing of Kuyper's favourite—Psalm 89:7–8:

How blessed, Lord are they who know the joyful sound,
Who, when they hear Thy voice, in happiness abound!
With stedfast step they walk, their countenances beaming
With brightness of the light that from Thy face is streaming;
Exalted by Thy might from depths of desolation,
They praise fore'er Thy Name, Thy justice and salvation.

Thou art, O God, our boast, the glory of our power;
Thy sovereign grace is e'er our fortress and our tower;
We lift our heads aloft, for God, our shield is o'er us;
Through Him, through Him alone, whose presence goes before us,
We'll wear the victor's crown, no more by foes assaulted,
We'll triumph through our King, by Israel's God exalted.

On his tombstone were engraved the words:

Dr. A. Kuyper
Born October 29, 1837
And fallen asleep in his Saviour
November 8, 1920

Kuyper's influence remains powerful today. Many throughout the international Reformed community continue to wrestle with the implications of Kuyper's declaration: 'God's majesty and sovereignty require that we believe God's Word, not because of what it says, but because *it is His Word,* not because we think it beautiful and true, but because *He has spoken it.'*

Seven

'Most God-beloved Father': Eusebius of Samosata in the Letters of Basil of Caesarea[1]

Michael A. G. Haykin

By 376, Basil of Caesarea's (*c.*329–379) long-standing friendship with his mentor Eustathius of Sebaste (*c.*300–*c.*377) had completely disintegrated.[2] His relationship with Eustathius had been one of the most significant friendships of his life and stretched back twenty years to

[1] I am delighted, through the means of this essay, to honour Prof. Peter Barnes for his church-focused scholarship that is grounded in a love of the Lord Jesus and his word. His work has been a great encouragement to me.
In the preparation of this paper, I am deeply indebted to Dr. C. Berry Driver, Jr., Associate Vice-President of Academic Resources at the Southern Baptist Theological Seminary and the head librarian of the seminary's James P. Boyce Centennial Library, as well as the staff of the library, and Jordan H. Edwards, one of my doctoral students.

[2] For Basil's life and thought, see especially Paul Jonathan Fedwick, *The Church and the Charisma of Leadership in Basil of Caesarea* (1979 ed.; repr. Eugene, OR: Wipf and Stock, n.d.); Andrew Radde-Gallwitz, *Basil of Caesarea: A Guide to His Life and Doctrine* (Eugene, OR: Cascade Books, 2012); Stephen M. Hildebrand, *Basil of Caesarea* (Grand Rapids, MI: Baker Academic, 2014). On his friendships, see especially J.-R. Pouchet, *Basile le Grand et son univers d'amis d'après sa correspondance: Une stratégie de communion* (Rome: Institutum Patristicum 'Augustinianum,' 1992).
On Eustathius and his pneumatology, see especially Wolf-Dieter Hauschild, 'Eustathios von Sebaste,' *Theologische Realencyklopädie*, 10 (1982): 548–549; Michael A. G. Haykin, *The Spirit of God: The Exegesis of 1 and 2 Corinthians in the Pneumatomachian Controversy of the Fourth Century* (Leiden: E. J. Brill, 1994), 27, n.86. On Eustathius' career, see also Friedrich Loofs, *Eustathius von Sebaste und die Chronologie der Basilius-Briefe: Eine Patristische Studie* (Halle: Max Niemeyer, 1898); Jean Gribomont, 'Eustathe de Sébaste,' *Dictionnaire de Spiritualité*, IV/2 (1961): 1708–1712; C.A. Frazee, 'Anatolian Asceticism in the Fourth Century: Eustathios of Sebastea and Basil of Caesarea,' *The Catholic Historical Review*, 66 (1980): 16–33; J. Gribomont, 'Eustathius of Sebaste' in *Encyclopedia of Ancient Christianity*, ed. Angelo Di Berardino et al. (Downers Grove, IL: IVP Academic, 2014), 1:882.

the time of Basil's conversion in the mid-350s. At the very beginning of his Christian life Basil had purposely sought out men whose lives were marked by godliness and whom he could regard, in his own words, as 'fathers and guides of my soul on the journey to God.'[3] Eustathius was initially such a man, but by the late 360s and early 370s it became apparent to Basil that there were significant differences between them when it came to Trinitarian doctrine. Eustathius was largely unconcerned about questions of dogma such as the nature and status of the Holy Spirit, and it was undoubtedly because he was not a theologian that none of his writings have been transmitted. As Wolf-Dieter Hauschild once described the keynote of his pneumatology, 'the Holy Spirit was... a charismatic reality primarily to be experienced.'[4] Eustathius appears to have been quite happy to affirm the Nicene Creed as it stood, but he had a deep aversion to expanding it to include a dogmatic assertion with regard to the Spirit. He was committed essentially to a Binitarianism that was hostile to any conglorification of the Spirit with the Father and the Son. His refusal to take a clear stance on the Spirit's deity is well captured by a remark he reputedly uttered at a synod in 364 when the question of the Spirit's ontological status was raised: 'I neither choose to name the Holy Spirit God nor dare to call him a creature.'[5]

Basil retained his friendship with Eustathius, though, in part with the hope of bringing his old friend around to a robust confession of the Spirit's deity. Basil's irenicism, though, made his own orthodoxy suspect to some. In late 372 and early 373, Theodotus of Nicopolis (d.375), a leading bishop in northern Asia Minor, began to pressure Basil to clarify his own position on the Spirit as well as his relationship with Eustathius. Meletius of Antioch (d.381), another key supporter of the Nicene Creed, shared Theodotus' view.[6] Basil, by associating with a suspected heretic, was himself dogmatically suspect! Basil found himself in an unenviable position. On the one hand, he was beginning to be

[3] *Letter* 204.6. All translations of Basil's works are by the author unless otherwise indicated. The Greek text used has been that of the four volumes of Roy J. Deferrari, *Saint Basil: The Letters* (Loeb Classical Library; Cambridge, MA: Harvard University Press/ London: William Heinemann, 1926–1934).

[4] Hauschild, 'Eustathios von Sebaste,' 548–549.

[5] Socrates, *Church History* 2.45.

[6] For Meletius' theological views, see Haykin, *Spirit of God*, 33–37.

criticised by a circle of Eustathius' followers for doctrinal convictions regarding the Spirit that were increasingly unacceptable to many of Eustathius' Pneumatomachian partisans. On the other hand, his close ties to Eustathius were making him dogmatically suspect to a number of his episcopal colleagues and some of his monastic friends.[7]

During the summer of 373 Basil began to pressure Eustathius to commit himself to a more robust Trinitarianism. After two meetings Basil was actually sanguine about Eustathius' theological orientation. As he told Eusebius of Samosata (*c.*310/330–380), who, as shall be seen, would replace Eustathius in the 370s as Basil's chief mentor and friend: 'we found, with God's help, that he was sincerely following the entirety of the orthodox faith.'[8] At the second of these meetings, in August of 373, Eustathius signed a statement of faith in which he affirmed:

> [We] must anathematise all who call the Holy Spirit a creature, and all who so think; all who do not confess that he is holy by nature, as the Father is holy by nature and the Son is holy by nature, and refuse him his place in the blessed divine nature. Our not separating him from Father and Son is a proof of our right of mind. For we are bound to be baptised in the terms we have received and to profess belief in the terms in which we are baptised, and as we have professed belief in, so to give glory to Father, Son and Holy Spirit. Thus we must hold aloof from the communion of all who call him a creature, as from open blasphemers. One point must be regarded as settled; the remark is necessary because of our slanderers. We do not speak of the Holy Spirit as unbegotten, for we recognise one Unbegotten and one Origin of all things, the Father of our Lord Jesus Christ. Nor do we speak of the Holy Spirit as begotten, for by the tradition of the faith we have been taught one Only-begotten. We have been taught that the Spirit of truth proceeds from the Father, and we confess him to be of God without creation.[9]

That fall, though, when Eustathius was to ratify this statement of faith at a meeting with Theodotus and Meletius, he failed to show. Instead, he renounced his signature on the statement and, at a series of Pneumatomachian synods, denounced what he described as the

---

7 Haykin, *Spirit of God*, 31–36.

8 Basil, *Letter* 98.

9 Basil, *Letter* 125.3.

doctrinal innovations of Basil and openly slandered him as a Sabellian.[10] Basil was so stunned by this turn of events and the betrayal by one of his closest friends that, in his words, 'my heart was crushed.'[11] During this difficult time, it was another friendship, namely, that with Eusebius of Samosata that was a source of theological strength and spiritual encouragement for the bishop of Caesarea during the most difficult, though extremely fruitful, period of his life.[12]

'Most God-beloved Father'

Given the fact that by 361 Eusebius was already regarded as 'a bishop of great moral authority,'[13] his birth should be placed probably in the first two decades of the fourth century.[14] As bishop of Samosata, a city of military and political significance on the upper Euphrates River about 150 miles north-east of Antioch on the Orontes, Eusebius strongly supported the election of Meletius to the see of Antioch in 361.[15] Antioch had been something of an anti-Nicene stronghold since the exile of

---

[10] For details, see Haykin, *Spirit of God*, 38–39.

[11] Basil, *Letter* 244.4.

[12] The key ancient sources for Eusebius' life are Theodoret, *Church History* 2.27–28; 4.12–13; 5.4; and Sozomen, *Church History* 6.4. For a Greek life of Eusebius that follows Theodoret more or less, see François Halkin, 'Une vie grecque d'Eusèbe de Samosate,' *Analecta Bollandiana*, 85, nos.1–2 (1967): 5–15. There is also a Syriac life of Eusebius; for a French translation of this life, see Paul Devos, 'Le Dossier syriaque de S. Eusèbe de Samosate,' *Analecta Bollandiana*, 85, nos.1–2 (1967): 95–240.
For more recent studies, see Henry Robert Reynolds, 'Eusebius (77), bishop of Samosata' in *A Dictionary of Christian Biography and Literature*, ed. Henry Wace and William Piercy (London: John Murray, 1911), 342–343; M. Spanneut, 'Eusèbe de Samosate,' *Dictionnaire d'histoire et géographie ecclésiastique*, 15 (1963): 1473–1475; J.-R. Pouchet, 'Eusèbe de Samosate, père spirituel de Basile le Grand,' *Bulletin de Littérature Ecclésiastique*, 85, no.3 (1984): 179–195; Markus Vinzent, 'Eusebius of Samosata (Saint)' in *Religion Past & Present: Encyclopedia of Theology and Religion*, ed. Hans Dieter Betz *et al.* (Leiden: Brill, 2008), 4:667; J. Gribomont, 'Eusebius of Samosata' in *Encyclopedia of Ancient Christianity*, ed. Di Berardino, 1:880.

[13] Gribomont, 'Eusebius of Samosata,' 880. In *Letter* 98, dated summer 373, Basil refers to Eusebius' 'venerable age.' See also Pouchet, 'Eusèbe de Samosate,' 181.

[14] Gribomont, 'Eusebius of Samosata,' 880. In the words of Raymond Van Dam, Eusebius 'belonged to the generation of Basil's father' (*Families and Friends in Late Roman Cappadocia* (Philadelphia, PA: University of Pennsylvania Press, 2003), 35.

[15] Theodoret, *Church History* 2.27–28. See also Pouchet, 'Eusèbe de Samosate,' 182–183.

Eustathius of Antioch (fl.320s–330s) in 327–328,[16] and thus Eusebius' support of and subsequent friendship with Meletius led to various Western bishops and even Peter II of Alexandria (d.381) viewing both men with deep suspicion and even regarding them as 'Ariomaniacs,' as Basil put it.[17] In 363, though, Eusebius was present with Meletius at a synod at Antioch in which both men forthrightly affirmed their acceptance of the Nicene *homoousios*.[18] Nonetheless, a schism ensued between Meletius and those who supported him, including Eusebius, and those, like the Western bishops, who regarded Meletius as an interloper, maintained that Eustathius was the rightful bishop, and thus supported his heir, Paulinus II (d.388).[19]

The first extant letter of Basil to Eusebius was written five or six years after the Antioch synod in either the latter months of 368 or shortly after the advent of 369 and in a lapidary conclusion Basil identified the bishop of Samosata as a spiritual mentor. Basil told Eusebius that he longed to be filled with the 'great treasures of wisdom' that his correspondent possessed.[20] Presumably the two men had met one another personally before this letter. When Basil was ordained bishop of Caesarea in the fall of 370, Eusebius made the journey from Samosata to take part in the episcopal election. Gregory of Nazianzus (*c*.329–389), who had strongly urged Eusebius to attend, recalled Eusebius' presence as one that filled the hearts of the congregation at Caesarea with

---

[16] For the date, see Sophie Cartwright, 'Eustathius of Antioch in Modern Research,' *Vox Patrum*, 33 (2013), t.59: 478 and n.84.

[17] Basil, *Letter* 266.2. See also Basil, *Letter* 214.2.

[18] Sozomen, *Church History* 6.4. See also R. P. C. Hanson, *The Search for the Christian Doctrine of God. The Arian Controversy 318–381* (1988 ed.; repr. Grand Rapids, MI: Baker, 2005), 581, 651–652.

[19] For details of this schism, see Radde-Gallwitz, *Basil of Caesarea*, 58–59, 135–137.

[20] Basil, *Letter* 27. For the date, see Loofs, *Eustathius von Sebaste*, 50; and Wolf-Dieter Hauschild, *Basilius von Caesarea: Briefe* (Stuttgart: Anton Hiersmann, 1990), 1:178. Paul Jonathan Fedwick places it in the spring of 370: 'A Chronology of the Life and Works of Basil of Caesarea' in his ed., *Basil of Caesarea: Christian, Humanist, Ascetic. A Sixteen-Hundredth Anniversary Symposium* (Toronto, ON: Pontifical Institute of Mediaeval Studies, 1981), 1:11.
For the significance of this letter, see Pouchet, 'Eusèbe de Samosate,' 184–195. Roy J. Deferrari could not be more wrong when he says in his note to his translation of this letter that it 'is of no particular interest except as containing one of the many complaints expressed by Basil against the ill-health which followed him through life' (*Saint Basil: The Letters*, I, 156–157, n.1).

'courage and joy.'[21] Basil would also have been deeply encouraged that such a 'noble guardian of the Faith and watchful ruler of the churches,' as he once called Eusebius, made the arduous journey to lend his support to Basil.[22] Basil wrote again to Eusebius a few months after this ordination, either in December 370 or January of the following year. In this letter he informed Eusebius that he was not only looking forward to the coming of spring after two months of heavy snowfalls that had kept the Cappadocians indoors for much of the time, but was hopeful that Eusebius could revisit Caesarea so that he and his church might 'gain new strength through his good teaching.'[23]

In two further letters from the summer of 373 Basil addressed Eusebius as the 'most God-beloved Father,' another indication that Basil considered Eusebius to be his spiritual mentor.[24] That summer or autumn Basil again wrote to Eusebius and told him that he was eager to meet with him so as to 'consult about many things and learn many things.' In fact, Basil continued, he knew of no one like Eusebius who had 'such perfect wisdom and experience garnered from many labours for the churches.'[25] The following year, Basil again commended Eusebius, this time for his foresight and zeal for the spiritual health of the churches in their part of the Empire, 'writing letters, visiting them in person, leaving no act undone, no word unspoken.'[26]

---

[21] Gregory of Nazianzus, *Letter* 42 and 44. See also Van Dam, *Families and Friends*, 36.

[22] Basil, *Letter* 136. This letter is to be dated in 374; thus Wolf-Dieter Hauschild, *Basilius von Caesarea: Briefe* (Stuttgart: Anton Hiersmann, 1973), 2:15. See also Radde-Gallwitz, *Basil of Caesarea*, 93–94.

[23] Basil, *Letter* 48. For the date, see Loofs, *Eustathius von Sebaste*, 30–31, n.6; Hauschild, *Basilius von Caesarea: Briefe*, 1:194.

[24] Basil, *Letter* 98.2; 128.2. For the date of these two letters, see Loofs, *Eustathius von Sebaste*, 32–33; Hauschild, *Basilius von Caesarea: Briefe*, 2:163, n.91. Loofs places *Letter* 98 in the summer of 372 (*Eustathius von Sebaste*, 25). In his *Letter* 120 to Meletius of Antioch, Basil called Eusebius 'the most God-beloved bishop.' This description of Eusebius occurs again in Basil, *Letter* 181, 219, and 266. In a letter to Eusebius' nephew, Antiochus, Basil called Eusebius 'the great man' (*Letter* 146). Gregory of Nazianzus also spoke of Eusebius' eminent virtue and remarkable 'communion with God' (Basil, *Letter* 167). Though transmitted as Basil's letter, this text is actually from Nazianzen. See Hauschild, *Basilius von Caesarea: Briefe*, 2:171, n.185.

[25] Basil, *Letter* 138.2. For the date, see Loofs, *Eustathius von Sebaste*, 30; Hauschild, *Basilius von Caesarea: Briefe*, 2:165, n.116.

[26] Basil, *Letter* 136.2.

Although they were rare, Basil clearly treasured his actual face-to-face meetings with Eusebius.[27] And yet, he was also thankful that when they could not meet they could still speak to one another through the medium of the letter. There were times when Basil felt that their letters to one another were like shadows compared to the reality of actually meeting.[28] Nonetheless, when one of Eusebius' letters arrived at a particularly difficult juncture in Basil's life, he compared its effect upon him to the way sailors must feel when, in rough seas, they see 'a beacon fire kindled from afar' on dry land.[29]

During the pneumatological debates of the 370s that saw the total collapse of his friendship with Eustathius, Basil came to rely deeply upon Eusebius as both mentor and friend. Raymond Van Dam has rightly noted that during this decade the two men came to share 'a deep emotional bond.'[30] But their relationship was not without its tensions.

'Turning Back to Blues and Greens'

When Silvanus of Tarsus died in 369, and there appeared in the diocese Pneumatomachi who maintained that the Spirit belongs to the creaturely realm, Basil turned to Eusebius for advice and wisdom to deal with the situation as it was threatening to blow the whole church there apart.[31] Now, Basil had a number of ongoing medical conditions, which he frequently mentioned in his letters to Eusebius,[32] and as such had a multitude of medical illustrations at hand. In this letter Basil likened relief from the distress caused by the pneumatological quarrel in the Tarsus church to anaesthetic drugs given by doctors to patients

---

[27] See references to such in Basil, *Letter* 27, 34, 48, 95, 127, 136, 138, 145, and 162. See also Basil's letter to Eusebius' nephew, Antiochus, *Letter* 146.

[28] Basil, *Letter* 162.

[29] Basil, *Letter* 100.

[30] Van Dam, *Families and Friends*, 36. Van Dam makes this assertion since 'Eusebius was one of the few correspondents from whom Basil solicited advice about his family.'

[31] Basil, *Letter* 34. For the date, see Loofs, *Eustathius von Sebaste*, 50; Hauschild, *Basilius von Caesarea: Briefe*, 1:181, n.173. For details regarding the theological crisis in Tarsus at this time, see Basil, *Letters* 113–114. Also see Michael A.G. Haykin, 'And Who is the Spirit? Basil of Caesarea's Letters to the Church at Tarsus,' *Vigiliae Christianae*, 41 (1987): 377–385.

[32] In the following letters to Eusebius, for example, Basil related to his friend details of his various illnesses: *Letter* 30, 34, 100, 136, 138, 141, 145, 162, 198, 237.

suffering intolerable pain. Where was he to find similar relief from the spiritual distress caused by the quarrels at Tarsus? Basil suggested two sources—first, prayer and then, contemplation of the person of Eusebius. With regard to the latter he wrote:

> Though we are indeed distressed, we experience this consolation: that we can contemplate your kindness and alleviate the soul's distress by thinking of you and remembering you. For just as the eyes, after looking intently at glistening objects, obtain some relief by turning back to blues and greens, so also, to our souls, the memory of your gentleness and gracefulness is like a gentle touch that wipes away the pain. …May the Lord graciously grant you to us and to his churches for the benefit of our life and correction of our souls, and may he count me worthy of another beneficial meeting with you.[33]

Basil's language here is yet further evidence of the fact that he clearly regarded Eusebius as a spiritual mentor, one whose wisdom would not only benefit the Church but also Basil personally. Basil used a chromatic illustration to drive home to Eusebius the benefit he had derived from him. After one's eyes have looked at a brilliant object—and here Basil probably had in mind the sun—it was difficult to focus, and it was a relief to look at the blue sea and green vegetation of this world. Similarly, Basil found relief from preoccupation with the problems of the Tarsus church by thinking about the kindness of Eusebius.

The 'Evangelical and Guileless Way of Life'

In the summer of 373, Basil was dealing with a yet greater pneumatological challenge, namely, the views of Eustathius of Sebaste that have been detailed above. Basil had asked Eusebius to meet with the bishop of Sebaste and ask him to answer what Basil termed 'simple, clear, and easily remembered' statements: 'Whether we refuse to admit into fellowship those who do not embrace the Nicene Creed; and whether we refuse to have any part with those who dare to call the Holy Spirit a creature.'[34] Eusebius subsequently met with Eustathius, but the answers that the latter had given to Basil's mentor were anything but clear from Basil's point of view. In Basil's words, Eustathius,

[33] Basil, *Letter* 34.

[34] Basil, *Letter* 128.2.

> instead of answering my questions word for word, has concocted the statement which you have sent me, and this not from simplemindedness, as might be imagined, nor yet from his inability to realise the outcome. But what he reckons is this, that by repudiating my proposition, he will expose his true character to the people; but, if he agrees with us, he will depart from that middle position that has so far seemed preferable to him to any other. So do not let him outwit us, nor let him deceive your Wisdom with the others. Let him send a succinct answer to the question, whether he agrees or denies communion with the enemies of the faith. If you get him to consent to these things and send me such truthful answers as I pray for, then I have been wrong in all that has gone before. I take all the blame upon myself. And then ask from me a proof of humility. But, while none of these things have happened, pardon me, most God-beloved father, if I am unable to approach God's altar with hypocrisy.[35]

Basil had told Eusebius at the outset of this letter that he genuinely desired peace to rule in the churches and he was fully prepared to give his life to this end. But such peace could not be achieved at the expense of truth, for that would entail an abandonment of their 'evangelical and guileless way of life,' Basil's paraphrase, as it were, of Acts 4:32 ('those who believed were of one heart and one soul),' a Bible text that dominated his thought about the nature of what constituted genuine Christian community.[36] Basil concluded by telling Eusebius that if Eustathius was not prepared to make an orthodox confession, then Eusebius should quit writing to him about the possibility of reconciliation with his former mentor.[37]

Given Basil's normal deference to Eusebius in their correspondence, Basil's tone in this letter is at first surprising. In fact, it is nothing less than unique among Basil's letters to Eusebius. One explanation is that, for Basil, rectitude on the subject at hand, namely the rejection

---

[35] *Basil, Letter 128.2, trans.* Blomfield Jackson in *A Select Library of Nicene and Post-Nicene Fathers of the Christian Church,* 2nd series, Volume 8, ed. Philip Schaff and Henry Wace (New York, NY: The Christian Literature Company, 1895), 197, altered.

[36] Emmanuel Amand de Mendieta, *L'Ascèse monastique de saint Basile: essai historique* (Maredsous, Belgium: Éditions Maredsous, 1948), 129, n.88; Fedwick, *Church and the Charisma of Leadership*, 22.

[37] Basil, *Letter* 128.1, 3.

of the creaturehood of the Spirit, outweighed the strongest claims of human friendship, even with such a man as Eusebius.[38]

'Moses Prayed Continually'

During their correspondence Basil frequently mentioned his need for and appreciation of Eusebius' prayers.[39] For example, in the autumn of 373, Basil sought Eusebius' advice regarding three specific issues: how best to respond to the Western bishops regarding the resolution of the schism in Antioch, how to help those in Sebaste who had rejected what Basil called the 'festering ulcer of Eustathius' wicked doctrine,' and how to fulfil a request for Basil to appoint a bishop in the city of Iconium though the city lay outside of his diocese.[40] Illness prevented Basil from meeting with Eusebius in person, and thus he asked his mentor to send him written answers to the three queries. But if he did not have time to do that, then Basil wanted him to pray:

> Pray that what is pleasing to the Lord may come into my mind. And in your synod request that we be remembered, and pray for us yourself, and also include the people as you pray, that we might be counted worthy to serve so as to please the Lord in the days and hours of our pilgrimage that remain.[41]

One of Basil's last extant letters to Eusebius was written two years later in the fall of 375. In the previous year the Homoian Emperor Valens (328–378) had removed a number of Nicene bishops from their charges, among them Eusebius, who had been banished to Thrace.[42] Eusebius could no longer shepherd his people in person but he could

---

[38] Van Dam, *Families and Friends*, 142.

[39] See, for example, Basil, *Letter* 27, 30, 100, 141, 162, and 239.1. If Basil also sent *Letter* 213 to Eusebius, as J.-R. Pouchet has cogently argued, it is another excellent example of Basil's desire for and reliance upon Eusebius' prayers. See J.-R. Pouchet, 'Essai de décryptage de la Lettre 213 de S. Basile,' *Studia Ephemerides 'Augustinianum', 27 (1988): 487–502*. This entire volume was a collection of essays in memory of Jean Gribomont (1920–1986).

[40] Basil, *Letter* 138.2.

[41] Basil, *Letter* 138.2.

[42] Theodoret, *Church History* 4.12–13; Spanneut, 'Eusèbe de Samosate,' 1474.

still engage in 'earnest prayer on behalf of the churches,' even as Moses had prayed unceasingly during Israel's battle with the Amalekites.[43] This comparison with Moses was among the highest compliments that Basil could give to Eusebius, for Basil regarded the Israelite leader as 'a paragon of self-sacrificial love, contemplation, [and] nearness to God.'[44]

Coda

If Basil had lived to hear of Eusebius' death in 380, it would have been added confirmation of his opinion of Eusebius as a holy man and godly mentor. After Valens' death at the Battle of Adrianople (August 9, 378), his successor Gratian (359–383) recalled Eusebius along with others who had been exiled. According to Theodoret of Cyrrhus' (*c.*393–*c.*458) rendition, and admittedly Eusebius is one of his heroes,[45] the exile was on his way back to Samosata in 380 and stopped in Dolica in Syria to appoint a bishop over the town's church that had been previously under the control of the Homoians. Upon entering the town, an Homoian woman threw a tile from the roof of her house at Eusebius, managing to split his skull and fatally wounding him. While dying, Eusebius made his friends and co-workers promise to refrain from seeking to punish the woman, for he had forgiven her, clearly patterning his death after those of Jesus and Stephen.[46] This is the only thing that is often remembered about Eusebius of Samosata: he was the sole example of an orthodox martyr in the post-Constantinian church of the fourth century. But, as this essay has sought to show, Eusebius' mentorship of and friendship with Basil of Caesarea during the doctrinal watershed of the 370s is of vital importance and should be remembered in any account of the Cappadocian's formulation of the Holy Spirit's deity.

---

[43] Basil, *Letter* 241. For the date of the letter, see Wolf-Dieter Hauschild, *Basilius von Caesarea: Briefe* (Stuttgart: Anton Hiersmann, 1993), 3:212, n.275.

[44] Andrea Sterk, *Renouncing the World Yet Leading the Church: The Monk-Bishop in Late Antiquity* (Cambridge, MA/London, England: Harvard University Press, 2004), 62.

[45] Cyrrhus and Samosata belonged to the same Roman province in the fourth century, Euphratensis. See Angelo di Berardino with Gianluca Pilara, ed., *Historical Atlas of Ancient Christianity* (St. Davids, PA: ICCS Press, 2013), 97.

[46] Theodoret, *History of the Church* 5.4.

Eight

A.W. Pink and the Quest for Reformed Identity

Brett Lee-Price

It is likely not an overstatement to assert that Arthur Walkington Pink (1886–1952) was one of the leading proponents of Reformed soteriology in the early-to-mid-20th century. Pink's advocacy of the doctrines of grace was a rarity during a period when such a robust form of Calvinism was unpopular and, indeed, practically non-existent. But, and further to the point, Pink's promotion of such foundational principles through both his seminal title, *The Sovereignty of God*, and his long-running periodical, *Studies in the Scriptures*, was to be influential in the doctrinal retrieval of such beliefs decades after his death. It is as John J. Murray aptly noted; Pink served as a 'link between the Calvinism of C. H. Spurgeon and the rediscovery of the doctrines of grace under the ministry of Dr. D. M. Lloyd-Jones'.[1]

However, did Pink solely intend to encourage the retrieval of the doctrines of grace? Or was he hoping, through his writings, to motivate the recovery of something greater, such as a more robust profession of the Reformed framework—with all its theological trimmings? And, if the latter is true, is it then right to see A.W. Pink as solely a Calvinistic theologian or also a Reformed one? While this may, at first, seem to some like a distinction without a difference, it would be incorrect, as Richard A. Muller has rightly asserted, to treat the doctrines of grace, or what are commonly called the five points of Calvinism, as the 'absolutely primary basis for identifying someone as holding the Calvinistic or Reformed faith'.[2] Likewise, the late R. C. Sproul argued that while

---

[1] John J. Murray, *Catch the Vision: Roots of the Reformed Recovery* (Darlington, England: Evangelical Press, 2007), 34.

[2] Richard A. Muller, 'How Many Points?' *Calvin Theological Journal* 28 (1993): 426.

the five points were absolutely central to the Reformed faith, they simply did not 'exhaust this system of doctrine'.[3]

At first, this may sound truistic, yet modern-day Christians have continuously demonstrated an inability to grasp and clearly distinguish the difference. A person being Reformed is still often conflated with and bandied around as one holding merely to the five points. The *Young, Restless, Reformed* descriptor epitomises such an approach.[4] While adherence to the doctrines of grace is often taken as the defining marker of Reformed identity, with little regard for the broader doctrinal framework historically accompanying it, such a reductionist perspective overlooks the rich heritage of Reformed thought, which is not merely a soteriological construct but encompasses an entire theological system that includes a distinctive hermeneutic, a confessional tradition, and a covenantal framework. Without these integral components, the Reformed label loses its historical and theological precision, leading to a broad yet shallow application that misrepresents the tradition it seeks to uphold.

While Pink's theological emphasis was undeniably Calvinistic, the question remains whether he should be classified as a Reformed theologian in the fullest sense. Matthew Bingham rightly cautions against the misapplication of the Reformed label, stating that 'the Reformed tradition represents a far richer and more complex theological heritage than this, and to promiscuously include within its boundaries any and all who honour God as fully sovereign simultaneously negates the utility of the 'Reformed' label and obscures the actual theological and ecclesial identities of the groups to which it is wrongly applied.'[5] The challenge, then, is to determine whether Pink's theological corpus aligns sufficiently with this broader Reformed tradition or whether his divergence disqualifies him from such classification.

---

[3] R. C. Sproul, *What is Reformed Theology? Understanding the Basics* (Grand Rapids, MI: Baker Books, 1997), 30.

[4] Collin Hansen, *Young, Restless, Reformed: A Journalist's Journey with the New Calvinists* (Wheaton, IL: Crossway, 2008). See also Jeremy Walker, *The New Calvinism Considered: A Personal and Pastoral Assessment* (Darlington, UK: Evangelical Press, 2013).

[5] Matthew Bingham, ''Reformed Baptist': Anachronistic Oxymoron or Useful Signpost?' in *On Being Reformed: Debates over a Theological Identity*, Christianities in the Trans-Atlantic World, eds. Crawford Gribben and Scott Spurlock (Milton Keyes, UK: Palgrave Macmillan, 2018), 30.

This paper seeks to interact with this question by examining Pink's theological writings, his doctrinal commitments, and his engagement with the historical Reformed tradition. While some may argue that his Baptist identity and lack of formal confessional allegiance place him outside the Reformed camp, a closer analysis reveals that his theological methodology, biblical hermeneutic, and commitment to systematic theology bear the marks of Reformed thought. By assessing his theology in the light of the broader contours of Reformed identity—particularly its *principia theologiae*, confessionalism, and covenantal structure—this paper will argue that A.W. Pink, despite certain divergences, can indeed be considered a Reformed theologian.

Reformed? Setting a Taxonomical Framework

Of course, attempting to consider Pink as Reformed is not without its problems. Pink was, for most of his life, a Baptist. Simply his position on baptism would be enough in some quarters to deny him any right to the classification of being 'Reformed'. The rest of his theology would bear little to no relevance in such a decision. Yet, this begs the question, what does the label *Reformed* actually mean?

It is noteworthy that the usage of any label can be complex, and certainly the use of some labels can be an affair of the Machiavellian order. Their use is inevitable, but labels can carry connotations that are not always helpful in specific situations. While labels can be employed appropriately to distinguish and differentiate, they can also be used in a highly charged way to express a sectarian or partisan spirit beyond what ought to be charitably acceptable. However, this is not to deny labels their rightful place. A label like 'Reformed' helps us to identify the unique qualities of a particular strand within the Christian tradition. The immediate concern is then not only one of definition, but also of qualification. Subsequently, the question as to the entailment of the Reformed label is pertinent if we are to attempt any clarity on whether the categorisation of Pink as Reformed can indeed be deemed legitimate.

Furthermore, the people who attempt to create such a definition need to be mindful of the problems with the modern elevation of self-identification and the desire to belong. Such attempts have been identified by others.[6] Whether such critiques are legitimate or not, the reality is that one needs to be conscious of the modern trajectory that places, as Carl Trueman notes, the 'onus for meaning [...] with the human self as constructive agent.'[7] Arguably, the most reasonable approach, in seeking definitional clarity around the contours of Reformed identity, is to allow historical social markers to speak without, as much as possible, any form of anachronistic projection taking place. What constitutes the understanding of the Reformed label should be the Reformed themselves as made evident through the theological and sociological frameworks that they held.

So, then, what is meant by Reformed? Certainly, at a minimum, it is an understanding that someone is operating within the theological structure of the great traditions that descend from the Reformation, notably those which trace their descent from the likes of Geneva, Strasbourg, and Zurich. It would also entail, by consequence, that one holds to a predestinarian soteriology, often identified as Calvinism, yet not solely held or articulated by Calvin alone. This much would be true but alone would be insufficient. Indeed, more critical to Reformed thought was a certain understanding, approach, and method to Scripture. This paper is certainly unoriginal in asserting that the absolute core of Reformed thought, and subsequent Reformed identity, is a particular *principia theologiae*.[8] Specifically, the *principia theologiae* entailed a careful fidelity to Scripture, recognising both its supremacy and its authority in being the guiding light for the Christian, subjecting all else to its legitimacy. The *principia theologiae* firmly establishes that theology begins with God as the ontological foundation (*principium essendi*) and Scripture as the cognitive foundation (*principium cognoscendi*), revealed and understood through the Spirit's work. As Auguste Lecerf

[6] See D. G. Hart, 'Baptists Are Different,' in *On Being Reformed: Debates over a Theological Identity*, Christianities in the Trans-Atlantic World, eds. Crawford Gribben and Scott Spurlock (Milton Keyes, UK: Palgrave Macmillan, 2018), 53–68.

[7] Carl R. Trueman, *The Rise and Triumph of the Modern Self: Cultural Amnesia, Expressive Individualism, and the Road to Sexual Revolution* (Wheaton, IL: Crossway, 2020), 71.

[8] See Fred H. Klooster, 'The Uniqueness of Reformed Theology: A Preliminary Attempt at Description,' *Calvin Theological Journal* 14:1 (1979): 39. I cannot help but echo Klooster's sentiments: 'I had expected to say something new, something apparently more profound. Perhaps there is nothing more profound that can be stated, even today, than this simple Reformed conviction concerning the Scriptural principle.'

(1872—1943), who arguably divides his volume, *Introduction à la Dogmatique Réformée* (1931) between both *principium*, observes, 'Calvin and the Swiss Reformers subordinated a legitimate concern with salvation to the restoration of a sense of the sovereign independence and exclusive authority of God. Thus Calvinism developed a stricter conception of the formal authority of Scripture. . . '[9] This approach was to provide the methodological framework that undergirded subsequent theological thought, recognising the not insignificant epistemological reality of the archetypal/ectypal distinction and, subsequently, the creator/creature divide.[10] This principle also rightly acknowledged the absolute centrality of God, via Scripture, as the authoritative basis of order and theological structure.[11] Rather than leading to the stark theological extremities of biblicism on the one hand and mere traditionalism on the other[12], the principle was consciously cognisant of the past, recognising its import but not doing so in any manner that would corrode Scripture's authority.[13]

It is this *principia theologiae*, which Muller describes as 'the *sine qua non*, the necessary and irreducible ground of theology'[14], which served as the formative basis of Reformed thinking and from which all doctrinal outworking was subsequently derived. Positions on theology proper, Christology, anthropology, et al., far from being developed by virtue of simple proof-texting, were deduced based on the reasonable textual, contextual, and structural implications. The understanding

---

9 Auguste Lecerf, *An Introduction to Reformed Dogmatics*, trans. Andre Schlemmer (Grand Rapids, MI: Baker Book House, 1981), 13.

10 Lecerf, *An Introduction to Reformed Dogmatics*, 21; Richard A. Muller, *Post-Reformation Reformed Dogmatics*, 4 vols. (Grand Rapids, MI: Baker Academic, 2003), 1:234; See also R. Scott Clark, *Recovering the Reformed Confession: Our Theology, Piety, and Practice* (Phillipsburg, NJ: P & R Publishing, 2008), 150; B. B. Warfield, *Calvin and Augustine*, ed. Samuel G. Craig (Philadelphia, PA: Presbyterian and Reformed, 1956), 288; A. A. Hodge and B. B. Warfield, 'Inspiration,' *Presbyterian Review* 6 (1881): 226–28.

11 Herman Bavinck, *Reformed Dogmatics*, ed. John Bolt, trans. John Vriend, 4 vols (Grand Rapids, MI: Baker Academic, 2003), 1:64–65. Note that this thought finds specific expression through the reality of the Westminster Confession starting with the doctrine of Scripture.

12 Warfield, *Calvin and Augustine*, 291.

13 R. Michael Allen, *Reformed Theology*, Doing Theology (London, England: T&T Clark, 2010), 138; Carl R. Trueman, *The Creedal Imperative* (Wheaton, IL: Crossway, 2012), 123.

14 Muller, *Post-Reformation Reformed Dogmatics*, 1:430.

and emphasis given to this principle was located throughout the writings of Calvin and his Reformation contemporaries.[15] Such a common commitment ensured that unity in Reformation thought was evident within the pages of a great deal of Reformation and post-Reformation writings—unity which was not simply the result of shared experience and theological expression. Commenting on this consistency, R. Scott Clark aptly remarks:

> There was a remarkable degree of agreement on the main lines of Reformed theology. Judging by the theology of the classical period of Reformed theology, when our vocabulary and categories were developed, we can speak of a Reformed doctrine of Scripture, a Reformed understanding of the nature of theology, and Reformed doctrines of God, man, Christ, salvation, church, and sacraments. There was a Reformed piety organised around the Word, the sacraments, and prayer. There was common Reformed understanding of the principle by which worship was to be conducted, when, and even how often. Thus there can even be said to have been a Reformed practice.[16]

This principle was also evidenced in the composition of confessions, with confessions providing a, if not *the*, sensible expression of the method. The embrace of confessionalisation was an acknowledgement not only of the commitment to this method but also particularly of the reality that the medium of confessions provided an orderly outworking of this principle into thought. Notably, this reality was acknowledged in the bringing together of multiple doctrinal subjects into a single and concise statement. Confessions were to serve as common declarations on significant doctrines whereupon fellowship, of an ecclesiastical fashion, could be established. Most were intended to be relatively succinct documents which, by the establishing of crucial theological markers, aimed to emphasise both unity with those who were of like tradition and variance with those who were not.[17] In a significant way, the embracement of confessionalism, as made evident through the act of confessionalisation, was to signify the understanding that the

---

[15] Klooster, 'The Uniqueness of Reformed Theology,' 43–44.

[16] Clark, *Recovering the Reformed Confession*, 154; Trueman, *Creedal Imperative*, 131.

[17] Trueman, *Creedal Imperative*, 109; J. V. Fesko, *The Need for Creeds Today: Confessional Faith in a Faithless Age* (Grand Rapids, MI: Baker Academic, 2020), 23.

utilisation of such documents was an important feature of being Reformed, particularly in how these documents, through the use of the principle, appropriately distilled fundamental truths from Scripture.

Indeed, this prevalence of confessions in Reformed thought, which signifies their importance, legitimately brings into question any form of Calvinistic expression that professes doctrinal loyalty to predestinarian soteriology while rejecting the accompanying, or overarching, confessional framework.[18] Being Reformed ought to, then, as it has historically, denote a commitment not only to the Reformed tradition, as in a subscription to the theological method, but also to the medium which was subsequently employed—specifically, a commitment to confessionalism. Such an understanding is inherently perceptible through the plethora of confessions that stretched from the Reformation (ca. 1520) to the (so-called) High Orthodox (ca. 1640) periods. While each had its local and varying contextual emphases, the unity in methodological commitment is unarguably evidenced through such confessions as the Belgic Confession (1559), the Thirty-Nine Articles (1562), Second Helvetic Confession (1564), Irish Articles of Religion (1615) and Westminster Confession of Faith (1646). Each, in turn, demonstrated the importance of doctrinal articulation but did so specifically as that articulation was derived from a consensual theological method. Thus, one can recognise that while variance on a number of topics existed, that a standardisation on a number of essential subjects—including on the nature of God, the *historia salutis,* and the nature of *justificatio sola fide*—was a result of this shared methodological dedication.[19] In many respects, the universality of the Synod of Dort (1618–1619), which sought to put an end to the doctrinal machinations of the Remonstrants, was predicated upon, and drew authority from, the recognition of this shared unity among its delegates.

Therefore, this theological unity, based on a methodological consensus and displayed through confessionalisation, is why Clark

---

[18] While a church may affirm election apart from a formal confession, the historical Reformed tradition has always articulated its theological commitments through confessionalisation. Thus, to reject confessionalism is not necessarily to reject election, but it does mark a departure from the structured theological identity that has historically defined Reformed Christianity.

[19] Trueman, *Creedal Imperative,* 131.

is rightly justified in saying that 'the word [Reformed] denotes a confession, a theology, piety, and practice that are well known and well defined and summarised in ecclesiastically sanctioned and binding documents.'[20] A Reformed contour had started to form based on a consistent approach to Scripture, where unity of thought on issues which were understood as central matters, such as the common commitment to predestinarian soteriology, was apparent. Of course, while there was, arguably, diversity on certain allowable points, and this is to be explored later, there remained a common commitment to a specific theological method shared by the Reformed world, and confessionalism was to serve as a chief expression of this consensual commitment.

However, the outworking of this Reformed method was not limited to the writing of, and the subsequent holding to, confessions and the doctrinal subjects articulated therein. This principle was also to establish a particular hermeneutic, a particular way that Scripture was to be understood—namely, through the lens of covenants. Drawing from the existential reality of the Creator/creature divide, Heinrich Bullinger and others recognised that God largely dealt with his people covenantally; this was to be an area that would be significantly developed by the Reformers' 17th-century successors on both the Continent and the British Isles. As a result, theologies would be developed that recognised, and gave due weight to, the controlling paradigm that covenants provided for helping God's people understand the continuity (and discontinuity) of God's unfolding providential and redemptive acts in both the Old and New Testaments, particularly in view of the interpretive grid of law and gospel. While other theological subjects, such as the tripartite division and threefold use of the law and the regulative principle of worship, were also to be significantly developed during the same time, it was covenant theology that, in many respects, was to play a significant part in Reformed thought within the 17th century. It was to become, as has been noted by others, 'an organising principle in Reformed theological systems.'[21]

---

[20] Clark, *Recovering the Reformed Confession*, 3.

[21] Guy Prentiss Waters, J. Nicholas Reid, and John R. Muether, 'Introduction,' in *Covenant Theology: Biblical Theological, and Historical Perspectives*, eds. Guy Prentiss Waters, J. Nicholas Reid, and John R. Muether (Wheaton, IL: Crossway, 2020), 35.

Seeking to comprehend and articulate how respective covenants in Scripture related to one another seized the imagination of a vast number of 17th century writers, particularly as the covenants related to the nature and composition of the church. Almost completely, Reformed thought across Europe was to become covenantal in approach. Indeed, so intertwined did the understanding of covenant theology become with Reformed thought during this period that the theologian John Hesselink was well warranted to state that 'Reformed theology is covenant theology'.[22] While the scriptural principle was the methodology by which all other doctrines were derived, covenant theology was to be the system by which such doctrines were to be subsequently ordered.

It is at this point that it is likely worth taking stock of the genius of the Reformed tradition as it has, so far, been articulated above. While it is possible to go further and comment upon other doctrines that were also commonly held, the purpose of the above is to evidence that at the heart of the Reformed tradition was the *principia theologiae* which shaped how those within the tradition approached Scripture, followed by the utilisation of confessions which provided the written outworking of the employed method, and accompanied by a covenantal view which provided the organisational hermeneutic.

Including Particular Baptists: A Taxonomical Challenge?

Much of what is outlined above, though intended as a succinct summary, would not, generally, be considered controversial by those who would see themselves as being 'Truly Reformed', modern-day gatekeepers of Reformed identity. It may be considered somewhat sparse due to the lack of detail on several other theological distinctives that were expressly held. However, it could well be argued that many such distinctives, such as the Reformed view of the law, of worship, or even Sabbatarianism, were themselves derived from the application of the *principia theologiae*, particularly through the utilisation of covenant theology and their enshrinement by means of the act of confessionalisation.

---

[22] I. John Hesselink, *On Being Reformed: Distinctive Characteristics and Common Misunderstandings* (Ann Arbor, MI: Servant Books, 1983), 57.

However, it is when one argues for the inclusion of the Particular Baptists within the Reformed tradition for holding to, effectively, the nub of the theology articulated above that one encounters particularly fierce resistance. The most outspoken oppose any inclusion of Particular Baptists within the tradition, due to their variance on baptism, ecclesiology, and covenant theology.[23] Such opposition is evident enough within the work of esteemed Presbyterian scholars R. Scott Clark and Darryl G. Hart, who both question the right of Particular Baptists to sit at the Reformed table.[24] Often, in these arguments, Presbyterianism and the Dutch Reformed traditions are held as the benchmark of Reformed legitimacy. Yet, the question must be asked: why is 1646 the standard by which Reformed theology must be assessed? Or, to put it differently, must an assessment of Reformed theology be benchmarked against the standard of the Presbyterianism of the 1640s?

After all, such an understanding either denies or unduly simplifies the legitimate variance within the Reformed tradition of the 17th century and instead paints it as being much more monolithic than is frankly warranted. While the overarching *principia theologiae* was uniformly held, its outworking in regard to both covenant theology and ecclesiology was still being fleshed out.[25] The development and trajectory of Reformed covenant theology, while trending towards bicovenantalism through the influence of John Ball (1585–1640), was still being established, and no position was completely unanimous. Edmund Calamy (1600–1666) in his *Two Solemne Covenants Made Between God and Man*

[23] Whilst it does not explicitly engage with the content of the printed debate, *On Being Reformed: Debates over a Theological Identity* (Milton Keyes, UK: Palgrave Macmillan, 2018), this section is written with this in the immediate background.

[24] Both D. G. Hart and R. Scott Clark have made it known that they don't believe Baptists, of any stripe, belong to the Reformed tradition; whilst this is seen implicitly in Hart's *Calvinism: A History* (New Haven, CT: Yale University Press, 2013), and much more explicitly on R. Scott Clark's Heidelblog (https://heidelblog.net), it is worth perusing their relevant chapters in *On Being Reformed,* D. G. Hart, 'Baptists Are Different,' and R. Scott Clark, 'A House of Cards? A Response to Bingham, Gribben, and Caughey'.

[25] For a tracing of the development of covenant theology within the English landscape, see Richard L. Greaves, 'The Origins and Early Development of English Covenant Thought,' *The Historian* 31:1 (1968): 21–35. Also, see Samuel D. Renihan's chapter, 'Unity and Diversity in Reformed Covenant Theology,' in *From Shadow to Substance: The Federal Theology of the English Particular Baptists (1642–1704)* (Oxford, UK: Regent's Park College, 2018), 18–66.

(1647), provided a contemporaneous survey of a variety of positions held at the time, noting that certain independents held to positions distinctive from the bicovenantalism later articulated by the Westminster Confession of Faith. Some proposed a fourfold covenant structure, while others, such as Jeremiah Burroughs (1599–1646), held to a threefold covenant, with two covenants of works that were given to Adam and to Israel after Egypt, and then a covenant of grace made with Christ.[26] Other expressions also existed. John Cameron (1579–1625), for example, introduced a fivefold covenant schema, distinguishing between absolute covenants (eternal and Noahic) and hypothetical covenants, including the subservient Mosaic covenant, which prepared for grace.[27] In contrast, Thomas Cartwright (1535–1603) adhered to a more traditional bicovenantalism yet emphasised the conditional obligations of faith and repentance, stressing human responsibility within the covenant of grace.[28] Others, such as John Owen (1616–1683), have been understood by some scholars as holding to an altogether unique position.[29] While the underlying theological grid and theme of law and gospel united the views, the precise Reformed/covenantal expression varied.[30]

---

[26] Edmund Calamy, Sr. *Two Solemne Covenants Made between God and Man: viz. the Covenant of Works, and the Covenant of Grace. Clearly Laid Open, Distinguished, and Vindicated from Many Dangerous Opinions; the Right Knowledge of Which Will Be Very Profitable to All Those That Have Escaped the First, and Are Confirmed in the Second at the Sacrament* (1647).

[27] Richard A. Muller, 'Divine Covenants, Absolute and Conditional: John Cameron and the Early Orthodox Development of Reformed Covenant Theology,' *Mid-America Journal of Theology* 17 (2006): 11–56; Renihan, *From Shadow to Substance,* 48–57.

[28] Greaves, 'English Covenant Thought,' 29.

[29] Willem van Vlastuin, 'The Fruitfulness of a Paradox: The Doctrine of the Covenant in Wilhelmus à Brakel (1635–1711) Reapplied,' in *Covenant: A Vital Element of Reformed Theology,* Studies in Reformed Theology 42 (Leiden, Netherlands: Brill, 2021), 283–284; Joel R. Beeke and Mark Jones, 'The Minority Report: John Owen on Sinai,' in *A Puritan Theology: Doctrine for Life* (Grand Rapids, MI: Reformation Heritage Books, 2012), 293–303.

[30] Muller comments that the history of early Reformed covenantal thought is 'rather fluid and variegated' in 'Divine Covenants, Absolute and Conditional,' 37. Likewise, Herman Hoeksema notes, 'There has never been any unanimity about this subject among Reformed people. In fact, it cannot even be said that there is a single covenant concept which has won for itself the exclusive name of Reformed in distinction from all other views' (Herman Hoeksema, *Believers and Their Seed: Children in the Covenant* [Grand Rapids, MI: Reformed Free Publishing Association, 1977], 13). See also Beeke

Similarly, comprehensions of the composition of the church, as well as its governance, were likewise debated. Excluding the Anglican tradition, which had its own Reformed pedigree, Presbyterianism and Congregationalism disputed the nature and structure of the church and the question of whether there was to be a national, visible church that held structural political authority or individual congregations, each with their own independent authority. While most delegates to the Westminster Assembly concluded the former, which was to be enshrined within the Westminster Confession, the Congregationalist minority would later revise the Confession in 1658 to reflect Congregational polity.[31]

However, despite the divergence of thought between Presbyterians and Congregationalists in the 17th century, both generally recognised each other's mutual inclusion within the Reformed tradition. When debates arose, as they did, they were conducted in recognition of this reality and in an esteem that was generally reciprocated by both sides. Indeed, acknowledging their shared heritage and theological approach, Presbyterian-Congregational relations were typically cordial, as both struggled against the dominant establishment church, seeking worship and church practices that conformed to Reformation principles and conformity of the national church to what was Scripturally warranted.

Within this context, the Particular Baptists appeared, emerging from Congregationalism in the mid-1630s. The link of the first prominent Congregationalist church, the Jacob-Lathrop-Jessey church, to Particular Baptists has been well noted[32], whereby several groups,

---

and Jones, 'The Puritans on the Old and New Covenants,' in *A Puritan Theology: Doctrine for Life* (Grand Rapids, Michigan: Reformation Heritage Books, 2012), 284.

[31] Although, earlier in 1648, the Congregationalists in New England adopted the *Platform of Church Discipline,* commonly called the Cambridge Platform. Written by Richard Mather, with additional content incorporated from John Cotton, this document served to justify Congregational polity and defend the orthodoxy of the New England churches. The same Synod that adopted the Cambridge Platform was also to adopt the Westminster Confession as their confession of faith, agreeing in substance whilst differing on some issues (e.g., polity).

[32] A. C. Underwood, *A History of the English Baptists* (London, UK: Kingsgate Press, 1947), 57–58; Michael A.G. Haykin, *Kiffen, Knollys, and Keach: Recovering Our English Baptist Heritage,* 2nd ed. (Peterborough, Canada: H&E Publishing, 2019), 21–25.

having grappled with the theological and biblical grounds for infant baptism, left the church to establish new churches with the understanding that baptism and church membership were reserved for professing believers. While the latter belief was held by Congregationalists, who believed in the ecclesiastical doctrine of churches being composed of visible saints, these first Particular Baptists struggled to reconcile this concept with the practice of infant baptism, a point noted by Hart, who observed that an 'important consequence of the Congregational decision to limit church membership to those who could prove an experiential acquaintance and appropriation of the gospel was to raise doubts about the practice of infant baptism.'[33]

Yet despite the divergence between Congregationalists and the emerging Particular Baptists, the two groups maintained amiable and intertwined relationships.[34] Congregationalist leaders such as Thomas Goodwin (1600–1680), Jeremiah Burroughs, and Philip Nye (1595–1672) upheld irenic relations with Particular Baptist leaders like John Spilsbery (1593–1668), Hanserd Knollys (1598–1691), and Henry Jessey (1603–1663).[35] Many Particular Baptists continued to identify with the Congregationalists, collaborating and sharing much of their doctrinal and ecclesiological framework. As Matthew Bingham aptly observes, the early Particular Baptists 'were simply congregationalists who modified one piece of their existing doctrinal framework.'[36] They did not perceive themselves as 'Baptists' but as adherents of the Congregational way who, through consistent application, arrived at a baptistic conclusion. They argued that if the church comprises visible saints and baptism is the entryway into the church, then baptism must be reserved for those giving credible evidence of conversion. Yet

---

[33] D. G. Hart, *Calvinism: A History* (New Haven, CT: Yale University Press, 2013), 113.

[34] James M. Renihan, *Edification and Beauty: The Practical Ecclesiology of the English Particular Baptists, 1675–1705*, Studies in Baptist History and Thought (Milton Keynes, UK: Paternoster, 2008), 11; Matthew Bingham, *Orthodox Radicals: Baptist Identity in the English Revolution*, Oxford Studies in Historical Theology (Oxford, UK: Oxford University Press, 2019), 39.

[35] Bingham, *Orthodox Radicals*, 47, 52, 57; Benjamin Stinton, *A Repository of Divers Historical Matters Relating to the English Antipedobaptists Collected from Original Papers of Faithful Extracts* (1712), 18; reprint, *Transactions of the Baptist Historical Society*, 1:4 (1910): 243–244.

[36] Bingham, *Orthodox Radicals*, 44.

this theological development did not fracture their relationships with others in the broader movement. On the contrary, collaboration endured, as evidenced by accounts from the 1650s of Congregationalist ministers advising members who rejected paedobaptism to travel to London to receive baptism from Jessey himself.[37]

Following Charles I's execution and the establishment of the Protectorate under Oliver Cromwell (1599–1658), the standing of the Particular Baptists improved significantly. Their legitimacy was recognised, and, alongside Presbyterians and Congregationalists, they were included in official administrative roles, such as the Commission of Triers, a 38-member body formed in 1654 to evaluate the qualifications of parish ministers.[38] It was during this period that John Owen was to collaborate closely with the Particular Baptists, serving with them on such committees and later defending them against their fiercest critics.[39]

This era also saw efforts to create a confession aimed at building a broader Reformed consensus while excluding groups like Socinians, Quakers, and Arminians. The resulting document, *A New Confession of Faith, or The First Principles of the Christian Religion Necessary to Bee Laid as a Foundation by All Such as Desire to Build on unto Perfection* (1654), was drafted by figures such as Goodwin, Owen, Nye, Thomas Manton (1620–1677), and Richard Baxter (1615–1691). All except Baxter were involved in Cromwell's Triers and Ejectors scheme.[40] However, a glaring omission in the confession seems to be the complete absence of any mention of baptism. Evidently, Particular Baptists were seen as part of official English Reformed orthodoxy.

During the Restoration and the enactment of the Clarendon Code, particularly the Act of Uniformity in 1662, Nonconformist ministers faced heightened threats of persecution and arrest. In response,

---

[37] Bingham, *Orthodox Radicals*, 124.

[38] Hart, *Calvinism*, 88.

[39] Crawford Gribben, 'John Owen, Baptism, and the Baptists,' in *By Common Confession: Essays in Honor of James M. Renihan*, eds. Ronald S. Baines, Richard C. Barcellos, and James P. Butler (Palmdale, CA: RBAP, 2015), 62–63, 66.

[40] Beeke and Jones, *A Puritan Theology*, 310–311; Crawford Gribben, *John Owen and English Puritanism: Experiences of Defeat*, Oxford Studies in Historical Theology (Oxford, UK: Oxford University Press, 2017), 153.

Congregationalist and Particular Baptist churches frequently collaborated to sustain their ministries when pastors were detained. Mid-20th century historian Gerard G. Cragg observed:

> In some districts Baptists and Congregationalists were so associated that the denominational loyalty of a particular church might not be clear. One of the most remarkable examples of united action for common (though limited) ends was provided by the Baptists, Presbyterians and Congregationalists of Bristol. There was no question of their sacrificing anything of their independence or autonomy, but in the face of a threat to their very existence they concerted plans to frustrate the expectations of their foes. As a first step, the four dissenting congregations chose two men from each, and the committee of eight so formed became responsible for initiating such action as would be most likely to protect the dissenters from the worst ravages of persecution.[41]

The two Particular Baptist congregations in Bristol (Pithay and Broadmead) and the Congregational church accepted a formula of compromise. However, the Presbyterian church was reluctant to recognise any minister who was not formally trained, and consequently, the joint services did not proceed.[42] However, regardless, joint days of prayer were held each quarter; fast days were also observed whenever one of the congregations requested or the committee suggested them, and an agreed-upon procedure for dealing with informers' attacks on such joint gatherings was devised.

While a close relationship between Congregationalists and Particular Baptists continued throughout the 17th century, exceptions arose in specific contexts. One notable instance of tension occurred in 17th-century Massachusetts Bay, where sectarian divisions emerged. John Owen and other independent clergy notably addressed these tensions by writing a letter to the governor of Massachusetts, criticising the colony's treatment of Baptists.[43] In contrast, other Congregationalist regions, such as the nearby Plymouth Colony, demonstrated a

---

[41] Gerald R. Cragg, *Puritanism in the Period of the Great Persecution, 1660–1688* (Cambridge, UK: Cambridge University Press, 1957), 183.

[42] James M. Renihan, ed., *Faith and Life for Baptists: The Documents of the London Particular Baptist General Assemblies, 1689–1694* (Palmdale, CA: RBAP, 2016), 122.

[43] Gribben, *John Owen and English Puritanism*, 240.

more amicable and accepting attitude toward Baptists, reflecting the diversity of responses to Baptist practices within the broader Congregationalist tradition.[44]

Indeed, this relationship between Particular Baptists and Congregationalists extended beyond mere unity during tribulation. The concept of 'union chapels' persisted well into the 18th and 19th centuries, symbolising their shared fellowship. These chapels often hosted joint worship services, with ministers from both traditions alternating leadership roles.[45] This practice was particularly evident during the colonisation of Australia in the 19th century, where cities like Sydney and Brisbane witnessed Congregationalists and Particular Baptists worshipping together until their numbers grew sufficiently to establish separate churches for each persuasion.[46]

From their inception, Particular Baptists maintained close fellowship with Congregationalists and were broadly regarded as part of the wider Reformed tradition. The regular occurrence of joint worship underscored how Congregationalists viewed Particular Baptists as firmly within the bounds of Reformed orthodoxy. Theologically, the two groups were nearly identical, with both also following the principle that churches should consist solely of members—visible saints—who covenanted together. They diverged principally on the proper subjects of baptism. While both rejected the inclusion of children as full members based solely on their parents' faith, Congregationalists maintained the practice of infant baptism as a sign of the child's covenantal relationship, as mediated through their believing parents, though this did not grant them automatic church membership. Full membership required a personal profession of faith and a formal covenant commitment.[47] Particular Baptists, by contrast, saw baptism itself as a sign of

---

[44] Francis J. Bremer, *One Small Candle: The Plymouth Puritans and the Beginning of English New England* (Oxford, UK: Oxford University Press, 2020), 184.

[45] Anthony R. Cross, *Baptism and the Baptists: Theology and Practice in Twentieth-Century Britain* (Eugene, OR: Wipf & Stock, 2000), 92–93.

[46] Ken R. Manley, *From Woolloomooloo to 'Eternity': A History of Australian Baptists* (Milton Keynes, UK: Paternoster, 2006), 1:26–27; David Parker, *'Strange Bedfellows': Rev. Charles Stewart, Brisbane's First Baptist Minister, and the United Evangelical Church* (Brisbane, Australia: Baptist Historical Society of Queensland, 1998), 28–29.

[47] Crawford Gribben, *An Introduction to John Owen* (Wheaton, IL: Crossway, 2020), 43; Gribben, *John Owen and English Puritanism*, 120.

personal inclusion in the New Covenant and therefore reserved it for those who could give evidence of regeneration.

However, beyond simple ecclesiastical unity with Congregationalists, a shared theological heritage was evident in several ways. The *Second London Baptist Confession of Faith* was written in 1677 and circulated publicly in 1689. Particular Baptists largely adopted the Congregationalist revision of the Westminster Confession of Faith—the *Savoy Declaration of Faith and Order*—mostly following its edits and adjustments with few exceptions.[48] So too, the earlier London Baptist Confession of Faith, published in 1644, and revised in 1646, was largely derived from earlier Congregational documents.[49] This approach demonstrated that the Particular Baptists, as James Renihan argues, 'were declaring with some vigour their own desire to be placed in the broad stream of English Reformed Confessional Christianity.'[50]

Likewise, Particular Baptists were, as was typical of the Reformed tradition of the 17th century, *covenantal*. Noting this point, Ligon Duncan states, 'Covenant theology, not dispensationalism, is the native soil of not only Presbyterian, Congregational, and evangelical Anglican traditions but also of historic Baptist biblical theology.'[51] While not necessarily monolithic in adopting a particular covenantal structure, as was also typical of the period[52], several Particular Baptists utilised John Owen's approach to the unity and discontinuity of the old and new

---

[48] James M. Renihan, *To the Judicious and Impartial Reader: A Contextual-Historical Exposition of the Second London Baptist Confession of Faith*, Baptist Symbolics Volume 2 (Cape Coral, FL: Founders Press, 2022), 10–11.

[49] Richard P. Belcher and Anthony Mattia, *A Discussion of the Seventeenth-Century Particular Baptist Confessions of Faith* (Southbridge, MA: Crowne Publications, 1990), 3–5; William L. Lumpkin, *Baptist Confessions of Faith* (Chicago, IL: Judson Press, 1959), 81.

[50] Renihan, *Edification and Beauty*, 20. Whilst Renihan is referring to the methodology behind the Second London Baptist Confession, the same could arguably be said for both the first and second confessions.

[51] Ligon Duncan, foreword to *Covenant Theology: Biblical, Theological, and Historical Perspectives* (Wheaton, IL: Crossway, 2020), 26.

[52] See Matthew C. Bingham, 'The Covenantal Theology of John Spilsbery,' in *Journal of the Institute of Reformed Baptist Studies* 3:1 (2016): 65–96; Samuel Renihan, ''Dolphins in the Woods': A Critique of Mark Jones and Ted Van Raalte's Presentation of Particular Baptist Covenant Theology,' *Journal of the Institute of Reformed Baptist Studies* 2:1 (2015): 82.

covenants within the schema of the covenants of works and grace.[53] Adopting Owen's hermeneutical treatment in his understanding of both the Abrahamic and Mosaic covenants,[54] Nehemiah Coxe (1650–1689), a well-respected Particular Baptist minister, for example, noted happily the publication of Owen's third volume on Hebrews due to its alignment to his own thoughts on the difference of administration *and* substance between old and new covenants.[55]

This consistent theological unity between Congregationalists and Particular Baptists testifies to the adherence of the Particular Baptists to the very same hermeneutic approach, *viz.*, the *principia theologiae*, that was adhered to within the greater Reformed tradition. This, in turn, explains why, outside the position of baptism (which, as Hart rightly noted above, was a logical outworking of Congregational ecclesiology and, arguably, covenantal expression),[56] Particular Baptists adopted most positions that aligned with the Reformed tradition, particularly that expressed in 17th-century England. These included positions on the regulative principle of worship[57] and the moral law (including Sabbatarianism).

---

[53] On the debate on the legitimate use of John Owen by the Particular Baptists, note Pascal Denault, *The Distinctiveness of Baptist Covenant Theology: A Comparison between Seventeenth-Century Particular Baptist and Paedobaptist Federalism*, 2nd ed. (Vestavia Hills, AL: Solid Ground Christian Books, 2017), 33–36; Beeke and Jones, *A Puritan Theology*, 725–741; and Renihan, 'Dolphins in the Woods,' 63–89.

[54] Renihan, 'Dolphins in the Woods,' 73–75.

[55] Nehemiah Coxe, 'The Preface to the Reader,' in Nehemiah Coxe & John Owen, *Covenant Theology: From Adam to Christ* (Palmdale, CA: Reformed Baptist Academic Press, 2005), 30.

[56] This was noted contemporaneously in the 17th century. In a debate between Particular Baptist minister Thomas Delaune and Joseph Whiston, Delaune makes note of the dissonance between Owen's theological treatises and practices: 'What the *Doctor* supposes to *Infants being in the Covenant, in his Judgement or practice* concerns not the matter in hand. . . . And, I am as certain, that the *Doctors* discourse of the Covenant, wholly excludes them from any such title. And if Mr. *Whiston* can no better reconcile the *Doctors* words to his *Practice*, he had better have held his peace.' Thomas Delaune, *Truth Defended: Or, a Triple Answer to the Late Triumvirates' Opposition in Their Three Pamphlets, Viz. Mr. Baxter's Review, Mr. Wills His Censure, Mr. Whiston's Postscript to His Essay, &c.* (London: Printed for the author, 1677), 20, as quoted in Samuel Renihan, 'Dolphins in the Woods,' 71–72. Italics original.

[57] The adherence to the regulative principle of worship is evident within 2LBCF 22.1. However, the outworking can also be seen in the arguments of Particular Baptists on

This is why, when contrasted against many of the modern attempts to define Reformed theology, such as those provided by John R. de Witt[58], R. C. Sproul[59], and R. Michael Allen[60], the consensual positions such as the centrality of God, the sole authority of Scripture, the law-gospel distinction, the commitment to the ministry of the Word, and a commitment to 'two-kingdom' cultural engagement, as well as a commitment to an overarching prism of covenant theology, are all positions that Particular Baptists could, and can, agree with. This is because they were committed to the same *principia theologiae* of the greater Reformed tradition. This explains, when commenting on the 18th-century Baptist intellectual powerhouse, John Gill (1697–1771), why Richard A. Muller can note that 'English Baptist theology is in large part an intellectual and spiritual descendant of the thought of those Reformers, Protestant orthodox writers, and Puritans who belonged to the Reformed confessional tradition.'[61]

Of course, the most significant point of divergence, one could argue, was the point of baptism, a notable point of discontinuity from the greater Reformed consensus, as observed by Isaac Watts

---

the subject of baptism. See John Spilsbery, *A Treatise Concerning the Lawfull Subject of Baptism* (London: Henry Hills, 1652), 62–63; or Benjamin Keach, *Gold Refin'd, Or, Baptism in Its Primitive Purity* (London: Printed for the author, 1689), 147–149.

[58] John R. de Witt, *What is the Reformed Faith?* (Edinburgh, UK: The Banner of Truth, 1981)

[59] R. C. Sproul, *What is Reformed Theology? Understanding the Basics* (Grand Rapids, MI: Baker Books, 1997)

[60] Of the three, R. Michael Allen makes it clearest that Baptists are to be excluded from the 'Reformed' identifier. In one of his books, he states, 'While such use of the term 'Reformed' may be very handy in certain settings (e.g., differentiating predestinarian Baptists from other Baptists), it cannot be allowed to serve as the primary meaning. As the term will be used in this book, then, one cannot be both baptistic and identified as 'Reformed' in as much as baptistic ecclesiology depends on a sharp distinction between Israel and the church, thereby disagreeing with the Reformed way of affirming the unity of the covenant of grace.' (R. Michael Allen, *Reformed Theology*, Doing Theology [London: T&T Clark, 2010], 5.) Of course, attempting to untangle Baptist ecclesiology from Congregational ecclesiology is no easy feat, and any lack of a connection needs to be argued for as opposed to being assumed.

[61] Richard A. Muller, 'John Gill and the Reformed Tradition: A Study in the Reception of Protestant Orthodoxy in the Eighteenth-Century,' in *The Life and Thought of John Gill (1697–1771): A Tercentennial Appreciation,* Studies in the History of Christian Thought, ed. Michael A. G. Haykin (Leiden, Netherlands: Brill, 1997), 51.

(1674–1748), the Congregational minister and hymnist, 'They differ not from Calvinists in their doctrine, unless in the article of infant baptism: they generally deny any children to be in the covenant of grace, and so deny the seal of the covenant to them. They deny baptism by sprinkling to be real and true baptism.'[62] However, as noted above, their approach represented 'the last stage in the evolution of English Separatism as it moved forward to its logical outcome in believer's baptism.'[63] This position was likely reached as an outworking of the *principia theologiae* rather than being at odds with it. Nevertheless, from the Particular Baptists' point of emergence onwards, it did not prevent them from being accepted within greater Reformed orthodoxy during the Interregnum under Oliver and Richard Cromwell and most notably in Congregational circles.

Ironically, noting the general theological alignment of Particular Baptists within the Reformed orthodoxy of the 1650s, one cannot help but wonder whether Particular Baptists were more faithful stewards of the tradition and, indeed, held to a closer alignment to 1640s Presbyterianism than even certain expressions of Presbyterianism that have developed since.[64] The confessional drift that was to take place throughout the 18th and 19th centuries was to put many Presbyterian denominations at odds with confessional fidelity—a point lamented by Charles Hodge (1797–1878), who remarked: 'To adopt every proposition contained in the Westminster Confession and Catechisms is more than the vast majority of our ministers either do or can do. To make them profess to do it is a great sin. It hurts their consciences. It fosters a spirit of evasion and subterfuge.'[65] So too, within the Australian

---

[62] Isaac Watts, 'From Dr. Watts to His Brother Enoch Watts' in *The Sermons and Practical Works of the Late Isaac Watts, D.D.* (London, 1805), 109. Notice that Watts remarks that Baptists differ in their view of baptism because they understand that the substance of the covenant of grace is different.

[63] Underwood, *A History of the English Baptists*, 56.

[64] See Lefferts A. Loetscher's *The Broadening Church: A Study of Theological Issues in the Presbyterian Church Since 1869* (Philadelphia, PA: University of Pennsylvania Press, 1957). For a more localised analysis, see Peter Barnes' *Theological Controversies in the Presbyterian Church of New South Wales, 1865–1915: The Rise of Liberal Evangelicalism* (Lewiston, NY: Edwin Mellen Press, 2008).

[65] Charles Hodge, *The Church and Its Polity* (London, UK: Thomas Nelson and Sons, 1879), 332. See also Peter Barnes, 'Scottish and American Approaches to the Westminster Confession of Faith,' in *Read in the Light: The 1901 Declaratory Statement of the Presby-*

landscape, the introduction of the Declaratory Statement in the mainline Presbyterian Church of Australia, contained in the Basis of Union as adopted in 1901, allowed for liberty of opinion regarding positions expounded in the Westminster Confession of Faith which were 'not essential to the doctrine therein taught'. However, as noted by John McClean, 'there is no attempt to delimit what is essential'[66]. Instead, as McClean observes, 'All of this suggests that the [Declaratory Statement] was composed with the intent of establishing a theological position which differed from that of the WCF—though the extent of the difference is not clearly determined.'[67]

Indeed, to deny the Particular Baptists a seat at the Reformed table fails to take into consideration the organic relationships that existed as Particular Baptists emerged from Congregationalism in the 1630s, and further developments that unfolded within the Reformed tradition during the period of the Interregnum (1649–1660). Instead, modern proponents, such as Clark and Hart, who try to deny such links attempt to present an understanding of the Reformed tradition that halts in 1649—a benchmark of which many modern adherents to Presbyterianism would subsequently fall short. It would be odd indeed if the overarching theological conformity of the Particular Baptists to the Reformed tradition, due to shared commitment to the *principia theologiae*, was discounted due to the singular doctrinal divergence of baptism[68], a position that aligns more with the position of Rome and additionally acts as a wilful dismissal of several centuries of Particular Baptist and Congregational relations. However, this is not to say that there

terian Church of Australia, eds. Paul F. Cooper and David A. Burke (Stanhope Gardens, NSW: Eider Books, 2019), 9–25.

[66] John McClean, 'The Declaratory Statement: Help or Hindrance?' in *Read in the Light: The 1901 Declaratory Statement of the Presbyterian Church of Australia,* eds. Paul F. Cooper and David A. Burke (Stanhope Gardens, NSW: Eider Books, 2019), 251.

[67] John McClean, 'The Declaratory Statement,' 252.

[68] Matthew Bingham makes a similar observation, wherein he argues that, rather than making infant baptism the *sine qua non* of the Reformed tradition, 'a far more reasonable basis upon which to differentiate the Reformed tradition would be the covenantal framework which undergirds both Reformed paedobaptism and the Reformed theological system as a whole.' See Matthew Bingham, ''Reformed Baptist': Anachronistic Oxymoron or Useful Signpost?' in *On Being Reformed,* 45. As this paper argues, a more foundational position is to understand the continuity of the theological methodology, of which federalism is a principal outworking.

are not those who *do* acknowledge the inclusion of Particular Baptists within the Reformed family. Herman Bavinck (1854–1921), who used 'Reformed' and 'Calvinism' synonymously, observed that '[Calvinism] is not limited to one church or other, but—in a variety of modifications—constitutes the animating element in Congregational, Baptist, Presbyterian, Dutch Reformed, and German Reformed churches, and so forth.'[69] Likewise, as we have also noted above, Richard A. Muller, whose Reformed credentials are not to be taken lightly, acknowledges the diversity of Reformed thought by noting that 'The Baptist churches, whether in England or in America, are certainly to be regarded as branches of the Reformed movement.'[70] Evidently, denying Particular Baptists' use of (and their right to use) the taxonomical label raises significant issues on theological and, particularly, historical grounds.

A. W. Pink: A Reformed Theologian?

Having then established that Particular Baptists ought to be rightly considered part of the Reformed tradition, we now turn to Arthur W. Pink and the question at hand: Can Pink himself be considered part of this tradition? While there is little doubt that Pink ranks among the foremost expositors of sovereign grace in the 20th century, his inclusion within Reformed theology warrants closer examination. Individuals such as John J. Murray and Richard P. Belcher have argued that Pink not only stood firmly within the Reformed tradition but also played a significant role in its revival within the English-speaking world between the late 1950s and early 1970s.[71]

Despite this recognition, few works have rigorously explored how Pink's theology aligns with the Reformed framework. Richard P. Belcher's works, such as his book *Arthur W. Pink: Predestination*, provide a valuable starting point, comparing Pink's soteriology to the

---

[69] Bavinck, *Reformed Dogmatics*, 1:201.

[70] Richard A. Muller, 'Reformed Theology between 1600 and 1800,' in *The Oxford Handbook of Early Modern Theology, 1600–1800*, Oxford Handbooks, eds. Ulrich L. Lehner, Richard A. Muller and A. G. Roeber (Oxford, UK: Oxford University Press, 2016), 169.

[71] John J. Murray, *Catch the Vision*, 162; Richard P. Belcher, 'Arthur W. Pink,' in *Bible Interpreters of the 20th Century: A Selection of Evangelical Voices*, eds. Walter A. Elwell & J. D. Weaver (Grand Rapids, MI: Baker Books, 1999), 141.

Reformed confessions.[72] Belcher concluded that while Pink exhibited some minor variations from these confessional standards, he remained 'a safe guide' in the study of Reformed theology, particularly on predestination.[73]

However, contextualising Pink within the Reformed tradition is not without its challenges. His theology underwent an significant shift between the mid-1920s and early-1930s, moving from an early dispensational premillennial framework to an increasingly covenantal and Reformed outlook. This transition, evident in his writings, leads to what some have described as a distinction between 'early Pink' and 'later Pink'.[74] As one dispensational commentator noted, Pink eventually came 'to believe the only balanced biblical teaching came from the Reformation and the Puritan era.'[75] Therefore, it is necessary to trace his theological trajectory before assessing Pink's theology against the Reformed framework established above.

Pink's Early Dispensationalism

Born in 1886, Pink's early ministry years unfolded within the dispensationalist circles of the Fundamentalist movement, shaped by the broader Fundamentalist-Modernist controversy that dominated the early 20th century. Converted in 1908 after renouncing Theosophy, Pink's passion for ministry led him to Moody Bible Institute in 1910, though he left after six weeks, dissatisfied with the program's depth. Securing his first pastoral charge in Silverton, Colorado, Pink was, for much of the next decade, to become a prominent figure in the dispensationalist-fundamentalist community, forming ties with influential

[72] Belcher's book, *Arthur W. Pink: Predestination,* compares Pink's predestinarian theology against the Philadelphia Confession of Faith and largely draws from his ThD dissertation, Richard P. Belcher, 'Predestination: A Comparative Analysis of the Theology of A. W. Pink in Relation to the Westminster Confession of Faith' (ThD diss., Concordia Seminary, 1981).

[73] Belcher, 'Predestination,' 188.

[74] Belcher, *Arthur W. Pink,* 139–140; Iain H. Murray, *The Life of Arthur W. Pink* (Edinburgh, UK: Banner of Truth, 2004; reprint, 2017), 180–190; Mal Couch, 'Pink, Arthur,' in *Dictionary of Premillennial Theology,* ed. Mal Couch (Grand Rapids, MI: Kregel Publications, 1996), 306.

[75] Couch, 'Pink, Arthur,' 306.

leaders like Arno C. Gaebelein and contributing regularly to *Our Hope*, a flagship dispensational publication.

By this time, dispensationalism's growing influence had permeated nearly every denomination, including the Anglican, Baptist, and Presbyterian traditions. Writing in 1890, R. L. Dabney (1820–1898) observed that there 'was a large number of religious teachers in the other evangelical churches, who, without actual separation, have adopted the chief doctrinal views' of dispensationalism.[76] With its theological framework rooted in a distinct hermeneutic, dispensationalism eroded traditional Reformed interpretations, particularly those grounded in covenant theology. Its rejection of covenantal continuity as well as its emphasis on stark divisions between dispensations undermined historical doctrines central to Reformed thought. As John Murray (1898–1975) observed in his critique: 'The 'Dispensationalism' of which we speak as heterodox from the standpoint of the Reformed Faith is that form of interpretation, widely popular at the present time, which discovers in the several dispensations of God's redemptive revelation distinct and even contrary principles of divine procedure and thus destroys the unity of God's dealings with fallen mankind'.[77] Indeed, John Nelson Darby (1800–1882), a key proponent of dispensationalism, vehemently opposed covenant, or federal, theology, labelling it 'a mischievous fable'. Darby critiqued foundational Reformed doctrines such as God's covenant with man and the moral law as outlined in the Westminster Confession, asserting that, together, they were a 'grave and fundamental error' and had 'tainted the whole evangelical system everywhere'.[78] His influence shifted theological priorities away from the unity of Scripture and covenantal interpretation, reshaping the theological landscape of the time.

---

[76] Robert L. Dabney, 'Theology of the Plymouth Brethren,' in *Discussions, Vol. 1: Theological and Evangelical*, ed. C. R. Vaughan (Harrisonburg, VA: Sprinkle Publications, 1982), 169.

[77] John Murray, 'The Reformed Faith and Modem Substitutes,' *The Presbyterian Guardian* (February 3, 1936), 143. Quoted in Edwin H. Rian, *The Presbyterian Conflict* (Philadelphia, PA: Committee for the Historian of the Orthodox Presbyterian Church, 1992), 164.

[78] John Nelson Darby, 'Presbyterianism: A Reply to 'The Church and The Pulpit,'' in *Collected Writings of J. N. Darby* (Oak Park, IL: Bible Truth Publishers, 1972), 14:528.

Despite gaining recognition as a capable Bible teacher in dispensationalist circles, Pink's theological convictions began to evolve. Troubled by the man-centred focus of contemporary evangelism and its neglect of doctrines like divine sovereignty and human depravity, Pink turned to the works of Jonathan Edwards (1703–1758) and Puritan literature for support. Between March 1917 and July 1918, he wrote *Sovereignty of God;* the first edition was to marshal supporting quotes from Edwards, James Ussher (1581–1656), John Trapp (1601–1669), John Brown (1784–1858), Moses Stuart (1780–1852), Charles Hodge (1797–1878) and the Westminster Larger Catechism to defend the doctrine of reprobation.[79]

However, writing on the doctrine of predestination and election had set Pink on a theological journey. While familiar with Reformed and Puritan authors, he now commenced a voracious reading diet between 1918 and 1920, reading the complete volumes of Edwards, Manton, Goodwin, and Owen. His growing Calvinism strained relationships within the dispensationalist-fundamentalist circles where he had once gained prominence and, by 1920, several prominent leaders denounced him for promoting the 'deadly poison' of Calvinism.[80] Yet, while Pink's commitment to Reformed soteriology was already solidified, his dispensational framework remained intact, though increasingly questioned.

Towards the end of 1922 and beginning of 1923, Pink wrote a series of articles in *Studies in the Scriptures,* including 'The Saint and the Law'. These writings challenged the typical dispensationalist rejection of the moral law and the Sabbath, arguing for the abiding relevance of the law in the Christian life. Pink intended to 'recover some of the truths known and practiced by our fathers, and which are largely lost to the rising generation'.[81] By 1926, Pink's work began to hint at covenant-

[79] Arthur W. Pink, *The Sovereignty of God* (Swengel, PA: Bible Truth Depot, 1918), 273–275.

[80] Brett Lee-Price, 'The Context, Writing, and Impact of *The Sovereignty of God,*' afterword to *The Sovereignty of God* (Lansvale, NSW: Tulip Publishing, 2022), 253–54.

[81] Arthur W. Pink, *Studies in the Scriptures,* eds. I. C. Herendeen and Arthur W. Pink, 2:1 (1923): 1. For the articles, see Arthur W. Pink, 'The Saint and the Law,' *Studies in the Scriptures,* eds. I. C. Herendeen and Arthur W. Pink, 1:12 (1922): 268–75; Arthur W. Pink, 'Are Believers Under the Law?' *Studies in the Scriptures,* eds. I. C. Herendeen and Arthur W. Pink, 2:1 (1923): 9–13; Arthur W. Pink, 'The Moral Law the Rule of Conduct

al ideas, but his framework remained predominantly dispensational. In his series *Gleanings from Exodus*, Pink introduced the concept of the Mosaic covenant as a 'covenant of works', a development that showed his growing alignment with covenant theology. However, his writings were still couched within a dispensational structure.[82]

Pink's deepening engagement with, and renewed study of, John Owen was to become instrumental in his shift. Initially dismissive of Owen's writings—remarking in 1919 that they 'did not appeal to me at all'—Pink experienced such a profound change of perspective that by 1925, he was frequently citing Owen's works. Indeed, Owen's theology was to become a cornerstone of Pink's works, as is particularly evident in his commentary *Epistle to the Hebrews* (1928–1938), whereby Owen is cited 222 times, far more than any other author. Pink commenced 1930 with a series of articles in his *Studies in the Scriptures*, titled *The Everlasting Covenant*, outlining 'the eternal agreement entered into by the Persons of the Godhead'.[83] Pink came to affirm the classical Reformed distinction between the covenant of works and the covenant of grace, while also emphasising the eternal 'everlasting covenant'—what many label the intratrinitarian covenant of redemption.[84] He further rejected dispensational distinctions between Israel and the church, critiquing the exclusion of Old Testament saints from the church.[85] In

---

to Believers,' *Studies in the Scriptures*, eds. I. C. Herendeen and Arthur W. Pink, 2:2 (1923): 42–45.

[82] Arthur W. Pink, 'Gleanings from Exodus,' *Studies in the Scriptures*, 5:4 (1926): 61 (Arthur W. Pink, *Gleanings in Exodus* (Chicago, IL: Moody Press, 1981), 153); Arthur W. Pink, 'Gleanings from Exodus,' *Studies in the Scriptures* 5:8 (1926): 61 (Pink, *Gleanings in Exodus*, 175). Interestingly, the first and clearest mention of covenant theology in Pink's literature is in an article by the Australian Particular Baptist Daniel Allen (1824–1891), 'A Perverted Gospel,' reprinted in *Studies in the Scriptures* 5:1 (1926): 22–23. Pink's qualified dispensationalism can be particularly seen in 'Gleanings from Exodus,' *Studies in the Scriptures* 5:4 (1926): 82–86. It must also be added that there is a very early schema of how Pink saw the covenants unfolding in Scripture, including the Adamic covenant, in Pink's earlier 'Gleanings in Genesis,' released in *Our Hope*, particularly in his treatment of Genesis 8 (Arthur W. Pink, 'Gleanings in Genesis,' in *Our Hope* 21:10 [1917]: 218–19.)

[83] Arthur W. Pink, 'The Everlasting Covenant,' *Studies in the Scriptures* 9:1 (1930): 13.

[84] See Arthur W. Pink, 'The Epistle to the Hebrews,' *Studies in the Scriptures* 10:1 (1931): 2–9. (Arthur W. Pink, *An Exposition of Hebrews* [Grand Rapids, MI: Baker Books, 1997, reprint 2006], 436–447.); Arthur W. Pink, 'The Epistle to the Hebrews,' *Studies in the Scriptures* 10:2 (1931): 26–32. (Pink, *An Exposition of Hebrews*, 448–459.)

[85] Arthur W. Pink, 'The Epistle to the Hebrews,' *Studies in the Scriptures* 10:6 (1931): 127.

1934, Pink wrote: 'The worst mistakes made by the 'dispensationalists' grow out of their failure. . . to see the organic union between the Mosaic and Christian economies. . . to perceive that the 'old covenant' and the 'new covenant' were but two different administrations under which the blessings of the 'everlasting covenant' are imparted; [and]. . . to distinguish between the spiritual remnant and the nation itself'.[86] Between 1933 and 1938, Pink further wrote a series of articles titled 'A Study on Dispensationalism' and 'The Divine Covenants'. These writings crystallised his decisive break with dispensationalism and his complete embrace of covenant theology.

Reflecting on his earlier dispensationalist views, Pink confessed in 1935:

> For fifteen years I was misled by much of their writings, but after I began to study the Puritans, I soon discovered how far they were astray on almost every doctrine; and today I have no hesitation in saying that the writings of J.N.D [Darby] and C.H.M [Mackintosh] are full of error, although in a very subtle form, which can only be detected by one having a deep and wide grasp of the truth.[87]

Likewise, in an earlier letter to John C. Blackburn, a Southern Presbyterian minister and grandson of theologian John Girardeau (1825–1898), Pink elaborated further on his growing disenchantment with dispensationalism. He wrote in 1934 that he had fallen 'considerably out of love with' the doctrine. Observing that the lives of early and contemporary premillennialists 'compare most unfavourably with the godly Puritans', he resolved to re-examine dispensationalism's foundations. Aware of the danger of swinging to extremes, Pink 'sought to proceed the more slowly and cautiously'. And after almost five years, Pink stated he had 'now arrived at some positive (probably 'settled') conclusions.'[88]

(Pink, *An Exposition of Hebrews*, 503.)

[86] Arthur W. Pink, 'The Epistle to the Hebrews,' *Studies in the Scriptures* 13:10 (1934): 220. (Pink, *An Exposition of Hebrews*, 888.)

[87] Arthur W. Pink, letter to Lowell Green, 7 July 1935, in *Letters of Arthur W. Pink* (Edinburgh, UK: Banner of Truth, 1978), 65.

[88] Arthur W. Pink, Letter to John C. Blackburn, 3 February 1934, *Letters of Arthur W. Pink,*

Subsequently, Pink was also to repudiate his earlier dispensational works, such as *The Redeemer Returns* and *The Antichrist*—the latter of which had been praised by a dispensational commentator as 'the most complete work on the subject'.[89] As his theological convictions shifted, Pink became one of dispensationalism's most vocal critics, labelling it a 'poison' and a 'modern heresy'. Oswald T. Allis (1880–1973) would later note that Pink and Philip Mauro (1859–1952) were among the most active opponents of dispensationalism.[90] In a striking critique, Pink, towards the end of his life, would write: 'Consciously or unconsciously, dispensationalists are, in reality, repeating the sin of Jehoiakim, who mutilated God's Word with his penknife (Jer. 36:23). Instead of 'opening the Scriptures' (Lukw 24:32), they are bent in closing the major part of them from God's people today. They are just as much engaged in doing the devil's work as are the Higher Critics, who, with their dissecting knives, are wrongly 'dividing the word of truth' (2 Ti 2:15).' He further accused dispensationalists of 'seeking to force a stone down the throats of those who are asking for bread'. Acknowledging that his 'severe and solemn indictments' would not be palatable to all, he asserted that 'medicine, though sometimes necessary, is rarely palatable'.[91]

Such sharp critiques of dispensationalism cemented Pink's position as a theological outcast. His Calvinism had already strained his relationships within the fundamentalist circles he once frequented, and his outspoken opposition to dispensationalism further isolated him. Richard Belcher observed, 'When Pink left dispensationalism, he was going against the grain of many. And as he began to write against it, he no doubt offended many more.'[92] Like evangelist Rolfe Barnard (1904–1969), who was 'ostracised. . . by his former friends' in the 'fundamentalist circles in which he had been moving' and saw invitations to larger platforms dry up due to his own Calvinism several decades

65. A graduate of Columbia Theological Seminary, Rev. John Cavitt Blackburn (1889–1959) was to have some connection with Westminster Theological Seminary, preaching on the Annual Day of Prayer the same year of J. Gresham Machen's death.

[89] Couch, 'Pink, Arthur,' 306.

[90] Oswald T. Allis, *Prophecy and the Church* (1946; reprint, Phillipsburg, NJ: Presbyterian & Reformed Publishing, 1974), 15.

[91] Arthur W. Pink, 'Application of the Scriptures,' *Studies in the Scriptures* 31:8 (1952).

[92] Belcher, *Arthur W. Pink*, 141.

later,[93] Pink found himself increasingly relegated to smaller, more obscure audiences. His theological convictions, which were becoming increasingly rooted in Reformed principles, left him without a home in the polarised religious landscape of his time. As one biographer, Aaron Menikoff, noted, as a 'Calvinist who argued against dispensationalists, he [Pink] became a pariah even among fundamentalists.'[94]

Pink and the Principia Theologiae

Early in his ministry, Pink embraced a dispensationalist approach that emphasised sharp discontinuities in God's dealings with humanity across redemptive history. However, his extensive engagement with Reformed and Puritan writers, notably John Owen, marked a decisive shift toward the theological unity and covenantal continuity foundational to Reformed thought. His theological journey between 1925 and 1935 represented more than a mere adjustment—it was a reorientation of his method, affirming the sufficiency and authority of Scripture as the cohesive narrative of God's redemptive work. This section will demonstrate how Pink's theology reflects the key elements of the *principia theologiae*, particularly Scripture as the *principium cognoscendi* and God as the *principium essendi*.

Pink's approach to Scripture was marked by an unwavering commitment to its preeminence, rooted in his conviction that God, as the Ultimate Being, authored and sustains His Word. Writing in his first book, *The Divine Inspiration of Scripture* (1917), Pink declared that to deny the divine authorship of Scripture had serious consequences: deny 'that the Bible is, without any qualifications, the very Word of God, and you are left without any ultimate standard of measurement and without any supreme authority.'[95] Holding firmly to the inerrancy and infallibility of Scripture, Pink espoused a verbal plenary inspiration view that aligned with the Fundamentalist circles to which he

[93] John F. Thornbury, 'Rolfe Pickens Barnard,' in *Sermons of Evangelist Rolfe Barnard, 1904–1969*, ed. Eulala Bullock (Greenville, SC: n.p., 1982), 1:xvi.

[94] Aaron Menikoff, 'Arthur W. Pink (1886–1952),' in *A Noble Company: Biographical Essays on Notable Particular-Regular Baptists in America*, ed. Terry Wolever, vol. 11 (Springfield, MO: Particular Baptist Press, 2018), 457.

[95] Arthur W. Pink, *The Divine Inspiration of the Bible* (Swengel, PA: Bible Truth Depot, 1917), 7.

initially belonged. However, Pink's theological method went beyond uncritical adherence to any system. He consistently placed Scripture as the starting point for understanding God, humanity, and salvation, refusing to allow any human authority to impose limitations on Scripture that it did not set on itself. This commitment is evident even in his early divergence from dispensationalism on matters such as the moral law, a position that set him apart from many dispensationalists.

As Pink increasingly engaged with Reformed hermeneutics, mainly through Puritan writings, his work began to reflect a deepening conviction that Scripture is a unified narrative of God's redemptive plan. His hermeneutic became grounded in the principle of the analogy of faith (*analogia fidei*), an interpretive approach that became central to his exegesis after the 1930s. Pink articulated this conviction, writing: 'Scripture, not logic, is our rule of faith, and not one or two statements taken out of their contexts, but the whole analogy of faith.'[96] He believed that proper context, combined with the analogy of faith, set the boundaries for the meaning of Scripture, ensuring both fidelity to the text and theological coherence.

This commitment is most evident in his later works, including *The Interpretation of the Scriptures* and *The Application of the Scriptures*, published in *Studies in the Scriptures* between 1950 and 1953. Pink cautioned against unwarranted restriction and over-generalisation, asserting that 'we must ever beware of unwarrantably restricting the scope of a verse. And, on the other hand, be constantly on our guard against making general what is manifestly particular. It is only by carefully taking heed to the general Analogy of Faith that we shall be preserved from either mistake. Scripture ever interprets Scripture, but much familiarity with the contents, and a diligent and prayerful comparing of one part with another, is necessary before anyone is justified in dogmatically deciding the precise meaning or application of any passage.'[97] For Pink, Scripture's unity required careful, prayerful study that recognised its coherence while safeguarding against misinterpretation.

---

[96] Arthur W. Pink, 'Epistle to the Hebrews,' *Studies in the Scriptures* 11:3 (1932): 54. (Pink, *An Exposition of Hebrews*, 601.)

[97] Arthur W. Pink, 'Application of the Scriptures,' *Studies in the Scriptures* 31:6 (1952).

Though Pink upheld the absolute supremacy of Scripture, he was deeply appreciative of creeds and confessions, but only as subordinate documents *to* Scripture in a way that embodied *Sola Scriptura*. In a 1925 sermon, he affirmed, 'I have a great respect for John Calvin, and under God am greatly indebted to his writings, but I call no man master. If Calvinism does not harmonise perfectly with this Book, then away with his teachings, or any other man's. We are bound by no human creed or catechism. Our creed is, what saith the Lord?'[98] However, Pink viewed Reformed confessions as helpful tools, habitually using them as secondary standards after Scripture to discern and critique what he saw as 'novel theological teachings' that had infiltrated the church.[99]

Interestingly, despite his own Baptist convictions, Pink often cited the Westminster Confession of Faith and highly regarded it as a faithful summary of biblical doctrine.[100] He quoted from it extensively throughout *Studies in the Scriptures*. He very rarely quibbled with its wording, disagreeing only in its chapter on sanctification, believing some elaboration was needed.[101] Yet he remained adamant that readers should 'test everything' by the Word of God. Writing in 1950, he stated: 'While I am satisfied that, for the most part, the Thirty-Nine Articles of the Church of England, and the Westminster Confession of Faith and Catechism, were drawn up by godly and scholarly men; nevertheless, they were finite and erring men, and therefore, if we value our souls, we

---

[98] Arthur W. Pink, 'The Sovereignty of God,' *Studies in the Scriptures* 4:10 (1925): 238.

[99] Pink often qualified precisely why he cited confessions, to, firstly, show that his teachings were in unison to the 'scripturally-instructed fathers', and, secondly, to show how other teachings were not. Note Arthur W. Pink, *The Sovereignty of God* (Lansvale, NSW: Tulip Publishing, 2022), 125–126; Arthur W. Pink, 'The Doctrine of Election,' *Studies in the Scriptures,* 17:6 (1938): 187 (Arthur W. Pink, *The Doctrines of Election and Justification* [Grand Rapids, MI: Guardian Press, 1976], 46–47).

[100] Arthur W. Pink, 'The Doctrine of Reconciliation,' *Studies in the Scriptures* 25:12 (1946): 279; Arthur W. Pink, 'The Doctrine of Election,' *Studies in the Scriptures* 17:6 (1938): 187 (Pink, *The Doctrines of Election and Justification,* 46–47.)

[101] Pink's main critique of the Westminster Confession and the other Reformed confessions on sanctification was their omission of the believer's positional sanctification in Christ. Additionally, he felt that certain phrases did not fully capture the believer's experience—particularly the struggle with sin and an increasing awareness of its depth. In Pink's view, the wording risked discouraging believers by implying a smoother progress in holiness than Scripture and experience attest. See Arthur W. Pink, 'The Doctrine of Sanctification,' in *Studies in the Scriptures* 15:2 (1936): 58–61.(Arthur W. Pink, *The Doctrine of Sanctification* [Fearn, Ross-Shire, UK: Christian Heritage, 1998], 122–128).

shall test everything in them by the Word of Truth. Other writings may be ancient, learned, interesting, and even edifying, yet none of them was 'given by inspiration of God' (2 Tim. 3:16)! The Holy Scriptures are the only perfect standard.'[102]

Yet Pink also rejected shallow biblicism that disregarded the church's historical tools, warning against the belief that self-interpretation alone was sufficient. He reminded readers that God often works through secondary means, writing that believers should not 'forget what is God's common and usual method in supplying the wants of His creatures—mediately and not immediately, by secondary causes and human agents.'[103] Indeed, while Pink did not demand a strict subscription to any confession, he saw them as vital tools for believers—not merely for intellectual assent but as aids to experientially encountering the truths they faithfully summarised.[104] This emphasis is evident throughout Pink's writings, perhaps most strikingly in his 1948 caution: 'Reader, you may be an ardent 'Calvinist,' subscribe heartily to the soundest 'Articles of Faith,' assent sincerely to every sentence in the Westminster Confession and Catechism, and yet be dead in trespasses and sins'.[105]

Indeed, for Pink, while the most pressing issue of his day was the departure from Scripture, such a decline manifested in the widespread rejection of Reformed truths and old divinity. Near the end of his life, he was to lament: 'During the past century, there was an increasingly marked departure from doctrinal preaching. Creeds and confessions of faith were disparaged and regarded as obsolete. The study of theology was largely displaced by engaging the mind with science, psychology, and sociology. The cry was raised, 'Give us Christ, and not Christianity,' and many superficial minds concluded that such a demand was both

---

[102] Arthur W. Pink, 'Divine Inspiration of the Scriptures,' *Studies in the Scriptures* 29:4 (1950): 90.

[103] Arthur W. Pink, 'Interpretation of the Scriptures,' *Studies in the Scriptures* 19:8 (1950): 187.

[104] Arthur W. Pink, 'Sermon on the Mount,' *Studies in the Scriptures* 22:4 (1943): 78 (Arthur W. Pink, *An Exposition of the Sermon on the Mount* [Grand Rapids, MI: Guardian Press, 1975], 382); Arthur W. Pink, 'John's Gospel,' *Studies in the Scriptures* 3:9 (1924): 196–197 (Arthur W. Pink, *Exposition of the Gospel of John* [Grand Rapids, MI: Zondervan Publishing House, 1975), 91.]

[105] Arthur W. Pink, 'The Doctrine of Revelation,' *Studies in the Scriptures* 27:12 (1948):

a spiritual and pertinent one. In reality, it was an absurdity, an imaginary distinction without any vital difference'.[106] For Pink, Scripture and confessions were to work together to foster not merely orthodoxy but also orthopraxy—a lived faith rooted in the Word of God.

However, if Pink's high view of Scripture reflects his alignment with the *principium cognoscendi*, his theology also reveals a profound understanding of the *principium essendi*—God as the ultimate Source and Foundation of all reality. For Pink, the supremacy of Scripture could not be separated from the God who authored it. His writings consistently emphasise that all creation, history, and revelation find their ultimate origin and purpose in the being of God. Pink's theology is rooted in the conviction that God's essence underpins every aspect of existence, from the eternal decrees that shape history to the glory displayed in creation.

Indeed, this alignment is particularly evident in Pink's treatment of God's sovereignty, self-sufficiency, and the purpose of creation. His works consistently reveal a profound conviction that everything exists by God's will and for His glory—a central motif running from his early work, *The Sovereignty of God*, and contemporary articles[107] to his later writings, such as *The Attributes of God*. Pink frequently emphasised that creation's ultimate purpose is to manifest God's glory, a reality most fully displayed in the act of redemption. In *The Sovereignty of God*, he asserts, 'From all eternity God designed that our world should be the stage on which He would display His manifold grace and wisdom in the redemption of lost sinners'.[108] This 'manifestative glory,' a term Pink often used (and which he likely derived from Thomas Goodwin),[109] refers to the outward revelation of God's inherent greatness,

---

[106] Arthur W. Pink, 'The Doctrine of Mortification,' *Studies in the Scriptures* 31:10 (1952).
[107] See Arthur W. Pink, 'God's Sovereignty and Christian Prayer,' *Our Hope* 11:1 (1919): 421–424.
[108] Pink, *The Sovereignty of God*, 97–98.
[109] Pink's use of the term 'manifestative glory' closely aligns with Thomas Goodwin's frequent employment of the phrase, particularly in *Christ Our Mediator* (Thomas Goodwin, *The Works of Thomas Goodwin*, vol. 5, *Christ Our Mediator* [Edinburgh, Scotland: James Nichol, Publisher, 1862], 2–30.). Like Goodwin, Pink saw God's glory not merely as an intrinsic perfection but as something actively revealed through His works of creation and redemption. Pink recognised Goodwin as a 'deeply-taught man and so able an expositor,' (Arthur W. Pink, *Divine Healing* [Swengel, PA: Reiner Publications, n.d.],

power, and holiness, made known to His creatures through creation, providence, and redemption, all decreed solely by Him according to the good pleasure of His will. As Pink explains, if God 'be pleased to bring creatures into existence, His own supreme and sovereign will must be the sole cause, as His own *manifestative* glory is His ultimate end and design.'[110] For Pink, creation is not an autonomous entity but a theatre in which God's sovereignty, wisdom, and power are displayed for the purpose of glorifying Him.

However, this act of worship does not add to nor, in any way, alter God's essential or intrinsic glory.[111] God is all-sufficient in Himself—immutable, self-existent, and unchanging.[112] God's knowledge is perfect, whereas ours is finite and tainted. Though we are dependent upon His gracious self-revelation, He has made Himself known not only through Scripture but also through creation, providence, and ultimately in Christ.[113] He is the sovereign Creator, while we are fallen creatures desperately needing His infinite grace. As Pink described, this vast and infinite chasm 'divides the creature from the Creator'.[114] Pink was unequivocal in his assertion that God is sovereign in all aspects of existence and that all things unfold according to His eternal decrees. Nothing, as Pink insists, 'can come into being save that which He decreed before the foundation of this world'.[115] Every event in his-

---

22.) and much of his understanding of election and divine sovereignty—especially the idea that the world serves as a stage for the unfolding of God's redemptive plan—was shaped by Goodwin's exposition of God's eternal decree (See Pink's citations of Goodwin throughout *The Doctrine of Election*). For both men, creation exists primarily to make known the riches of God's grace in Christ, as the ultimate display of His manifestative glory.

[110] Emphasis original. Arthur W. Pink, 'Doctrine of Sanctification,' *Studies in the Scriptures* 14:12 (1935): 379 (Pink, *The Doctrine of Sanctification*, 108).

[111] Arthur W. Pink, 'Epistle to the Hebrews,' *Studies in the Scriptures* 16:10 (1937): 292. (Pink, *An Exposition of Hebrews*, 1219.); Arthur W. Pink, 'The Solitariness of God,' *Studies in the Scriptures* 32:10 (1953): 217, 240. (Arthur W. Pink, *The Attributes of God* [1975; reprint, Grand Rapids, MI: Baker Books, 1993], 9–10.)

[112] Arthur W. Pink, 'The Doctrine of Revelation,' *Studies in the Scriptures* 26:1 (1947): 16.

[113] Arthur W. Pink, 'The Doctrine of Revelation,' *Studies in the Scriptures* 26:9 (1947): 211.

[114] Arthur W. Pink, 'Doctrine of Election,' *Studies in the Scriptures* 17:7 (1938): 219 (Pink, *The Doctrines of Election and Justification*, 55.)

[115] Arthur W. Pink, 'Sermon on the Mount,' *Studies in the Scriptures* 21:11 (1942): 78 (Pink, *Sermon on the Mount*, 382).

tory, every decision of men, and every aspect of creation is under His sovereign authority, working toward His ultimate purpose.

Indeed, for Pink, election, in particular, was the most vivid demonstration of both God's sovereignty and grace. He writes, 'Nowhere does the sovereignty of God shine forth so conspicuously as in His acts of election and reprobation, which took place in eternity past, and which nothing in the creature was the cause of. God's act of choosing His people in Christ was before the foundation of the world, without the consideration of the fall, nor was it upon the foresight and footing of works, but was wholly, *of grace*, and all to the praise and glory of it'.[116] Pink held firmly to double predestination but rejected equal ultimacy, a position well within the Reformed consensus.[117] He consistently cited Calvin, affirming that God's election is not based on foreseen faith or human merit but rooted solely in His sovereign good pleasure.[118]

For Pink, election and reprobation are determined by God's sovereign will, yet man's actions remain secondary, serving as the ordained means through which God's decree is fulfilled.[119] God is the primary cause of all things, including election and reprobation, and this in no way infringes on man's responsibility or guilt. Pink clarifies that reprobation occurs 'upon His foreview of our defection in Adam, who was our natural head and representative'.[120] Though contingent upon God's decree, the creature's agency remains genuine and voluntary. As Pink explains, 'Man is a moral agent, acting according to the desires and dictates of his nature: he is at the same time a creature, fully controlled and

[116] Arthur W. Pink, 'Doctrine of Election,' *Studies in the Scriptures* 17:3 (1938): 92 (Pink, *The Doctrines of Election and Justification*, 25).

[117] For more information on Pink's Calvinism, refer to Richard P. Belcher's unpublished ThD dissertation, 'Predestination: A Comparative Analysis of the Theology of A. W. Pink in Relation to the Westminster Confession of Faith.' C.f. Paul Helm and Brett Lee-Price, 'The Differing Editions of *The Sovereignty of God*,' in *The Sovereignty of God*, eds. Paul Helm and Brett Lee-Price (Lansvale, NSW: Tulip Publishing, 2022), 269–300.

[118] Arthur W. Pink, 'Doctrine of Election,' *Studies in the Scriptures* 17:1 (1930): 28 (Pink, *The Doctrines of Election and Justification*, 11.) Pink frequently cited Calvin throughout his writings, particularly on the doctrines of election, God's sovereignty, and man's depravity.

[119] Arthur W. Pink, 'Doctrine of Election,' *Studies in the Scriptures* 17:2 (1938): 58 (Pink, *The Doctrines of Election and Justification*, 16.)

[120] Arthur W. Pink, 'Doctrine of Election,' *Studies in the Scriptures* 17:11 (1938): 348 (Pink, *The Doctrines of Election and Justification*, 82).

determined by his Creator. In each of these cases, the divine and human elements coalesce, but the divine dominates, yet not to the exclusion of the human'.[121] Consequently, God's decree is always concomitant with, or executed through, man's sinful actions. Reprobation (a sovereign, divine act) and sinfulness (man's own corrupt nature) are distinct but inseparably linked. The former unfolds through the means of the latter. The decree of reprobation does not create sin but permits it in such a way that it serves God's ultimate purpose; namely, the glorification of His justice and holiness.

Election, therefore, is not merely a display of sovereign will but how God magnifies His grace and the glory of Christ as Mediator. Pink notes, 'Obviously the very term 'salvation' implies sin, and that in turn presupposes the fall. But this determination of God to suffer His people to fall into sin and then deliver them from it, was entirely subservient to His prime design concerning the elect and the ultimate glory to which He ordained them'.[122] While God sovereignly ordains all things that come to pass, Pink carefully distinguishes that God is not the author of sin but its 'Orderer and Controller'.[123] Clarifying this distinction, he writes that God 'is not the Author of it in the same way that He is the Author of good. Sin could not proceed from a holy God by positive and direct creation, but only by decretive permission and negative action.'[124]

For Pink, God's decree of reprobation does not create sin but permits it in such a way that it serves His ultimate purpose; namely, the glorification of His justice and holiness. The decree of reprobation and the presence of human sinfulness are distinct yet inseparably linked. The former unfolds by means of the latter. Pink asserts, 'Nothing out of God can move Him: or be a motive to Him; His *will* is His rule, His glory His ultimate end.'[125] This theological framework is illuminating

[121] Arthur W. Pink, 'Doctrine of Election,' *Studies in the Scriptures* 18:11 (1939): 254 (Pink, *The Doctrines of Election and Justification*, 159).

[122] Arthur W. Pink, 'Doctrine of Election,' *Studies in the Scriptures* 17:11 (1938): 348 (Pink, *The Doctrines of Election and Justification*, 82).

[123] Arthur W. Pink, 'The Decrees of God,' *Studies in the Scriptures* 9:2 (1930): 25 (Pink, *The Attributes of God*, 13–14).

[124] Pink, 'Decrees of God,' 13–14.

[125] Arthur W. Pink, 'Doctrine of Election,' *Studies in the Scriptures* 18:3 (1938): 92 (Pink, *The Doctrines of Election and Justification*, 25.).

in showing Pink's alignment to the *principium essendi*, affirming that God's will is self-determined, unaffected by external influences, and entirely for His own glory. Thus, for Pink, recognising God as the *principium essendi* deepens reverence for His majesty and places humanity in its proper posture—utterly dependent on God's sovereign grace, entirely undeserving, yet recipient of His eternal mercy.

Pink and the Outworking of the Principia Theologiae

Yet, as indicated at the outset of this essay, it is highly improbable that Pink was content with merely passing on Calvinism in the narrow sense of its soteriology. Instead, his aim was for readers to grasp *the doctrine of grace* in its fullness—what he described as 'that sacred system of theology, all the fundamentals of the everlasting Gospel of the blessed God, that grand 'mystery' of His mind and will which sets forth to us the complete counsel and covenant of the Eternal Three, the record of God concerning His Son, by which He declares that 'he that believeth hath everlasting life.''[126] In other words, Pink's concern was not simply to uphold certain doctrines of salvation but to lead believers into a comprehensive embrace of God's nature and Word—that is, the *entire* Reformed framework. He sought to demonstrate how the underlying principles of Reformed theology, as underpinned by the *principia theologiae*, shaped not only doctrinal formulation but also devotion and practical Christian living. His focus was never confined to a small cluster of truths about salvation but extended to the totality of divine revelation. Indeed, while Pink did not always employ the precise technical language of academic theologians—a likely reflection of both his autodidacticism and his ministerial priorities—he unmistakably shared their core theological commitments. Instead of reducing Reformed identity to a handful of doctrines on election, he embraced a covenantal reading of Scripture and upheld the abiding validity of God's moral law, aligning himself with the broader contours of historic Reformed thought.

This stance flowed directly from his methodological commitments and reflected the same foundational position held by earlier Reformed

[126] Arthur W. Pink, 'Epistle to the Hebrews,' *Studies in the Scriptures* 15:4 (1937): 102 (Pink, *An Exposition of Hebrews*, 1167.).

thinkers. It also reveals a man keenly aware of his own theological convictions and the tradition he drew from. As his wife, Vera, would later note, 'Mr. Pink is a Puritan in reality and often says to me that he is 200 or 300 years out of his time'.[127] By employing these foundational principles, Pink crafted a far-reaching theological tapestry akin to that of the 17th-century divines, who sought to derive not only soteriological doctrines but also the entire framework of worship, ethics, and ecclesial order from God's authoritative revelation.

This Reformed method emerges vividly in Pink's covenant theology, mainly as he develops it from *The Epistle to the Hebrews* (1928–1938) and *The Divine Covenants* (1934–1938) onwards. To Pink, this unfolds as a progressive revelation of God's redemptive plan, beginning in the earliest pages of Scripture and reaching its consummation in the person and work of Christ. Pink argues that the promise of redemption first hinted at in Genesis 3:15 is part of an eternal decree made by the Father and secured by the Son.[128] Pink develops a covenantal schema from these early expositions that distinguishes between two primary types of covenants: one based on human works (exemplified in Adam's covenant and the Sinaitic dispensation) and the other on divine grace. The former, he contends, exposes human inability to earn righteousness, while the latter—often identified with both the covenant of redemption and the covenant of grace, both belonging to, as Pink termed it, the everlasting covenant—is the eternal, unconditional promise of salvation that finds its full expression in Christ.[129]

For Pink, the covenant of redemption (the eternal agreement between the Father and the Son) is not a separate redemptive plan but is, in fact, the source and foundation of the covenant of grace. Such was its importance that Pink observed that a failure to understand its relation to Christ's mediatorial work was the reason why there had been 'so many fruitless controversies upon the atonement'.[130] Indeed,

---

[127] Vera Pink, Letter to Evelyn Green, 6th September 1936 (Murray, *The Life of Arthur W. Pink*, 172).

[128] Arthur W. Pink, 'The Divine Covenants,' *Studies in the Scriptures* 13:8 (1934): 178 (Arthur W. Pink, *The Divine Covenants* [Grand Rapids, MI: Baker Book House, 1983], 15.).

[129] Arthur W. Pink, 'The Epistle to the Hebrews,' *Studies in the Scriptures* 10:2 (1931): 27. (Pink, *An Exposition of Hebrews*, 450.)

[130] Arthur W. Pink, 'The Everlasting Covenant,' *Studies in the Scriptures* 32:11 (1953): 249.

he makes clear that Christ's mediatorial work, His atoning death, and His resurrection are the fulfilment of *the* eternal promise, a promise determined 'before the foundations of the world were laid'.[131] For Pink, the everlasting covenant stands behind all God's dealings with humanity from eternity, rendering the covenant of works with Adam both temporary and preparatory. In that light, he maintains that God initially entered into a covenant of works with Adam, requiring perfect obedience as the condition for life. Citing Hosea 6:7, Pink states: 'There was an original covenant made with Adam and all mankind in him. . . It was a covenant of works, and had no mediator.'[132] Once Adam broke that covenant, it 'ceased as soon as sin entered the world', because God had already purposed a way of redemption through the promise of grace.[133] Nevertheless, the Adamic arrangement established the universal moral obligation of obedience, along with the just penalty for disobedience—a principle that continued to highlight humanity's need for a perfect Mediator.

Pink further points out that the Sinaitic covenant 'exemplified the Adamic' by containing works-oriented features—though it did not serve as a second covenant of works for eternal salvation. As Pink puts it in his December 1953 article 'The Everlasting Covenant Administered,' 'The Abrahamic covenant was followed by the Sinaitic, which was the very antithesis of the other, the former being one of pure grace, the latter one of works.'[134] Yet, unlike Adam, Israel was never intended to earn a right standing before God purely by obedience to the Law; rather, the Abrahamic promises remained in force, ensuring that Israel lived under a gracious pledge of redemption. In Pink's understanding, the Sinaitic system instead recapitulated a works principle

---

[131] Arthur W. Pink, 'Dispensationalism,' *Studies in the Scriptures* 12:5 (1933): 110.

[132] Pink, 'Hebrews,' *Studies in the Scriptures* 10:2 (1931): 26. (Pink, *An Exposition of Hebrews*, 448.)

[133] Pink, 'Hebrews,' *Studies in the Scriptures* 10:2 (1931): 26. (Pink, *An Exposition of Hebrews*, 448.)

[134] Likewise, in Pink's much earlier *Epistle to the Hebrews*, he notes, 'Previously, God had made a covenant with Adam (Hosea 6:7), and in some respects the Covenant at Sinai adumbrated it, for it was chiefly one of works. So too He had made a covenant with Abraham, which in some respects adumbrated the Everlasting Covenant, inasmuch as it was one purely of grace.' Arthur W. Pink, 'The Epistle to the Hebrews,' *Studies in the Scriptures* 10:1 (1931): 6. (Pink, *An Exposition of Hebrews*, 442.)

at the national level (due to the 'if-then' language), thereby exposing human frailty and reinforcing the necessity of the everlasting covenant in Christ, whose redemptive obedience would ultimately fulfil all that Adam—and, by extension, Israel—could not accomplish.

Pink, therefore, turns from the post-Fall covenant of works dynamic to unfold his understanding of the covenant of grace intimately tied to the everlasting covenant. He consistently teaches that, once humanity fell, God revealed a gracious arrangement whose saving provisions were rooted in Christ's future mediation, initially declared in Genesis 3:15. As he succinctly puts it, 'God had provided a way of salvation for His own elect apart from their personal obligation to sinless obedience', so that 'no sinner was ever saved but by virtue of the new covenant and the mediation of Christ therein'.[135] The Abrahamic, Sinaitic, and Davidic covenants served as typological shadows, successively unveiling aspects of that one gracious plan, with Old Testament saints benefiting from Christ's suretyship in a promise form.[136] In this respect, Pink concedes that while these older covenants presented different emphases—Abrahamic being more purely gracious and Sinaitic containing national obligations—they nevertheless belonged under a single overarching economy of salvation.

Yet Pink just as firmly stresses that this covenant, even though graciously proclaimed from Genesis 3:15 onward, was not *formally* inaugurated until Christ's atoning death on the cross.[137] He explains that the old covenant 'could not be abrogated till its curse had been borne', indicating that only once Christ satisfied its demands by His death was its fullest legal force 'made manifest' in a testamentary sense (cf. Heb. 9:16–17).[138] Consequently, there is an undeniable *discontinuity* in Pink's framework when comparing the old and new covenants:

[135] Arthur W. Pink, 'Hebrews,' *Studies in the Scriptures* 10:2 (1931): 27. (Pink, *An Exposition of Hebrews*, 450.)

[136] Arthur W. Pink, 'Divine Covenants,' *Studies in the Scriptures* 15:7 (1935): 206 (Pink, *Divine Covenants*, 77.); Arthur W. Pink, 'Application of the Scriptures,' *Studies in the Scriptures* 31:8 (1952).

[137] Pink, 'Hebrews,' *Studies in the Scriptures* 10:2 (1931): 28–29. (Pink, *An Exposition of Hebrews*, 451–452.)

[138] Pink, 'Hebrews,' *Studies in the Scriptures* 10:2 (1931): 29. (Pink, *An Exposition of Hebrews*, 454.); Arthur W. Pink, 'The Divine Covenants,' *Studies in the Scriptures* 15:12 (1938): 368 (Pink, *Divine Covenants*, 303–304.)

while the Old Testament saints truly participated in the benefits of Christ's future mediation, they did so by looking forward to a promise; the definitive ratification and complete clarity of the covenant of grace arrived only at Calvary. Thus, although Pink highlights a unifying gracious thread running through the entire Old Testament, he consistently portrays the new covenant as unique and final—completing, superseding, and formally enacting what had been promised and 'shadowed' under earlier dispensations.

Indeed, Pink's covenant theology charts a middle ground that shows some semblance of both alignment and discontinuity with both what is called 1689 Federalism and the classic Westminsterian one-covenant, multiple-administrations schema, without fitting squarely into either system. On the one hand, his Baptist convictions and insistence that the new covenant was *formally ratified only at the cross* echo 1689 Federalism's strong emphasis on discontinuity before and after Calvary; on the other hand, his repeated references to the Abrahamic and Sinaitic covenants as subservient 'administrations' of the same gracious plan recall the Westminster view of a single covenant of grace unfolding progressively. Pink's reliance on John Owen pervades his works: Pink is largely in agreement with John Owen's interpretation of Hebrews 8:6–13, which insists that the 'new covenant' is neither a sheer novelty nor a mere administration of the old covenant. Instead, it is a 'substantially distinct covenant,' established in Christ, while the essence of its grace was 'virtually administered. . . in the a way of a promise' going back to Genesis 3:15.[139] Pink repeatedly endorses Owen's approach, stating that salvation in all ages has been by the promise rather than 'by virtue of' the old covenant[140]—both share a robust view of Christ's suretyship as operating even for Old Testament saints, while stressing that the Mosaic economy pointed forward to the cross without completely duplicating the covenant of works. Owen's writings, in turn, powerfully shaped Pink's exegesis of Hebrews and his overarching insistence on the centrality of the everlasting covenant.

[139] Pink, 'Hebrews,' *Studies in the Scriptures* 10:2 (1931): 29. (Pink, *An Exposition of Hebrews*, 441.); Arthur W. Pink, 'The Divine Covenants,' *Studies in the Scriptures* 8:15 (1938): 236–237. (Pink, *The Divine Covenants*, 279.)

[140] Pink, 'Hebrews,' *Studies in the Scriptures* 10:2 (1931): 28–29. (Pink, *An Exposition of Hebrews*, 450–452.)

Pink stands in a distinctively Particular Baptist lineage, one that blends Owen's insights with classic Reformed categories and produces a covenantal framework both conversant with and somewhat independent of standard 17th-century confessional divisions.

Another hallmark of Pink's alignment with Reformed theology is his robust emphasis on the moral law's continuity and binding authority for the believer. He rejected the notion that the coming of Christ annulled the moral law, arguing instead that Christ came to fulfil it by His perfect obedience, His atoning sacrifice, and His confirmation of its spiritual depth.[141] For Pink, the law was not a means of salvation but the enduring standard of righteousness by which Christians are to regulate their lives. He lamented the growing trend among evangelicals to discard the law, criticising what he called the 'modern outcry against the Law,' in which many falsely assumed that grace nullified moral obligation.[142] He argued that such a perspective was entirely foreign to biblical teaching and undermined the very holiness to which Christians are called.

Iain H. Murray observes that Pink's unwavering commitment to the moral law—including the Sabbath—distanced him from the broader fundamentalist movement, noting that it completed such alienation.[143] Many fundamentalists, influenced by dispensational theology, treated the moral law as a relic of the Jewish economy, but Pink saw this as a grievous error that threatened to erode the church's moral foundation. 'Divine grace does not set aside its recipient's responsibility, nor does the believer's obedience render grace any the less necessary', he insisted, emphasising that while believers are freed from the law's condemnation, the law was never abolished as their rule of life.[144] This position mirrored the historic Reformed confessions, which assert that the law continues to function in such a capacity.[145]

---

141 Arthur W. Pink, 'The Law and the Saint,' *Studies in the Scriptures* 2:7 (1923): 211. (Arthur W. Pink, *The Law and the Saint* [Swengel, PA: Reiner Publications, n.d.], 26–27.)

142 Arthur W. Pink, 'Dispensationalism,' *Studies in the Scriptures* 13:1 (1934): 10.

143 In Murray's words, this commitment 'made his alienation from Fundamentalism complete' (Murray, *The Life of Arthur W. Pink*, 180).

144 Arthur W. Pink, 'Divine Covenants,' *Studies in the Scriptures* 15:11 (1935): 336. C.f. Arthur W. Pink's *The Law and the Saint*, which is dedicated to this specific subject.

145 See *WCF, SFDO, 2LBCF 19.6*. In a letter to one reader, Pink noted his continuity with 'leading Puritans… Jonathan Edwards and Spurgeon' who taught 'the moral law is the

Pink also strongly opposed antinomian tendencies that sought to sever the law from the gospel. He argued that law and grace are not in opposition to each other but rather complementary: the law reveals sin, driving sinners to Christ, and grace enables obedience to that same law. 'The principles of law and gospel are not contradictory, but supplementary', he wrote, echoing the classic Reformed understanding of the law's threefold use: as a mirror to judge personal behaviour, as a restraint on sin, and as a guide for Christian living.[146] His theological framework reflected that of Calvin, Owen, and the Westminster divines, all of whom maintained that the moral law remains binding, not as a covenant of works but as a standard of holiness.[147]

His treatment of the Sabbath further demonstrates his alignment with Reformed theology. Pink upheld the Sabbath as a creation ordinance, reaffirmed in the Decalogue and perpetuated under the new covenant as the Lord's Day. He denounced efforts to relegate the Sabbath to a mere Jewish institution, arguing instead that it is a divinely instituted moral requirement for all people.[148] This conviction placed him squarely within the Puritan tradition, which saw Sabbath observance as a vital means of honouring God and fostering spiritual growth. As in all his writings on the law, Pink sought to uphold the grandeur of God's righteousness, ensuring that grace never became a pretext for lawlessness.

A further dimension illustrating Pink's Reformed orientation was his adoption of the classical principle that only Scripture determines the nature and content of public worship. This aligns with the traditional regulative principle: Pink insists worship must be drawn directly

---

Christian's rule of life!' Arthur W. Pink, letter to Lowell and Evelyn Green, 27 February 1938, *Letters of Arthur W. Pink*, 93.

[146] Arthur W. Pink, 'Divine Covenants,' 333; Arthur W. Pink, 'Dispensationalism,' *Studies in the Scriptures* 14:4 (1934): 85; Arthur W. Pink, 'The Ten Commandments,' *Studies in the Scriptures* 20:2 (1941): 48.

[147] Throughout his treatment on the moral law in *Studies in the Scriptures*, Pink cites from the Westminster Catechism ('Dispensationalism,' *Studies in the Scriptures* 14:1 [1934]: 11), Calvin ('The Ten Commandments,' *Studies in the Scriptures* 20:2 [1941]: 48), and Owen ('Dispensationalism,' *Studies in the Scriptures* 14:6 [1934]: 132), as well as many other Reformed theologians, in support of his position.

[148] Arthur W. Pink, 'The Holy Sabbath,' *Studies in the Scriptures* 18:2 (1939): 40; Arthur W. Pink, 'The Ten Commandments,' *Studies in the Scriptures* 20:6 (1941): 144.

from biblical prescriptions. He routinely chides human innovations that deviate from the sufficiency of God's Word in worship practice, denouncing such intrusions as man's will rather than God's revealed mind.[149] By doing so, Pink situates himself among Calvin and the Puritans, who insisted that worship's form and substance must derive from explicit biblical sanction—again, a direct application of the *principium cognoscendi*.

Pink's approach to societal and political matters also reflects what is frequently termed a 'Two Kingdoms' outlook. He maintained that while the state is divinely instituted to uphold moral equity—which is rooted in the moral law—its proper role is distinct from that of the church. In his writings on national accountability, Pink points to Genesis 9 as the moment when 'the sword of magisterial authority' was first committed to humanity, obligating governments to promote justice and restrain evil, yet not imposing religious uniformity or ceremonial legislation.[150] He thus denied that Mosaic civil ordinances should be replicated verbatim in secular states, warning that God never mandated them for the entire New Testament era.[151] Pink insisted that while the moral law abides for all and must inform public ethics, the state's jurisdiction extends only to administering societal order and not to coercing spiritual fidelity.[152]

Within this framework, the church remains a spiritual institution, serving under Christ by administering Word and sacrament, rather than seeking to wield civil authority. Pink emphasised that God alone binds the conscience in religious matters, and any enforcement of uniform worship by the government intrudes upon Christ's unique prerogatives as Head of the church. Hence, Pink championed a pluralistic stance, which honours 'the fear and dread' of man's accountability before God yet stops short of forcing distinctively Christian worship or

[149] Arthur W. Pink, 'The Ten Commandments,' *Studies in the Scriptures* 20:4 (1941): 96; Arthur W. Pink, 'The Holy Sabbath,' in *Studies in the Scriptures* 19:3 (1940): 61.

[150] Arthur W. Pink, 'Gleanings in Genesis,' *Our Hope* (October 1917), 221–222 (Arthur W. Pink, *Gleanings in Genesis* [Chicago, IL: Moody Press, 1922], 115.)

[151] Arthur W. Pink, 'The Holy Sabbath,' *Studies in the Scriptures* 18:8 (1939): 187; Arthur W. Pink, 'Epistle to the Hebrews,' in *Studies in the Scriptures* 16:11 (1937): 326 (Pink, *An Exposition of Hebrews*, 1232.)

[152] Arthur W. Pink, 'Private Judgement,' in *Practical Christianity* (Grand Rapids, MI: Baker Books, 1990), 169.

sacraments on non-believers.[153] His vision essentially upholds a duality of spheres: the church exercises spiritual rule over believers, while the civil order governs civic justice for all—two domains subject to one sovereign Lord but not collapsed into one.[154]

It is when we turn to Pink's ecclesiology, though, that we come to the greatest dissonance with the Reformed tradition. While not extensively developed in his writings, the small amount of work that has been written shows some continuity with Reformed theology, particularly in its Congregationalist expression. His early pastoral ministry, beginning in a Congregational church in Silverton, Colorado and later extending to Baptist congregations, demonstrated a firm commitment to regenerate church membership. Pink largely held that local churches should consist solely of those giving credible evidence of personal faith, aligning with the Congregationalist principle that the covenant people of God, under the new covenant, must be composed of self-consciously professing believers—*visible saints.*[155] In his article 'The Churches of God', Pink outlined his vision of a New Testament church, emphasising adherence to apostolic doctrine, the maintenance of ordinances, strict discipline, and active evangelism as essential characteristics. He regarded such a church as 'the only institution on this earth ordained, built, and approved of by the Lord Jesus Christ'.[156] Yet, Pink was also reluctant to view the New Testament as providing a fixed, exhaustive blueprint for church governance. He maintained that while the Scriptures supply clear principles for church order, they do not prescribe a rigid pattern in every detail, allowing for a measure of Spirit-led discretion in structuring local assemblies.[157]

However, despite his theological convictions, Pink became increasingly disillusioned with the visible church, culminating in his withdrawal from formal church membership in his later years. While he continued to uphold the biblical concept of the church as the body

---

153 Pink, 'Private Judgement,' 171.

154 Arthur W. Pink, 'The Path of Duty,' *Studies in the Scriptures* 23:6 (1944).

155 Arthur W. Pink, 'Goats,' *Studies in the Scriptures* 13:6 (1934): 142; Arthur W. Pink, 'Baptismal Address: Matthew 28:19,' unpublished sermon, 10 July 1928, 9–10. In the possession of the Arthur W. Pink Archives.

156 Arthur W. Pink, 'The Churches of God,' *Studies in the Scriptures* 11:12 (1927): 281.

157 Pink, 'Epistle to the Hebrews,' *Studies in the Scriptures* 16:11 (1937): 325. (Pink, *An Exposition of Hebrews*, 1231.)

of Christ, he came to believe that true believers should separate from unfaithful institutions, seeking spiritual nourishment through personal study and small gatherings rather than through structured church involvement.[158] This perspective placed him at odds with the broader Reformed tradition, which, while acknowledging the presence of error in visible churches, maintains that even imperfect congregations remain the ordinary means through which God dispenses grace.[159] Thus, while many of, if not most of, Pink's theological writings resonate deeply with Reformed doctrine, his ecclesiology largely reveals a reactionary response to the failings of contemporary churches rather than a robust confessional commitment to the visible and institutional church.

Conclusion: A Puritan Out of His Time

Arthur Walkington Pink stands as a unique figure in the landscape of 20th-century theology—not merely as a proponent of Calvinistic soteriology but as one who increasingly advocated a theological system firmly rooted in Reformed thought. While he may not have identified himself with the Reformed tradition in a strict confessional sense, the depth and consistency of his theological writings demonstrate an unmistakable adherence to its core tenets. His work reflects the distinctive marks of Reformed theology: a commitment to the sovereignty of God, a high view of Scripture as the *principium cognoscendi*, and a theological method that sought to interpret all redemptive history through the lens of God's covenantal dealings with His people. Pink's doctrinal framework was thus not a mere retrieval of Calvinistic soteriology but a sustained and systematic articulation of the broader Reformed tradition, even if he never formally adopted its nomenclature.

One of the key reasons Pink is often overlooked as a Reformed theologian is his lack of formal association with the confessional Reformed tradition, as well as his unique, often idiosyncratic, style of theological expression. Unlike many of his Reformed contemporaries, who worked within ecclesiastical structures or academic institutions, Pink was largely self-taught, shaping his theological understanding

---

[158] Arthur W. Pink, 'A Call to Separation,' *Studies in the Scriptures* 7:4 (1928): 72.

[159] See *WCF* 25.5, *SFDO*, *2LBCF* 26.3.

through intense personal study rather than formal seminary training. Consequently, he did not always utilise the same technical vocabulary as those operating within historically Reformed frameworks. This may have contributed to the perception that he was an independent thinker rather than one firmly situated within a theological tradition. Nevertheless, his theology—rooted in exegetical rigour, covenantal continuity, and a robust view of divine sovereignty—remains unmistakably Reformed in substance.

Furthermore, Pink's Reformed orientation is evident in the theological influences he endorsed and recommended to his readers. His extensive citations of Puritan and Reformed divines—figures such as Thomas Manton, John Owen, Stephen Charnock, and Matthew Henry—demonstrate that he drew heavily from the wellsprings of classic Reformed orthodoxy. The theological library he promoted was not eclectic or broadly evangelical but both distinctively and consistently Reformed. This is particularly significant, as it suggests that, even if Pink did not always employ the traditional language of Reformed systematic theology, he consciously directed his audience toward sources that embodied that very tradition. In this way, Pink functioned as a conduit for the transmission of Reformed theology to a new generation, particularly within Baptist and independent circles where such theological resources had been largely neglected.

Moreover, Pink's theological trajectory over time further underscores his Reformed identity. A careful tracing of his works from the 1910s through to the 1930s and beyond reveals a deepening commitment to Reformed theology. While his early writings bore the marks of a fervent fundamentalist zeal, his later works became more theologically mature, increasingly reflecting the rich contours of Reformed thought. His engagement with covenant theology, his fuller articulation of the doctrines of grace, and his growing affinity with Puritan divines all demonstrate that Pink's theological development was one of increasing alignment with Reformed orthodoxy. What emerges is a picture of a man who did not begin as a Reformed theologian in the fullest sense but became one over time—a reality that is often overlooked by those who critique his Reformed credentials.

Ultimately, Pink saw himself as a Puritan out of his time. He was a theologian who belonged to a different era, not just because of his theology but because of his method—eschewing institutional recognition, prioritising the careful exposition of Scripture, and labouring in near obscurity for the sake of doctrinal fidelity. In this sense, A.W. Pink's legacy is not simply that of a Calvinist or even a Baptist theologian but of a true heir of the Puritan tradition—a Reformed thinker whose work, despite its unconventional path, rightly belongs within the great stream of Reformed theology.

Nine

'FIGHTING LARRY' - DEFENDER OF THE FAITH?
Rev. Dr J. Laurence Rentoul (1845–1926)

Rowland S. Ward

The Rev. Dr J. Laurence Rentoul taught in the Theological Hall of the Presbyterian Church of Victoria for over 40 years until his death in 1926. During this period he was the best-known spokesman of the Presbyterian Church and extremely influential. There is a not altogether satisfactory overview of his life by Stuart Macintyre in the *Australian Dictionary of Biography* but I have not been able to locate any other significant article on a many-sided man who trained several hundred ministers. Further, not a great deal of attention has been given to his formative years in Ireland that help explain his public stance on various issues. This essay aims to provide a careful appraisal of his life before and after he came to Victoria in 1879 at the age of 34.

Family Background

The Rentoul/Rintoul name appears to be of French origin, not surprising given the Auld Alliance between Scotland and France. In Scotland the name dates from as early as about 1320 at which time there was in Kinross, near Loch Leven, a landed estate called Rentoule with the final e pronounced as a distinct syllable.[1] A man in the parish called James Rintoul (1762–1839) aspired to Christian ministry and was offered by the proprietor, Lord Kinnoul, any of five parishes of the Established

[1] The foundational source is 'J. Laurence Rentoul of Ormond College' in Robert S. Rantoul, *Some Material for a History of the Name and Family of Rentoul-Rintoul-Rantoul* (Salem: Salem Press, 1885) 8–17. JLR spelled his name Laurence and this is the spelling in the Presbytery of Coleraine minutes for 1870. In other public records in Ireland the spelling is invariably Lawrence as is also the case for his uncle and nephew.

Church of Scotland at his disposal, but Rintoul would not accept any of them.[2] Rather, he adhered to the Antiburgher section of the Secession Church which had originated from a number who had withdrawn from the Established Church in the 1730s. Both branches of the Secession Church around 1800 were impacted by 'New Light' and were becoming more relaxed compared to their former somewhat sectarian strictness. The adherence to the old covenants faded, earlier acceptance of the principle of religious establishments was given up, and tolerance of others holding an orthodox Christian faith increased.

In 1791 James Rintoul was sent as a licentiate of the orthodox Antiburgher division of the Secession Church to the church of Ray, Manorcunningham in Co. Donegal, then one of the largest congregations of that denomination in Ireland. There he was ordained and served, changing the spelling of his name to Rentoul to match that of his second cousin and friend in the Synod of Ulster at Ballykelly, the Rev. Robert Rentoul. In 1793 James married Anne Cunningham Reid, the daughter of Margaret Cunningham and the Rev. Robert Reid. Margaret was a direct descendant of Army chaplain Hugh Cunningham, one of the founders of the Presbyterian Church in Ireland in 1642. James Rentoul was a natural leader of men and an eloquent and powerful preacher in a parish of 443 families in 1814.[3] He was prominent in facilitating the union of the Burgher and Antiburgher branches to form the United Secession Church in 1818 and was chosen the first Moderator. It embraced 97 ministers, about 70 of these from the Burgher section.[4]

Three of James' four sons were ordained. Alexander succeeded his father in 1822 and was a great champion of tenant rights as were his brothers. In the Synod of Ulster, the main Presbyterian body, Arian views had been tolerated but in the 1830s subscription to the Confession was enforced. Alexander was Secession Moderator in 1840 when union with the Synod of Ulster was achieved, although he and his two ministerial brothers, James Buchan (ordained 1824) and John Lawrence

[2] *Belfast News-Letter*, 11 May 1870.

[3] John W. Lockington, *The Rentouls: A Presbyterian Dynasty* (Belfast: Presbyterian Historical Society of Ireland, 2016) 9.

[4] David Stewart, *The Seceders in Ireland* (Belfast: Presbyterian Historical Society, 1950) 204.

(ordained 1833), only joined the union in 1841. They wanted assurance on the exclusive use of the Psalter in public worship.[5]

John Laurence Rentoul, the subject of this essay, was the 4th son of the Rev. James Buchan Rentoul and was born on 6 July 1845[6] in the Bann Valley at Garvagh, a village 18 kms south of Coleraine having a population of 841 in 1841.[7] He grew up in what we might call a Levitical family steeped in Presbyterian history. In common with the majority Roman Catholic population of Ireland, he resented 'the privileges, exclusivism and social superiority of the Episcopal [ie. Anglican] Church of Ireland'[8], supported, as it was, by tithes levied on everyone working the land. The family nevertheless shared the common Protestant concern about the influence of the Roman Catholic Church if Home Rule was given. The population of Belfast increased from 20,000 in 1800 to 120,000 in 1859, a third of these Roman Catholics.[9] The 1830s onwards for decades saw considerable agitation over farm-tenant's rights by Roman Catholics and Presbyterians who wanted fair rents, fixed tenure and compensation for improvements from the mostly Tory Anglican landowners. Rentoul recalled scenes of his youth when electors, stalwart farmers who attended his father's church, were 'pushed or dragged up to the polling booth by the landlord and the landlord's agent to vote against their conscience, under threat of eviction'.[10] In the 1830s and 1840s there was also concern to see renewal of spiritual life,

---

[5] Stewart, *The Seceders*, 266–267.

[6] It was commonly reported that Rentoul was 80 at his death in April 1926 and so states the official death certificate. As there is no reason to doubt the day and month of his birth, this would make his year of birth 1845. Dr J. W. Lockington, author of *The Rentouls*, advised me [email 19 November 2019] that JLR was baptised on 10 August 1845 in his father's church (now known as Main Street Presbyterian, Garvagh) so 1845 is confirmed. I imagine there was confusion between 'age 80' and 'in his 80th year', hence the gravestone in the St Kilda Cemetery, Monumental Grave Compartment A Grave 146 gives 1846, as also Stuart Macintyre's article in the *Australian Dictionary of Biography*.

[7] *The Parliamentary Gazetteer of Ireland*, Vol. 2 (Dublin: A Fullerton & Co., 1846) 250. The population was 798 in 1861.

[8] Finlay Holmes, *Our Irish Presbyterian Heritage*^{2} (Belfast: PCI, 1992) 106; the Church of Ireland was disestablished in 1869.

[9] J. T. Carson, *God's River in Spate: the story of the religious wakening of Ulster in 1859*^{2} (Belfast: Presbyterian Historical Society, 1994) 52. Note the valuable introduction by Prof. R. F. G. Holmes, i-xvii.

[10] *The New Zealand Tablet*, Vol. XXVIII, issue 32, 10.

as formality had a fair hold in many places, and there was a build-up to the revival which broke out in 1859. This was accelerated no doubt by the famine of the 1840s, the industrialisation of textile work in the north from the traditional home-based operation, and the news from America of revival in the eastern half of the United States in 1857–58.[11]

J. Laurence Rentoul's father[12] was one of the four ministers appointed to speak on the revival at the Presbyterian Assembly held in Londonderry in May 1858.[13] His uncle and namesake at Ballymoney experienced two 'visitations' of the Spirit in his congregation in 1859.[14] However, while the revival invigorated church life, largely through its effect on those already church-goers, it did tend to soften the definite contours of the Reformed Faith by the emphasis given to religious experience; Baptists and Brethren also gained considerably.[15] Meanwhile, in the intellectual world, Friedrich Schleiermacher (1768–1834) had sought to free Christianity from criticism. He understood religion as 'the feeling of absolute dependence' which meant that an infallible Scripture was no longer needed. One did not need worry about the Bible's literary origins and dates of composition since it was the essential religious ideas of Scripture mediated through inspired but fallible men that mattered, and these could not be overthrown by criticism. The piety of those in the pew could be nurtured by those who did not hold the old position of plenary inspiration.[16] The intuition and emotion fostered by Romanticism also had its impact.

[11] A valuable article is Andrew Holmes, 'The Experience and Understanding of Religious Revival in Ulster Presbyterianism c. 1800–1930' in *Irish Historical Studies*, Vol. 34 No. 136 (November 2005) 361–385.

[12] Note the obituary for J. B. Rentoul in *The Presbyterian and Messenger of the Churches* [PCNSW] 5 March 1887, 83–84.

[13] Carson, *God's River in Spate*, 12; also John W. Lockington, *The Rentouls*, 29–30.

[14] Carson, *God's River in Spate*, 43.

[15] See R. F. G. Holmes in Introduction to J. T. Carson.

[16] Andrew R. Holmes, 'Biblical Authority and the Impact of Higher Criticism in Irish Presbyterianism, ca. 1850–1930', *The Historical Journal*, Vol. 52, No. 3 (September 2009) 615–640.

Student Days

Young Laurence was evidently a gifted child. It is said that he became classics master at an Anglican school in the west of Ireland and for a time was a tutor in Munster in the south,[17] so he probably already had Greek and Latin. In 1865 he began studies at the Queen's College in Belfast where the influence of Prof. George Lillie Craik (1798–1866) was significant in his English literature studies. In 1866 he took the prize in the literature and language of the period before Chaucer (1343–1400) offered by the *Early English Text Society* (founded in London in 1864). He graduated BA in 1867 with second class honours and MA in 1868 with first class honours and the gold medal in history, English literature and political economy. He also gained an exhibition in law. Despite a brilliant career before him,[18] Rentoul abandoned a course in law for theology and enrolled at the Assembly's College in Belfast in 1868. It is not clear what caused this change of direction but a letter to Professor Samuel Angus in Sydney dated 21 August 1923 is relevant.

> I thank you for your letter received today. The strong claim of friendship, I need scarcely say, makes difference of conviction on truth which (to me) are matters of life and death the more sorrowful. These things and allegiance to them transcend all claims of friendship or kinship, as Christ said. In my case I had, just when the dream of my life was within my acceptance as realised, to be 'mulch in the loss of all things' which made life's future a naturally bright and ambitious prospect. 'The excellency of the knowledge' for which that prospect was abundant is what, as I now perceive, you are bent upon striking away, if you can.[19]

This letter, written shortly after Rentoul had realised the seriousness of Angus's modernist theological position, suggests a spiritual crisis was the cause of Rentoul's career change. We have no detailed information but the same letter speaks of coming to a living faith via doubt and uncertainty 'through Gethsemene and by the way of the Cross and of the empty tomb and of the Easter certainty'.

---

[17] *Argus* (Melbourne), 16 April 1926, 11.

[18] Apparently, he rejected the offer of a secretaryship in the Liberal Association of Ulster with an attractive salary and an opening in politics, J. W. Lockington, *The Rentouls*, 36.

[19] Original in Samuel Angus file, Ferguson Library (PCNSW), Sydney.

There were 29 students in the 1868–69 class at the Assembly's College, almost all graduates of Queen's. Robert Watts was the thoroughly orthodox and inspiring Professor of Theology and devotee of Charles Hodge at Princeton. W. D. Killen was the capable Professor of Church History and J. G. Murphy the diligent Professor of Hebrew who had already written commentaries on Genesis and Exodus. Henry Wallace taught Christian Ethics which covered science and religion as well; he was a good thinker but not very effective in class. John Rogers taught Sacred Rhetoric and Catechetics while Dr Josias Porter (1823–89) held the Chair of Biblical Criticism which covered Old and New Testament. Porter had studied in the College of the Free Church in Edinburgh. He was ordained in 1846 and served Newcastle on Tyne. From 1849–59 he was the Irish Church's missionary to the Jews based in Damascus. A popular writer he was ineffective in the needed area of assessment of higher criticism but valuable in college administration. The normal course at Assembly's College was three years with the session running from November to April inclusive with a week's vacation at the end of the year, and most subjects were only studied for two sessions.[20] Rentoul did well in his studies and seemingly the duration of the course was reduced in his case because of existing attainments. He was President of the Theological Society 1869–70,[21] took the First prize in the senior Hebrew Class at the close of that academic year and also collected a £10 scholarship.[22]

On 5 April 1870 the matter of his two trial discourses preparatory to being licensed was raised at the Presbytery of Coleraine. One was approved by the Committee involved, the other on the Establishment Principle was not. Rentoul alleged that 'the spirit of Christ's teaching was opposed to the establishment principle' and that 'the principle of establishment was wholly antagonistic and foreign to Christianity.'[23] Even so, the discourse was sustained by the Presbytery on a 6–3 vote. Rentoul's father, who was the Clerk of the Presbytery, agreed with his son's views, and the Rev. Robert W. R. Rentoul of the same presbytery

---

[20] Robert Allen, *The Presbyterian College Belfast 1853–1953* (Belfast: William Mullan & Sons, 1954) 146–147. Dr Watts noted that at Princeton there were three sessions each of nine months.

[21] *Belfast News-Letter,* 21 March 1870.

[22] *Belfast News-Letter,* 14 April 1870. The sum of £10 in 1870 equals about £1,300 in 2024.

[23] *Belfast News-Letter,* 7 April 1870; although acknowledged on 12 April 1870 as not exact quotations from his discourse, they were for substance correct.

wrote several letters in the *Coleraine Chronicle* in support of his younger brother. In rebutting sneers against ministers' sons by another correspondent, Robert wrote:

> We *are* Presbyterian ministers' sons. But we are not sons of such Presbyterian ministers as, from mere worldly motives, struggle through the dirt, carrying with them the coarseness and vulgarity of their birth and training; we are sons of Presbyterian ministers who came from Scotland for the love of God, and were noble men in every sense. Men of low birth are always envious of ministers' sons, because they are superior to them in talents, manners, training and in every respect.[24]

Not surprisingly, such snobbish comments intensified feelings and Robert was directed to withdraw certain statements and apologise, although some, including his father, dissented from this decision.[25] Robert's remarks certainly indicate something of the sense of superiority in the Rentoul clan. The upshot of a rather public spat was that, after deciding on 3 May 1870 to refer the matter to the Assembly, the Presbytery on 21 May 1870 finally resolved to licence young Rentoul. At the meeting on 31 May his father explained that his son held:

> that Christ is King of Nations, that it is the duty of the civil magistrate to further the interests of religion by punishing certain violations of the moral law and that he only objects to the State having power to interfere with the internal arrangements of the Church and take order in ecclesiastical affairs.[26]

The Presbytery concluded these views were not out of line with the standards of the church and that 'the difficulties of this case arose from a misunderstanding' and therefore resolved to grant him a licence. This

---

[24] *Belfast News-Letter*, 11 May 1870. In the period 1840–1870 about 66% of Presbyterian ministers were sons of farmers and 10% sons of ministers, John M. Barkley, *Fasti of the General Assembly* (Belfast: Presbyterian Historical Society, 1986) 81.

[25] *Belfast News-Letter*, 12 May 1870. On 6 September 1870 Robert duly apologised publicly before his presbytery.

[26] I owe details of the Presbytery record to the Rev. Dr John W. Lockington, 6 December 2019.

was duly done on 6 June 1870 and he was transferred to the Presbytery of Belfast. The newly-minted licentiate was teaching English Language and Literature for an hour three days a week at Mrs Byers' Educational Establishment for Young Ladies in Belfast in September 1870.[27] Other movements have not been traced but one can imagine Rentoul continuing wide reading and reflecting on the issues of the age.

The two great matters impacting Christianity were Higher Criticism and Evolution theory. Higher Criticism considers how the text came to be composed and matters such as authorship, sources, editing and type of literature. Here there was much controversy since those who treated Scripture like any other merely human document commonly rejected the supernatural and reconstructed the history behind the text by naturalistic assumptions about the evolution of religion. Rentoul rejected the naturalistic assumptions of the negative critics but was accepting of some modifications to traditional doctrine. As regards evolution, Darwin's *On the Origin of Species* was published in 1859, when the idea of progress and development by natural laws was already current in other areas such as geology, but it is not likely Rentoul was impacted greatly until the application to man was more specially argued by Darwin in his *The Descent of Man,* published in February 1871.

First Charge – St George's, Southport, England

Rentoul declined a call to the Academy Street Church in Belfast[28] in July 1871 but accepted a call from Southport within the Presbytery of Liverpool of the English Presbyterian Church. In 1881 Rentoul claimed that he went to England because 'the half Orange presbytery he stood before condemned him and would not give him a licence. He therefore went from Ireland to England where breath was freer and the bosom broader'.[29] But given he was already licensed it was perhaps ordination

[27] *Belfast News-Letter,* 15 September 1870.

[28] *Belfast News-Letter,* 5 July 1871. Thirty-seven seat-holders were in favour and twelve against. The congregation relocated to Berry Street, Belfast in 1876.

[29] *Argus,* 2 March 1881, 7. The 'Orange' reference is to the Loyal Orange Institution, named after the Dutch Protestant prince William of Orange who defeated James II in 1688. It was formed in 1795 and committed to upholding the Protestant succession. In the earlier years Episcopalian landholders were prominent but after Catholic emancipation in 1829 Presbyterians were drawn into it.

in Ireland he was seeking to avoid. The Irish Church did not countenance higher critical views at this time and perhaps Rentoul felt himself needing 'a broader bosom', while of course there was a generous stipend and prospects on offer in England.

The Southport congregation had become a preaching station in March 1869. In May 1870, when there were 82 members, it was made a sanctioned charge eligible to call its own minister.[30] However, there were only 37 members[31] and no building when Rentoul was ordained and inducted on 18 January 1872 with his father and older brother Alexander present. Apparently Rentoul did not preach at Southport before receiving a call but was recommended to the congregation by a person now unknown.[32] Perhaps Alexander Rentoul, who had been ministering 20 miles away in Liverpool since 1866, suggested his brother. At any rate, Rentoul had a successful ministry. A site in Lord Street was purchased and a building erected seated for 500. Rentoul chose St George's as the name and by the close of 1875 all the property expense of about £7,000 had been paid.[33]

The opening service on 10 September 1874 was conducted by the Rev. J. Oswald Dykes (1835–1912) of London. Dykes had existing connections with Victoria as in 1865 this talented former assistant to the Rev. Dr Robert Candlish of Edinburgh had arrived in Melbourne to seek recovery of his health. This so improved that soon he was preaching for the ageing Rev. Dr Adam Cairns of East Melbourne, assisting in theological education and facilitating the reconciliation of some who had stayed out of the union forming the Presbyterian Church of Victoria [PCV] in 1859. Dykes, since 1869

[30] Graham Morrison, *St George's Presbyterian Church Southport, Diamond Jubilee 1874–1934*, 2.

[31] Information Leaflet accessed at https://www.stgeorgessouthport.org.uk/informationleafletaboutourchurch.htm

[32] Graham Morrison, 3.

[33] Graham Morrison, 7.

minister of Regent Square Church in London, received a commission to secure a minister for the new East St Kilda Church in Melbourne. Rentoul announced to the congregation in July 1878 that he had accepted the invitation Dykes had extended. There were then 300 members at Southport. They were keen to retain Rentoul's services, but he felt it his duty to go. He married Annie Rattray at Southport on 30 October 1878. His wife's sister Jessie remained a member at Southport until her death in 1931.[34] Alfred, his younger brother, married Annie and Jessie's younger sister Caroline in 1881.

Leipzig

Rentoul proceeded to the University of Leipzig where on 20 November 1878 he was enrolled as a 'listener' and audited some classes.[35] Negative literary criticism had not raised its head in the Assembly's College but a man of Rentoul's intelligence would have been very well aware of the wider world of thought that was developing. Professor Murphy had written against Bishop J. W. Colenso's views on the Pentateuch in 1863,[36] the same year that A. B. Davidson (1831–1902), the careful pioneer of the higher critical approach to the Old Testament, had in effect begun his long career as Professor of Hebrew at the Free Church of Scotland College, Edinburgh.[37] Certainly Rentoul met and presumably studied with the relatively conservative Lutheran commentator Franz Delitzsch (1813–90), who taught at Leipzig 1867–90, and whose cautious

---

[34] Graham Morrison, 9. Rentoul was to visit his old church in 1906.

[35] Obituaries for Rentoul typically note that he continued his theological studies in Leipzig but give no further detail. Petra Hesse of the Leipzig University Archives was able to advise me on 6 December 2019 that Rentoul was a 'listener' in the winter semester but she could not determine whose lectures he attended.

[36] J. G. Murphy, *The Nineteen Alleged Impossibilities of Pt. I. of Colenso on the Pentateuch, Shown to be Possible. With a Critique on P. II* (Belfast 1863, 104pp). Also note Josias L. Porter's *The Pentateuch and the Gospels* (Belfast 1864). Of his time as a theological student Rentoul stated (*Argus*, 18 March 1908, 7): 'The answers of the theologians of the time to Colenso had filled him with uneasiness, they were so unconvincing.'

[37] Davidson was Hebrew tutor 1858–63 and assistant to the eccentric Rev. Prof. John 'Rabbi' Duncan 1863–70 and thereafter Professor. Duncan was not the man to prepare students to face the challenges of the time and Davidson was already moving in the newer critical way. See also Allan Harman, *The Background to 'Believing Criticism' in the Free Church of Scotland, RTR* 81, 3 (December, 2022) 208.

approach would underlie Rentoul's teaching at Ormond College.[38] Perhaps he also met Delitzsch's strictly conservative literary collaborator C. F. Keil (1807–88) who lived in the town, and even Adolf Harnack, who was teaching at Leipzig until 1879.[39] However, he did not meet B. B. Warfield whose attendance at Delitzsch's lectures occurred in the winter of 1876/77.

At a farewell in London on 23 April 1879, Dykes stated:

> I did not select Mr Rentoul merely on account of his eminent scholarship, and wide culture, and fine social sympathies. In addition to these qualities he has, in my opinion, a higher quality still. The faith he holds and teaches is not one which he has accepted from others as a mere parrot cry. He has made it his own by the honest, manful wrestling of his own brain and heart, through the doubts and mental difficulties of our own age. Therefore he is, in my opinion, all the more able to sympathise with the mental unrest of a young and self-reliant community, and to present the faith of the Gospel to them as a reasonable and persuasive thing, speaking its message in the practical language of our present century.[40]

Clearly, Rentoul had continued intellectual study during his time at Southport. The evolution of man was much discussed in the 1870s. In 1887 Rentoul stated that 'he had been at first strongly inclined to Darwinism, and was prepared to believe it now if it could be proved'.[41] However, he accepted that Rudolf Virchow (1821–1902), the great German physician and pathologist, had shown evolution to be unscientific. One presumes the controversy that erupted in 1877 following

---

[38] Don Chambers, *Theological Teaching and Thought in the Theological Hall of the Presbyterian Church of Victoria 1865–1906* (Parkville: Ormond College, 1967) 32–33.

[39] Both Keil and Delitzsch were confessional Lutherans and their joint OT Commentary came out in 1861. In his later work the ever-devout Delitzsch made concessions to higher critical theories of the literary history of the Old Testament. In 1877 Delitzsch translated the New Testament into Hebrew to further evangelistic efforts among the Jews. However, his son Friedrich (1850–1922), the noted Assyriologist, went in the opposite direction. Like many in Germany at the time, he came to reject the Old Testament as unfit for Christians and regarded its Jewish authors as inferior people. Cf. the assessment by Raymond F. Surburg, 'The Influence of the Two Delitzsches on Biblical and Near Eastern Studies' *Concordia Theological Quarterly* 47.3 (July 1983) 225–240.

[40] *Argus*, 14 June 1879, 9.

[41] *Christian Colonist* [South Australia], 11 November 1887, 6.

Virchow's statements rejecting Darwin's hypothesis led Rentoul to this conclusion. Virchow was an outspoken critic of evolution until the end of his life as well as opposing the theories of racial superiority that he feared would (and did) gain support from it, but he was not an overtly religious person. For him, as for Rentoul, it was a scientific question, and Rentoul did not believe it to be detrimental to the doctrines of the fall and redemption.

At his farewell in London, Rentoul was presented with a numerously signed address by ministers and members of the Presbyterian Church of England. They wrote that they had hoped

> your wide culture, your admirable literary faculty, and your earnest Christian feeling might long have been at the disposal of the Church ... Your peculiar gifts are not so plentiful that we can do otherwise than grudge the loss of them. But we rejoice to know our loss will be the gain of a sister Church occupying a most important field...[42]

Second Charge – St George's, East St Kilda, Victoria

Rentoul and his wife sailed from Plymouth on the *SS Aconcagua* on 24 April 1879 and arrived in Melbourne on the evening of 8 June. The call was placed in his hands by the Presbytery on 12 June, he preached the following Sunday and was officially inducted on 23 June 1879.

The Presbyterian Church of Victoria had begun work in East St Kilda in 1866, largely at the instigation of merchant-politician James McCulloch (1819–93), the Premier of Victoria on four occasions between 1863 and 1877, who lived nearby. It proved difficult to secure a suitable permanent minister but more definite moves in 1876 led to plans for a building to be erected on the one acre site in Chapel Street granted by the Government in 1866. It adjoined on the north side All Saints Church of England and on the south side the Orderly rooms previously used for church services.[43] The foundation stone was laid by Sir James

[42] Full text in *Argus*, 14 June 1879, 9.

[43] McCulloch's attempt to secure the more prominently located two acre Free Presbyterian property on the corner of Alma Road and Chapel Street, East St Kilda was rebuffed, Arthur Paul (ed.), *The Presbyter*, July 1879, 69. Its bluestone church opened in January 1864 was seated for 200 and designed capable of extension to double its seating

McCulloch on 21 April 1877 and the first stage of the planned building was opened on 1 October 1877. The stipend paid to Rentoul was £800 per year, more than twice the average, and reflected the wealth of some of the congregation's members, although Rentoul stressed there was no class system and all were welcome. His arrival brought immediate growth in the congregation and the building was soon too small. The balance of the originally planned building was therefore erected and the extended building opened for worship on Sunday 3 October 1880, seated for about 600.[44] An imported organ arrived 2 years later and replaced the harmonium.

Rumours about the views of the Rev. Charles Strong, minister of the Scots Church in Melbourne since 1875, had reached England and in 1878 Rentoul had asked Oswald Dykes if Strong held the central truths. Dykes did not know but he thought Melbourne would not stand Strong if he was not orthodox.[45] Hardly had Rentoul arrived in Melbourne than his work as a parish minister was overshadowed by the growing controversy over Strong's theology that, impacted by philosophical idealism, cut Christianity from its historical moorings and reduced it to ideas. Thus the root and essence of Christian doctrine was reduced to the human consciousness rather than to the objective supernatural facts on which Christian faith rests.

Strong Case

The November 1879 PCV Assembly, Rentoul actively supporting, recommended against the 'progressive' (or should one say 'provocative'?) *Presbyterian Review* with which the Rev. Charles Strong was associated. In April 1881 the Melbourne Presbytery expressed its 'concern and pain' over Strong's article on the Atonement in the secular *Victoria Review* published in October 1880. In August 1881, J. C. Stewart, an elder of Scots Church and the PCV Law Agent, caused 'no small sensation' throughout the church by his assault on the Confession of Faith, which led to his suspension by the Presbytery of Melbourne the following month. The speech made by Rentoul on this occasion is revelatory of

capacity, cf. *Leader* (Melbourne) 23 January 1864, 2.

[44] Description appears in *Argus*, 2 October 1880, 8.

[45] *Herald* (Melbourne), 20 September 1883, 3 (part of Rentoul's speech in the Presbytery).

his own position.[46] Far from wanting to defend 'scholastic Calvinism', Rentoul had, on his own testimony, persuaded those more conservative than himself, such as the Rev. Alex Yule,

> to act with me along a clear middle line, in saving our church and its faith – on the one hand from those who would shatter its historic basis, the certainty of its historic facts and gospel; on the other hand, from those who would narrow and shackle it into all the minute network of doctrinal propositions of the 16th and 17th century.[47]

Rentoul did not touch directly on the inspiration of Scripture in his powerful address. That would have been to upset needlessly many holding the older position. Rentoul in effect regarded inspiration as limited to its saving message so that incidental errors or mistakes on other matters could be allowed as well as some diversity in assessment of its literary composition. He cared little for what he called 'non-essentials', and had long thought a shorter creed desirable,[48] but he could not and would not concede 'the centre-point of the battle—the divine ever-living person of our Lord Jesus Christ, risen with redemption from the dead.'[49] He described himself as 'an evangelical broad churchman'. He claimed his experience in seeking licence in Belfast in 1870, had given him 'a strong desire never to take part in any judicial action'[50] While his recollection of what took place in 1870 is not quite correct, he certainly reflected the increasingly common view that heresy cases were best avoided in favour of a positive statement of a church's position or an administrative procedure.

In 1881 the Assembly took steps to draw up what was called a Declaratory Act. It was approved but not adopted in November 1882.

---

[46] For complete text of Rentoul's speech see Rowland S. Ward, *Presbyterians in Australia: Origins, Conflicts and Progress 1803–2018* (Wantirna: New Melbourne Press, 2018, 2021) 129–136.

[47] 'The Late Rev. Alex Yule, MA', from an In Memoriam Service by Rev. Prof. Rentoul, MA, DD, preached 5 May 1907, *The Messenger* (1907), 332; cf. D. Chambers, *Theological Teaching*, 32 who correctly notes that Rentoul's statement 'appears to contain much truth'.

[48] Rentoul on 8 September 1881 in Ward, *Presbyterians*, 130.

[49] Rentoul on 8 September 1881 in Ward, *Presbyterians*, 136.

[50] *Argus*, 2 March 1881, 7.

The legal force of the Act was therefore dubious while, to the extent it purported to vary commitment to 'the whole doctrine' of the Confession of Faith, it was in conflict with the trust commitments which governed church property. Amendment by Parliament would be necessary to ensure the Act's full validity. Nevertheless, its practical effect was to give some measure of relief in subscription and adjust the church to the current mood, as well as clarifying some disputed points raised by Stewart. The Rev. Murdoch Macdonald (1832–1906) of the influential Toorak congregation played a significant role in drafting the Declaratory Act. Rentoul, through the debate over Strong, contributed the substance of the requirement in the Act to give

> a chief place to the central and most vital doctrines, with those objective supernatural facts on which they rest, especially the incarnation, the Perfect Obedience and Expiatory Death, and the Resurrection and Ascension of our Lord, avoiding such forms of teaching as might be fitted to weaken or destroy the faith of the people in the same.

Rentoul's position was not really different from men like the brilliant William Robertson Smith (1846–94). Smith had been removed from his Chair of Old Testament at the Aberdeen Free Church College in 1881, not by a judicial finding of heresy but by an administrative decision.[51] Controversy about Smith became significant in 1875 following the publication of an article by him entitled 'Bible' in the 9th edition of *Encyclopaedia Britannica*. Yet at least as early as November 1869 Smith was stressing that revelation is personal and not a communication of doctrines. He claimed that the early Protestant Reformers emphasis on experimental conviction had 'soon passed over into a lifeless orthodoxy out of which rationalism arose'.[52] He held:

> The theology of a living Church does not start from the mere outward form and vehicle of Christianity, be that form never so divine, but from

---

[51] For the progress of higher criticism in the Free Church of Scotland see Kenneth R. Ross, *Church and Creed in Scotland: The Free Church case 1900–104 and its Origins* (Edinburgh: Rutherford House, 1988) 154ff.

[52] J. S. Black & J. Chrystal (eds.), *Lectures and essays of William Robertson Smith* (London: A. & C. Black, 1912) 153.

> the true substance of Christianity which the Church knows she has already grasped.[53]

This meant that Christian faith and criticism of the Scripture as to its literary composition and inaccuracies on other matters of history or science were compatible. One could and should hold unswervingly to the incarnation, the sinless life and atoning death and real resurrection of Christ. In February 1878, in words often quoted, Smith put it this way:

> If I am asked why I receive Scripture as the Word of God and the only rule of faith and life, I answer with all the Fathers of the Protestant Church, 'Because in the Bible is the only record of the redeeming love of God, because in the Bible alone I find God drawing near to man in Jesus Christ, and declaring to us in Him, His will for our salvation. And this record I know to be true by the witness of His Spirit in my heart, whereby I am assured that none other than God himself is able to speak such words to my soul.'[54]

So what we have is a very significant redefinition of revelation and inspiration. Revelation was regarded in orthodoxy as the content of the Scriptures, all being inspired by God. The Spirit of God works by and with the word illuminating the believer to saving knowledge and assurance. Under the new scheme, revelation was confined to God's acts in history. In short, revelation was not co-extensive with Scripture but consisted of a kernel in Scripture. The kernel consists of the record of God's acts for our redemption, discerned by particular inspired men who have passed it on to us along with the fallible husk of their own limitations. But, said critics, we are supposed to have confidence in this kernel of revelation because of the testimony of the Holy Spirit even though the Spirit who reveals Christ to us reveals a Christ who tells us 'the Scriptures are inspired by God and cannot be broken'. A very unsatisfactory and unstable position indeed.

---

[53] Black & Chrystal, 155.

[54] W. R. Smith, *Answer to the Form of Libel Now Before the Free Presbytery of Aberdeen* (Edinburgh: David Douglas, 1878) 21.

Smith was not discreet in propagating his views about the nature and literary composition of Scripture. In 1877 the Rev. Marcus Dods vented similar views about revelation and inspiration. His case had been dropped in May 1878 because the Assembly had its hands full with the Smith case. Only in 1889 would action against him arise but censure for his views was not supported.[55]

Third Charge – Ormond College Theological Hall, Melbourne

The Presbyterian Theological Hall had commenced in 1865 under the Rev. Dr Adam Cairns' leadership with various other ministers providing assistance. Cairns (1802–81) retired in 1872 but a new Principal was not appointed. There were seven students in the 1865 intake but that number was not reached in after years and in fact declined to a low of three in 1871. However, numbers began to increase and reached 16 in 1877. Endeavours to secure teaching staff from overseas were made, but without success. Wealthy pastoralist Francis Ormond (1829–89), an elder at Toorak, provided most of the funds for the erection of a residential college attached to the university that would also house the Theological Hall, and this made advance possible. The Assembly of 1880 reappointed three existing professors but also five lecturers, including Murdoch Macdonald of Toorak and Laurence Rentoul of East St Kilda, all on an annual basis.

At the Assembly of 1882 it was agreed to seek from the United Kingdom, using the good offices of Oswald Dykes, a Principal who would also be a Professor. A second professor would be chosen from among local men, if a stipend for him was secured, and both positions would be permanent. Failure to secure a man from the old country would mean both positions would be filled from local men. No overseas man was secured and the Assembly therefore asked the eleven regional presbyteries to nominate local men. Most presbyteries nominated the Rev. Murdoch Macdonald of Toorak and the Rev. Laurence Rentoul of East St Kilda,[56] ministers of two of the wealthiest congre-

[55] See also Marcus Dods, *The Bible, its Origin and Nature.* The Bross Lectures (New York: Charles Scribner's Sons, 1905) and the review of this book by B. B. Warfield, *Works*, Vol X (New York: OUP, 1932) 118–127.

[56] The Rev. A. J. Campbell narrated the steps taken in detail to address claims of parti-

gations. In November 1883, the General Assembly duly appointed these two men and they were inducted on 24 March 1884. Rentoul's stipend was a generous £800 a year, the same as he had received at East St Kilda. Rentoul received a DD (*honoris causa*) from the Faculty of the Presbyterian Church in Ireland on 4 April 1884,[57] while Macdonald, who had published a well-received book in 1875 entitled *The Covenanters of Moray and Ross*, received a DD from Rutgers College in New Jersey in 1886.

The appointments caused some controversy with accusations of partisanship from supporters of Strong. A minor dispute about Rentoul's stipend due from St George's erupted in the press. The Rev. Dr Peter Mercer (1821–1902), who had been Moderator 1882–83 and who had had a major teaching role since 1869, was aggrieved at being passed over and resigned his other denominational roles as secretary and treasurer of the PCV. He had been close to Strong in the production of the provocative *Presbyterian Review* the Assembly had disapproved in 1879, but apart from any theological concerns about him, he was probably regarded as rather old for the post.

Given their prominent contributions both to the silencing of the *Presbyterian Review*, and dealing with the crisis over Strong, it is not surprising that Macdonald and Rentoul were the two men appointed. Macdonald (1832–1906) was a Highlander ordained in the Free Church of Scotland in 1863 whose personal position was conservative, but who wanted to avoid division over believing criticism.[58] He had responsibility for Church History and Systematic Theology and generally followed the line taken at Princeton by Charles and Alexander Hodge.[59] Rentoul's portfolio covered Hebrew and Old Testament, Greek and New Testament as well as Apologetics. As one denomination among many, the PCV had to compete for adherents. It needed the support of wealthy pastoralists and businessmen and it still had a close connection with the churches of the United Kingdom from which migrants and ministers came. The new mood in progressive Melbourne, as well

---

sanship, *Argus*, 25 March 1884, 6.

[57] *Belfast News-Letter*, 5 April 1884.

[58] For Macdonald's views on subscription see *Argus*, 9 September 1881, 6.

[59] Chambers, *Theological Teaching*, 32; similarly Chambers in Stuart McIntyre (ed.), *Ormond College Essays* (Melbourne University Press, 1984) 108.

as Scotland, could not be ignored but the increasing impact of secular and unbelieving thought had to be challenged. In Rentoul the PCV had a man who was reassuringly implacably insistent on the central redemptive facts, and in Macdonald a man who was orthodox but not reactionary or bigoted. They were rather different men but they could work together, an important factor given the tensions in the church.

The Hall course ran from March to August and was extended to six months in 1885. Rentoul included study of Franz Delitzsch's *Old Testament History of Redemption* which had been published in English translation in 1881. It presupposed Deutero-Isaiah and a late date for Daniel, but did not enter in any major way into critical questions which were, however, covered by Rentoul's lectures.[60] An interesting summary of the course at Ormond taken by the Rev. John Mathew, the top student 1884–87, is available, and his appreciation of Rentoul's 'liberating' teaching about Scripture on this originally strictly orthodox student is evident.[61] The number of students would fluctuate between 15 and 24 between 1885 and 1903. In the latter year two-thirds of PCV ministers were Australian trained compared to one-third sixteen years before.[62] Ormond was far ahead of training arrangements in New South Wales, and PCV students could sit for the Edinburgh BD. Rentoul lectured each morning and attended pastoral duties and correspondence in the afternoons. He was made Principal in 1906. The Master of Ormond until 1915 was his friend John MacFarland but Rentoul did not get on so well with MacFarland's successor, D. K. Picken (1879–1956). Picken was a former mathematics professor whose religious views were certainly not aligned with Rentoul's but were mainly expressed in the furtherance of ecumenical endeavours with the Australian Student Christian Movement formed in 1896.

---

60 Delitzsch also acknowledged at least four hands participated in the codification of the Pentateuch, but he questioned the ages assigned by critics and insisted that the historical certainty of 'the fundamental faith of redemption-history' did not depend on the conclusions they drew - 'The New Criticism', *The Hebrew Student*, Vol.1, No. 2 (May 1882) 7.

61 Malcolm D. Prentis, *Science, Race and Faith: A Life of John Mathew* (CSAC: Sydney, 1998) 84–91; see also the Rev. R. L. Taylor's article 'Practical Reply to T.J.S.', *Presbyterian Monthly* May 1891, 140–141; Chambers, *Theological Teaching*, 34–36.

62 Chambers in Stuart Macintyre (ed.), *Ormond College*, 112.

Higher Criticism in Australian Controversy

Rentoul held that the doctrines of the fall and redemption were based on the consciousness of sin in human experience and the deeply embedded need of redemption and not on 'the external prosaic verbal interpretation' of the Genesis story which reduced 'the perennial beauty and truth of the narrative to an ancient fable'.[63] Although he remained a theistic evolutionist,[64] it is clear Rentoul remained personally sceptical that Darwin's particular theory of the descent of man from lower forms of life could explain his intellectual, moral and spiritual powers. Only creative power could account for these. He was not alone in this. Scottish theologian James Orr (1844–1913), Rentoul's notable contemporary, was a theistic evolutionist too. However, Orr held to a real historic fall from original righteousness by the progenitors of the human race, and death as a consequence, although he considered Genesis 3 had something of an allegorical dress.[65] Rentoul was not as conservative as Orr and did not consider the religious truth of Genesis affected whether the narrative is taken 'as couched in figurative language or as an exact historical narrative'.[66] In 1887 Rentoul thought man's time on earth could be scientifically maintained as no more that 8,000 years even though some argued for 100,000,[67] but I suspect he was not so confident of the lower date in later years.

In 1889 Andrew Harper (1844–1936), Principal of Presbyterian Ladies' College, was appointed to take over the Hebrew and Old Testament part of Rentoul's teaching load. Harper was extremely capable but he held to higher critical views about Scripture along the lines of his friend and fellow student, William Robertson Smith, and his view

---

[63] *Argus*, 14 July 1914, 11.

[64] His latest reported statement is in the *Weekly Times* [Victoria], 18 July 1925, 7. He states: 'So far as I know, no educated man, and certainly no Protestant Church is opposed to evolution.' While expressing his reservations about true Darwinian theory, he cites Joseph LeConte (d.1901) and Canon (later Bishop) E. W. Barnes (1874–1953) as 'outstanding Christian teachers who have held Darwinian theory *holus bolus*'. Barnes later gained notoriety as a radically modernist English bishop and member of the Eugenics Society.

[65] James Orr, *The Christian View of God and the World* (Edinburgh: Andrew Elliot, 1893) 210–217.

[66] *Argus*, 2 August 1921, 8.

[67] *Christian Colonist* [Adelaide], 18 November 1887, 6.

of the atonement was such that he affirmed the fact but understood it in terms of the teaching of McLeod Campbell and F. D. Maurice and so rejected penal substitution.[68] These views in 1872 had precluded Harper's ordination, but there was no difficulty in him securing ordination in 1893.

The PCV magazine, the *Presbyterian Monthly*, had been edited for many years by the Rev. James Ballantyne (1818–96), an old school conservative. It had not been controversial but carried news and other edifying material. However, in 1889 when Marcus Dods was appointed by the Free Church of Scotland Assembly to the New Testament chair in Edinburgh, there was considerable outcry. The Free Church Assembly of May 1890 followed Robert Rainy, the 'pope' of the Assembly, in countering the conservative action which had also been brought against Professor A. B. Bruce. In effect, the Assembly voted to permit a view of inspiration that allowed for errors if only the great saving truths were maintained. From June 1890 to May 1891 a series of articles on higher criticism appeared in the *Presbyterian Monthly* directed at 'Victorian critics' (ie. Rentoul and Harper) by one who was only 18 months out of the Theological Hall, the Rev. T. Jollie Smith (1858–1927).[69] Jollie Smith penned his articles in response to the defence of Dods and Bruce by Rentoul and Harper. But it was too late. Liberal evangelicalism had gained the field in Scotland and also in Victoria. Jollie Smith himself was not a champion of verbal inspiration, as sometimes claimed,[70] but an opponent of modernist assumptions like Rentoul. Whatever Rentoul thought of Smith's initial salvo, later they were close. Rentoul's support of T. Jollie Smith for the Hebrew and Old

---

[68] See Harper's letter in *Argus*, 7 November 1883.

[69] Smith was a brilliant scholar. He served Naracoorte (SA) 1890–1903; *pro tem* lecturer in Hebrew, Ormond College 1904; Malvern East (Ewing Memorial) 22.6.1905–1922; Professor of Old Testament, Ormond College 1923–27. Among other accomplishments he introduced the study of Japanese at Melbourne University.

[70] See T. J. Smith, *Studies in Criticism and Revelation* (New York: Fleming H. Revell Co., 1925) and his specific allowance of 'human imperfection and human ignorance' in 'the divinely guided record of the divinely given revelation' (p. 170). Don Chambers incorrectly terms Smith 'an unrepentant fundamentalist' in McIntyre, *Essays*, 117, but Ian Breward's *ADB* article on Smith rightly speaks of him 'as not so much a fundamentalist as an enemy of modernist assumptions'.

Testament chair in 1922 reflects the choice of someone not markedly different from himself on critical questions.

There was a final rear-guard action. In March 1894, the Rev. George MacInnes (1846–1908), deli vered his address as NSW Moderator proclaiming the death of 'verbal inspiration'. It sparked considerable controversy.[71] Questioned for his response, Rentoul attractively argues at length just this position,[72] although he avoids much of the inflammatory language used by MacInnes. At the Federal Assembly on 21 September that year, the Rev. Duncan McEachran (1826–1913) of Carlton (Melbourne), gave an address as retiring moderator which dealt with the inspiration of Scripture in a modest but orthodox way.

Rentoul *circa* 1895

Another conservative, the Rev. Alex Yule of Parkville, read a paper in which he rejected theories which postulate a rationalistic or naturalistic view of Scripture but advanced three theories of inspiration that he said may be fairly claimed 'to be tenable and not merely tolerable under the Westminster Confession':[73] The first is verbal inspiration of the originals, the orthodox view exemplified by Charles and Alexander Hodge of Princeton. The second is the view that inspiration varies in quality or intensity. Yule thinks this can be held along with complete loyalty to the Confession although he does not particularly like it and he says it lacks explicit support in the Confession. The third view is that the Scriptures are inspired as to their moral and spiritual truth so as to

[71] The Rev. G. D. Buchanan (1853–1920) as incoming Moderator of the Presbyterian Church of Queensland in 1894 advanced similar views (*Queenslander*, 12 May 1894, 880). He was deposed for a moral offence in 1900, advocated Christian Socialism in South Africa, latterly fraternised with the Bahai Faith and died in the USA.

[72] *Sydney Telegraph*, 23 April 1894, 5.

[73] Published as *The Westminster Teaching on Inspiration* (Melbourne: Rae Bros., 1894) 32pp. Cf. George Tait, *The Bible - How to Think of It* (Melbourne: Harston Partridge, 1919) being the Alexander Love Lectures delivered at Ormond College.

be the rule of faith and life and that this is what the Holy Spirit testifies to the believer.

The third view had been advancing for 20 years past, and with the death of older men such as the Rev. Dr Robert Steel (1827–93) of St Stephen's Sydney, the shift that had occurred could be asserted more openly as by MacInnes in his NSW Moderator's address. The shift is well described in the Rev. Peter Barnes' published doctoral dissertation, *Living in a Half-way House: The Rise of Liberal Evangelicalism in the Presbyterian Church of New South Wales 1865–1915*.[74] Andrew Harper, who married Robert Rainy's daughter in 1892, was editor of the *Presbyterian Monthly* 1895–1902 and in 1901 moved to NSW to become the leading theological teacher there. Both he and Rentoul supported Yule's proposal that Yule's three positions be an acceptable peace platform.[75] On that basis the church moved on. But the change was much more significant than might at first appear. Harper was well aware of the implications and that the change on inspiration did not end with itself.[76] Rentoul's public statements put the best face on it:

> ...the authority of scripture depends on it being an adequate record through which the inner life and manifestation of God's character and grace, especially in his Son Jesus Christ, are made visible to men...Even if you could prove little blunders in the outer record, or defective knowledge, for example, in statements affecting matters of science or dates or various other matters, it would not in the least affect the truth and authority of the inner substance of the revelation of God's character and personality and redeeming grace for man.[77]

---

[74] Revespress Publications, Sydney 2007. In essentially the same form it was republished as *Theological Controversies in the Presbyterian Church of New South Wales 1865–1915* (New York: Edwin Mellon Press, 2008).

[75] *The Presbyterian*, 6 October 1894, 5.

[76] *Presbyterian Monthly*, December 1892, 397; see also Harper's lecture 'The influence of modern critical studies on the spiritual value of the Bible'- *Daily Telegraph* (Sydney), 14 April 1903, 3.

[77] 'The Verbal Theory. A Chat with Professor Rentoul' *Daily Telegraph* (Sydney) 23 April 1894, 5. Of course there is a sense in which Rentoul is right. The general trustworthiness of Scripture could provide a firm basis for Christianity. Yet, as Warfield says (*Works*, Vol. 1., 211): ' We do not think the doctrine of plenary inspiration is the ground of Christian faith, but if it was held and taught by the New Testament writers, we think it an element in the Christian faith; a very important and valuable element;...'

Some movement in Rentoul's higher critical views would be likely given the unstable foundation, just as is found in Delitzsch's final work *Messianic Prophecies in Historical Succession* (a translation of lectures in 1887 published in 1891), but I doubt much of any significance.[78]

Rentoul and Church Union

The desire to see greater unity among the colonial Presbyterian churches led to Conferences 1879–85, to a Federal Assembly from 1886 and ultimately to the Presbyterian Church of Australia [PCA] in 1901 as a federal union of the state-based churches, but with certain powers, especially doctrine, ceded to the new body. Rentoul, PCV Assembly Moderator in 1894–95, was significant in opposition. While wanting a simplified creed and supporting wider union among Protestants, the great concern he expressed was the maintenance of high standards for ministerial training.[79] These were slipping anyway by the mid-1890s what with financial shortages.

Wider union among Protestants was a theme of the PCA from its beginning and gained traction given Dr Andrew Harper, the prominent liberal-evangelical, gave his support to a Basis approved in 1918 largely in line with a similar proposal in Canada which was to lead to the United Church there in 1925. In 1908 David S. Adam (1859–1925) had became Professor of Church History and Theology at the Theological Hall in Melbourne. Although, ironically enough, Adam was from the Glasgow idealist philosophical tradition to which Charles Strong belonged,[80] he does not seem to have been overly provocative in the

[78] G. B. Stevens, *The Theology of the New Testament* (1899) was used in the Senior Class for many years being supplanted by H. A. A. Kennedy, *The Theology of the Epistles* (1919). Both held the newer theology but Stevens was a rather dogmatic American and Kennedy a scholarly Scot.

[79] Rentoul had been an Australian delegate to the *Alliance of Reformed Churches Holding the Presbyterian System* meeting in Toronto in 1892. When he spoke about the Presbyterian Church in Australia he said, '...they had seen the folly of forcing upon men shibboleths of extensive creeds not at all essential to living, thinking Christianity. They had seen the need of battling only for central truths which were the common foundation of Christendom,—not Calvinism nor Arminianism, but Christ Himself.' *Proceedings of the Fifth General Council* (Toronto: Hart and Riddell, 1892) 215–216.

[80] Adam was recommended as of 'the definite evangelical school' which meant to Scottish liberals that he sought to make the gospel meaningful in a changing world. Cf. Don

Hall setting. He was thoroughly ecumenical and a strong supporter of union with Methodists and Congregationalists. Rentoul, naturally enough for one of his background, strongly opposed the obliteration of the 'historic memories' of the Presbyterian Church in such a union. Rentoul was Moderator-General 1912–14 and in 1919 President of the newly formed Presbyterian Defence Association to oppose wider Church Union. The modernist Rev. Professor Samuel Angus of Sydney was Vice President. His argument against union was philosophical and theological and practical.[81] The proposed Basis drew heavily on the Canadian Basis that produced the United Church there in 1925, and was neither strictly orthodox or radically modernist and so still too specific and dogmatic for men like Angus.[82] The anti-unionist effort increased support modestly in most States, particularly among elders but dramatically in Victoria where 69.7% support in a second vote in state Assemblies in 1923 was achieved and some States failed to meet the constitutional threshold. For the time being wider union was dead and achieved only in 1977.

Rentoul the Controversialist

As well as a strong stand for Sabbath observance,[83] Rentoul had a number of battles with the claims of Rome. The Roman Catholic Archbishop Thomas Carr gave several lectures on 'The primacy of the Roman Pontiff'. Rentoul's public lectures in response were published in 1896 as *The Early Church and the Roman Claim,* including in an Appendix the correspondence between the two men in the public press.[84] Carr's poor scholarship was evident and Rentoul's book went

---

Chambers in McIntyre, *Ormond College Essays*, 113–114.

[81] Susan Emilsen, *A Whiff of Heresy: Samuel Angus and the Presbyterian Church in New South Wales* (University of New South Wales Press, 1991) 104–116.

[82] For Angus see Ward, *Presbyterians,* 249–269; also S. McN. Bonnington, 'The Religion About Jesus or The Religion Of Jesus? The Theological Formation of The Rev Dr Samuel Angus (1881–1943)' (unpublished PhD Thesis, Australian University of Theology, Sydney, 2024).

[83] Further to footnote 79 above, note Rentoul's comment in 1892 on the Sabbath in *Proceedings*, 343: 'on the vast harm in individual Christian life and Church life by the existence and reading of the Sunday newspaper' but also (at p. 223) his sensitivity in dealing with the State on sabbath observance matters.

[84] The book is readily accessible at <archive.org>. Rentoul also wrote three books of

to six printings. That Rentoul remained on good terms with Carr and his successor Daniel Mannix (1864–1963) reflects that all of them were Irish patriots who had common negative experiences from the English establishment, while the Rentoul clan, and Rentoul's father in particular, had played a prominent role in seeking tenant rights there. Rentoul was always kindly on a personal level and was respected by those who might strongly disagree with him on a particular issue. He supported Home Rule for Ireland in 1890s, and gave the public St Patrick's Day address in March 1901.[85] He was in favour of the introduction of Bible reading in public schools that had been excluded by the secularists, but not the way the 1904 referendum proposed to do it. Many thought him inconsistent but he saw it as an attempt to Protestantise the schools and divide society.[86] While in 1920 Rentoul conceded the rights of an Irish Free State, he was concerned about violence along the border with the dissenting counties of the north and had a decided preference for British law over Roman dominance and IRA thuggery.[87] Mannix took Ormond Rentoul (see below) into Roman Catholic institutional care when Rentoul's daughters could not cope.

In the interest of avoiding the social problems he saw in the United States, Rentoul supported the White Australia policy enshrined in the Immigration Restriction Act passed by the Commonwealth Government in 1901.[88] He was foundation chair of the Peace and Humanity Society in 1900 along with Charles Strong whose theology he had opposed while remaining his friend. The Society campaigned strongly against the Boer War. Rentoul saw it as a war of capitalist interest energised by jingoism but he was not in principle a pacifist. His concern for the underdog and those whom he regarded as oppressed by the powerful is evident and so any difficulty he might have had with involvement in the Great War was soon overcome. He was Chaplain General, A.I.F. in 1914–17, supported conscription but protected some of his students who in conscience refused to join up. He was appointed OBE in 1920 for his contribution to the war effort on the recommendation of Governor

poetry and a number of small items.

[85] *The Herald* (Melbourne), 16 March 1901, 4. It was a rousing address for a United Australia.

[86] *The Advocate*, 19 July 1902, 11–12; *Geelong Advertiser*, 6 May 1904, 4.

[87] *The Age* (Melbourne), 4 August 1920, 9.

[88] *The Herald*, 16 March 1901, 4.

General Sir Ronald Munro Ferguson, and this despite Fergusons' support of the Boer War.

Family Life

Laurence and Annie had six children. The first two—James and Elsie—died in infancy. Annie (1882), the third child, lived to a great age and died in 1978 unmarried. She taught Greek, Latin and ancient history at Presbyterian Ladies College with great distinction from 1913 and collaborated with Ida (1888–1960) in some of her sister's early work as an illustrator in the fairy tradition. Ida married in 1909 Arthur Outhwaite (1876–1938) and in later years lived with her sister Annie. John Noel Rentoul (1884) was no intellectual. Although having injured a leg in a railway accident, he signed up for the Great War in 1915 but if he had been maimed or injured he and his wife and child would have been dependent on the elderly Dr. Rentoul and his wife (who was in poor health following an accident). They already had responsibility for the youngest child, Alexander Ormond Rentoul (1892–1973). A gifted lad, Ormond 'lost his reason' in a breakdown in 1909 and was admitted to Mt Ida House in East Hawthorn in July 1910. Discharged in 1912 he was cared for within the family who employed a person to assist, but the Rentouls were not particularly wealthy. John's enlistment was promptly cancelled by the intervention of his brother-in-law.[89]

To recuperate his strength Rentoul regularly spent part of his summer holidays bicycling in Tasmania or trout fishing in New Zealand with his friends such as the Rev. Samuel Robinson (1841–99) of St Kilda; John MacFarland (1851–1935), the Master of Ormond and a great administrator; and H. B. Higgins (1851–1929) politician and judge. These men were all Ulstermen. He also enjoyed gardening.

Rentoul stumbled and fell at Spencer Street Railway Station (now Southern Cross) on 15 April 1926. He was carried into the cloak room but it was too late. His last words were an apology to the porter who tended him for the inconvenience he had caused him. In a lengthy obituary *The Age* wrote:

---

[89] See National Archives of Australia, Series B2455 (First AIF, Personnel dossiers) Rentoul, John Noel.

> Dr. Rentoul will long be remembered for his erudition, his versatility, his great powers of debate, his forceful and uncompromising opinions. But, though he was a ferocious debater, an antagonist to be feared on the public platform, and though his sermons were strong in tone and vigorous in delivery, as a private individual he was the kindest of men, generous to a fault, possessed of a most winsome manner. He would do anything to help anyone - even a foe. As one churchman said, 'He would hit you hard between the eyes, flooring you, and then he would give all his assistance in helping you to rise.' He was an energetic speaker, and many of the Presbyterian assemblies are remembered for his debate. He was impatient of restraint, and despite all the protests of a chairman, he would speak for an hour and a half when the limit was supposed to be ten minutes. Small surprise that he earned the name of 'Fighting Larry,' for he was ever ready to enter into a controversy with anyone and he was a great controversial correspondent. He was possessed of keen wit which he used to best advantage whenever he found an opportunity.[90]

I put a question mark in the title of this essay. Rentoul was certainly a remarkable man bordering on genius, as many said, but Rentoul was not a defender of the full-orbed Reformed faith, nor of the doctrine of Scripture that was the heritage of Christendom. However, he did aim to defend the heart of Christian faith against a secular onslaught and only those who do not think that they too are creatures of their own time should be quick to condemn. His colleague Jollie Smith said:

> I never knew anyone whose heart was so anchored in the Gospel of 'God be merciful to me a sinner.' The Cross was all in all to him...The one hymn he would always have was: 'Mine is the sin, but thine the righteousness;/ Mine is the guilt but thine the cleansing blood;/ Here is my robe, my refuge and my peace –/ Thy blood, thy righteousness, O Lord my God.' [Horatius Bonar]

The Rev. K. D. Forster (1875–1945), who studied under Rentoul, wrote a half dozen verses on Rentoul's passing. I quote the last to conclude this study:[91]

[90] *The Age*, 16 April 1926, 9. Other important tributes are in *The Presbyterian Messenger*, 23 April 1926 and 30 April 1926.

[91] *The Presbyterian Messenger*, 23 April 1926, 267. JLR's will was dated 16 August 1916 and the estate was valued at £1,191.14.6d. His wife was to receive the income for her

His soul has passed!

That mighty soul which dwelt in such frail shell;

And those great mysteries of which he sought to tell,

To him are plain at last.

---

life, then half the income to daughter Annie and half for the benefit of his son Ormond. Ultimately the estate was to be divided equally between surviving children or their children.

Part 3
The Outworking in Biblical Theology

Ten

The Age of Augustus and the Age of Jesus Christ: Reading Luke 1–4 in its Historical Pastoral Context

Wesley Redgen

This chapter is a plea to all who read the New Testament (which should be everyone who names Jesus Christ as Lord) to re-capture the vision of the riches of insight that can be found in reading the Scriptures in their historical pastoral context. The New Testament is a deeply theological document. However, it does not deliver its theological truths to us as an ahistorical theology textbook. Luke, the topic of this investigation, presents God the Son breaking into human history incarnated as the Jewish Christ in First Century Palestine under the rule of the Roman Emperor Augustus. Luke's presentation of Jesus comes to us in the form of an historical work written for a real man, Theophilus, who had the pastoral need to 'have certainty concerning the things [he had] been taught' (Luke 1:4). The Scriptures are written to be read theologically, historically and pastorally.[1]

My prayer is that this case study, which reads Luke 1–4 in its historical pastoral context, will strengthen our resolve always to read the New Testament historically. May we experience the pleasure and appreciate the value of historical endeavour in reading our New Testaments. Why should the church historians and historical theologians have all the fun?

The main thesis of this chapter is that when Luke 1–4 is read in its historical pastoral context, it becomes clear that Luke is writing to give Theophilus and the wider readership 'certainty concerning the things

[1] It is right to be wary of historical criticism practiced in a way that undermines the Scriptures' authority, inspiration and inerrancy. However, if this leads us to shy away from reading the Scriptures historically, we have let the pendulum swing too far in the other direction.

[they have] been taught.' After a consideration of the historical and pastoral relationships between Luke, Paul, and Theophilus and associates, this chapter will consider three ways in which Luke 1–4 brings certainty. First, it provides historical certainty as to the facts about Jesus which they had received through Paul's gospel. Secondly, it gives certainty that Jesus is the Christ in the face of opposition from the local synagogues. Thirdly, it brings certainty in Jesus the Christ in the midst of their historical and cultural world that promoted the Roman emperors as the divine bearers of salvation and peace. At no stage does this historical research change our understanding of the theological truths. However, it brings those truths into sharper focus and shows how these truths were always designed to be applied to bring certainty to Christians living in a world that challenges those truths.

Luke, Theophilus, and the Pauline Churches: Why the Identity of Luke and Theophilus Matter

From one perspective, the answer to why Luke wrote his Gospel is clear and simple: to tell us about Jesus. All humanity needs salvation in Jesus. However, he did not construct his Gospel in a theological vacuum separated from the world in which he and his readers lived. Luke wrote to Theophilus 'that you may have certainty concerning the things you have been taught' (Luke 1:4).[2] As Luke sat writing with a multitude of historical eyewitness accounts on the table before him, his knowledge of Theophilus and Theophilus' need of certainty shaped his editorial choices of what to include and what to leave out. Luke was not just writing a theological account of Jesus, or just a history. His Gospel is historical, theological, and pastoral all at the same time. The first step toward reading Luke 1–4 in its historical pastoral context is to consider the identities of Luke, Theophilus, and those beyond Theophilus whom Luke also expected to read Luke 1–4.

Luke: Paul's Co-worker

Paul's references to Luke reveal that Luke was one of Paul's co-workers who travelled with him around the Mediterranean. In Philemon 24,

[2] Unless otherwise noted, biblical quotations in this chapter are from the ESV.

Paul lists Luke as one of his inner circle of co-workers who ministered to him in prison, and acted on his behalf beyond the prison. In Colossians 4:14 Paul calls Luke 'the beloved physician.' This suggests a close relationship; possibly, also that Luke was Paul's personal doctor. When Paul later wrote to Timothy from jail toward the end of his life, many of Paul's co-workers either had deserted him, or Paul had sent them off to continue the gospel work in other places. Luke alone was still with Paul (2 Tim. 4:11).

Luke's own account of Paul's ministry journeys in Acts confirms his involvement in many of the events of Paul's ministry. Taking note of when Luke uses 'we' in his accounts of Paul's journeys informs us where and when Luke was a participant in the action with Paul.[3] Luke first joined Paul while Paul was in Troas on his second journey (Acts 16:8–10). He accompanied Paul as far as Philippi, but the account no longer uses 'we' as Paul moved on to Thessalonica (Acts 16:40). This suggests that Paul left Luke in Philippi. Four years later, as Paul returned back through Philippi, Luke resumes using 'we' (Acts 20:3–5). Luke re-joined Paul and continued with him to Jerusalem (Acts 21:17). The fact that Luke resumed accompanying Paul from the same place that Paul had left him suggests that Paul may have left Luke in Philippi as his co-worker to carry on the Philippian ministry for him. Luke had done his job in Philippi and now Paul needed him for the next stage of ministry.[4] He remained with Paul until they arrived in Rome two years later (Acts 28:1). Although we have no knowledge of Luke's movements in the intervening two years between Paul's first imprisonment in Rome (Acts 28) and his second imprisonment prior to his execution, Luke (alone) was still with Paul right at the end (2 Tim. 4:11).[5]

---

[3] Questions about the historical veracity of the Lucan corpus have only emerged in recent centuries and have been answered adequately. E.g. I. H. Marshal, *Luke: Historian and Theologian* (1971 reprinted and updated, Downers Grove, IL: IVP, 1998).

[4] This suggested reconstruction of the 'silent' four years cannot be conclusively asserted. However, it makes the most sense of the available evidence. Nor does this reconstruction rule out that Luke may have made trips to other places for Paul in that four-year period. Whether the details of this reconstruction are accepted or not, the basic premise stands that Luke was one of Paul's trusted co-workers.

[5] Approx. AD 64. This was during Nero's persecution of Christians following the fire of Rome.

Therefore, even though we have no extant letter from Paul to Luke, such as Titus and Timothy received, Luke was a long-term co-worker in Paul's ministry. He would have been known and respected in many of the Pauline churches as one of Paul's trusted inner circle of co-workers.

Theophilus: Luke's Patron

Luke's Gospel is addressed to 'most excellent Theophilus.' We have no evidence of the specific identity of Theophilus. However, the historical context guides us to certain conclusions.

Luke wrote to give Theophilus 'certainty concerning the things you have been taught' (Luke 1:4). Theophilus had already been taught about Jesus. The word translated 'taught' was used commonly in early Christian writings for the basic instruction of new believers.[6] He was most likely a believer. However, Theophilus was not the average congregational member. He was high on the social ladder. The address 'Most Excellent' (κράτιστε) implies that Theophilus was a person of influence in society.[7] The term was used commonly of people of the equestrian order.[8] In Acts 23:26 it is used of Felix, who was an equestrian and prefect over Judea.[9] The style of Luke's Gospel is consistent with this. Luke and Acts both are written in polished Greek for a well-educated readership.[10] The introduction (Luke 1:1–4) conforms to the opening

[6] '**κατηχέω**,' in Danker, Fredrick W., Walter Baer, William F. Ardt, and F. Wilbur Gingrinch, eds. *A Greek-English Lexicon of the New Testament and other Early Christian Literature*. 3rd ed. (Chicago: University of Chicago, 2000), 534. The English word 'catechize' is derived from this word.

[7] Some have speculated that because Theophilus means 'friend of God,' he was a fictitious character who is representative of all Christians. However, the use of the title κράτιστε, together with the patronal dedication formula, would be out of place for such a purpose. Theophilus was a common Greek name.

[8] BGAG '**κράτιστος**, η, **ον**,' 565. While the common English translations rightly imply nobility and honour, the etymology of the word implies power and influence. In a society driven by glory and honour, the two concepts were inter-related. People with power and influence were the nobility who were honoured.

[9] Felix was Governor of Judea, which came under the Roman Province of Syria. Felix was Prefect answerable directly to the Governor of Syria who was answerable directly to the Emperor.

[10] Marshall, *Luke*, 39–40. The exception is where Luke was alluding to the LXX or sometimes in parts of stories unique to his Gospel. He appears to do this to capture authen-

paragraph of a well-written history of the time.[11] Luke also has many features in common with moral biographies of the time.[12] Such literary works were designed to be read aloud in performance in polite society. It was common practice to dedicate these works to a patron who had sponsored the writing.[13] Theophilus was probably Luke's patron. This both honoured Theophilus as Patron, and also Theophilus' name gave the work credibility. So, while Luke's Gospel is addressed to Theophilus, it was always intended for a wider readership, for whom the dedication to 'most excellent Theophilus' had meaning.[14]

The Intended Readers Beyond Theophilus: The Pauline Churches

So who constituted Luke's intended wider readership? The obvious answer is the Pauline churches. However, why would Luke write to the Pauline churches in a style that was appropriate for the elite of the Greco-Roman world? A quick survey of the cities Paul visited in Acts, and of the cities to which he wrote letters, soon reveals that Paul focused on the centres of influence within the Greco-Roman world: Roman

---

tically, for effect, the unpolished language of his original Jewish source. (Compare how a modern preacher may quote the language of the KJV at times or how, in story mode, we may slip into the language style of the character in the story.) Luke consistently corrected and polished Mark's Greek in passages where Mark was his source. Wesley Redgen, *A Comparison of the language and grammar of the parallel passages in Luke and Mark* [Unpublished Thesis BA (Hons) (Classical Greek) UNE, 1994].

[11] Darryl W. Palmer, 'Acts and the Ancient Historical Monograph' in *The Book of Acts in its First Century Setting, Vol.1*. Edited by Bruce W. Winter and Andrew D. Clarke (Grand Rapids, MI: Eerdmans, 1993); W. J. McCoy, 'In the Shadow of Thucydides' in *History, Literature, and Society in the Book of Acts*. Edited by Ben Witherington III (Cambridge: CUP, 1996), 3–32. For a contrary viewpoint see: Loveday C. A. Alexander, 'The Preface to Acts and the Historians' in *History, Literature, and Society in the Book of Acts*. Edited by Ben Witherington III (Cambridge: CUP, 1996), 73–103.

[12] Charles H. Talbert, 'The Acts of the Apostles: Monograph or *bios*?' in *History, Literature, and Society in the Book of Acts*. Edited by Ben Witherington III (Cambridge: CUP, 1996), 58–72.

[13] E.g. Josephus, *Contra Apionem* 2.1 'In the first volume of this work, my most esteemed Epaphroditus, I demonstrated the antiquity of our race ... '

[14] There was a Bishop Theophilus in Antioch in the mid-second century. Perhaps there is some connection? Perhaps a son or grandson?

provincial capitals of the Empire (Syrian Antioch, Paphos, Pisidian Antioch,[15] Philippi, Corinth, Ephesus, Rome); the larger Greek cites around them (Thessalonica, Athens, Troas); and Roman colonies (Iconium, Lystra, Derbe). Although many other Greek cities and Roman colonies are mentioned (E.g. Perge, Assos, Amphipolis, Colossae, Laodicea), the big picture is that Paul moved East to West, from centre of influence to centre of influence.[16] By the time Luke wrote, several decades after the earlier events of Acts, there were now churches in many other lesser Greek cities and Roman colonies surrounding these larger centres, but the original Pauline church plants were their mother churches (Acts 19:10).[17]

Acts shows us that Paul's churches often rose out of his synagogue preaching. However, while they included a foundation of Jewish members, many of them included Gentiles right from the start (Acts 13:43–48; 14:1; 17:4, 12, 34; 18:8). Consistently, the gospel spread quickly among the Gentiles of the city and region (E.g. Acts 13:49, 19:10). Two of Paul's earliest letters were written to predominantly Gentile congregations even though the churches started in the synagogues (Gal. 4:8; Acts 13:14, 14:1; 1 Thess. 1:9; Acts 17:1–2).

Not only were the early churches a mixture of Jews and Gentiles, they also included people from a variety of positions on the social scale. For example, the church in Philippi began with a wealthy merchant, a prison guard's household, and, perhaps, a slave girl (Acts 16:14, 18, 33). Soon after, Paul described the Macedonian churches giving despite their own extreme poverty (2 Cor. 8:1–2). The church in Corinth started with the households of a Roman God-fearer and the ruler of the synagogue (Acts 18:7–8). Later, Paul could write (1 Cor. 1:26–27) that not many of them were noble or powerful by the world's standards.

---

[15] Anchora was actually the capital of Galatia but Pisidian Antioch was the second city and the centre of influence on the main Roman road through the south of the province. The governor's prefect was based in Antioch to watch over the South of the province for the governor based in Anchora.

[16] The exception to the pattern is where the Lord in his wisdom forbade Paul to enter Asia (Ephesus) (Acts 16:6). Paul later backtracked to cover that base.

[17] Note how the church in Colossae was planted by one of Paul's disciples, presumably from Ephesus during Paul's time there. By the time John wrote Revelation, Ephesus was ringed by churches in the surrounding cities of Asia.

Although Paul highlights that 'not many were noble or powerful' to make his theological point, both Acts and Paul's letters note that these first Gentile converts included people of influence (Acts 16:14–15; 17:4, 12, 34; 18:7–8). These people would have become the patrons of the new churches. Luke does not spell this out because Theophilus and the Pauline churches understood how it all worked. Under Roman law it was illegal to gather as an unregistered association. Synagogues and churches, along with a myriad of other religious cults of the day, found their place in the Greco-Roman cities as registered associations. In fact, the words 'synagogue' (συναγωγή) and 'church' (ἐκκλησία) were both common words that described the gathering of registered associations of many types.[18] Such associations needed an influential patron to give them legitimacy, and often met in the patron's house. These rich, influential patrons were the public face of the association, the association's protector in society, and, often, became the leader of the association by default because of their social standing. Theophilus himself was probably one of these church patrons. Paul's greetings, in the introductions and conclusions of his letters, to the people in whose house the church met are culturally appropriate greetings to such patrons of the churches (Rom. 16:3–5, 10, 11; 2 Tim. 4:19). In most cult-based associations this leader/patron was also the officiating priest of the association's god. However, churches differed from their pagan (and even Jewish) counterparts in two significant ways. First, social leadership of the church was not the means of self-accumulation of honour and influence that it was in most associations. The church patrons were not to lord it over their clients as their pagan counterparts did. They were to be brother protectors of the socially lowly members under one Lord and master.[19] Secondly, the Pauline churches practiced a distinction between what we might call 'spiritual leadership' (pastor and teacher, elders and overseers, deacons) and the social leadership (patrons and head of the synagogue/church). It is not clear how these

[18] Philip A. Harland, *Associations, Synagogues, and Congregations* (Minneapolis: Fortress, 2003), 177–78.

[19] Luke's focus on the poor throughout his Gospel is highlighting this for the Pauline churches. Much more could be said about how Luke's Gospel promotes values and practices that were counter-cultural to the normal practice within associations and Greco-Roman society as a whole. However, that is another study.

two strands of leadership co-existed because the Scriptures focus on the appointment of, and instructions to, the 'spiritual leadership.' From some of Paul's greetings, it seems that some people were both patrons and ministry leaders (E.g. Philemon 1–2). Judge argues that the gospel spread quickly in cities because the influential converts spread the gospel through their client base.[20]

In summary, the social world of the Pauline churches for whom Luke wrote was that of the Greco-Roman cities of the Empire. Their membership was predominantly Gentiles. Although the churches contained people from all stations in life, they were led by the elite in whose houses they met and under whose patronage they were protected. Theophilus was one such patron. Luke wrote in the style of an educated historian for two reasons. First, because he was an educated historian. Secondly, he wrote in the style that the elite patron leaders of the Pauline churches expected for reliable history.[21]

Luke dedicated his work to Theophilus, but his intended audience was always the wider circle of the Pauline churches. The important point is that Luke and his readers knew each other. They understood Luke's position of authority as a loyal co-worker endorsed by the apostle Paul (2 Tim. 4:11) and, following Paul's death, as one of the guardians Paul entrusted to guard the good deposit (2 Tim. 1:13; 2:2). Luke, on his part, understood their context and pastoral struggles. It does not matter that we do not know any more than we do about Theophilus' identity or location. Acts and Paul's letters show us that while the specific details of each city and church varied, there were common issues that regularly arose for Christians living in the Greco-Roman cities of the Empire. These predominantly Gentile churches of the Empire needed certainty in three main areas. First, they needed certainty that the gospel they received from Paul (and his co-workers) was historically reliable. Secondly, they needed certainty that Jesus was the promised Christ in the

[20] E. A. Judge, *The First Christians in the Roman World* (Tübingen: Mohr Siebeck, 2008), 465, 530.

[21] While Mark's Gospel is reliable and inspired, the educated elite patrons of the Pauline churches would have been embarrassed to have its street Greek read aloud in their homes. A Gospel account suited to educated Greco-Romans was needed to enhance the spread of the gospel message among the cities of the Empire.

face of opposition from the local synagogue. Thirdly, they needed certainty that Jesus was the Lord, as they lived under the shadow of the Roman expectation of loyalty and devotion to the Emperor. After dealing with the first two in brief, the rest of this chapter shall focus on how Luke 1–4 applies its message to address this third, all-invasive aspect of life in the Greco-Roman cities of the Empire.

Historical Pastoral Issue 1: The Need of Eyewitness Certainty About Jesus' Life, Death and Resurrection

Luke wrote because he knew the Pauline churches needed the certainty of a reliable eyewitness account. Paul, their spiritual father, by self-acknowledgement was not an eyewitness of the life, death, (pre-Pentecost) resurrection or ascension of Jesus. By the time Luke was writing (approx. AD 70–80), the Jesus about whom Paul preached had lived, died and risen several decades earlier in another country and cultural setting. There were few living eyewitnesses. Perhaps John was the only apostle still alive. Mark's Gospel existed already, but the authority behind it was Peter and it was not written in a style of Greek respected by the Greco-Roman elite.[22] Matthew's Gospel probably also already existed, but it was written with an orientation to Jewish Palestinian concerns. Luke wrote to give the Pauline churches historical eyewitness certainty from someone they knew and trusted with known connections to Paul.

He also wrote in the literary style of a credible Roman historian acceptable to the elite in the Greco-Roman cities of the Empire. He fixed the dates of the key events by the reigns of the Roman Emperors and Governors (Luke 2:1–2, 3:1), so that they could understand how it lined up with their world. This literary and historical style did not make his account more reliable than the previous Gospels, but it enhanced its acceptance as reliable history for his intended readers.

[22] Although Peter and Paul's conflict in Antioch (Gal. 2) was long resolved, its memory may have lingered in the Pauline churches.

Historical Pastoral Issue 2: The Need for Certainty in the Face of Synagogue Opposition

Acts makes clear that one of the key threats faced by the Pauline churches was opposition from the local synagogue in two forms: a contrary gospel and persecution. They often refuted Paul's teaching that Jesus was the Christ and that justification was by faith alone, not by works prescribed by the Torah (E.g. Acts 13:38–45). Paul often needed to write letters to his churches and his co-workers to defend his gospel from others who presented a Jewish synagogue gospel that was not a gospel at all (e.g. Gal. 1:6–7; 1 Cor. 1:22–24; Col. 2:16–17; 1 Tim. 1:6–7; Titus 1:10). By the time Luke wrote, several decades after Paul, Paul's churches were still in that same pastoral situation. The synagogue's teaching still remained a serious threat to Paul's gospel.[23] A serious pastoral question they faced was, 'Why did the Gentile Pauline churches believe Jesus was the Jewish Christ, when the synagogue did not?' Luke 1–4 is designed to give them certainty that Jesus was indeed the prophesied Christ.[24]

However, the pastoral situation was more complex than just the theological question of Paul's gospel versus the synagogue's 'gospel.' Acts records how the Jews were often quick to stir up persecution against Paul and his gospel (e.g. Acts 13:50; 14:2–5; 14:19). The Jews even made accusations to the Romans that Paul's gospel that Jesus was the Christ was a message of treason to Caesar (Acts 17:2–8).[25] At times, Paul's letters encourage his churches to endure persecution from the Jews (e.g. Gal. 3:4, 4:29).

---

[23] Mitchell comments that Judaising tendencies remained a problem in the churches of Asia, even into the Fourth Century. S. Mitchell, Anatolia: *Land, Men, and Gods in Asia Minor, 2 Vols.*
(Oxford: Clarendon, 1993), 2:35.

[24] As Luke and Acts unfold, the message is built that they as Gentiles who are justified by faith are indeed the heirs of the promises of the age of the Christ. In contrast, unbelieving Jews who attend the synagogue are not heirs because they have rejected their own Christ.

[25] Luke and Acts also make clear that the Jews are culpable for rejecting their own Christ.

As Luke wrote a decade or two later, despite the Roman-Jewish war, the Jews of Asia Minor and Greece were still influential in the cities where Paul's churches were located.[26] Revelation links the persecution of the Christians in Smyrna (Rev. 2:9) and Philadelphia (Rev. 3:8–10) to the local synagogues.[27]

This raises a more intense pastoral question: 'Why should the churches persevere in faith in Jesus as the Christ if that could lead to the synagogue stirring up persecution?' Luke's extended presentation of Jesus as the prophesied Christ in Luke 1–4 runs deeper than simply assuring the Pauline churches that Jesus is the Christ. It was designed to give certainty that Jesus is the Christ in the face of opposition from both the local synagogue and from certain people with Judaising tendencies that arose from within the churches. This is a study in itself, but is not the focus of this chapter.[28]

Historical Pastoral Issue 3: The Need for Certainty in the World of the Roman Caesars

Luke historically dates the birth of Jesus vaguely within the reign of Herod (Luke 1:5). However, he specifies the exact time of Jesus' birth within the reign of Caesar Augustus and Caesar's Governor of the province of Syria (Luke 2:1–2). He precisely dates the beginning of Jesus' ministry within the reign of the Roman Emperor Tiberius, and of the Emperor's governor and client kings (Luke 3:1–3). This signals for the reader that the long-anticipated Christ arrived within the reign of Augustus Caesar. Although Luke was writing for Christians living several decades after the reign of Augustus Caesar, the man and the myth still dominated the psyche of the entire Roman Empire. This juxtaposition

---

[26] The Emperors Vespasian (AD 69–79) and his son Titus (AD 79–81) had led the Roman forces against the Jews in the Jewish war (AD 66–72). Although Titus' brother Domitian (AD 81–96) had not served in the war, his actions against the Jews as Emperor showed he had no love for them. However, the Jews of Asia Minor and Greece had taken no part in the war and so were considered as loyal to Rome.

[27] The persecution in Pergamum is unlikely to have come from the Jews (Rev. 2:13–14).

[28] See Wesley Redgen, *The Gospel Meets Persecution in Galatia: An historical reading of Galatians in the light of Acts 13:13–14:23* (Unpublished PhD, University of Queensland, 2016). A book by the same title is in production.

of the arrival of the promised Christ with the reign of Augustus Caesar prompts the reader to draw comparisons. In order for modern readers to understand the natural comparisons that the original readers would have made, a brief overview of the public persona of Augustus Caesar and his successors is needed.

The Dawning of the Age of Augustus

Octavian Caesar defeated Marc Antony in 31 BC, ending the Roman civil wars that intermittently had rolled on for decades. He was proclaimed 'imperator' (leader) by the army and honoured by the Roman Senate with the name 'Augustus,' which means 'revered.'[29] His victory brought peace and saved the Roman world from devastating protracted civil wars.[30] It enabled the Romans to stop fighting among themselves and instead focus on securing their borders and maintaining peace within those borders. He quickly fortified his military and political position. Augustus had the political cunning never to declare himself sole ruler. Rome was still technically a republic ruled by the Senate. Nevertheless, the influence and authority of one man controlled the Senate, the legions, the chief priesthood, and the significant provinces.

In addition, he also embarked on a program of propaganda to ensure his authority and honour as 'the revered one' was unquestioned. It was common practice for the leading noble Roman families to trace their ancestry back to a god. However, up until this point, no Roman leader had dared to suggest that any recent ancestor had possessed divinity. Augustus, who was the adopted son of his uncle Julius Caesar, initiated an innovation when he had the Senate declare the deceased Julius Caesar deified. This entitled Augustus to be called 'the son of a god.'

Augustus also commissioned the poet Virgil to write the *Aeneid*, a history of Rome from mythological time to the present. The *Aeneid* positioned Augustus as the descendant of Rome's founder, Aeneas,

---

[29] 'Roman Emperors' in *DNTB*, 969.

[30] His coins regularly feature the goddesses Victory and Peace. Paul Zanker, *The Power of images in the Age of Augustus* (Ann Arbor, MI: University of Michigan Press, 1990), 54, 55, 188.

and as the fulfilment of prophecies of Rome's destiny. Virgil hailed the reign of Augustus (31 BC – AD 14) as the beginning of a whole new golden age:

> This, this is he whom so often you hear promised to you, Augustus Caesar, son of a god, who shall again set up the golden age in Latium amid the fields where Saturn once reigned and shall spread his empire ... to a land that lies beyond the stars. (*Aeneid* VI, 791–5 published 19 BC)

Horace, likewise, proclaimed the reign of Augustus as the beginning of a new age:

> Thine age, O Caesar, has brought back fertile crops to the fields, … has wiped away our sins and revived the ancient virtues, … and the fame and majesty of our empire were spread from the sun's bed in the west to the east. As long as Caesar is the guardian of the state, neither civil dissension nor violence shall banish peace. (*Odes* 4.15, published 13 BC)

One of the most significant landmarks in Augustan Rome was the *Ara Pacis Augustae* (The Altar of Augustan Peace) commissioned by the Senate and consecrated in 9 BC. The symbolism on this altar is rich. On one panel is Aeneas, the founder of Rome, veiled as priest, sacrificing with his sons. On another panel is Augustus, veiled as chief priest (Pontifex Maximus), with his family leading the Roman Senate in sacrifice. Augustus was re-founding a new Rome. The peace of Rome (*Pax Romana*) was dependent on peace from the gods (*Pax Deorum*). Augustus had achieved it all. As Imperator he had brought military and political peace. As Pontifex Maximus he ensured divine peace.

The message was clear. Augustus was the son of a god, the saviour of the world who had inaugurated a new age of peace. Surviving inscriptions demonstrate the extent to which this message from Rome was embraced enthusiastically across the cities of the Empire. Even during Augustus' lifetime the rise of temples to worship various members of the Imperial Augustan family was rapid and widespread, especially

One scene on the Ara Pacis depicting Aeneas, veiled as priest, sacrificing with his sons at the original founding of Rome. (Photo by Gillian Law)

A corresponding scene on the Ara Pacis depicting Augustus Caesar, veiled as Pontifex Maximus, leading the Roman Senate in sacrifice. (Photo by Gillian Law)

throughout the Greek east where most of the Pauline churches were located.[31] These imperial cult temples dominated the landscape of the cities. There were multiple factors that fed into this rapid rise. For the present topic, it is sufficient to note that it happened.[32] A few examples of public inscriptions from the Greco-Roman cities of the Empire will suffice to demonstrate the extent of the veneration of Augustus. These are all from Roman Asia Minor, south of Ephesus (modern South-West Turkey).

An inscription under a statue of Caesar Augustus in Myra in Lycia (undated):

> The God Augustus, Son of God, Caesar, absolute ruler of land and sea, the Benefactor and Saviour of the whole cosmos, the people of Myra [have set up this statue].

An inscription from a public Calendar in Priene (dated 9 BC):

> Whereas the Providence which has guided our whole existence and which has shown such care and liberality, has brought our life to the peak of perfection in giving to us Augustus Caesar, whom it filled with virtue for the welfare of mankind, and who, being sent to us and to our descendants as a saviour, has put an end to war and has set all things in order.

An inscription from Halicarnassus (dated after 2 BC):

> Since the eternal and deathless nature of the universe has perfected its immense benefits to mankind in granting us as a supreme benefit, for our happiness and welfare, Caesar Augustus, Father of his own Fatherland,

---

[31] There was not just one Imperial cult to Augustus. There were multiple Imperial cults devoted to various members of the Imperial family; e.g. in Ephesus, there was a temple to the deified Julius Caesar. From AD 89 there was a temple to the Flavian Dynasty. In Corinth, the main Imperial cult temple was to Octavia (Augustus' older sister who was, by logic, the daughter of a god and also deified after her death). For a comprehensive discussion of the topic see S.R.F. Price, *Rituals and Power: The Roman Imperial Cult in Asia Minor* (Cambridge: CUP, 1984).

[32] Price, *Rituals and Power*, 5–7.

> divine Rome, Zeus Paternal, and Saviour of the whole human race, in whom Providence has not only fulfilled but even surpassed the prayers of all men: land and sea are at peace, cities flourish under the reign of law, in mutual harmony and prosperity; each is at the very acme of fortune and abounding in wealth; all mankind is filled with glad hopes for the future, and with contentment over the present; [it is fitting to honour the god Augustus] with public games and with statues, with sacrifices and with hymns.

As the empire passed from Augustus to his Julio-Claudian successors, and then to the Flavian dynasty, 'the Peace of Augustus' (*Pax Augustea*) was retitled 'the Peace of Rome' (*Pax Romana*).[33]

The Post Augustan World of Theophilus

By the time Luke wrote, the Julio-Claudian dynasty had collapsed with the demise of the reputation of Nero and his subsequent suicide (AD 68). In the early years of Nero's reign (AD 54–68), he was praised as reviving the age of Augustus.[34] However, those hopes fell flat. None of Augustus' Julio-Claudian successors quite lived up to his glory, at least not to the image and the myth.

Following the suicide of Nero in disgrace, the civil wars of AD 68–69 disposed of three successive emperors in one year before the Flavian dynasty gained the upper hand. The Flavian dynasty (AD 69–96), which had emerged victorious from the civil wars of AD 68–69, still fashioned itself as Augustan.[35] All later Emperors attempted to position themselves as Augustus' successors in an attempt to carry the glory of his reputation and authority. The cults of the deified Augustus and the Julio-Claudian dynasty still dominated both the landscape and

---

[33] The earliest extant use of *Pax Romana is from Seneca, De Clementia* I, 4.

[34] Calpurnius Siculus I. 42; Seneca, *Apocoloyntosis* 4.I, 8–32; *De Clementia* I, I.

[35] The Imperial cult temple that dominated Ephesus (after AD 89) is known to tourists as the Temple of Domitian because of the colossal statue of Domitian found there. However, inscriptions show that this temple was designated to 'the *sebastoi*' (the Greek translation of the Augustans), when it was in fact devoted to the Flavian dynasty (Vespasian AD 69–79, Titus 79–81, Domitian 81–96). While the temple of Ephesus' patron goddess Artemis was one of the wonders of the ancient world, it was a few kilometres out of town. The city itself was dominated by the temple to the Augustans (= Flavians).

the psyche of the Greco-Roman cities of the Empire. In some cities, this continued even into the second century. The utopian ideal of the age of Augustus still encapsulated how Augustus' successors wished their reigns to be viewed and expressed the hopes and dreams of the Greco-Roman cities of the Empire. However, all now realised that the salvation and peace inaugurated by the age of Augustus was far from enduring. The shine of the glory of the age of Augustus was fading.

There was also another, darker side to the story. The Peace of Rome had two sides to it. On the one hand, it did bring freedom from war (generally speaking), safe and efficient trade and travel, economic security and infrastructure benefits to the cities and all who lived in them.[36] On the other hand, the price for it all was subjugation and domination by Rome (along with taxes and conscription to the auxiliary forces attached to the legions). It was not uncommon for Roman officials to exploit the provinces over which they ruled for their own personal financial benefit. It is debatable whether the average non-Roman across the Empire enjoyed the salvation and peace in the way the Roman propaganda boasted or whether they were more the victims of the *Pax Romana* rather than the beneficiaries.[37]

For the significant Jewish population of the Empire, the Jewish War of AD 66–72, including the destruction of Jerusalem and the temple, could hardly have endeared them to the salvation and peace of the *Pax Romana*. Even the less devout and more Romanised among the Jews must have felt their Jewish hopes dashed, rather than fulfilled.

This was the world of the Pauline churches. A world where the salvation and peace of the *Pax Romana* was the ideal and hope held out by those who ruled the cities. A world where citizens were required to pledge loyalty to the Emperor, often in the form of offerings to Augustus and Roma.[38] Yet it was also a world where, even for the 'true believers,' the shine had gone off the golden age inaugurated by

---

[36] Infrastructure benefits such as roads, aqueducts, fountains, baths, theatres, etc.

[37] Tacitus (*Histories* IV 17, 2) records the words of Civilis prince of the Batavians (a German tribe who rebelled against Rome in AD 69), 'he reminded them of the miseries that they had endured so many years while they falsely called their servitude a peace.'

[38] Even well into the reign of the Flavians, the combined worship of Augustus and Roma remained the most common Imperial cult.

Augustus. A world where for some the Peace of Rome was actually code for subjugation and domination by Rome.

Into this world, Luke proclaims the arrival of Jesus the Christ, the Son of God, to bring salvation and peace, and he explicitly sets the inauguration of his kingdom within the reign of Caesar Augustus. This historical context brings clarity to Luke's intention. For the Pauline churches living within this social milieu, Luke 1–4 is setting up a deliberate contrast between the glorious age of Augustus and the age of Israel's Messiah, our Lord Jesus Christ.[39]

Reading Luke 1–4 in Its Historical Pastoral Context

For the Pauline Churches living in this world, Luke explicitly locates the incarnation of Christ within the reign of Augustus to compel his readers to understand Luke 1–4 in this context. This juxtaposition of Christ with Caesar works to deliver 'certainty of what they had been taught' in two different, but complementary, ways.

Christ and Caesar: speaking the language of their world

Luke is presenting Christ to the Pauline churches of the Greco-Roman cities in cultural models they could grasp easily. For example, Augustus as saviour provides a conceptual framework for Gentiles with little or no knowledge of the Old Testament to understand that Jesus is the saviour who brings peace. As they grew in their knowledge of the Scriptures, the Old Testament and Pauline concepts of peace with God would refine and sanctify their understanding of peace and even supplant Augustus as the conceptual framework through which they first understood the coming of the Christ.

To be clear, Augustus and the successive Roman emperors did not determine Luke's understanding of the identity and ministry of Jesus. His understanding and presentation of Jesus as the Christ was based firmly on the prophetic promises of the Old Testament, the historical events of the birth of Jesus, and the teaching of Paul and the other apostles. He understood Jesus from the divine self-revelation. However, Luke as historian and theologian crafted the way he communicated

[39] Luke starts his first volume juxtaposing Christ with Caesar. He finishes his second volume with Paul in Rome preaching the gospel unhindered. This is no coincidence. Luke does this deliberately.

that divine revelation to enable the Greco-Roman Pauline churches to perceive Jesus in the cultural categories by which they understood the world.

If the divine sovereignty over world history is taken seriously, it could even be suggested that the Lord had shaped world history to provide the non-Jewish world with conceptual categories by which to understand the Christ, who is the saviour of all humanity, not just of the Jews. For example, did the Lord by divine providence raise up Caesar Augustus to became emperor and proclaim himself saviour of the world, in order to prepare the Roman world's thinking for the coming of Christ the Saviour? If so, then the Holy Spirit was simply guiding Luke to use this phenomenon, which the Lord had prepared already for his use.

Christ and Caesar: forcing the comparison

The juxtaposition of Christ with Caesar transcends a model for communication. In a world where Caesar and Rome demanded loyalty and submission, to articulate the context of the rule of Caesar, then a call for trust and obedience to another king and saviour intrinsically sets up conflict.

In the face of societal demands for their trust and allegiance to Caesar, Luke wrote to assure the Pauline churches that they could have confidence that the Christ whom Paul preached was the true Lord of all. The Pauline churches constantly encountered pressure from their fellow city dwellers to return to the cultic calendar of their city and honour the gods of Rome and of their city as all their neighbours did.[40] In this, Theophilus and the Pauline churches found that their faith in Christ as Lord positioned them at odds with the cities in which they lived. Luke's comparisons with Caesar were designed to leave the

---

[40] The term 'fellow citizens' has been avoided because only a certain percentage of those living in the Greco-Roman city were actually citizens. Mitchell in his landmark work on Roman Asia Minor concludes:

'One cannot avoid the impression that the obstacle which stood in the way of the progress of Christianity, and the force which would have drawn new converts back to conformity with the prevailing paganism, was the public worship of the emperors. … it was not a change of heart that might win a Christian convert back to paganism, but the overwhelming pressure to conform imposed by the institutions of his city and the activities of his neighbours.' Mitchell, *Anatolia,* 2:10.

Pauline churches with certainty that Jesus is the true Son of God, who brings salvation and peace … and Caesar is not. Luke 1–4 sets up the contest. The rest of Luke's Gospel and Acts unpacks how, despite being crucified by Rome, Christ is Lord.

A Clash of Two Ages (the Age of the Christ Versus the Age of Augustus)

Although they used different terms, Luke's presentation of the arrival of the Christ and the Roman presentation of Augustus Caesar both spoke of the fulfilment of respective much-anticipated golden ages.[41] Both messages called their hearers to place their hopes and dreams in the respective Caesar and Christ in whom these hopes were incarnated. The end goal of both messages was to foster trust and loyalty.

Luke 1–4 uses a variety of terms that signify that the prophesied Davidic Christ has arrived to usher in the Kingdom of God. This is encapsulated in the angel's words in Luke 1:32–33: 'the Lord God will give to him the throne of his father David, and he will reign over the house of Jacob forever, and of his kingdom there will be no end.' This is not an isolated reference. Luke 1–2 overflows with similar ideas.[42] The arrival of Jesus is the arrival of the prophesied and long-awaited age of the Christ, the son of David and the kingdom of God.[43]

Rome's presentation of Augustus as the fulfilment of the mythological Roman golden age was propaganda manufactured after the event by poets such as Virgil and Horace.[44] Nevertheless, it was still the official public message held out to bring glory to Caesar and his rule. By the time Luke was writing, the Caesars continued to be promoted as the successors of Augustus and the incarnation of the hope of the Empire.

As these two golden ages, inaugurated by Christ and Caesar respectively, both presented themselves as the sole object of hope in this

---

[41] This topic could also be considered from the angle of eschatology. The prophesied kingdom of God finds its *eschatos* in the person of the Christ. Virgil's *Aenid finds its eschatos* in Augustus.

[42] Luke 1:19, 69; 2:4, 2:25–26, 38.

[43] As stated above, giving certainty that Jesus was the Christ in the face of synagogue opposition to Paul's gospel was also a key aim here. However, that is not the focus of this chapter.

[44] Quoted on p. 8.

world, Luke wrote to give historical grounding and certainty to the Pauline teaching that the Kingdom of God had arrived in Christ, who is the only true object worthy of their hope.[45]

A Clash of Two Sons of God (the Son of God Versus the Son of a God)

Both Christ and Caesar were proclaimed to be of divine descent. As modern readers of Christian theology, we immediately see the difference in English between the terms 'the Son of God' and 'the son of a god.' However, this distinction was not clear for the Pauline churches from the Greek vocabulary or grammar alone. Context is needed.[46] Nor did the Greco-Roman worldview encourage the types of ontological analysis of such terms in which our Christian theology engages. The approach of their culture was more pragmatic. This does not mean it was any less real or spiritual for them. It was simply a pragmatic spirituality. Caesar was powerful. He brought the types of blessings the gods brought. The Roman Senate had declared Caesar's deceased father to be divine. There was no expectation that anyone would analyse the matter theologically. However, there were political, social and religious expectations that they would accept it.

In the face of societal pressure to acknowledge the Caesars as the son of a god, Luke's presentation of Christ brought certainty to his hearers' faith. Luke both proclaims that Christ is the Son of God prophesied in the Old Testament and, at the same time, articulates exactly what that means. First, he clarifies of which God Christ is the Son. In Luke 1:32 an angel proclaims that Jesus 'will be called the Son of the Most High.'[47] Although the angel uses this euphemism for God, it is

---

[45] Hope is a key concept in Pauline teaching. Paul often presents Christ as the hope of the Gentiles. (E.g. Rom. 15:12; Eph. 2:12).

[46] The difference between 'God' and 'a god,' could be grammatically vague and required context. Context also is needed to know which 'God' or 'god' is implied. The term 'god' implied a god rather than a lesser spiritual being. However, there was still an immense pantheon of different types of gods who contended for power and honour within a hierarchy.

[47] 'The Most High' was also a common term for Yahweh from the Old Testament, which delineated him above other gods. Diaspora Judaism adopted the term: perhaps for the same reason or, perhaps, in order to avoid saying or writing the divine name. Irena Levinskya, *The Book of Acts in its First Century Setting, Vol 3: Diaspora Setting* (Grand Rapids, MI: Eerdmans, 1996), 83–104.

clear from the reference to David and Jacob that Yahweh is implied.[48] Secondly, he clarifies that Christ does indeed share divine essence with Yahweh. In Luke 1:35, an angel proclaims that He will be the 'Son of God' by divine conception, not by imperial adoption, or by senatorial decree.[49] Thirdly, Luke clarifies that angels proclaim Christ[50] and demons publicly fall before him.[51]

Luke wrote to bring certainty to the Pauline churches that, despite any grammatical vagueness or societal expectations, there is absolute clarity that Christ is the true Son of God … and Caesar is not. Christ was procreated by the Holy Spirit of the one creator God. Caesar was purported to be the adopted son of a human whom the Senate had declared divine after death by the process of apotheosis. Even then, the deified Caesar became one demi-god among many. Luke assures them that Christ was the true Son of God. Caesar was not in the same league.

A Clash of Two Sources of Salvation

Paul's churches lived in a world where Augustus Caesar's statues publicly presented him as the military saviour of the world.

Into this context Luke 1–4 proclaims the birth of Jesus as the arrival of the saviour of all mankind. The command of the angel to Mary to name the child 'Jesus' reveals that he will be a saviour. His name Jesus

---

[48] This is also clear from numerous other references in Luke 1–4. The context of the temple in Jerusalem for the angelic proclamation to Zechariah, for Jesus' references to his Father's house, and for Satan's temptation of Christ all imply Yahweh. Mary and Zechariah's quotes from the Old Testament in Luke 1:46–55 and 1:68–79 imply Yahweh. The Davidic references throughout Luke 1–4 imply Yahweh. Other verses that are not as explicit, but contribute to the overall picture: Luke 2:49; 3:23, 38; 4:3, 9.

[49] The terms 'Christ' and 'Son of God' as used in the Old Testament of the human Davidic Christ on the throne in Jerusalem did not intrinsically imply divinity. When passages such as Psalm 2, Psalm 110, or 2 Samuel 7 were read by a non-Christian monotheistic Jew, they were taken to describe the Davidic kingship's special relationship to God but were never taken to imply that the Davidic dynasty shared any essence with God. Luke's inclusion of the angel's proclamation of Christ's divine conception does not contradict the Old Testament, but shows that such Old Testament passages did in fact prophetically point forward to one anointed Davidic Son of God who would share divine essence with Yahweh.

[50] Luke 1:26–38; 2:8–14.

[51] Luke 4:33–35, 41.

In this presentation of Augustus Caesar his naked figure symbolises divinity. In his hand he holds the orb usually held by the goddesses Victory and Peace. (Photo by Gillian Law)

This presentation of Augustus Caesar in his military glory proclaimed that he had conquered the known world and brought peace. (Photo by Gillian Law)

is the Greek version of Joshua which means 'YHWH saves' (Luke 1:31). Zechariah's prophecy overflows with thanks to God using past tenses to say that, in the yet unborn Jesus, God already had acted to bring salvation.[52] The angelic announcement to the shepherds proclaims, 'to you is born this day in the city of David a Saviour, who is Christ the Lord' (Luke 2:11).[53] The angels confirm that Zechariah was interpreting the situation correctly. The Davidic Christ is indeed a saviour. The words of the prophets Simeon and Anna likewise recognise the arrival of salvation simply in the birth of Jesus. Simeon says, 'my eyes have seen your salvation' (Luke 2:30). Anna speaks of Jesus to all who were waiting for 'the redemption of Jerusalem' (Luke 2:38). The truth that Jesus Christ is saviour of the world was not an invention of Paul. It had good historical foundations, even from the moment of Christ's birth.

In the social context where Caesar was proclaimed saviour of the known world, these proclamations establish Christ as a rival to Caesar. Who is the true saviour of the world? Christ or Caesar? Luke did not intend this as a provocative challenge to Caesar in the public square. He wrote for the Pauline churches. His aim was to lay the foundation to bring certainty that Christ is the saviour … and Caesar is not.

'Christ is saviour' was a big claim when all knew that Christ was crucified by Caesar. In both Jewish and Roman thought, a crucified

[52] When Zechariah says that God 'has raised up a horn of salvation for us in the house of his servant David' he demonstrates that he understands Jesus to be the Davidic Christ who would save Israel (Luke 1:69). No doubt he and Elizabeth had compared notes with Mary regarding their respective angelic visitations. Zechariah's prophecy continues in the same vein, thanking God 'that we should be saved from our enemies' (Luke 1:71) and 'delivered from the hand of our enemies' (Luke 1:74). When he changes to address his child John in Luke 1:76 his prophecy that John's ministry would 'give knowledge of salvation to his people' (Luke 1:77) does not make John the saviour but fully understands that John was preparing the way for the Lord (Luke 1:76) who would bring that salvation through Christ.

The concept that 'salvation' is known 'through the forgiveness of their sins' unfortunately cannot be discussed at this point. While Christians take this for granted, it is not the first concept that would have sprung to the original hearers' minds when they anticipated salvation through the Christ.

[53] Although the angels announce that the Christ is the Lord (the Christ is YHWH), the original recipients of the angels' proclamation, as pre-resurrection Jews, have not grasped yet that the Christ is one with YHWH, but a different person. Only post-resurrection do the Jewish apostles understand the full implications of the angels' words.

saviour was no saviour at all. Luke does not attempt to resolve this dilemma in Luke 1–4. He simply lays out the historical record to bring assurance to the Pauline churches that Christ came into the world proclaimed as the long-anticipated saviour by God through prophetic and angelic announcements. Luke will take the rest of Luke and Acts to resolve how Christ can indeed be saviour when he was crucified as a criminal by Rome. He will turn out to be a very different type of saviour to Caesar.[54]

A Clash of Two Sources of Peace

The Romans designated the age of Augustus primarily with the term *Pax Augustae* (the Peace of Augustus). The angels proclaimed that Christ came to bring 'peace on earth' (Luke 2:14) at the time when the *Pax Augusta* (the Peace of Augustus) ruled. Luke forces his Greco-Roman readers, living a few decades later under the *Pax Romana,* to consider the comparison between the Peace of Rome and the peace that Jesus Christ brought. It is clear from a full reading of Luke and Acts that comparing the *Pax Romana* to the peace of Jesus Christ is not comparing apples to apples. The natures of each type of peace were very different. The peace of Jesus Christ was not a peace comprised of military subjugation of competing political and military forces. Luke 1–4 does not resolve this dilemma of differing proclamations of peace. It simply lays out the proclamation that Christ brought 'peace on earth.'

Under the original Jesus (Joshua), the conquest of the Promised Land brought peace and blessing in the land. (It was a rather imperfect conquest and peace, but conquest and peace it was.) Zechariah prophetically anticipated that this Jesus would bring a similar type of salvation and an age of peace: 'that we, being delivered from the hand of our enemies, might serve him without fear' (Luke 1:74). Zechariah's prediction that his son John would 'give light … to guide our feet into the way of peace' (Luke 1:79) recognises that in John would point people to the Christ who would bring an age of peace.[55]

---

[54] A resolution which Luke 24:19–21 and Acts 1:6 show that not even Jesus' disciples understood until Pentecost.

[55] By the incorporation of prophecies from Isaiah, Luke communicates that Jesus' peace transcends the peace (rest in the land) that the original Joshua brought.

Zechariah's prophetic anticipation is well founded. It sets the stage for the angels to proclaim that the birth of Christ will bring 'peace on earth among those with whom he is pleased' (Luke 2:14). The angelic proclamation also demonstrates that the juxtaposition of Christ and Caesar was richer than simply who was the real bringer of peace. In the same way that the Romans believed that the *Pax Romana* was only possible because they were careful to maintain the *Pax Deorum* (the peace of the gods), Luke demonstrates that the peace of Christ is in fact the peace of God.

Julius Caesar presented veiled as Pontifex Maximus. The Pontifex Maximus (Chief Priest) was responsible for overseeing sacrifices and rituals to ensure the Pax Deorum, upon which the Pax Romana depended, was maintained. (Photo by Zachary Brasch)

Peace was a key concept in the Pauline gospel. 'Therefore, being justified by faith, we have peace with God through our Lord Jesus Christ' (Rom. 5:1).[56] Luke wrote to bring certainty to the Pauline churches that Christ was the one who brought peace to the world. The

[56] The author's translation.

fully developed Luke and Acts leave the reader in no doubt that Christ brings real peace and Caesar does not.

In conclusion, Luke, as Paul's co-worker, had watched him on many occasions craft a pastoral letter to meet the needs of specific congregations. After Paul's departure from this life, Luke picked up the mantle and wrote to meet the ongoing pastoral needs of the Pauline churches. Although he wrote history, not a pastoral letter, he was still following Paul's model. Luke crafts the historical presentation of the arrival of the Christ into history in a way that organically blends history and Christology together to address the needs of the Pauline churches living in the Greco-Roman cities of the Empire.

The angelic pronouncements encapsulate the key pillars of the Christology of Luke 1–4. 'For unto you is born this day in the city of David a Saviour, who is Christ the Lord' (Luke 2:11). 'Glory to God in the highest, and on earth peace among those with whom he is pleased!' (Luke 2:14). It is no coincidence that these key elements of Luke's Christology are central to both Paul's gospel and the public presentation of the Caesars. Both Luke and Paul shaped their respective letters and history to exhort the Pauline churches to faith in Christ while confronted by a culture that demanded trust and allegiance to another who claimed to be the son of god who brings salvation and an age of peace.[57]

In one sense, Luke 1–4 'brings certainty concerning the things you have been taught' by showing the Pauline churches that even from the moment of his birth, the prophetic and angelic proclamations testified to the arrival of the Kingdom of God in the person of Christ.

In another sense, the fact that these proclamations were making direct confrontational counter claims to those of Caesar raises for examination the challenges to their faith in Christ that the Pauline churches faced on a daily basis. Faith is strengthened not by hiding one's head in the sand and ignoring the challenges to our faith from the world

---

[57] These same key elements reappear when Luke introduces Jesus' ministry through Jesus' own articulation of his 'mission statement' in the synagogue in Nazareth (Luke 4:18–19).
He is the Christ (the Son of God): 'The Spirit of the Lord is upon me, because he has anointed me.'
He brings salvation: 'liberty to the captives … to set at liberty those who are oppressed.'
His salvation brings an age of peace: 'the year of the Lord's favour'.

but by looking those challenges in the eye and then fixing our eyes on the supremacy of Christ. Luke brings the Pauline churches certainty in the Pauline gospel by highlighting Christ's counter claims to Caesar in Luke 1–4, then showing them through the rest of Luke and Acts that Christ is the supreme Lord of all who reigns at the right hand of God and is building his kingdom through the witness to Christ.

Revisiting the Importance of Historical Endeavour in NT Reading

I hope this chapter has encouraged readers to utilise historical research in the pursuit of the truth of God's word. The Bible was written to be read historically. Paul calls us to be a good workman with nothing of which to be ashamed (2 Tim. 2:15). The appropriate response is to read the Bible in its historical context. It is true that Luke's purpose was mainly Christological. Christology is the key pillar in understanding any gospel. Having done his historical research, Luke wanted to present a clear picture of the person and work of Christ in order to assure the faith of his readers (Luke 1:1–4). However, this chapter has shown how key aspects of Luke's message are missed if we stop at a purely Christological approach. No part of the New Testament is purely theological. It is always theology applied to pastoral situations, to real life in our fallen world. Understanding the historical pastoral context does not change the Christology, soteriology or biblical-theological message of Luke. However, it shines light on how we should apply these truths to give certainty in the midst of a world that proclaims false saviours and false hopes of peace.

Historical research is a valuable tool to guide our reading of the New Testament to see the pastoral application organically embedded within the passage we are reading. (It is often implicit, not explicit, but it would not have been missed by the original readers.) Seeing how Luke pastorally applied Christology in his context guides us see how it applies in our context. Luke does not expect us to be 'creative' to invent a completely new pastoral application of this Christology for our context. He actually gives us the main thrust of the application; we simply need to re-contextualise to our context. We do not live in the shadow of the age of Augustus and the *Pax Romana*. However, the experience of many of our brothers and sisters in Christ throughout history has been one of conflict between our faith and the demands of ruling powers. Even for those of us who live in 'Christendom', our world has its own alternate saviours and promises of peace which call for our trust and allegiance. When read in its pastoral historical context, the appropriate application of Luke's message to our context crystalises. When the historical pastoral context enlightens our reading, a richness of understanding develops that organically applies the Christology in ways that Luke, and the Holy Spirit, always intended.[58]

[58] No Reformed confession that advocates sola scriptura understands that to mean reading Scripture a-historically.

Eleven

The Structure of Old Testament Revelation

R. Todd Stanton

Introduction

The biblical writers trace the beginnings of ancient Israel back to divine revelation.[1] Israel's deity, Yahweh, is portrayed as a god who appeared, who spoke, and who entered into a covenant with Israel. As a result, 'communication between Yahweh and Israel is integral to the biblical writings'.[2] It was fundamental to Israel's existence. The covenant is what identified Israel as a nation.[3] While there were many

---

[1] 'Divine revelation' is a theological construct used by scholars to define how deities communicated with humans in the Bible and the ANE; cf. K. van der Toorn, 'Revelation as a Scholarly Construct in Israel and Mesopotamia,' in *Theologie in Israel und in den Nachbarkulturen*, edited by M. Oeming, K. Schmid, A. Schüle. Altes Testament und Moderne Band 9 (Münster: LIT Verlag, 2004), 125–76; M. Nissinen, 'What is Prophecy? An Ancient Near Eastern Perspective,' in *Inspired Speech: Prophecy in the Ancient Near East: Essays in Honour of Herbert B. Huffmon*, edited by J. Kaltner and L. Stulman. Journal for the Study of the Old Testament Supplement Series 378 (London: T & T Clark, 2004), 25. J. Barr, *The Concept of Biblical Theology: An Old Testament Perspective*, (London: SCM, 1999), 484–86 discusses the problems that he and others have with the term 'revelation' but he resolves to its appropriateness. Unfortunately, there is a lack of uniformity amongst scholars on terminology. Similar terms are sometimes utilised: 'divine communication,' 'divine intermediation,' 'divine manifestation,' 'prophecy,' 'divination,' etc. My justification for 'revelation' comes from the Bible's own vocabulary, eg.: גלה 'reveal,' ראה 'see,' ידע 'know'. See the standard article of S. Talmon, 'The Concept of Revelation in Biblical Times,' *Literary Studies in the Hebrew Bible* (Jerusalem: Magnes Press, 1993) 192–215; and the discussion below. Cf. also J.H. Eaton, 'Some Misunderstood Hebrew Words for God's Self-Revelation,' *Bible Translator* 25: 1974, 331–38.

[2] A. Millard, 'Story, History, and Theology,' in *Faith, Tradition, & History*, edited by A.R. Millard, J.K. Hoffmeier, and D.W. Baker (Winona Lake: Eisenbrauns, 1994) 42.

[3] For a defense of the centrality of the covenant for HB/OT life see M. Kline, *The Structure of Biblical Authority*. Second edition (Eugene: Wipf and Stock,1989) 27–45; and J.B. Payne, *The Theology of the Older Testament* (Grand Rapids: Zondervan, 1962) 71–119. For the role of the covenant in biblical scholarship see R.A. Oden, 'The Place of Covenant

cultural similarities between Israel and her surrounding neighbours, it was having a god who (continually) gave revelation through a covenant that made her solely unique in the Ancient Near East (ANE). Accordingly, Alan Millard writes,

> Basic to Israel's existence was the covenant that God made with her at Mount Sinai. In this, Israel was different from her neighbours. Although other nations understood that that they should be loyal to their patron gods, there is no hint of an agreement of the sort described in the Bible, and no comparison can be made between those gods and Israel's God, who communicated consistently century after century and so gave grounds for hope of restoration after the people were exiled from their land.[4]

Divine revelation became ancient Israel's ontological, epistemological, sociological, historiographical, and theological foundation.[5]

Outlining The Problem

As significant as divine revelation was for ancient Israel, Yahweh's communication didn't always arrive by the same means and in the same manner throughout Israel's history. In fact, when we get a panoramic view of divine revelation in the Bible, the means by which it came seems to be wide and diverse. There doesn't seem to be any clear, comprehensive, or uniform structure to the way that Yahweh revealed himself.[6]

---

in the Religion of Israel,' in *Ancient Israelite Religion,* edited by P.D. Miller, P.D. Hanson, and S.D. McBride (Philadelphia: Fortress Press, 1987) 429–47.

[4] Writing in the foreword to D. Block, *The Gods of the Nations: Studies in Ancient Near Eastern National Theology*. 2nd edition (Grand Rapids/Leicester: Baker Academic/Apollos, 2000) 9.

[5] These categories are taken from J. Walton, *Ancient Near Eastern Thought and the Old Testament: Introducing the Conceptual World of the Hebrew Bible* (Grand Rapids: Baker, 2006) 332–34.

[6] So R. Rendtorff, 'Die Offenbarungsvorstellungen im Alten Israel,' in *Offenbarung als Gescichte,* edited by W. Pannenberg. 3rd edition (Göttingen: Vandenhoeck & Ruprecht, 1965) 23. Similar observations are made by others: 'one cannot apply a general, comprehensive concept of revelation to the Old Testament' [C. Westermann, *Elements of Old Testament Theology,* translated by D.W. Stott. Atlanta: John Knox Press, 1982] 26). 'It would surely be impossible to find a uniform concept of revelation behind all of the

Though history[7] (or providence) as well as nature/creation[8] certainly could reveal the character of Yahweh, but it was primarily the way that Yahweh 'spoke' that frustrates any type of systematisation. He had many ways of 'speaking'. For instance, though widespread divination was forbidden in Israel,[9] decisive knowledge of Yahweh's will could be known through lot casting (Lev. 16:8; Josh. 18:6, 8, 10; 1 Sam. 14:41) and the Urim and Thummim (Exod. 28:30; Lev. 8:8; Num. 27:21; 1 Sam. 23:2).[10] Apart from those two exceptions, however, Yahweh's

---

occasions of divine involvement throughout the Old Testament' (D.A. Knight, 'Revelation Through Tradition,' in *Tradition and Theology in the Old Testament*, edited by D.A. Knight [Philadelphia: Fortress Press, 1978] 143–80); and 'No single teaching, model, or dogma regarding revelation dominates the OT. [Yahweh] reveals himself in many ways and the text also describes his revelation in many ways' (C. Barth, *God With Us: A Theological Introduction to the Old Testament* [Grand Rapids, MI: Eerdmans, 1991] 46). 'Revelation in the Old Testament yields the picture of a very non-uniform situation in research, with respect both to how the problems are conceived and to the results of research,' R.P. Knierim, 'Revelation in the Old Testament,' in *The Task of Old Testament Theology* [Grand Rapids: Eerdmans, 1995] 139).

[7] The seminal study was done by B. Albrekston, *History and the Gods: An Essay on the Idea of Historical Events as Divine Manifestations in the Ancient Near East and in Israel* (Lund: CWL Gleerup,1967). For a critique and correction, though, see W.G. Lambert, 'History and the Gods: A Review Article,' *Orientalia* 39 1970: 170–77 and H.W.F. Saggs, *The Encounter with the Divine in Mesopotamia and Israel* (London: The Athlone Press, 1978) 64–92.

[8] Cf. J. Goldingay, *Approaches to Old Testament Interpretation* (Downers Grove: Inter-Varsity Press, 1981) 69; and J.D.G. Dunn, 'Biblical Concepts of Revelation,' in *Divine Revelation*, edited by P. Avis (London: Darton, Longman, and Todd, 1997) 1–3.

[9] Cf. F.H. Cryer, *Divination in Ancient Israel and its Near Eastern Environment: A Socio-Historical Investigation*. Journal for the Study of the Old Testament Supplement Series 142 (Sheffield: Sheffield Academic Press, 1994).

[10] Cf. C. Van Dam, *The Urim and Thummim: A Means of Revelation in Ancient Israel* (Winona Lake: Eisenbrauns, 1997).

'verbal' communication came via the 'prophet'.[11] Yet *how* it arrived at the prophet is the question in this discussion.[12]

Some[13] point to Numbers 12:6–8 as the key text in answering this question.[14] There Yahweh states, what appears rather forcefully, that he

---

[11] Not surprising but research into the study of divine revelation finds its way into the broader subject of ancient Israelite prophets and prophecy. This is understandable since it was the prophet who usually received the revelation. Receiving the revelation, however, was only one aspect of his work and thus there is quite a bit of sifting through the secondary literature to glean some help in this area. Moreover, the secondary literature on Israelite prophecy is quite overwhelming. For some helpful guides to the literature on Israelite prophets and prophecy see G.M. Tucker, 'Prophecy and the Prophetic Literature,' in *The Hebrew Bible and Its Modern Interpreters*, edited by D. A. Knight and G. M. Tucker (Minneapolis: Fortress, 1985) 325–68; J.J. Schmitt, 'Prophecy (Pre-exilic Hebrew),' in *The Anchor Bible Dictionary*, edited by D.N. Freedman (New York: Doubleday, 1992) vol. 5, 482–89; J. Barton, 'Prophecy (Post-exilic Hebrew),' in *The Anchor Bible Dictionary*, edited by D.N. Freedman (New York: Doubleday. 1992) vol. 5, 489–95; D.W. Baker, 'Israelite Prophets and Prophecy,' in *The Face of Old Testament Studies: A Survey of Contemporary Approaches*, edited by D.W. Baker and B.T. Arnold (Grand Rapids: Baker, 1999) 266–94; and the essays in Y. Gitay, *Prophecy and Prophets* (Atlanta: Scholars Press, 1997); M. Nissinen, *Prophecy in its Ancient Near Eastern Context: Mesopotamian, Biblical, And Arabian Perspectives*. SBL SymS 13 (Atlanta: Society of Biblical Literature, 2000). For much later periods see D.E. Aune, *Prophecy in Early Christianity and the Ancient Mediterranean World* (Grand Rapids: Eerdmans, 1983).

[12] This is why 'revelation' is a better choice than 'prophecy'. The focus is on Yahweh, not the prophet. As Preuss rightly defines, 'the study of the means and power that Yahweh used in order to make known or to disclose his presence and activity to his people through his appointed spokesman belongs to the theology of revelation'. See H.D. Preuss, *Old Testament Theology I*, translated by L.G. Perdue. The Old Testament Library (Louisville: Westminster/John Knox Press, 1995) 200.

[13] For eg. E.J. Young, *My Servants the Prophets* (Grand Rapids: Eerdmans, 1952) 38–55; and R.D. Culver, 'The Problem of Interpreting Old Testament Prophecy,' *Bib Sac* 114:1957, 204.

[14] A major hurdle in moving forward with any sensible interpretation of Numbers 12: 6–8 is finding a sensible translation from the MT. The difficulty concerns the juxtaposition of יהוה ('Yahweh') with נביאכם ('your prophet') in the phrase אם יהיה נביאכם יהוה. If taken together without emendation, it reads, 'If your prophet is Yahweh.' Yet emendation is the usual first call to order. To smooth out the difficulty and agree with the Peshitta and LXX, a common practice is to emend נביאכם into two words נביא בכם ('a prophet among you'). Thus, deleting יהיה from the phrase and making it the subject of the next clause, the translation is, 'If there is a prophet among you, I, Yahweh' (Cf. J. Kselman, 'A Note on Numbers 12: 6–8,' *Vetus Testamentum* 26: 1976, 505; and F.M. Cross, *Canaanite Myth and Hebrew Epic* (Cambridge: Harvard University Press, 1973) 203. More recently, however, there has been a shift in scholarship to avoid the emendation

speaks to prophets *only* in 'visions' and 'dreams'. Moses is the obvious exception; Yahweh speaks to him without mediation.[15] From this statement alone, it seems that dreams and visions appear to be the normal[16] modes of revelation in the literature.[17] Yet, the biblical corpus includes other means besides these two, alongside different types of representations:[18] messenger, fire, cloud, wind, glory, and face, among others.[19]

There are historical and theological questions that follow. Why so many means? Why so many changes? Why didn't the biblical writers describe Yahweh's revelation in a more consistent and uniform manner? Why did they choose sometimes to tell their readers the mode

---

by maintaining that אם יהיה נביאכם יהוה is an example of the so-called broken construct chain. This view was first promulgated by D.N. Freedman, 'The Broken Construct Chain,' *Biblica* 53: 1972, 534–36; and now is followed by commentators G. Wenham, *Numbers*. Tyndale Old Testament Commentary (Downers Grove: InterVarsity Press, 1981) 112; J. Milgrom, *Numbers*. Jewish Publication Society Torah Commentary (Philadelphia: Jewish Publication Society, 1990) 309; T.R. Ashley, *The Book of Numbers*. New International Commentary on the Old Testament (Grand Rapids: Eerdmans, 1978) 200–21. This view argues that the pronominal suffix 'you' is merely an intervention between the genitive construct of 'prophet' and 'Yahweh.' Therefore, it is understood as, 'if there is among you a prophet of Yahweh.' My own position is neither of these two solutions. I rather maintain the MT as it is, without emendation, and take more consideration of the Masoretic accents. Notice נביאכם in the MT has a disjunctive accent (*zaqeph qaton*) which normally would separate it from what follows. There is also an accent (*rebe'a*) above 'Yahweh' (יהוה) which would indicate that 'Yahweh' is the primary subject of the next clause. Thus, the translation is literally, 'if there is your prophet, I [supplied here as in the Targums], Yahweh in a vision . . .' This is only a possibility, but it does highlight the significance of text-critical work in the endeavour to move closer to authorial intentions.

[15] Note the emphatic לא כן ('not so!') in 12:7.

[16] Yahweh is described in the Bible as sovereign and omnipotent and thus free to deviate from what seems to be prescribed modes of revelation. Hence, why he has 'ordinary' means but there are exceptions.

[17] For example, Isaiah 1:1; Obadiah 1; Nahum 1:1; Habakkuk 2:2; Ezekiel 1:1.

[18] 'Representation' is the term used by L. Koehler, *Old Testament Theology*, translated by A.S. Todd (London: Lutterworth, 1957) 119. Jacob, on the other hand, prefers 'manifestation'. See Jacob, *Theology of the Old Testament*, translated by A.W. Heathcote and P.J. Allcock (New York: Harper & Brothers, 1958) 73–85.

[19] For a brief discussion of these titles with specific OT examples see H. Ringgren, *Israelite Religion*, translated by David Green (London: SPCK, 1966) 89–94; and G. Fohrer, *History of Israelite Religion*, translated by D.E. Green (Nashville: Abingdon, 1972) 164–71.

of revelation (i.e., vision[20], dream[21], or theophany[22], among others) and other times nothing at all? Was one mode more predominant in a particular period of Israel's life than other periods?[23] Is it possible to reconstruct a history of Yahweh's self-revelation and explain the reasons why he spoke and how he spoke when he did?

What about those times where no mode is mentioned when he speaks? Can we discern the means if they are not explicit?[24] Most of the time, the writers introduce Yahweh's speech in several linguistic forms: 'God said,' 'Yahweh said,' 'Thus says Yahweh, God of Israel,' 'Thus says Yahweh of hosts.' Why the mixture?[25] Was it purely random how the biblical writers chose to introduce Yahweh speaking? Are they just following their literary preferences? Or were they deliberate in their choices on historical or theological grounds?

Somewhat elusive, and yet perhaps the key to the overall underlying structure of biblical revelation, is the formula: דבר יהוה היה אל.

---

[20] Cf. A. Behrens, *Prophetische Visionsschilderungen im Alten Testament: Sprachliche Eigenarten, Funktion und Geschichte einer Gattung*. AOAT 292 (Münster: Ugarit-Verlag, 2002).

[21] Cf. J-M. Husser, *Dreams and Dream Narratives in the Biblical World,* translated by J.M. Munro (Sheffield: Sheffield Academic Press, 1999); and R. Fidler, *'Dreams Speak Falsely'? Dream Theophanies in the Bible: Their Place in Ancient Israelite Faith and Tradition* (Jerusalem: Magnes Press, 2005).

[22] J.J. Neihaus, *God at Sinai: Covenant & Theophany in the Bible and Ancient Near East* (Grand Rapids: Zondervan, 1995); and G. Savran, *Encountering the Divine: Theophany in Biblical Narrative*. Journal for the Study of the Old Testament Supplement Series 420 (London: T & T Clark, 2005).

[23] Payne divides divine revelation into ten 'historical stages' and observes different modes Yahweh used during each stage but in his report does not discuss the purposes or the significance why there was a change from one period to the next. See J.B. Payne, *The Theology of the Older Testament* (Grand Rapids: Zondervan, 1962) 44–63.

[24] See my attempt to discern the means by which Yahweh spoke to Noah in Genesis 6–9, though no mode is mentioned, R.T. Stanton, 'Asking Questions on the Divine Announcements in the Flood Stories from Ancient Mesopotamia and Israel,' in *Gilgamesh and the World of Assyria,* edited by J. Azize and N. Weeks. Ancient Near Eastern Studies Supplement Series 21 (Leuven: Peeters, 2007) 147–72.

[25] Studies on the linguistical aspect of marking direct discourse in the Hebrew Bible that includes divine direct discourse see S.A. Meier, *Speaking of Speaking: Marking Direct Discourse in the Hebrew Bible*. Vetus Testamentum Supplement 46 (Leiden: Brill, 1992) 273–326; G. Hatav, '(Free) Discourse in Biblical Hebrew,' *Hebrew Studies* 41: 2000, 7–30; and C.L. Miller, *The Representation of Speech in Biblical Hebrew Narrative*. Harvard Semitic Museum 55. 2nd edition (Winona Lake: Eisenbrauns, 2003).

What does 'the word of Yahweh came to PN (person's name) . . . saying' mean? In other words, how did the person receive Yahweh's word? Grether's 1934 study seems to be the benchmark when he states, '*Debar jahwe* is almost everywhere a technical term for the prophetic revelation'.[26] Obviously nothing since then has been majorly advanced when Arthur reports,

> How Yahweh revealed his word to a prophet is *not certainly known*. As a rule, the arrival of an oracle is announced without further elaboration: 'the word of Yahweh came to me'. Little or nothing is said about *the manner* in which the word was received.[27]

---

[26] O. Grether, *Name und Wort Gottes im Alten Testament*. BZAW 64 (Giessen: Töpelmann, 1934) 76. Cf. von Rad's agreement, 'There can be, therefore, no doubt but that this collocation was used as a technical term for an oral prophetic revelation' (G. von Rad, *Old Testament Theology II: The Theology of Israel's Prophetic Traditions* [New York: Harper & Row, 1960] 87). I obviously haven't checked every commentary that comments on the formula (within the last thirty years) but a high number of those that I did, *all* pass it off as just a phrase to introduce revelation. Nothing more is said. Most lean on Grether's work. As such, Sasson is typical: 'Grether studied this expression thoroughly and concluded that *debar-YHWH* is nearly everywhere *the* technical terminology for the opening of prophetic message, before and after the exilic periods' (J. Sasson, *Jonah*. Anchor Bible 24B [New York: Doubleday, 1995] 67, emphasis his).

[27] D. Arthur, *A Smooth Stone: Biblical Prophecy in Historical Perspective* (Maryland: University Press of America, 2001) 12, emphasis mine. See also Grabbe's comments, 'How the prophet obtained [the word of Yahweh] is not specified. It could have been audition or vision, or it could have been written by a scribe in his study . . . could have come through a trance state . . . could have come spontaneously or it could be the result of specific inquiry. In many cases, a variety of modes is possible, and we can only speculate on how it was received' (L. Grabbe, *Priests, Prophets, Diviners, Sages: A Socio-Historical Study of Religious Specialists in Ancient Israel* [Valley Forge: Trinity Press International, 1995] 111).

This statement seems to overgeneralise and understate the situation, for in some contexts, divine presence, perhaps a theophany,[28] seems to be involved with the word of Yahweh.[29]

The formula itself finds itself in a variety of syntactical shapes.[30] How do we account for this?[31] Is this purely a syntactical matter or could there be historical or theological answers for the differences? Add to this the difficulty of just translating the formula. The substantive דבר יהוה seems easy enough to understand[32] but what do we do

[28] Very significant are the comments by Fretheim, 'the word of God as a verbal event, particularly associated with the theophany has been neglected. Theophanies are in fact the vehicle for the most common and most articulate revelations from God' (T.E. Freitheim, 'Word of God' in *The Anchor Bible Dictionary*, edited by D.N. Freedman [New York: Doubleday, 1992] vol. 6, 965).

[29] For example, Genesis 15:1 says that the word of Yahweh came to Abram in a *vision*! The whole narrative is described as a person–to-person conversation that takes place outside. Lipton is wrong in reading the encounter as a dream (D. Lipton, *Revisions of the Night: Politics and Promises in the Patriarchal Dreams of Genesis*. Journal for the Study of the Old Testament Supplement Series 288 [Shefffield: Sheffield Academic Press, 1999] 172–218). Hamilton's comments on Genesis 15 as a theophany are fairly thorough (V.P. Hamilton, *The Book of Genesis: Chapters 1–17*. New International Commentary on the Old Testament [Grand Rapids: Eerdmans, 1990] 417–41). Other times where the formula indicates a theophany/vision are 1 Kings 19:9–11; Jeremiah 1:4–14; Ezekiel 20: 45–49; 37:15.

[30] See Grether, *Name und Wort Gottes im Alten Testament*, 63–67; J.I. Lawlor, 'Word Event in Jeremiah: A Look at the Composition's 'Introductory Formulas',' in *Inspired Speech: Prophecy in the Ancient Near East; Essays in Honour of Herbert B. Huffmon*, edited by J Kaltner and L. Stulman. Journal for the Study of the Old Testament Supplement Series 378 (London: T & T Clark, 2004) 231–40; K. Koch, 'The Language of Prophecy: Thoughts on the Macrosyntax of the debar YHWH and its Semantic Implications in the Deuteronomistic History,' in *Problems in Biblical Theology: Essays in Honor of Rolf Knierim*, edited by H.T.C. Sun and K.L. Eades (Grand Rapids: Eerdmans, 1997) 210–21. My own division of the formula was roughly plotted in a post-graduate seminar paper (R.T. Stanton, 'Building a New Comparative Model for Understanding Divine Revelation in the Hebrew Bible.' Unpublished Post-graduate Seminar Paper, University of Sydney, 2004, 4).

[31] Weippert suggests that variations in the phrase's syntax are due to a diversity of authors and sources (H. Weippert, *Die Prosareden des Jeremiabuches*. BZAW 132 [Berlin: de Gruyter, 1973] 72–74); and Neumann argues for a chronological development in the literary use of the phrase (P.K.D. Neumann, 'Das Wort, Das Geschehen ist . . . Zum Problem der Wortempfangsterminologi in Jer I-XXV,' *Vetus Testamentum* 23:1973, 171–217).

[32] I say seems easy enough but perhaps we need to look at it with new eyes. I doubt if דבר יהוה should always be understood as an impersonal subject. This would certainly be true of, say Chronicles, and other post exilic books, where there the use of 'the word

with the verb היה: 'The word of Yahweh *was present/happened/came/sent/arrived* (?) to PN'[33] Bible translations and commentaries seem to only guess at the translation.[34]

All this goes to show is that a re-evaluation of the formula is worth pursuing. This time, however, with some different lenses. There is no doubt that better textual and linguistical knowledge of the Hebrew will contribute to translation precision but perhaps stepping back and taking a historical and theological snapshot of Yahweh's self-revelation will bring clarity to the issue as well.

---

of Yahweh' in some contexts took on the deliberate nuance of '*Torah* of Moses' (see W.M. Schniedewind, *The Word of God in Transition: From Prophet to Exegete in the Second Temple Period*. Journal for the Study of the Old Testament Supplement 197 [Sheffield: Sheffield Academic Press, 1995] 130–62). What was the perception of דבר יהוה by the people in pre-exilic times? This is a formidable question and perhaps the *crux interpretum* of this whole study! See further discussion below.

[33] Part of the problem is that comparative philology hasn't been much help towards this verb. There is no verb in the other ancient Semitic languages that adequately represent the meaning of the Hebrew-Aramaic root היה. Thus, answers for the meaning of this verb will most likely have to be within the HB corpus. Cf. the comments by Bernhardt: 'to date the verb *hyh* is attested only in the Old Testament. There is a corresponding Aramaic root *hwh*, used in the Old Aramaic inscriptions in about the same way that *hyh* is used in the Old Testament. We must therefore assume that the root is peculiar to the Aramaic-Hebrew branch of Semitic' (K.-H. Bernhardt, 'הָיָה,' in *Theological Dictionary of the Old Testament*, edited by G.J. Botterweck and H. Ringgren , and translated by John T. Willis [Grand Rapids: Eerdmans, 1978] vol. 3, 369).

[34] Even Price and Nida's recommendations to Bible translators (on Jonah 1:1; 3:1) indicate their observation that there is something going on with the phrase than just generic prophetic terminology: 'In the Hebrew expression used here, God's 'word' is described as something with an almost independent existence in the same way as his spirit 'comes upon' Othniel (Judges 3:10), . . . Similarly, in Ezekiel the hand of the Lord 'comes upon' the prophet (1:3), where the word of the Lord is also said to come to him. Some translators have felt that an expression such as 'the Lord spoke to Jonah' is not really adequate to render the implications of the expression 'the word of the Lord came to Jonah.' In order to suggest something of the role of the prophet receiving a special message from the Lord, these translators have preferred an expression such as 'the Lord uttered a special message to Jonah' or 'the Lord revealed to Jonah what he should do.' In this way something of the emphasis of 'the word of the Lord coming' can be communicated, thus suggesting the prophetic role which Jonah was to have' (B.F. Price and E.A. Nida, *A Translators Handbook on the Book of Jonah* [Stuttgart: United Bible Society, 1978] 5).

In all of this, the proverbial 'so what?' perhaps arrives at this point. 'What's the relevancy?' 'Does it matter how Yahweh is described speaking to his people?' 'Isn't the product of revelation more important than the process?' Perhaps so, but I am encouraged that there has been a precedent among scholars for such inquiries. Noel Weeks' passing comment certainly begged the question, 'Abraham receives the message personally whether by the appearance of God to him, by visions or whatever.'[35] Sam Meier also speculates, 'In the scores of cases where the text simply reads, 'God said,' it is not clear if a theophany is to be presumed.'[36]

Such guesswork is worth pursuing but can the differences be explained? A typical starting point for such a discussion is to look outside of Israel and explain the differences as something that was either borrowed or accommodated from her neighbouring cultures.[37] In other words, Yahweh's means of revealing himself were similar to what was known in the ancient milieu of Israel in communicating with his people; Yahweh in a sense accommodated himself to what was familiar to Israel. The biblical text is clear that there were other views of the divine represented both inside and outside Israel. How do these interact with the biblical conception of divine communication?[38]

[35] N.K. Weeks, *Gateway to the Old Testament* (Edinburgh: Banner of Truth, 1995) 5.

[36] S.A. Meier, 'Theophany,' in *The Oxford Companion to the Bible,* edited by B.M. Metzger and M.D. Coogan (Oxford: Oxford University Press, 1993) 740.

[37] Representative of the Pan-Babylonianism concerning 'prophecy' is F. Nötscher, *Das Angesicht gottes schauen nach biblischer und babylonischer Auffassung*. 2nd Edition (Darmstadt: Wissenschatliche Buchgesellschaft, 1969). He argues that such 'revelatory' expressions are rooted in the world of Mesopotamian language and conceptuality since there are many Mesopotamian texts that have a 'prophetic' genre which attests to 'visions' and 'dreams'.

[38] It is quite normal that questions of this nature find themselves in the broader works on ANE prophets and prophecy. For an earlier, yet still helpful survey see F. Nötscher, 'Prophetie im Umkreis des alten Israel,' *Biblische Zeitschrift* 10: 1966, 161- 186. See also H. Huffmon, 'Prophecy (ANE),' in *The Anchor Bible* Dictionary, edited by D.N. Freedman (New York: Doubleday,1992) vol. 5, 477–82; and the more recent essays in J. Kaltner, J. and L. Stulman (eds.), *Inspired Speech: Prophecy in the Ancient Near East: Essays in Honour of Hebert B. Huffmon*. JSOTSup 378 (London: T & T Clark, 2004).

Old Testament Revelation as Yahweh's Self-Manifestation

Amidst all the questions of Yahweh's revelation above, there is one aspect that is not mysterious. Yahweh's revelation is rightly understood as his *self-revelation*.[39] The biblical writers go to great effort to convey this idea by their choice of verbs and verbal forms. In certain contexts, when Yahweh is the subject of the so-called 'revelatory' verbs (e.g., גלה 'reveal,'ראה 'see,' ידע'know')[40] in either the *niphal* or *hithpael* stems, the action seems to take on a tolerative sense. In other words, the verb combines the reflexive notion with the idea of permission. That is to say, Yahweh *allows* himself to be the object of sight/hearing to others.[41] 'The presupposition of revelation is that God is hidden from man's sight. Revelation, therefore, is God's unveiling or uncovering himself and his purposes.'[42]

Divine Revelation in the Ancient Near East

The general outlook for revelation in the ANE seems to be antithetical to this concept. The gods were anything but self-revealing. For the most part, unlike Israel, there was no revelation given by the gods regarding what they expected of human beings. Rather, people had to endeavour to stay in harmony with the status quo of society and civilisation. Thus,

---

[39] Often quoted, Rendtorff has accurately stated, '[Yahweh's] revelation in the strict sense of the word . . . generally means [Yahweh's] self-revelation' (R. Rendtorff, 'Die Offenbarungsvorstellungen im Alten Israel,' in *Offenbarung als Gescichte*, edited by W. Pannenberg. 3rd edition [Göttingen: Vandenhoeck & Ruprecht, 1965] 23).

[40] Cf. S. Talmon, 'The Concept of Revelation in Biblical Times,' *Literary Studies in the Hebrew Bible* (Jerusalem: Magnes Press, 1993) 192; and G.W. Bromiley, 'Reveal' in *The International Standard Bible Encyclopedia*, edited by G.W. Bromiley (Grand Rapids: Eerdmans, 1998) vol. 4, 161–171.

[41] Unfortunately, some of the contemporary English translations (eg., JPSB; NKJV, NASB, NIV, and ESV) sometimes fail to provide the full force and sense of the action of these verbs. For example, the NASB misses the *crux interpretum* of Genesis 12:7 by translating וירא יהוה אל אברם as 'And the LORD [Yahweh] appeared to Abram'. Rather, my own translation, I believe, does more justice to the Hebrew: 'And Yahweh *let Himself be seen* by Abram'. For some helpful discussions on these syntactical nuances see B.K. Waltke and M.O'Connor, *An Introduction to Biblical Hebrew Syntax* (Winona Lake: Eisenbrauns, 1990) 389 and Eaton, 'Some Misunderstood Hebrew Words for God's Self-Revelation,' 331.

[42] B.W. Anderson, 'The Old Testament View of God,' in *Interpreter's Dictionary of the Bible*, edited by G.A. Buttrick (Nashville: Abingdon, 1962) vol. 2, 419.

it was not revelation that provided knowledge of what the gods demanded in general; tradition was the source. When special instructions were necessary, revelation was looked for through divination.[43] Unlike Yahweh, the ANE gods were for the most part hidden from man[44] and knowledge of their will was only known through tradition.[45] To be sure, dreams and visions were part of the revelatory repertoire, but they were seen only 'as methods (though not extensively used) among the wider techniques of divination, and were occasionally deliberately solicited.'[46] Biblical revelation, on the other hand, as remarked above, was

---

[43] Divination was one of the common means of determining the will of the deity in Mesopotamia, as well as elsewhere in the ANE, and in this way has some links with prophecy. For an up-to-date survey on divination (and prophecy) in the ancient world, see the essays in S.I. Johnston (ed), *Religions of the Ancient World: A Guide* (Cambridge: The Belknap Press of Harvard University Press, 2004) 370–92. Also helpful is G.A. Beckman, 'How Religion Was Done' in *A Companion to the Ancient Near East*, edited by D.C. Snell (Oxford: Blackwell, 2005) 352; and J. Walton, *Ancient Near Eastern Thought and the Old Testament: Introducing the Conceptual World of the Hebrew Bible*, 239–74. Fuller treatments are given by J. Vervant, *Divination et Rationalité* (Paris: Seuil, 1974); I. Starr, *The Ritual of the Diviner*. Bibliotheca Mesopotamica 12 (Malibu: Undena, 1983); and A. Jeffers, *Magic and Divination in Ancient Palestine and* Syria. SHCANE 8 (Leiden: Brill, 1996).

[44] Characteristic of this are the following testimonies: 'I wish I knew that these things were pleasing to one's god! What is proper to oneself is an offence to one's god, what in one's own heart seems despicable is proper to one's god. Who knows the will of the gods in heaven? Who understands the plans of the underworld gods? Where have the mortals learnt the way of a god?' (W.G. Lambert, *Babylonian Wisdom Literature* [Oxford: Clarendon, 1960] 41) and 'The plans of the gods are as far from us as the centre of heaven: to understand them properly is impossible, no one can understand them' (Ibid., 76).

[45] 'In part such knowledge [what the gods wanted] was, of course, given with the tradition. The gods were certain to want their temples looked after, their cult performed correctly, their festivals celebrated at the proper times, and attention and reverence from their people generally. But these—one might call them the 'standing' orders—were not all. Situations were bound to develop in which the divine will might not be so clear . . . For such cases—one might call them the 'specific' orders—the ruler had to rely on messages from the gods in dreams or visions, on signs and portents, or on one of the traditional ways in which one would approach the gods and obtain—if one was lucky—an answer' (T. Jacobsen, 'Mesopotamia,' in *The Intellectual Adventure of Ancient Man* [Chicago: University of Chicago Press, 1976] 84).

[46] P.T. Collins, 'Dreams,' in *Dictionary of the Ancient Near East*, edited by P. Bienkowski and A. Millard (Philadelphia: University of Pennsylvania Press, 2000) 95. Cf. J. Black J. and A. Green, *Gods, Demons and Symbols of Ancient Mesopotamia*. Austin: University of Texas Press, 1992) 71.

rarely solicited. Thus, divination was the normal or ordinary means of divine revelation in the ANE.[47]

The closest thing that comes to biblical revelation in the ANE, in the sense we are describing it, comes from Mari where what seems unsolicited visions and dreams are attested.[48] Malamat describes it as 'intuitive prophecy;'[49] that is, the various prophets[50] receive the revelation without resort to mantic or oracular devices and techniques. In other words, the revelation appears to be divinely inspired, or better, divinely initiated.

This compares quite nicely with the biblical texts since this is also the predominant characteristic of biblical revelation. However, despite the similarities, Malamat admits, 'the prophetic utterances [at Mari] have almost nothing comparable to the socio-ethical or religious ideology of biblical' revelation.[51] Furthermore, documentation concerning this type of revelation at Mari is mostly restricted to a very short period, perhaps only to the final decade (or less) of Zimri-Lim's reign. On the other hand, the biblical texts attest to the same phenomenon for centuries. Thus Mari 'represents a synchronous picture, a cross-section at one particular point in time, while the Bible gives a diachronous view, tracing the development of the phenomenon over a period of time.'[52]

---

[47] Contrast that with Yahweh's normal means of self-revelation in 'dreams' and 'visions'. See the discussion above.

[48] Literature comparing Mari with the Bible is legion. Two balanced works on comparing Mari with Israel come from the pen of Robert Gordon. See R.P. Gordon, 'From Mari to Moses: Prophecy at Mari and in Ancient Israel,' in *Prophets' Visions and the Wisdom of Sages*, eds. H.A. McKay and D.J.A. Clines. Journal for the Study of the Old Testament Supplement Series 162 (Sheffield: Sheffield Academic Press, 1993), 63–79; and R.P. Gordon, 'Where Have All the Prophets Gone? The 'Disappearing' Israelite Prophet against the Background of Ancient Near Eastern Prophecy,' *Bulletin for Biblical Research* 5 (1995): 67–86.

[49] See A. Malamat, 'Intuitive Prophecy – A General Survey' in *Mari and the Bible* (Leiden: Brill, 1998), 59–82.

[50] Malamat distinguishes between two types of prophets: the 'accredited' prophet who receives revelation while fully conscious (i.e., 'vision'); and the 'lay' prophet through 'dreams' (Malamat, 'Intuitive Prophecy,' 74). Apart from this general distinction nothing else is further advanced.

[51] Malamat, 'Intuitive Prophecy,' 59.

[52] Malamat, 'Intuitive Prophecy,' 62. Among those who have questioned the usefulness of the Mari letters for the interpretation of biblical prophecy/revelation is E. Noort, *Untersuchungen zum Götterbescheid in* Mari. AOAT 202 (Neukirchen-Vluyn: Neukirchener

Finally, perhaps most significant is that this type of revelation at Mari is atypical of the rest of the ANE.

Just from that brief sketch, the character and conception of revelation in the ANE seems to be very much at odds with the one the biblical writers portray for Israel. In light of the general outlook, can we legitimately say as a whole that Yahweh's character, concept, and means of revealing himself were 'similar' to what was known in the ANE? Did Yahweh operate on the same plane as the other gods? Even if he did, that doesn't explain why he chose one method in one place and another mode somewhere else.

Ironically, however, there is one observation between divine revelation in the ANE and divine revelation in the Bible that is curiously similar. Neither one of them form a coherent pattern. As Ringgren and others have pointed out, biblical revelation just like its Near Eastern counterpart 'is not a homogenous phenomenon.'[53]

Furthermore, we need to add that comparisons between the Hebrew Bible (HB) and ANE texts that do not have methodological rigour will not produce any formidable conclusions on why there was such nonuniformity of divine revelation in the Bible.[54] As Schaper has correctly pointed out:

> whoever wants to form an opinion on the compatibility of Israelite and Judean prophecy and its perceived Neo-Assyrian counterpart probably should not start with a definition of prophecy as is sometimes the case, but with a phenomenological account of the respective texts and the ways in which they have been preserved and transmitted . . . the position of these [ANE prophetic] texts in the world of Assyrian and Babylonian literature

Verlag, 197), 93–110.

[53] H. Ringgren, 'Prophecy in the Ancient Near East,' in *Israel's Prophetic Tradition*, edited by R. Coggins, A. Phillips, and M. Knibb (Cambridge: Cambridge University Press, 1982), 11.

[54] Comparative studies between the OT and the ANE are still in methodological disarray. For a balanced and sensible approach, see the work of Noel K. Weeks. In particular, read his 'The Ambiguity of Biblical 'Background',' *The Westminster Theological Journal* 72 (2010): 219–35; and 'Problems with The Comparative Method in Old Testament Studies,' *The Journal of the Evangelical Theological Society* 62:2 (2019): 287–306.

is very different from that of their supposed Israelite and Judean equivalents in the corpus of ancient Hebrew literature.[55]

Building a New Paradigm For Old Testament Revelation

Methodologically, the typical approach to understanding the means and manner by which Yahweh revealed himself has been to focus on the terminology that surrounds the phenomenon. That is, attention is normally given to those terms used for the different prophetic figures and for the verbal forms of their activities that imply certain things about how Yahweh revealed himself to the recipient. As a result, research into the subject is towards those passages of Scripture that describe Yahweh's modes (i.e., visions, dreams, and theophanies) and the person who receives them (i.e., the prophets).

Comparative studies, as we noted earlier, is usually the next step since 'revelation' from a deity was something claimed in every culture, even if it was unsolicited. The discussion then, however, for reasons mentioned above, inevitably falls within 'prophecy,' which is normally just a comparison of basic forms as well as basic motifs.[56] Similar terminology for 'vision,' 'dream,' and even the so-called 'prophetic trance' (i.e., ecstasy)[57] are pointed out but little has been done to explain the

---

[55] J. Schaper, 'Prophecy in Israel and Assyria: Are We Comparing Apples and Pears?' in*'Thus Speaks Ishtar of Arbela': Prophecy in Israel, Assyria, and Egypt in the Neo Assyrian Period,* eds. R. P. Gordon and H.M. Barstad (Winona Lake, IN: Eisenbrauns, 2013), 227–28. Cf. also E. Cancik-Kirschbaum, 'Prophetismus und Divination: Ein Blick auf die keilschriftlichen Quellen,' in *Propheten in Mari, Assyrien und Israel,* FRLANT 201, eds. M. Köckert and M. Nissenen (Göttingen: Vandenhoeck & Ruprecht, 2003), 33–53. See also the comments by E. Noort, *Untersuchungen zum Gottesbescheid in Mari. Die 'Mariprophetie' in der alttestamentlichen Forschung,* AOAT 102 (Kevelaer: Butzon und Bercker/ Neukirchen-Vluyn: Neukirchener Verlag, 1977), 91–92.

[56] See the helpful survey by M. Weinfeld, 'Ancient Near Eastern Patterns in Prophetic Literature,' *Vetus Testamentum* 27: 1977, 178–95. Reprinted in R.P. Gordon (ed.), *The Place is Too Small for Us: The Israelite Prophets in Recent Scholarship*. SBTS 5 (Winona Lake: Eisenbrauns, 1995) 32–49.

[57] Receiving the revelation by 'trance,' typical outside of Israel, unfortunately, has been forced upon the Hebrew prophets as well. Since ecstasy was evidently a common characteristic of Canaanite 'prophecy' (cf. 1 Kings 18), the possibility of a Canaanite derivation for Israelite prophecy was suggested in the past. Now with Mari, which includes ecstasy, perhaps being closer to the Hebrew phenomenon as a whole, is looked upon now favourably as the forerunner of Israelite prophecy. It should be observed, how-

relationship between ancient Hebrew prophecy/revelation and the non-Israelite forms, if any.[58]

Working off of superficial comparisons, in my opinion, will not produce any formidable conclusions why there was such nonuniformity of divine revelation in the Bible. In fact, it would be, in my judgement, methodologically incorrect to restrict divine revelation in Israel and the ANE only to those passages where certain terms are found.[59] The picture is much bigger than just the so-called 'prophetic' vocabulary. While not totally abandoning the old model, it is my assertion that the study of divine revelation needs to be diverted from its usual conversation and head in another direction.

The usual question is how did the 'prophetic' figures receive the divine message? Granted, the question is a natural one to ask since we are accustomed to read prophetic texts from the Bible in much the same way we read ANE prophetic texts. However, it should not be under emphasised that the majority of ANE texts are all anthropocentric, not theocentric.[60] The Bible, with all its genres—including the revelatory/prophetic texts—seems to be written from a theological perspective.[61] The biblical writers were intentional, writing history with a purpose.

ever, as Gordon suggests, 'that when prophets are represented as sometimes pleading and even arguing with God, the usefulness of ecstasy as an explanation of their experience becomes questionable' (R.P. Gordon, 'A Story of Two Paradigm Shifts,' in *The Place is Too Small for Us: The Israelite Prophets in Recent Scholarship*, edited by R.P. Gordon [Winona Lake: Eisenbrauns, 1995] 8). See also similar comments made by S.B. Parker, 'Possession Trance and Prophecy in Pre-exilic Israel, *Vetus Testamentum* 28: 1978, 280. Furthermore, I would lump ecstasy, if there is such a thing in Israel, under the category of divination, not something characterized by the normal definition of Yahweh's self-revelation.

[58] Something that Gordon has encouraged: more research in answering the question(s) of the relationships in prophetic terminology between the cultures. (Gordon, 'A Story of Two Paradigm Shifts,' 30).

[59] Malamat has begun this with some of the non-prophetic Mari texts. See A. Malamat, 'The Secret Council and the Prophetic Involvement in Mari and Israel,' in *Prophetie und geschichtliche Wirklichkeit im alten Israel*, edited by R. Liwak and S. Wagner (Stuttgart: Kohlhammer, 1991) 231–36. He has argued that the references to the 'royal council' in the Mari texts may have provided the model for the mythological divine court or 'council of the gods' that formed the background to the commissioning of a number of Near Eastern (and Israelite) prophets.

[60] Saggs, *The Encounter with the Divine in Mesopotamia and Israel*, 128.

[61] J. Van Seters, *In Search of History: Historiography in the Ancient World and the Origins of*

> Israelite writers composed consecutive histories of their people unique in the ancient Near East, aware of the continuity of events in a way other nations were not . . . Where Hebrew writers differed from their contemporaries was in the concept of a single god in control of events, who had a purpose in view and revealed his will to his people, whereas the gods of other nations acted to maintain a current situation or to change it at their individual whims, people suffering because of divine quarrels.[62]

As a result, if we want to make sense of how Yahweh revealed himself, the question needs to be turned around. Rather, not how did the biblical writers describe the 'prophetic' figure receiving divine revelation but how did the biblical writers describe Yahweh sending his message?

Thus, the language of revelation, not just the phenomenon, must be taken into consideration. If, as the Rabbis often mentioned, Yahweh employed the everyday language of human beings in order to communicate his will[63], then our understanding of biblical revelation may be found in correlating human institutions with metaphors for the divine realm.[64] In other words, I believe biblical revelation would be better understood when we discover the analogies within Israel and the broader ANE world that Yahweh may have employed as the accommodation of his revelation. In my opinion, the two key analogies that the biblical writers utilised in revelation were kingship and covenant.

Biblical History (New Haven: Yale University Press, 1983) 361.

[62] A. Millard, 'Historiography,' in *The Dictionary of the Ancient Near East,* edited by P. Bienkowski and A. Millard (Philadelphia: University of Pennsylvania Press, 2000) 146. Longman and Reid make similar observations, 'The Bible is about Yahweh. It is His self-revelation. The Bible, however, is not about Yahweh in the abstract; it is about God in relation to mankind. Furthermore, this relationship is not so much described as it is narrated. There is a historical dimension to biblical revelation. Thus, a proper biblical theology must take into account the subject matter of the Bible, the divine-human relationship, and the fact that the Bible's message is told through time' (T. Longman III and D.G. Reid, *God is a Warrior* [Grand Rapids: Zondervan, 1995] 15).

[63] This opinion *dibberah torah kileshon benei'adam* is found in Sifrei 112:11; Yev. 71a, Ket. 67b; Ned. 3a-b; Git. 41b; Kid. 17b; BM 31b, 94b; Sanh. 56a, 64b, 85b, 90b; Mak. 12a; Av. Zar. 27a; Zev. 108b; Ber. 31b; Arak. 3a; Her. 11a; Nid. 32b, 44a.

[64] For the subject of metaphors in the Bible see P. van Hecke, *The Metaphor in the Hebrew Bible*. Bibliotheca Ephemeridum Theologicarum Lovaniensium 187 (Leuven: Peeters, 2005) and P. Grelot, *The Metaphor in the Hebrew Bible*. Bibliotheca Ephemeridum Theologicarum Lovaniensium 187 (Leuven: Peeters, 2001).

Old Testament Revelation as Royal Administrative Correspondence

The picture of Yahweh as king may well be the 'leading image in the Old Testament,'[65] if not the 'predominant relational metaphor used in the Bible.'[66] Koehler even goes as far as to state,

> Yahweh is seen as the ruling Lord and this is the one fundamental statement in the theology of the Old Testament. Everything else derives from it. Everything else leans upon it. Everything else can be understood with reference to it and only it.[67]

Many agree that the kingship of Yahweh is the central theme of the Hebrew Bible.[68]

This is analogy. Analogy requires 'that one started from the object to be explained in order to construct 'calculated imaginations' around

---

[65] J.C.L. Gibson, *Language and Imagery in the Old Testament* (Peabody: Hendrickson Publishers, 1998) 121.

[66] M. Brettler, *God is King: Understanding an Israelite Metaphor*. Journal for the Study of the Old Testament Supplement 76 (Sheffield: Sheffield Academic Press, 1989) 160. Aaron has recently reevaluated Brettler's thesis and has suggested that descriptions of Yahweh as king may not always be metaphorical. 'I would maintain that the expression 'God is King' was, at certain stages in Israel's history, understood *literally* and that precisely because of this, some biblical passages argued for the limitations of the conceptualization of this image' (D.A. Aaron, *Biblical Ambiguities: Metaphor, Semantics, and Imagery* [Leiden: Brill, 2001] 35, emphasis his). In other words, the relationship between Yahweh and Israel went beyond purely the metaphorical. Yahweh was not like a king to Israel; he *was* the king to Israel. The (suzerain/vassal) covenant between Yahweh and Israel established Yahweh as their own personal God-King. The earthly king (eg., David) was a mere vice-regent. As a result, it is perhaps better to refer to the royal characteristics ascribed to Yahweh more analogical than metaphorical.

[67] Koehler, *Old Testament Theology*, 30.

[68] Representative of this position is S. Mowinckel, *He That Cometh* (New York: Abingdon, 1956) and J. Gray, *The Biblical Doctrine of the Reign of God* (Edinburgh: T&T Clark, 1999). See also statement made by Smith, 'The study of the ancient Near Eastern literature puts the concept of Yahweh into perspective, and the biblical literature suggests that the kingship or sovereign rule of Yahweh is of central importance in developing a biblical theology of the Old Testament' (G.V. Smith, 'The Concept of God/The Gods as King in the Ancient Near East and the Bible,' *Trinity Journal* 3: 1982, 37).

it to explain it.'[69] 'The principle of analogy facilitated a moving from the better known to the lesser known.'[70] As Millard rightly points out 'analogy is basic to the work of modern historians.'[71]

Therefore, if 'at best all language about [Yahweh] is analogical,'[72] then, how we understand analogy is critical.[73] Words used to describe Yahweh and his acts must inevitably be human words, but, naturally, they do not have quite the same meaning when applied to him as when they refer to men. This means that when we speak of Yahweh as king, we do not assign him *all* the attributes of human kingship. He is king '*par excellence*, whose kingship surpasses that of any human monarch.'[74] In other words, understanding the social analogies—or better, the conceptual analogies—of divine revelation is the ultimate goal here.

An example of this approach is in Holtz, who does exactly this in in his pursuit of understanding prayer in the Hebrew Bible.[75] Building on Moshe Greenberg's idea that prayer in the Hebrew Bible is modelled upon social analogies, he understands that when ancient humans communicated with the deity in prayer, they utilised, by analogy, the same kinds of social conventions and norms they would use to communicate with other humans, especially a social superior.[76] That is, in biblical and

---

[69] J. Bottero, *Religion in Ancient Mesopotamia*, translated by Teresa Lavender Fagan (Chicago: University of Chicago Press, 2001) 77.

[70] J.L. Crenshaw, 'The Contemplative Life in the Ancient Near East,' in *Civilizations of the Ancient Near East*, edited by J. Sasson (New York: Charles Scribner's Sons, 1995) vol. 4, 2450.

[71] A.R. Millard, 'Story, History, and Theology,' in *Faith, Tradition, & History*, edited by A.R. Millard, J.K. Hoffmeier, and D.W. Baker (Winona Lake: Eisenbrauns, 1994), 40.

[72] G. Wenham, *Genesis 1–15*. Word Biblical Commentary 1 (Fort Worth: Word, 1987), 40.

[73] Regarding the analogical nature of religious texts in the ANE, Jacobsen said, 'The core of all religion, the numinous experience, can only be suggested in metaphors and cannot be described. For an outsider to a civilization its metaphors do not readily come to life and so one can easily lose their religious content altogether and be left with their empty form' (Jacobsen 1995, vol. 4, p. 2750). Handy's work is illustrative of this (L.K. Handy, *Among the Host of Heaven: The Syro-Palestinian Pantheon as Bureacracy* [Winona Lake: Eisenbrauns, 1994]). He argues that the structure of the pantheon worshipped at Syria-Palestine mirrored the social structure of the city-states in that region.

[74] Brettler, *God is King: Understanding an Israelite Metaphor*, 33.

[75] S.E. Holtz, *Praying Legally*, Brown Judaic Studies 364 (Providence: Brown Judaic Studies, 2019).

[76] Cf. M. Greenberg, *Biblical Prose Prayer as a Window to the Popular Religion of Ancient Israel*, Taubman Lectures in Jewish Studies (Berkeley: University of California Press,

other ANE sources, prayer is an opportunity to make one's case before divine judges, which means prayers were formulated using courtroom or trial language, including demands for judgement, confessions, and accusations. 'The presence of these legal concepts reveals ancient Near Eastern thoughts about what takes place when one prays'.[77]

In the end, Holtz sets out to pursue the understanding of the 'frame of mind' of the petitioner in his prayer, what he calls a 'forensic theology of prayer'.[78] Could a 'forensic theology of divine revelation' also be produced? Could biblical revelation reflect something similar, where Yahweh's revelation reflected the royal state correspondences of the day? Did Yahweh accommodate his 'language' in political, diplomatic, and even legal terminology?[79]

If we build on the analogy that Yahweh is King, then could our starting point for understanding his self-revelation be placed within that reference? If so, to understand the analogy, one has to appreciate how the kings of the ANE administered their kingdoms.

Using secular, or social, analogies to explain religious language is not necessarily tied only to the Bible though. The other ANE nations also worked from the political analogy to express their religion as well. As Bottéro points out, 'the theological system paralleled so perfectly the political one that it anticipated, just as on earth, a full assembly of the gods.'[80] In other words, a similar image, transposed from the politi-

1983). 'In one section . . . Greenberg pursues what he calls 'the social analogy,' or the 'inter-human speech patterns' that constitute the model for speech between humans and God' (Holtz, *Praying Legally*, 3).

[77] Holtz, *Praying Legally*, 127.

[78] Holtz, *Praying Legally*, 1.

[79] Theologians refer to the phenomenon of God revealing himself to human understanding as 'divine accommodation'. Stephen Benin defines it as God adjusting divine revelation 'to the disparate intellectual and spiritual level of humanity at different times in history' (S.D. Benin, *The Footprints of God: Divine Accommodation in Jewish and Christian Thought* [Albany: SUNY Press, 1993], xiv). In other words, God adjusts to the low level of the addressees to speak to them in words they understand best. For a brief introduction to the subject, see P.M. van Bemmelin, 'Divine Accommodation in Revelation and Scripture,' *Journal of the Adventist Theological Society* 9 (1998): 221–229. Cf. F.L. Battles, 'God Was Accommodating Himself to Human Capacity,' *Interpretation* 31:1 (1977): 19–38.

[80] J. Bottéro, *Mesopotamia: Writing, Reasoning, and the Gods*, trans. Z. Bahrani and M. van De Mieroop (Chicago: University of Chicago Press, 1992), 213.

cal authority on earth, directed the religious ideology in Mesopotamia. Thus, the hierarchy among the gods was nothing more than a reflection of the bureaucracy on earth.[81] The logical conclusion, then, was 'like king, like god.' Kings kept administrative records, a bookkeeping of sorts, and so did the gods.[82] As a result, it would seem natural to think that corresponding/communicating to the god would be done in similar ways to communicating to a king. That was done, of course, through letters.[83] It is understandable, then, that when one wanted to pray to his god, he would come to the temple and deposit before the god a letter-prayer.[84] Speiser explains:

> Because no individual god in the Mesopotamian pantheon was really omnipotent, the purposes of the cosmic society were difficult to fathom. The mortal ruler was forever intent on pleasing the cosmic powers. Often, he found himself obliged to appease them. There were times when the need was urgent to establish direct contact with the distant gods. In a literate society distances can be neutralised through writing. It is logical, therefore, in these circumstances, that the kings of historic Mesopotamia

[81] See Handy, *Among the Host of Heaven.*

[82] cf. S.M. Paul, 'Heavenly Tablets and the Book of Life,' *Journal of the Ancient Near Eastern Society* 5 (1973): 345–53.

[83] For a general, yet very helpful, discussion on letters throughout the ancient world, see 'Letters' in *Brill's New Pauly – Antiquity, Volume 7 (K – Lyc),* eds. H. Cancik and H. Schneider (Leiden: Brill, 2005).

[84] For a list of the most important texts in this genre, see R. Borger, 'Gottesbrief,' in *Reallexikon der Assyriologie und Vorderasiatischen Archaologie,* ed. D. O. Edzard (Berlin: Walter de Gruyter, 1957), 3: 575–76. On interpretations of the letter-prayers, see W.W. Hallo, 'Individual Prayer in Sumerian: The Continuity of a Tradition,' *Journal of the American Oriental Society* 88 (1968): 71–89; W.W. Hallo, 'Letters, Prayers, and Letter-Prayers,' in *Proceedings of the Seventh World Congress of Jewish Studies: Studies in the Bible and the Ancient Near East,* ed. David Krone (Jerusalem: Magnes Press, 1981), 17–27; S.R. Keller, 'Written Communications Between the Human and Divine Spheres in Mesopotamia and Israel,' in *Scripture in Context.* Vol. IV, *The Biblical Canon in Comparative Perspective,* eds. K.L. Younger, Jr., W.W. Hallo, and B.F. Batto. Ancient Near Eastern Texts and Studies 11 (Lewiston: The Edwin Mellen Press, 1991) 299–309; J.H. Tigay, 'On Some Aspects of Prayer in the Bible,' *AJS Review* 1 (1976): 363–379. Letter-prayers weren't the only 'genre' of prayers throughout the ANE (see T. Longman, 'The Psalms and Ancient Near Eastern Prayer Genres,' in *Interpreting the Psalms: Issues and Approaches,* eds. P.S. Johnston and D.G. Firth [Leicester: Apollos, 2005], 41–59), but it is rather interesting, however, that this practice can be found across a long period of time, from Neo-Sumerian to Neo-Assyrian periods.

> should write to their gods, even as they were themselves petitioned by their own subjects.[85]

In response, the petitioner would have most likely hoped for a reply by the same means. The Mesopotamian gods 'were envisioned as partaking in a two-way avenue of communication whereby they both received and wrote letters'.[86] Receiving a letter from a god, however, was indeed rare[87] so the gods resorted to 'writing' by other means (e.g., extispicy, lecanomancy, libanomancy, astrology, and augury = divination).

Religion with Yahweh can be seen with the same secular analogies. Yahweh also keeps records. He has a 'book of life'[88] and a 'book of remembrance'.[89] As such, if an Israelite wanted to pray, there is good reason to believe that he, too, would have written a letter to Yahweh. Though no such letter exists explicitly, there is good evidence that some of the Psalms[90] originated first as letters. For instance, David, as Yahweh's king and administrator of the covenant (cf. Deut. 17:18–20) would have wanted to correspond with Yahweh on the affairs of the

---

[85] A. Speiser, 'Ancient Mesopotamia,' in *The Idea of History in the Ancient Near East*, ed. R.C. Dentan. American Oriental Series 38 (New Haven: Yale University Press, 1955), 63. Cf. also Jacobsen's comments on letter-prayers in Jacobsen, 'Mesopotamia,' 205. A few Egyptian letter-prayers are attested as well. See E. Wente, *Letters from Ancient Egypt*. SBL Writings from the Ancient World Series 1 (Atlanta: Scholars Press, 1990), 219.

[86] Keller, 'Written Communications,' 300.

[87] Keller provides a helpful discussion on the few such texts that have been discovered (300–304).

[88] See Paul, 'Heavenly Tablets and the Book of Life,' 345–53.

[89] See D.C. Deuel, 'Malachi 3:16: 'Book of Remembrance' or Royal Memorandum? An Exegetical Note,' *The Masters Seminary Journal* 7:1 (1996), 107–111.

[90] Roger Tomes has recently provided a very helpful comparative methodology for the psalms. Instead of comparing them with the religious texts of Mesopotamia, Egypt, and Canaan, he, rather, shows how the letters of the ANE are an equally rewarding analogue. In other words, he suggests, like this paper, that the cult of ancient Israel should be observed and studied with secular analogies. 'Praise of and prayer to the deity are close enough to praise of and appeals to the king for them to sound very much alike. Either psalms are religious versions of secular discourse, or address to the king is modelled on religious discourse' (R. Tomes, *'I Have Written to the King, My Lord': Secular Analogies for the Psalms*. Hebrew Bible Monographs 1 [Sheffield: Sheffield Phoenix Press, 2005], 8).

state, and thus, it is very likely that, just as he would have corresponded to an earthly king with a letter, he equally sent a letter to his heavenly king.[91]

It was Yahweh's reply, or correspondence, however, that set him apart from other ANE deities. Not only does he indeed reply, but also it would seem that his correspondence (or revelation) operates likewise to the administrative correspondence of the known day. In the ANE, kings used documents to administrate their kingdoms.[92] They preserved some texts in the royal archives as records of administrative decisions; others were dispatched and carried by messengers to officials who would carry out the actions commanded within. The correspondence of these documents played a vital role in the transmission of information. ANE kings built sophisticated networks of roads and relay stations[93], in essence a postal system, to provide the exchange of correspondence. With a communication infrastructure in place, they were able to expand their empires considerably.[94] Through the dispatching of oral and written missives the officials administered their areas of responsibility and established and maintained diplomatic

---

[91] Hallo ('Individual Prayer in Sumerian: The Continuity of a Tradition,' 71–89) speculates that the prayer of Hezekiah (Isa. 38) and a few of the psalms, specifically the Davidic *miktām* psalms (Psalms 16, 56–60) are the closest parallels to the Sumerian letter-prayers. He speculates that they may well have originated as royal inscriptions. (Interestingly, the LXX translates *miktām* as *stēlographia,* i.e., 'stela inscription').

[92] For an excellent example of how different types of administrative documents were used in the ANE, see D.C. Deuel, 'Apprehending Kidnappers by Correspondence at Provincial Arrapha,' in *Mesopotamia and the Bible: Comparative Explorations,* eds. M. Chavalas and K.L. Younger (Grand Rapids: Baker Academic, 2002), 191–208.

[93] Meier notes the antiquity of the system: 'The evidence confirms that the Persians were not the initiators of a sophisticated postal and relay system but were the heirs of a long tradition. Ur III, Old Babylonian and Neo-Assyrian monarchs are known to have maintained a communication network which permitted the rapid flow of information essential to the welfare of the palace' (S.A. Meier, *The Messenger in the Ancient Semitic World*. Harvard Semitics Museum 45 [Atlanta: Scholars Press, 1988], 128–29).

[94] Cf. W.L. Westermann, 'On Inland Transportation and Communication in Antiquity,' *Political Science Quarterly* 43: 1928, 375–76; A.D. Crown, 'Tidings and Instructions: How News Traveled in the Ancient Near East,' *Journal of the Economic and Social History of the Orient* 17: 1974, 264–65; B.J. Beitzel, 'Travel and Communication (OT World),' in *The Anchor Bible Dictionary,* edited by D.N. Freedman (New York: Doubleday, 1992) vol. 6, 644–48.

relations with other regions.[95] As a result, messengers played critical roles in the correspondence systems.[96]

Drawing upon these trappings of ANE kingship and administrative correspondence we can get a better picture of not only what Yahweh is like but also how he works. Yahweh possesses a throne, manifests attributes of kingship, and gathers about himself courtiers among who are messengers and scribes—a so-called divine council.[97] In his role as Sovereign *par excellence*, the biblical writers describe Yahweh as the exalted and transcendent king who dispatches his messengers from his heavenly court to direct the affairs of his people. Thus, Yahweh uses administrative correspondence metaphorically to 'communicate' his message and transcendence.[98]

Equally important in the manner in which the biblical writers describe Yahweh's self-revelation is how they portray Yahweh's character. The two are significantly correlated. Not only is he portrayed as the supreme and incomparable[99] God-King, but he is a God-King who happily reveals his will to his subjects. As Block points out:

> It is perhaps the gracious nature of [Yahweh's] dealings with his own people that distinguishes him from all other deities. He is not capricious, ego-

---

[95] A.R. Millard, 'Oral Proclamation and Written Record: Spreading and Preserving Information in Ancient Israel,' in *Michael: Historical, Epigraphical and Biblical Studies in Honor of Prof. Michael Heltzer*, edited by Y. Avishur and R. Deutsch (Tel Aviv: Archaeological Center Publication, 1999) 237–41.

[96] Cf. Meier, *The Messenger in the Semitic World*; J. Greene, *The Role of the Messenger and the Message in the Ancient Near East*. Brown Judaic Series 169 (Atlanta: Scholars Press, 1989); V.H. Matthews, 'Messengers and the Transmission of Information in the Mari Kingdom,' in *Go to the Land I Will Show You: Studies in Honor of Dwight W. Young*, edited by J.E. Coleson and V.H. Matthews (Winona Lake: Eisenbrauns, 1996) 267–74.

[97] Cf. M.E. Polley, 'Hebrew Prophecy within the Council of Yahweh, Examined in its Ancient Near Eastern Setting,' in *Scripture in Context: Essays on the Comparative Method*, edited by C.D. Evans, W.W. Hallo, and J.B. White (Pittsburgh: The Pickwick Press, 1980) 141–56.

[98] This means that there is a correlation between Yahweh's use of administrative correspondence and his 'relational distance' (i.e., transcendence) from his people.

[99] Cf. C.J. Labuschange, *The Incomparability of Yahweh in the Old Testament* (Leiden: Brill, 1966); and D.N. Freedman, 'Who is Like Thee Among the Gods,' in *Ancient Israelite Religion*, edited by P.D. Miller, P.D. Hanson, and S.D. McBride (Philadelphia: Fortress Press, 1987) 315–35.

> tistical, or self-indulgent, as are his rivals. The history of biblical revelation is a history of merciful condescension . . . Yahweh [continually] assures his people that his covenant with them is eternal, for he is distinctively on who keeps his word.[100]

In other words, the character of Yahweh and biblical revelation go hand-in-hand. Yahweh is unlike the highly capricious and elusive gods of the ANE who resort to 'hiding' their messages in sheep's entrails and the like. He makes himself known through a 'word,' that is something written.

This is why biblical religion is often referred to as the religion of the 'book'. No other ANE religion had such a 'book'. A book that is quite diverse but nevertheless unified. If Weeks is correct in placing the covenant early, and if we take the canonical shaping seriously[101], then it seems that it is the covenant between Yahweh and Israel that unites the biblical corpus together. After all, it is Israel and her relationship with Yahweh that seems to be the main subjects of the Bible. Seen in this way, the historical books are a history of the covenantal relationship. The wisdom books give practical advice on obeying the covenant.[102]

---

[100] D.I. Block, *The Gods of the Nations: Studies in Ancient Near Eastern National Theology*.2nd edition (Grand Rapids/Leicester: Baker Academic/Apollos, 2000) 151.

[101] Accepting the tri-partition of the TaNaKH as significant, the Torah/Pentateuch (or Covenant/Law) becomes the foundation for the Prophets and Writings. The final editors of the canon made this apparent by placing quite strategically the mandate to 'meditate on Torah' as the introduction to the other two partitions (Joshua 1:8; Psalm 1:2). More on this see J.C. Trebolle Barrera, 'Origins of a Tripartite Old Testament Canon,' in *The Canon Debate*, edited by L.M. McDonald and J.A. Sanders (Peabody: Hendrickson, 2002) 133–34. See also James M. Hamilton, 'Canonical Biblical Theology,' in *God's Glory Revealed in Christ: Essays on Biblical Theology in Honor of Thomas R. Schreiner*, edited by Denny Burk, James M. Hamilton Jr., and Brian Vickers (Nashville: Broadman and Holman, 2019) 59–73.

[102] In responding to those who see the nonhistorical nature of wisdom literature—absence of patriarchal promises, Exodus and Moses, the covenant and Sinai, the promise to David, and so forth—Waltke concedes that is largely so, 'yet Solomon, as king of Israel (Prov. 1:1), looked at humanity and his world through *the lens of Israel's covenants* and drew the conclusion that one could enter the world of wisdom only through the fear of the Lord (1:7)' (B.K. Waltke, 'Wisdom Literature,' in *The Face of Old Testament Studies: A Survey of Contemporary Approaches*, edited by D.W. Baker and B.T. Arnold [Grand Rapids: Baker, 1999] 297, emphasis mine). In other words, the Israelite sages could be regarded as 'covenant practitioners'. The covenant/law was black and white

The psalms are a reflection of their cultic worship of the covenantal deity. The king administrates the covenant (Deut. 17: 18–20). The priests teach the covenant and perform the covenant rituals (Mal. 2: 4–7). The prophets, as the 'messengers of Yahweh'[103] are his covenant enforcers.[104] Life in Israel centred on the covenant.[105]

Therefore, if biblical revelation is analogous to ANE administrative correspondence, what then was being administrated? In a word, the covenant. Biblical revelation and the purposes for which Yahweh revealed himself were to promulgate and administrate the covenant. In other words, all that Yahweh wanted to disclose about himself and his relationship with Israel is done through the program of covenant. Walton summarises it this way, 'in the plan of God, the goal is relationship, the objective is revelation, the mechanism is covenant, and the instrument is Israel'.[106] Consequently, the purpose of revelation is revealing and administrating a covenant whereby a relationship between Yahweh and people are established. Niehaus suggests something very close to this when he argues that Yahweh 'appears' in 'theophanic glory' as part of his covenantal administrations: 1) to initiate a covenant, 2) to instruct, encourage, or correct his covenant vassal, 3) to commission or encourage a prophet in a covenantal lawsuit, 4) to bring covenantal judgement against rebellious vassals, 5) to bring covenantal salvation to his covenantal vassal, and 6) to demonstrate his presence as a testimony to his covenant.[107]

---

but life yields moments when things are grey. For example, the law says do not commit adultery. The sage takes the law and extrapolates, giving practical advice; in this case, to the point of not even heading down the street of a prostitute (Proverbs 7).

[103] See J.S. Holladay, 'Assyrian Statecraft and the Prophets of Israel,' *Harvard Theological Review* 63: 1970, 29–51.

[104] Cf. H.B. Huffmon, 'The Covenant Lawsuit in the Prophets, 'Journal *of Biblical Literature* 78: 1959, 285–95.

[105] The centrality of the covenant in interpreting Scripture suggests that a sound biblical-theological approach necessitates interpreting the biblical narrative sequentially. As Dempster puts it: 'a particular sequence suggests hermeneutical significance'. See S. G. Dempster, *Dominion and Dynasty: A Biblical Theology of the Hebrew Bible* (Downers Grove: InterVarsity Press, 2004) 34.

[106] J. Walton, *Covenant: God's Purpose, God's Plan* (Grand Rapids: Zondervan, 1994) 60.

[107] Niehaus, *God at Sinai: Covenant & Theophany in the Bible and Ancient Near East* (Grand Rapids, MI: Zondervan Academic, 1995) 108–109.

With that in mind, it is worth going back and looking at the 'word of Yahweh' formula a bit closer. Taken in its ANE context, it resembles quite considerably to the pattern 'the word of the king;' which is understood as a royal command, a linguistic formula employed to describe the dictates of gods and kings.[108] Thus certain oracles, commands, and decisions originating with the gods may often be prefaced with 'the word of Ishtar,' 'the word of Nusku,' 'the word of Sin,' etc. In addition, Akkadian letters with an epistolary introduction, 'the word of the king,' is widely attested as a phenomenon of royal missives. It is perhaps this type of secular analogy that 'the word of Yahweh' formula should be understood. A full study cannot be given here but it is remarkable that in many contexts 'the word of Yahweh' is described as coming to the prophet in a dream or vision and what follows the formula appears to be a person-to-person conversation; indicating divine presence involved in the revelatory event (e.g., Gen. 15; Jer. 1).[109] Even without explicit evidence of divine presence in the text, the question remains: 'the word of Yahweh came . . .', but how did it come? Perhaps with the use of the ANE secular analogies, the word of Yahweh arriving to the prophet signifies the arrival of a messenger—a messenger of Yahweh. If 'the word of Yahweh' is correlative with 'the word of a king' and both are classified as messenger formula,[110] then it may be that the normal or ordinary means by which Yahweh revealed himself was through a messenger(s).[111]

108 For a good discussion of the formula and its ANE counterparts see Meier, *Speaking of Speaking: Marking Direct Discourse in the Hebrew Bible*, 314–19.

109 I address this more fully in R.T. Stanton, 'The Person in Old Testament Theophanies,' in *Proclaiming Truth, Pastoring Hearts: Essays in Honour of Deane J. Woods*, edited by R.T. Stanton and L.J. Crawford (Adelaide: ACM Press, 2003) 53–93.

110 Certain formulas in the biblical text, including this one, which are described as part of divine speech, are not attributed by all scholars as 'messenger formula'. Meier's discussion is fairly thorough (Meier, *Speaking of Speaking: Marking Direct Discourse in the Hebrew Bible*, 273–322. Wagner has recently readdressed the issue and believes the messenger theory is justified (A. Wagner, *Prophetie als Theologie: Die so spricht Jahwe-Formeln und das Grundverständnis alttestamentlicher Prophetie*. Forschungen zur Religion und Literatur des Alten und Neuen Testaments 207 [Gottingen: Vandenhoeck & Ruprecht. 2004]).

111 Polak recently observed that many of the Mari texts that include treaties/covenants have envoys, ambassadors, or messengers acting on behalf of the king in making the treaty alliance. The king was not always present. This, plus other formal similarities he points out, 'provide the justification for the structural comparison between the biblical

The transmission of the word of Yahweh from the prophet to the people already had an analogy to the ANE messengers promulgating the message of the king.[112] Why not then, the transmission from Yahweh to the prophet be done in like manner? This may very well be what is described in 1 Samuel 3. The chapter opens (3:1) with a crisis: revelation had not been given for some time to Israel; the word of Yahweh was only coming rarely.[113] The crisis is finally resolved when 'Yahweh revealed himself to Samuel at Shiloh with the word of Yahweh; and (therefore) the word of Samuel came to all of Israel' (3:21 – 4:1). Clearly, the means that the word of Samuel came to the people was either through Samuel going to the people and speaking to them himself or if not him directly, possibly through one of his messengers. Either way, the word of Samuel arrived to the people via a personal agent. Interestingly enough, the word of Yahweh to Samuel arrived the

covenant tradition and the treaty procedures of Mari and other kingdoms of the Old Babylonian period' (F. Polak, 'The Covenant at Mount Sinai in Light of Texts from Mari,' in *Sefer Moshe: The Moshe Weinfeld Jubilee Volume*, edited by C. Cohen, A. Hurvitz, and S. Paul [Winona Lake: Eisenbrauns, 2004] 119–34). For the analogy, he singles out Moses as the messenger (or 'mediator') for Israel in the covenant with Yahweh. Though he doesn't carry the analogy over to Yahweh, it is interesting to speculate. Understanding the role of messengers in the covenant process may bring new light to the מלאך יהוה passages (e.g., Judges 2:1) and מלאך הברית text (Malachi 3:1).

[112] See the important study by Holladay, 'Assyrian Statecraft and the Prophets of Israel' *The Harvard Theological Review* 63:1 (Jan 1970): 29–51.

[113] The expression 'the word of Yahweh' is mentioned three times (3:1, 7, 21), yet it does not once contain all the elements of the revelational formula 'the word of Yahweh came to PN'. Only in v. 1 does the verb היה occur with the construction, but even then, there is the absence of אל('to'). In addition, the translation of v. 1 in many of the English translations (e.g., NASB) unfortunately reads, 'and word from the LORD was rare in those days, visions were infrequent'. The Hebrew, however, conveys something slightly different: ודבר יהוה היה יקר. First notice that דבר יהוה is a construct relationship, but the translators omitted the definiteness of *'the word'*. Secondly, though 'from' can be a legitimate translation in some contexts, the preposition is an interpretive element not necessarily supported here. Furthermore, since היה is juxtaposed with דבר יהוה there is perhaps something more that the biblical writer wants to convey than 'was'. For example, the Targums read, 'And the word of the LORD became hidden in those days' (*Tg. Neb.*). Thus, if the biblical writer understood דבר יהוה not as a rhetorical formula, but perhaps as introducing divine presence, then there might be the idea that יקר ('rare') is acting adverbially (see the discussion in GKC §100d for the use of adjectives acting as adverbs). As a result, it is my opinion that the text would be better understood: 'and the word of Yahweh came rarely in those days'.

very same way. There was no ecstatic experience or some divine 'impression' placed upon his mind. The revelation in 1 Samuel 3 cannot be described by anything less than a person-to person conversation. Yahweh 'calls,' he 'stands', and he 'speaks' with Samuel. It is all described as 'something seen'.[114] The word of Yahweh coming to Samuel is paralleled to the word of Samuel coming to Israel (4:1). Having them both side by side gives us some insight on the means by which Yahweh reveals himself. In other words, it is the everyday non-theological context that provides colour for the metaphorical milieu used to depict Yahweh's communication.

Conclusion

Biblical revelation should be understood as Yahweh's administrative correspondence. Yahweh is king, Israel is his vassal, and what he administrates is the covenant. As a result, Yahweh's communication comes as 'the word of the king' = 'the word of Yahweh'.[115] In this, the biblical religion is rather distinctive.[116] Unlike His competitors in the

---

[114] המראה is normally translated 'a vision' not 'a dream'; contra R.K. Gnuse, *The Dream Theophany of Samuel: Its Structure in Relation to Ancient near Eastern Dreams and its Theological Significance* (Lanham: University Press of America, 1984). See additional comments by J. Sasson, 'The Eyes of Eli: An Essay in Motif Accretion,' in *Inspired Speech: Prophecy in the Ancient Near East: Essays in Honour of Herbert B. Huffmon*, edited by J. Kaltner and L. Stulman. Journal for the Study of the Old Testament Supplement Series 378 (London: T & T Clark, 2004) 181–84.

[115] Lawlor, 'Word Event in Jeremiah: A Look at the Composition's 'Introductory Formulas',' 231–43 has many good things to say regarding the דבר יהוה formula in Jeremiah but resorts to form criticism concluding that there is a literary or rhetorical use of the formula in the composition of the book. No attention is given to the phrase in a theophanic or covenantal context.

[116] The current trend in Old Testament studies is to make 'biblical prophecy' a subset of divination. See most recently the article and bibliography given in John H. Hilber, 'Israelite Prophecy in Its Ancient Near Eastern Context,' in H.H. Hardy II and M. Daniel Carrol R. (eds), *The State of Old Testament Studies: A Survey of Recent Research* (Grand Rapids, MI: Baker Academic, 2024), 132–45. This is but another attempt to suppress the distinctiveness of biblical religion. A thorough scholarship will prove that the Ancient Israelite religion, with all the internal and external evidence, will yield a different picture when contrasted with the ANE (e.g., monotheism vs. monolatry). In fact, if we have learned anything from Noel Weeks' book it is that there was no monolithic culture in the ANE; see N.K. Weeks, *Admonition and Curse: The ANE Treaty/Covenant Form as a Problem in Inter-Cultural Relationships*. Journal for the Study of the Old Testament Sup-

ANE world who are capricious and normally hidden, Yahweh makes his character and His word known freely and wilfully. It could be said that 'the great boon granted to Israel by Yahweh was the privilege of having revelation, the Torah from Sinai, as well as the admonitions of the prophets, concerning precisely what their God expected of them.'[117]

How did Yahweh reveal what he expected of them? The manner in which the biblical writers describe Yahweh's self-revelation should be seen consistent with his character. Therefore, divine revelation in the Bible, if we follow this thinking and contrary to popular opinion, is possibly uniform and homogeneous after all. Something that was the very opposite of divine revelation in the rest of the ANE.

How do we then explain the diversity of means that Yahweh employed for his self-revelation? I believe that it is necessary to explain the differences through the model just briefly sketched. Starting as Yahweh as king and his communication as administrative correspondence. Only a thorough historical-grammatical-comparative method to the texts will yield such a possibility.[118]

---

plement Series 407 (London: T & T Clark, 2004). While similar in many respects, each culture in its own right could claim distinctiveness. A discussion of ancient Israel's distinctiveness is furthered by P. Machinist, 'The Question of Distinctiveness in Ancient Israel,' in *A Highway from Egypt to Assyria: Studies in Ancient Near Eastern History and Historiography Presented to Hayim Tadmor*, edited by I. Eph'al and M. Cogan (Jerusalem: Magnes Press, 1990) 196–212.

[117] Walton, *Ancient Israelite Literature*, 24

[118] The full argumentation of my attempt to formulate a 'forensic theology of revelation' can be found in my unpublished University of Sydney PhD thesis, 'Biblical Revelation in its ANE Context'.

Part 4
The Outworking in Systematic Theology

Twelve

Limited or Universal Atonement? Why Not Have Both?

Jared Hood

Peter Barnes is a prolific author and has made a significant contribution to the Presbyterian Church of Australia. He is an incisive church historian and an erudite biblical scholar. One of his writings that I have particularly appreciated is an article he wrote for the *Reformed Theological Review*, 'The Free Offer of the Gospel'.[1] He argues for limited atonement and the free offer in a highly irenic way.

In grateful response to Peter's article, though without his wit and his sometimes slightly mischievous style, I would like to reflect upon limited atonement. Many see the doctrine as merely theological extrapolation, but of those who do accept it, some want to hold it alongside or subsumed by universal atonement. This is the question addressed now: 'Why not hold to both limited and universal atonement?' The question is not about the Cross in every respect but in its essential nature.[2] Did Christ give His life to satisfy for the sins of both his elect people and all people?

A broad view of options for understanding the extent of the atonement will be given first. Next, the data for limited atonement will, rather simply, be compiled with little exegetical argumentation, before seeking at greater length to place onto firmer ground the argument that

[1] Peter Barnes, 'The Free Offer of the Gospel,' *Reformed Theological Review 59*, no. 1 (April 2000), 28–36.

[2] J. I. Packer, 'Introduction: Penal Substitution Revisited,' in *In My Place Condemned He Stood: Celebrating the Glory of the Atonement*, eds. J. I. Packer and Mark Dever (Wheaton, IL: Crossway, 2007), 25; what John R. W. Stott (*The Cross of Christ: 20th Anniversary Edition* (Downers Grove: IVP, 2006), 195) called the 'heart of the Gospel.' Alternative theories of the atonement such as encouraged by Aulén are not in view here (Gustaf Aulén, *Christus Victor: An Historical Study of the Three Main Types of the Idea of the Atonement* (London: SPCK, 1965).

limited atonement inherently negates unlimited atonement. The data for unlimited atonement will then be considered, but in a way that tries to avoid the typical exegetical slogging match that usually accompanies this debate. The analogy of Scripture will be the key at this point. Finally, various theological arguments for limited atonement will be given—somewhat familiar territory, but hopefully still with some thoughtful emphasis.

A Biblical Debate?

Biblical Questions

Scripture seems to speak of the atonement in both limited and unlimited terms.[3] There are three ways of resolving the tension, as follows.

1. The atonement is only definite. The texts that appear to be indefinite will be understood to be:
    a. Not indefinite but definite.
    b. Not about the atonement (but probably about the free offer).

    Definite atonement was held by Anselm, the Reformed orthodox (Owen, Turretin), Whitefield, Bavinck, Hodge, Warfield, and Vos.[4]

2. The atonement is both definite and indefinite. John Davenant posited two divine decrees. In one decree, Christ died for all. In the other decree, Christ died for some. Still, the Cross was not quite 'for all' in the same way it was 'for some'. The Cross

[3] Terminology will not be debated: limited, definite, or intentional; indefinite, universal, general, or unlimited. When the nature of atonement is understood, the adjectives become redundant. If I made a purchase at a shop, no-one asks whether it was a limited purchase. The question is, 'What did you purchase?' It is intrinsically definite, and the purchaser has something to show for it (not that one wants to overstretch payment language).

[4] David S. Hogg, ''Sufficient for All, Efficient for Some': Definite Atonement in the Medieval Church,' in *From Heaven He Came and Sought Her: Definite Atonement in Historical, Biblical, Theological, and Pastoral Perspective*, eds., David Gibson and Jonathan Gibson (Wheaton, IL: Crossway Books, 2013), 75–96, argues that Aquinas and Lombard saw the atonement in definite terms.

is 'medicine' for the world but an effective satisfaction for the elect.[5]

3. The atonement is only indefinite. The texts that appear to be definite will be understood to be:
    a. Not definite but indefinite.
    b. Not about the atonement (but about salvation applied, about the accomplishment and application together, or otherwise vaguely understood).
    c. Definite but not mutually exclusive of universality ('many' being a subgroup of 'all').

Arminius, Amyraut, and Wesley held to unlimited atonement. Amyraut had Christ dying only for all and the Spirit applying that to some. The Cross itself did not guarantee faith and life for anyone.

Points 2 and 3c each produce the 'Why not both?' scenario. This study focuses on 3c, which, on closer inspection, is not actually a two-atonement view. It has the limited as a subset of the universal, so there is only one atonement. Christ died for the elect since he died for all. The review below will still have relevance to point 2, though the concept of a hypothetical universal divine decree will not be discussed.

Biblical Answers

One would think that exegesis would determine which of the above positions is correct, but there are other forces in play that give unlimited atonement a privileged position today. These forces include the following:

1. Group identity. Evangelical traditionalism is alive and well, and that tradition, since the 18th century, is weighted towards unlimited atonement.
2. Natural theology. We too easily think we know what God is like from general revelation. Axioms such as 'God loves all' and,

[5] John Davenant, 'A Dissertation on the Death of Christ' in *An Exposition of the Epistle of St Paul to the Colossians* (London: Hamilton, Adams, and Co., 1832), 2:344. There is considerable ambiguity and inconsistency. It is akin to the dispensationalist ascribing two meanings to the one word *parousia* (coming).

therefore, 'Christ died for all' feel instinctive. Even the 19th-century liberals, having jettisoned the Bible, still believed in God's universal love.

3. Postmodern worldview. Binary oppositions are restrictive and should be deconstructed. Dichotomies are to be resisted. The question is almost reflexive: 'Why not both?'
4. Political ideology. 'Equality' is enshrined in the classical Western tradition and weaponised in socialist political activism. Limited atonement, though, says that, in the central Gospel act, all are not equal. It sounds positively medieval (and in many respects, it is positively medieval and was swept aside by the 18th-century Enlightenment).
5. Theology of glory. In a pragmatic world that measures success by numbers, surely the greatness of God's great love is proved by an atonement that embraces the largest number of people.

The pressure to hold limited atonement is comparatively diminutive. Denominations may still require the doctrine, though confessional standards were mostly relaxed in the 19th century. That the great Reformed theologians affirmed limited atonement will influence some. However, this is not the overwhelming alliance of forces militating for a universal atonement. Advocates of limited atonement are more likely to be defensive and apologetic: 'Yes, I affirm limited atonement, but there might be mystery there. I don't want to be dogmatic.' Limited atonement ekes out its existence on a stark and lonely landscape.

The point is this: 'Be very strong to keep and to do all that is written' (Josh. 23:6). It does need to be a biblical debate, not a debate governed by hidden presuppositions and one's historical setting.

Limited Atonement Texts — They Are There, and They Cannot Be Silenced

The evangelical zeitgeist belittles limited atonement as only theological extrapolation rather than as being biblically based.[6] Advocates of

---

[6] David Broughton Knox, *D. Broughton Knox: Selected Works. Volume I: The Doctrine of God* (Kingsford: Matthias Media, 2000), 263, 'a textless doctrine'.

limited atonement can comply with the stereotype, feeling unsure of their exegetical ground and preferring theological arguments. However, dare one put it like this, 'theological extrapolation' is fake news. Scripture simply keeps speaking of a limited atonement.[7] The list below provides twenty examples of supporting verses (along with a passage about Christ's active obedience). Some might be surprised at the weight of the biblical witness.

The list is not complete. It omits most of the profuse first-person language: 'He bore *our* sins... a curse for *us*... the propitiation for *our* sins... suffered for *us*' (e.g., Titus 2:14, 'gave himself for us... a people for his own possession'). Limited atonement advocates are in a predicament here. The profuse data usually must be truncated to present a concise argument—giving the appearance of a lack of data and mere theological extrapolation.[8]

1. Stricken for the transgression of my people (Isa. 53:8).[9]
2. By his knowledge shall the righteous one, my servant, make many to be accounted righteous, and he shall bear their iniquities (Isa. 53:11).
3. You shall call his name Jesus, for he will save his people from their sins (Matt. 1:21).
4. The Son of Man came not to be served but to serve, and to give his life as a ransom for many (Matt. 20:28).
5. For this is my blood of the covenant, which is poured out for many for the forgiveness of sins (Matt. 26:28).
6. For even the Son of Man came not to be served but to serve, and to give his life as a ransom for many (Mark 10:45).
7. This is my blood of the covenant, which is poured out for many (Mark 14:24).
8. The good shepherd lays down his life for the sheep (John 10:11).

---

[7] David Gibson and Jonathan Gibson, 'Sacred Theology and the Reading of the Divine Word: Mapping the Doctrine of Definite Atonement,' in *From Heaven He Came and Sought Her: Definite Atonement in Historical, Biblical, Theological, and Pastoral Perspective*, eds., David Gibson and Jonathan Gibson (Wheaton, IL: Crossway Books, 2013), 38, where limited atonement is called a '*biblico-systematic* doctrine.'

[8] For a long list of atonement texts in the New Testament, see David L. Allen, *The Extent of the Atonement: A Historical and Critical Review* (Nashville, TN: B&H Academic, 2016), chapter 3.

[9] Unless otherwise noted, biblical quotations in this chapter are from the ESV.

9. I lay down my life for the sheep (John 10:15). Compare this with Ezek. 34:11–12: I myself will search for My sheep and will seek them out. As a shepherd seeks out his flock when he is among his sheep that have been scattered, so will I seek out my sheep, and I will rescue them.
10. He prophesied that Jesus would die for the nation, and not for the nation only, but also to gather into one the children of God who are scattered abroad (John 11:51–52).
11. Greater love has no one than this, that someone lay down his life for his friends. You are my friends (John 15:13–14).
12. Care for the church of God which he obtained with his own blood (Acts 20:28).
13. Therefore, as one trespass led to condemnation for all men, so one act of righteousness leads to justification and life for all men. For as by the one man's disobedience the many were made sinners, so also by the one man's obedience the many will be made righteous (Rom. 5:18–19).
14. Christ loved the church and gave himself up for her (Eph. 5:25).
15. Christ, having been offered once to bear the sins of many (Heb. 9:28)
16. To those who are elect exiles. . . according to the foreknowledge of God the Father, in the sanctification of the Spirit, for obedience to Jesus Christ and for sprinkling with his blood (1 Pet. 1:1–2).
17. The grace that was to be yours. . . when he predicted the sufferings of Christ (1 Pet. 1:10–11).
18. You were ransomed. . . not with perishable things. . . But with the precious blood of Christ. . . He. . . was made manifest in the last times for the sake of you (1 Pet. 1:18–20).
19. You were slain, and by your blood you ransomed people for God from every tribe and language and people and nation (Rev. 5:9).
20. Finally, the very first gospel verse in Scripture, Genesis 3:15: 'I will put enmity between you and the woman, and between your offspring and her offspring; he shall bruise your head, and you shall bruise his heel.' A universal atonement has Christ

> bruised by Satan for the sake of the seed of Satan. Genesis has the Warrior-Redeemer fighting for the people of God.[10]

Five observations should be made. First, every New Testament author is cited above except for James and Jude, who do not mention the atonement. In other words, limited atonement receives a consistent and pervasive testimony. It is not a deduction drawn from a few cherry-picked verses.

Secondly, few Old Testament texts have been cited, but this is not due to a lack of witness. The Old Testament frequently speaks about atonement in the sacrificial system but makes no provision for universality. Contrived arguments aside, it only presents typological atonement for the people of God.[11] If Gentiles want Israel's blessing, they need to obey the laws of Israel (Num. 9:14). One might retort that this is Old Testament racial myopia. Still, those who adhere to the unity of the covenants will see the implication. If limited atonement is in the Old Testament, it will be in the New.

Thirdly, some texts use the word 'many.' What does 'many' mean? Isaiah has the answer (also compare 'sheep' in Isa. 53:6 with John 10:11). In Isaiah, it is only the remnant coming through the exile that arrives safely at the new heavens and new earth. This is the 'offspring', separated from those who have 'rebelled' (66:22–24). This is the 'offspring' that is the product of the Servant's ministry in Isaiah 53 (53:10). This seed represents the 'many' for whom the Servant dies and whom the Servant justifies (53:10–11). Isaiah 53 solves the sin problem of the remnant.[12] 'Many' is a term referring to a particular group of people.

---

[10] See the similar and fuller discussion in Loraine Boettner, *The Reformed Doctrine of Predestination* (Grand Rapids, MI: Eerdmans, 1932), https://ccel.org/ccel/boettner/predest/predest.i.html.

[11] Paul R. Williamson, ''Because He Loved Your Forefathers': Election, Atonement, and Intercession in the Pentateuch,' in *From Heaven He Came and Sought Her: Definite Atonement in Historical, Biblical, Theological, and Pastoral Perspective*, eds., David Gibson and Jonathan Gibson (Wheaton, IL: Crossway Books, 2013), 238, 'Atonement in the OT is circumscribed by covenant and election and is therefore necessarily particular.'

[12] Cf. J. Alan Groves, 'Atonement in Isaiah 53,' in *The Glory of the Atonement: Biblical, Theological, and Practical Perspectives*, eds. Charles E. Hill and Frank A. James III (Down-

Fourthly, the above verses do not only speak of a definite *salvation* but also of a definite *atonement*. Only two verses have both the accomplishment and application of salvation in view. The others are specifically about accomplishment only (the atonement).

Fifthly, the point is that limited atonement texts are present in Scripture. Perhaps some could be interpreted as unlimited texts or not relevant to the discussion but surely not all of them. These limited atonement texts are there, and they cannot be silenced. This presents a significant problem for unlimited atonement, which is discussed next.

The Limited Excludes the Unlimited—Mutual Exclusivity

How do the limited atonement texts sit alongside the unlimited atonement texts? A committed 'universalist' (with a universal view of the atonement, not of salvation itself) might universalise every limited atonement text[13] or take the limited atonement texts as being only about salvation applied.[14] A typical approach is to affirm both universality and limitation. Carson expounds the limited focus of John 10:11–16 but sets it alongside the 'world' texts:

> However clearly this Gospel portrays Jesus as the Saviour of the world (4:42), the Lamb of God who takes away the sin of the world (1:29, 36), it insists no less emphatically that Jesus has a peculiar relation with those the Father has given him (6:37ff.), with those he has chosen out of the world (15:16, 19). So here: Jesus' death is peculiarly for his sheep, just as

---

ers Grove: IVP Academic, 2004), 87–89.

[13] Wesley comments on 11 of the texts in the list, taking them in two ways. First, they are about application, not accomplishment (Isa. 53:11; Matt. 1:21; Mark 14:24; John 11:51–52; 1 Pet. 1:10–11; Rev. 5:9—not 'redemption' but the 'fruit of it'), although the notes are too brief on some of these verses. Secondly, 'many' is universal: 'as many as spring from Adam', 'as many souls as needed such a ransom', 'many (that is, all men)', 'as many as are born into the world' (notes respectively on Matt. 26:28; Mark 10:45; Rom. 5:18–19; Heb. 9:28). John Wesley, *Wesley's Notes on the Bible* (n.p., 1754, 1765), https://ccel.org/ccel/wesley/notes/notes.i.html

[14] On John 10:11–16, see Richard C. H. Lenski, *The Interpretation of St. John's* Gospel, Commentary on the New Testament (Minneapolis, MN: Augsburg Fortress, 1943, 1961), 726. Jacobus Arminius, *Works of James Arminius*, 3 vols, vol. 3 (n.p., n.d.), https://ccel.org/ccel/arminius/works3/works3.i.html, 321, argued that William Perkins confounded the accomplishment with the application.

we elsewhere read that 'Christ loved the church and gave himself up for her' (Eph. 5:25).[15]

The outcome is that Scripture apparently says both of the following:

The atonement is for all.

The atonement is for some (the elect).

How can these two positions sit alongside each other, though? Is there not a contradiction here? Would not his paying for the sins of some exclude him paying for the sins of all? However, some argue, as it were, that the 'many' statements do not exclude the 'all' statements. 'Many' is a subcategory of 'all'.[16] Hence, the following conclusion results:

The atonement is for all, which includes some (the elect).

At least it does not give the atonement two meanings, as though Christ's death means one thing for all and something else for the elect, but there is still a problem.[17] The force of the 'some' texts needs to be

---

[15] D. A. Carson, *The Gospel According to John* (Leicester, UK: IVP, 1991), 387. D. A. Carson, *The Difficult Doctrine of the Love of God* (Leicester, UK: IVP, 2000), speaks more pointedly, connecting universality to the Cross's atoning sufficiency. However, 'sufficiency' has always been a red herring in the atonement debate, neither providing the reason for the free offer nor clarifying atoning intentionality. In what sense is the sufficiency 'for' all?

[16] David Broughton Knox, *D. Broughton Knox: Selected Works. Volume I: The Doctrine of God* (Kingsford: Matthias Media, 2000), 263. Jonathan Gibson, 'For Whom Did Christ Die? Particularism and Universalism in the Pauline Epistles,' in *From Heaven He Came and Sought Her: Definite Atonement in Historical, Biblical, Theological, and Pastoral Perspective*, eds. David Gibson and Jonathan Gibson (Wheaton, IL: Crossway Books, 2013), 292–93, notes others who take this approach.

[17] Francis Turretin, *Institutes of Elenctic Theology* (Phillipsburg, NJ: P&R, 1994), 2:460, saw the problem: 'Christ could not will to die absolutely for the elect without involving (by the law of contraries) a will not to die for the reprobate...All the passages adduced,

understood. That force is that definiteness excludes universality. The limited atonement texts do not only have the following meaning:

> The atonement is for some (the elect).

Their intended force is this:

> The atonement is for some *only* (the elect *and not others*).

Why should 'some (the elect)' be taken to be exclusive? Is it not a logical fallacy to infer unstated exclusivity? How is 'only' inferred? To explain this, a tedious argument follows.

The Rhetorical Implication of at Least Some Limited Atonement Statements

First, human language is not precise. It implies. It is elliptical. It does not always follow the patterns that the rules of logic would seem to dictate. For example, I might say, 'I am married to Cassie'. Does anyone conclude anything other than that I am married to Cassie *only*? I did not say 'only', but it is understood (although a different meaning might be intended if I lived in a different social context). These are language conventions.

Somewhat correlatively, in the legal context, there is the principle, *expressio unius est exclusio alterius*, the expression of one thing is the exclusion of another, which is somewhat equivalent to the regulative principle in a theological context. We are to do only what is commanded and are not free to do whatever is not prohibited. In other words, *only* is implied (even if not explicitly stated) in Scripture's commands.

Explaining when these conventions are present can be difficult. Context helps and will be addressed in a moment. Still, some observations about expressions in themselves can be made. First, the level of

---

if not explicitly yet implicitly include an exclusion in the description of those for whom Christ died (which cannot pertain to others).'

intensity or intentionality in a statement can indicate whether there is an unstated exclusion. The more important the topic or statement, the more likely that exclusivity is present. Statements expressing purpose are often significant statements. Hence, a statement about the focus of Christ's death is very likely to be meant exclusively: 'for many *only*', not for all.

Secondly, statements that specify number or enumerate are likely to be exclusive (whether the enumeration is exhaustive or examples of the class, *eiusdem generis*). 1 Peter 1:1 says that the letter is written to the pilgrims of 'Pontus, Galatia…' These are the primary recipients, even if a broader circulation was secondarily in mind. Hence, the enumeration implies *only*. The letter was not written primarily to those in Rome or Egypt. Neither was it written to non-pilgrims (non-Christians). Perhaps the enumerated are examples of a wider group, but that still gives a restriction ('Christians in Asia Minor (modern-day Turkey)'). If Peter had written, 'pilgrims in Rome, Asia, Egypt', he may have had in view all Christians in the ancient world.

Thirdly, as just indicated, restriction can be determined according to class. 'Christ died for the Ephesians' would not mean 'for the Ephesians only'. 'Ephesians' is part of the class of Christians—for Christians only and not non-Christians. The key is to see the class. More clearly, a statement that He gave His life 'for His sheep' would exclude 'goats' and 'wolves'. 'For His sheep' is not intended to mean 'for all animals', as it were. Again, 'for His friends' would not mean 'along with non-friends as a subgroup of all people'.

Universalists unconsciously infer a limitation according to class, just as limited atonement advocates consciously do, only universalists do it at a different stage. They reject 'many *only*' but read 'all *only*', as in '*human beings* only'. Is not 'all people' a subclass of all living things? Why not say that Christ satisfied for the sins of angels?

The discussion is tedious, but the point is that at least some texts are going to mean 'elect *only*'. It is difficult to believe that none imply exclusivity.

The Contextual Demand of At Least Some of the Limited Atonement Texts

Context clarifies the sense of at least some of the cited texts. When Jesus says that he lays down his life for his friends (John 15:13), 'friends', by context, is an exclusive group that omits non-friends. Verse 16 says that he specially chooses his friends: 'You did not choose me, but I chose you'. Verse 19 excludes from the circle of his friends the others of the rebellious world: 'I chose you out of the world'. The exclusivity of friends implies the exclusivity of the purpose in dying. Both the following will not be true, but the first rules out the second:

> I give my life for the friends—those chosen out of the world.
>
> I give my life for the non-friends—those not chosen out the world.

The Inexplicability of the Emphasis upon Particularity

Why would Scripture emphasise 'some' if—seemingly more gloriously—He gave His life for all? Were the scriptural authors selfishly fixated on their own salvation? Gibson draws on William Cunningham to say that the 'onus lies with proponents of a universal atonement to explain why Paul would employ limited or definite language if there really was no limitation in the intended object of the atonement.'[18]

Preachers who believe limited atonement can become tongue-tied when offering the Gospel, not being able to say, 'Christ died for you'. However, universalists have a more perilous predicament. How often will the universalist want to say, 'The Good Shepherd gave his life for the sheep'? It is a direct quote of Scripture, but universalists need to qualify it to the point of contradiction: 'The Shepherd died for his sheep, *but actually*, he died for all'. Limited atonement verses are effectively expunged from Scripture. It demonstrates again that 'many' and 'all' are mutually exclusive.

---

[18] Jonathan Gibson, 'For Whom Did Christ Die?' in *From Heaven He Came and Sought Her: Definite Atonement in Historical, Biblical, Theological, and Pastoral Perspective*, eds., David Gibson and Jonathan Gibson (Wheaton, IL: Crossway Books, 2013), 293.

Universal Texts and the Analogy of Scripture

Thus, there are limited atonement texts in Scripture, with implied exclusivity. Christ atoned only for the elect. What, then, should be done with the unlimited texts? At this point, the debate tends to descend into an exegetical slogging match. The advocate of universal atonement presents texts; the advocate of limited atonement (re)interprets them as limited or irrelevant to the discussion. There is a real problem here. The liberating doctrine of the atonement becomes hostage to the resolution of minutiae. There may be even 100 verses that clearly teach one position, but seemingly do so to no avail while a verse or two elude explanation.

All is not hopeless, though. The doctrine of the atonement can be set free by applying the well-known hermeneutical principle, the 'analogy of faith' or the 'analogy of Scripture'. The principle says that difficult texts do not hold clearer texts captive. Clearer texts take the lead, and difficult texts follow along (without flattening the richness of Scripture).[19] It is a God-honouring principle because it rests on belief in the divine authorship of Scripture. All Scripture, not just an individual text, is from God, and God does not contradict Himself. Some will heroically assert their understanding of the ambiguous text—baptism for the dead, a God who changes His mind—but zeal for the individual text ironically becomes unbiblical.

The 'analogy of Scripture' considers factors such as the following:

- Volume: a few texts do not supplant multiple uniform texts.
- Spread: a cluster of passages in one subsection of Scripture does not supplant the teaching of many authors across Scripture.
- Intensity: unexplained, metaphorical, and incidental statements do not supplant overt theological explanation.

---

[19] And with fair-minded 'common sense.' Pedantry can reduce any text to incomprehensibility. J. Ramsey Michaels, 'Atonement in John's Gospel and Epistles,' in *The Glory of the Atonement: Biblical, Theological, and Practical Perspectives*, eds. Charles E. Hill and Frank A. James III (Downers Grove, IL: IVP, 2004), 109, 112, remarkably finds that John's Gospel has no theology of atonement. However, whilst John 10:11 might not painstakingly say that Jesus 'dies in penal substitutionary atonement for the sins of' the sheep, Isa. 53:6 is presupposed.

- Contextual clarity: passages that fail to define terms by context do not supplant contextually clear passages.

On these measures, limited atonement is well established in Scripture, but what of unlimited atonement? Universal texts are categorised below into three groups: the 'saved the world' texts, the 'desires to save the world' texts, and the 'died for the world' texts.

'Saved the World' Texts

Three-quarters of 'Saviour' texts in the New Testament are exclusive. The Saviour is ours, Israel's, the body's, etc (18 of 24 uses). One text does not indicate whom he saves (2 Pet. 3:2). Still, in three texts, he is described in the following ways:

- 'Saviour of the world' (John 4:42),
- 'Saviour of all people, especially of those who believe' (1 Tim. 4:10), and
- 'Saviour of the world' (1 John 4:14).

Two similar texts have a saved world (without the word 'Saviour'):

- 'In Christ God was reconciling the world to himself, not counting their trespasses against them' (2 Cor. 5:19) and
- 'The Lamb of God, who takes away the sin of the world' (John 1:29—is this about salvation accomplished or applied?).

A universalist would be foolish to marshal these texts (again, remembering that 'universalist' here refers to a personal who believes in a universal atonement, not a universal salvation). They say too much. They are not only about the atonement. They are about the outcome of salvation. If 'world' must mean every person in human history, then every person is saved.[20]

---

[20] Frederick Dale Bruner, *The Gospel of John: A Commentary* (Grand Rapids, MI: Eerdmans, 2012), 202, forcefully underlines 'the world' and 'all people' in John 3:16 and 1 Tim. 4:10 as though that inherently proves the point and counters the 'theological

The universalist should learn from these verses. 'World' cannot possibly be 'every person' in these texts. The retort could be that 'Saviour' does not mean 'Saviour', but would this not twist the term to suit the doctrine—the very thing that advocates of limited atonement are accused of doing?

The main point is this: whether limiting 'world' or 'Saviour', some caution is needed with these verses. They should not be placed on equal footing with or be used to overturn clearer verses.

As to what the passages do mean, perhaps they indicate that Jesus is the *offered* Saviour. The free offer is not a universal atonement. More likely, 'world' is not what the universalists imagine. In John 4:42, it could easily mean all races, not Jews only, since it is said by Samaritans. 1 Timothy 4:10 has its own complexity. It could be alluding to Psalm 36:6, which says that God preserves (literally 'saves') people and animals.[21] Alternatively, perhaps Paul qualifies his thought in the next clause: 'the Saviour of all people, *by which I mean*...those who believe.'

'Desires All to Be Saved' Texts

- God 'desires all people to be saved' (1 Tim. 2:4).
- 'The Lord is...not wishing that any should perish' (2 Pet. 3:9).

The passages are not about the atonement and so are not relevant to the discussion. A universalist might say that God's desire must be given expression in atonement, but that is theological extrapolation, not exegesis.

The verses could be about God's desire to save all his people or all classes of people, or they could be about the free offer of the Gospel. God wants all to be saved, just as he wants all to love their neighbours and not to murder. This would be God's will of precept rather than decree, saying nothing about the decretal intentionality behind the Cross.

---

theory' of the L in TULIP. He misses the exegetical detail in his haste to support his own theological theory.

[21] Turretin, *Institutes*, 2:461.

'Died for All/the World' Texts

Most 'died for all' texts have both accomplished *and* applied salvation in view. Hence, if 'all/world' must be 'every person in history', every person is atoned for *and* saved. The advocate of unlimited atonement who does not believe in universal salvation would be foolish to rely on these texts.

- John 12:32 has Christ lifted up and drawing 'all people' to himself. The difficulty is that 'drawing' is what the Father does to bring the elect to Christ (John 6:44). 'All' cannot possibly mean every person unless the belief is that all are saved. 'All', in the plural, could easily mean 'all people groups'.
- 2 Cor. 5:14–15 says that Christ 'died for all'. Paul also uses the language of 'all' in Romans 5, but quickly swaps the language to 'many'. 2 Corinthians 5:19 adds that the 'world' is reconciled, so once again, 'all' and 'world' cannot possibly mean 'every person' unless the belief is that all are reconciled.
- Heb. 2:9 says that Jesus 'tasted death for everyone'. The next verse speaks of bringing 'many sons to glory', so 'all' is defined—all sons. Once again, 'all' cannot mean 'every person'.

2 Peter 2:1 does not help. Some 'deny the Master who bought them', but this only signifies that they deny the one whom they had previously claimed was their Redeemer.

There is a handful of 'died for all' texts that are more suggestive.

John 3:16, with John 6:51

Universalists may have become increasingly frustrated with this discussion. Why has John 3:16 not been mentioned? It is the linchpin of universal atonement.

The consensus is that 'world' in John uniformly signifies all people in rebellion against God. Thus, God loved fallen humanity. However, it is extraordinarily unlikely that this is John's point. He certainly does not say anything like it anywhere else. Other writers might say it, but not 'John the sectarian'.[22] That 'world' is not 'everyone' is evident when comparing John 3:16 with John 6:33 and John 6:51. Jesus does not just offer salvation to the 'world'; He actually provides it. 'He...gives life to the world'! Are all saved?

John does not use 'world' uniformly. This needs exploration elsewhere. One-quarter of the time, John's uses of 'world' are metaphorical, signifying 'openly, publicly, to many' (e.g. John 7:4; 12:19). In John 7:4, Jesus' brothers say, 'Show yourself to the world'. They only mean that He should go to Jerusalem, probably to be scrutinised by Israel's religious leaders. That is a very small 'world'! John 3:16 might mean, 'God loved so widely and openly that he gave his Son' (just as Moses lifted up the snake so openly to the repentant Israelites).

1 Timothy 2:6

Christ Jesus 'gave himself as a ransom for all'. 'All' need not be every person. In vv. 1–2, 'all people' is probably 'all kinds or classes of people', with 'kings and all who are in high positions' cited as an example of a class (unless one is meant to pray for every king in history!). Verse four adds that God 'desires all people to be saved', but that gives no further information for defining 'all'.

1 John 2:2

'He is the propitiation for our sins, and not for ours only but also for the sins of the whole world.' As with John 3:16, 'world' could easily be 'openly, widely' or as unrestrictive of ethnicity, 'not Jews only'. The context gives no assistance in defining 'world'.

---

[22] Robert H. Gundry, *Jesus the Word according to John the Sectarian* (Grand Rapids, MI: Eerdmans, 2002).

The important point is this: A universalist reading is possible in these passages, not because they clearly teach it, but because the contexts do not rule it out. 'All' and 'world' are not overtly defined, and the universalist exploits the ambiguity. The universalist too readily forces a presupposed definition of 'all' and 'world' upon the texts.

The universalist has an insurmountable hurdle. It is not enough to show that 'world' and 'all' can mean 'every person' in some texts. The universalist must prove that this is what is meant in these specific verses. The contexts are just not clear enough to allow such a dogmatic reading. Underlining, bolding, italicising, or loudly reciting 'world' and 'all' does not help. These verses are no sure basis for framing a doctrine of unlimited atonement.[23]

It could whimsically be put that to pit three or four ambiguously universalist texts against 20 limited texts gives the universalist position a 20 per cent likelihood of being correct. If the dozens more 'our' and 'us' texts that support limited atonement are included, the 20 per cent is probably halved (I have not counted all the texts). That ten per cent should be halved again since the universal texts do not positively affirm universalism but allow for it because of ambiguity. With a five per cent likelihood, how is this even a debate? All credit is given to the energy of the Arminian evangelists, but their zeal radically outpaces the biblical data.

Theological Considerations

Next, three theological arguments for limited atonement are presented to round out the discussion. These are not *mere* theological extrapolations. They might not rely on the handy, single proof text, but they rest on biblical teaching all the same.

---

[23] On the interpretation of these texts by Grotius and Dort, see Lee Gatiss, 'The Synod of Dort and Definite Atonement,' in *From Heaven He Came and Sought Her: Definite Atonement in Historical, Biblical, Theological, and Pastoral Perspective*, eds. David Gibson and Jonathan Gibson (Wheaton, IL: Crossway Books, 2013), 160–61. On Dort's doctrine of limited atonement, see Raymond A. Blacketer, 'Definite Atonement in Historical Perspective,' in *The Glory of the Atonement: Biblical, Theological, and Practical Perspectives*, eds. Charles E. Hill and Frank A. James III (Downers Grove, IL: IVP Academic, 2004), 317–322.

The Power of the Atonement: Legal Demand and Divine Integrity

Advocates of universal atonement see the atonement as a health elixir on offer at a graveyard. It would raise the dead if only the dead would reach out and take it. Unfortunately, to the universalist, the Cross has no power to raise the dead and so to enable them to take the tonic.

Indeed, from one perspective, the Cross does seem ineffectual and powerless. After all, there is a huge chronological gap between the Cross and its application to us 2,000 years later. It is 'only a historical fact' until it is 'subjectively appropriated'.[24] Everything seems dependent upon what I decide (or what the Spirit decides within me). Will I take the medicine in the cabinet?

The mistake is not seeing that legal, penal, and moral realities have consequences. For example, in the legal realm, the adopting parent *will* love the child. The newly wedded husband *will* provide for his wife. Of course, that is not quite true. Adoptions and weddings do not create love and care—but they do *demand* it. And *faithful* people keep their word. Legal demands in the hands of faithful people have consequences.

This is the act of atonement. Firstly, it is an accomplished, historical reality. It is not waiting to become atonement when I believe.[25] It already is atonement (which might confuse people if they have conflated atonement and justification).[26]

Secondly, it was a penal act. 'On that cross, as Jesus died, the wrath of God [God's justice] was satisfied'.[27] My Genesis 3 death sentence has been expended. To be sure, I was not justified (declared righteous) at the time Jesus died—my court date came around 1,945 years or so after the atonement—but still, back then, my debt was paid. God then was 'reconciled' and the 'hostility' was put to death, even though I was not then myself reconciled to God (Rom. 5:10; Eph. 2:16). Before I believed,

---

[24] Robert H. Culpepper, *Interpreting the Atonement* (Grand Rapids, MI: Eerdmans, 1966), 127.

[25] The language of Emil Brunner, *The Mediator: A Study of the Central Doctrine of the Christian Faith* (London: Lutterworth Press, 1934, 1946), 524, is inaccurate: 'in faith…the Atonement becomes real'.

[26] The atonement is *historia salutis*. Justification is *ordo salutis*.

[27] Citing the song, 'In Christ Alone', by Stuart Townend.

I was by nature a 'child of wrath' (Eph. 2:3), but that conceals God's true affections towards me and that Christ alone has experienced every last drop of God's wrath that I deserve (and I never get to stand before God and boast that I carried some it myself).

Thirdly, the atonement as a legal act established the new covenant. He 'puts an end to sin' and so 'makes a strong covenant' (Dan. 9:24, 27, in a messianic reading of the passage; or see Matt. 26:28). The covenant offers salvation to all but promises life to some.

Fourthly, the atonement was moral or legal obedience. It was the culmination of a righteous life: 'one act of righteousness' (Rom. 5:18).

What does God do with all that 2,000-year-old history in relationship to me now? This atonement, in the hands of the *faithful* God, produces results. For me, just as Christ was in the tomb on the Saturday, the Sunday must follow! Before I come to Christ, while there is no wrath for me, I still have the old legal status, 'guilty'. However, the faithful God must soon reconvene the court. The Genesis 2 covenant of works case must be reopened (as it were) because there is new evidence (Christ's righteous life). He 'sealed my pardon with his blood',[28] and at the time of the court's choosing, innocence must be declared.

Existential or personal realities also follow. With my debt paid, the Father no longer has any reason to exclude me and isolate me from his presence! I am soon given the Spirit of adoption, who works faith within me. God cannot fail to do these things. The Cross demands these things. '*This*, the power of the Cross'—God's faithfulness to his Son.[29]

The old argument stands: if Christ died for all, then all would be saved, but not all are saved, so Christ did not die for all. What utter faithlessness it would be to the Son to have him carry the sin of all but then to pour out eternal wrath on even one person.

One cannot have both here. If Christ died for all, the Cross is universal but powerless, and God is faithless, ignoring his own Son's death. Otherwise, Christ died for the elect only, and the atonement is definite and powerful, and God is faithful.[30]

---

[28] Citing the hymn, *Man of Sorrows*, by Philip Paul Bliss.

[29] Citing the song, 'The Power of the Cross', by Stuart Townend.

[30] There is the covenantal corollary. If Christ died for all, the New Covenant is a hypothetical covenant (as per Amyraut). It commands faith, but it cannot provide faith. The

The Power of Christ's Righteousness: The Reward of Resurrection

The correlative argument can be made regarding Christ's righteousness. First, follow the story of Christ's life. He lived a righteous life. He was killed but then publicly justified (or 'vindicated') in his resurrection.[31] The Spirit raised him, and that resurrection declared his righteousness to the world. As Paul puts it, he was justified by the Spirit and became a life-giving spirit (1 Tim. 3:16; 1 Cor. 15:45). This was his reward. Within the terms of the covenanted arrangement, the faithful God had no option but to so vindicate him. Christ's righteousness demanded it. Still, the reward came at the moment of God's choosing. It was not instantaneous but came 'three days' after Christ's death (in the Jewish way of counting).

However, Christ lived this righteous life for us and not just for himself. Thus, secondly, we plot our story in Christ's story. We share in his righteousness, and therefore we share in his reward. The faithful God must publicly vindicate us. Christ's righteousness demands our resurrection. It might come to us three days later or 2,000 years later but it must be ours.

What is the nature of our resurrection? In its first instalment, it is regeneration. It is the gift of the Spirit, and with that, the gift of faith. *This* is where our faith comes from. It results from Christ's righteousness and from us sharing in his reward. Regeneration is not justification, but it does prove that we are in the right with God.

This is the 'power' of Christ's righteous life lived for us. Would one then dare say that Christ's righteous life was lived for all people? Does He enter onto the court record for all people that they have met God's standards? If so, all people would be raised with Christ.

Gospel is only law. More generally on covenant and atonement, see Leon Morris, *The Atonement: Its Meaning and Significance* (Downers Grove, IL: IVP, 1983), 14–42.

[31] Richard Gaffin, 'Atonement in the Pauline Corpus,' in *The Glory of the Atonement: Biblical, Theological, and Practical Perspectives*, eds. Charles E. Hill and Frank A. James III (Downers Grove, IL: IVP Academic, 2004), 160. Cf. Richard B. Gaffin, *Resurrection and Redemption: A Study in Paul's Soteriology*, 2nd ed. (Phillipsburg: P&R, 1978).

Christ Our High Priest

Advocates of limited atonement have long pointed to the unity of the two dimensions of Christ's priestly ministry. He intercedes in heaven for some only—everyone in this debate agrees with that. Hence, he died for some only. John 17:9 is usually cited, 'I am not praying for the world'. The Old Testament high priest had only the names of Israel on his breastplate when making atonement.[32]

The argument does not always have the intended effect. As one who once held to a universal atonement position, I still wondered about matters such as the following:

1. Why Christ's work on Earth could not be universal while his heavenly work was limited.
2. Why John 17:9 should be taken to mean that he never prays for the world.
3. Whether the Old Testament type of high priest is being unduly pressed.

It would take a separate study to work through these issues.[33] Still, the teaching of Hebrews, and Hebrews 9:12 in particular, needs to be better understood. Hebrews insists that Jesus' atonement and intercession parallel the activity of the high priest on the Day of Atonement. I must take this seriously. Hebrews does not allow me to dismiss the Old Testament typology.[34]

Two points need emphasis. First, in the Old Testament, the priest's work was only for the people of God. In any ancient culture,

---

[32] Charles Hodge, *Systematic Theology*, 3 vols. (Grand Rapids, MI: Eerdmans, 1960), 2:553.

[33] See Stephen J. Wellum, 'The New Covenant Work of Christ: Priesthood, Atonement, and Intercession,' in *From Heaven He Came and Sought Her: Definite Atonement in Historical, Biblical, Theological, and Pastoral Perspective*, eds. David Gibson and Jonathan Gibson (Wheaton, IL: Crossway Books, 2013), 523–535.

[34] Remarkably, Steve Motyer, 'The Atonement in Hebrews,' in *The Atonement Debate: Papers from the London Symposium on the Theology of the Atonement*, eds. Derek Tidball, David Hilborn, and Justin Thacker (Grand Rapids, MI: Zondervan Academic, 2008), 146–47, avoids reading Hebrews in the light of the Old Testament and so avoids penal substitution in Hebrews.

priests served their nation or their devotees, and no others.[35] Hence, it is no surprise that throughout Hebrews, Christ's High Priestly work is always and only limited in focus:

- Our 'merciful and faithful High Priest' helps 'the offspring of Abraham' (Heb. 2:16–17).
- Christ Jesus is the High Priest of 'our' confession, we who are the 'holy brothers, you who share in a heavenly calling' (Heb. 3:1), and he who is the Son over the house (v. 6).
- 'We' have a High Priest (Heb. 4:14, 15; 8:1).
- He entered behind the veil as High Priest 'on our behalf' (Heb. 6: 19–20).
- He is a 'fitting . . . High Priest' for us (Heb. 7:26).
- Christ is High Priest 'over the house of God' (Heb. 10:21).

Christ's priestly work should not be confused with his role as Prophet and King, either. Even as Prophet and King, he primarily works for his people, although there are secondary, universal aspects. As Prophet, he evangelises and exposes guilt; as King, he preserves and judges. This says nothing about the extent of the atonement. Is there universality to his priesthood? See below on Psalm 110.

Secondly, the high priest did not only kill the Day of Atonement animal. He took the blood to God in the Holy of Holies. Hence, Jesus' act of atonement was not complete until he 'entered' the heavenly Holy of Holies 'with His blood' (NKJV) (not 'by'; Heb. 9:12). The satisfying of God is not ethereality, hidden in the divine decrees and the mind of God. Atonement is not a divine-Son-to-divine-Father transaction mysteriously completed at Christ's death. The satisfaction is human, physical, historical, bloody, and personal, and hence completed only at the session in God's manifest presence. In the old system, blood was taken behind the curtain as the proof of a poured-out life. Jesus ascends with his whole crucified self, body and soul, with the death wounds 'yet visible above, in beauty glorified'.[36]

---

[35] In Exodus 19:6, the line, 'kingdom of priests', is not directly about mission to the nations. The parallel line, 'holy nation', makes it clear that 'kingdom of priests' is about intimacy with God.

[36] Citing the hymn, *Crown Him with Many Crowns* (Matthew Bridges and Godfrey

Hebrews pervasively makes this connection from his earthly suffering to the heavenly presentation and relevance (1:3; 2:10–12; 4:14–16; 5:9; 7:26–8:1; 9:12; 9:24; 10:12; 12:2). This is in accord with Psalm 110, which mentions the Melchizedekian priesthood in the context of 'Sit at my right hand' (cf. the rapid movement in Hebrews 2 from incarnation and suffering to exaltation, relying on Psalm 22).

- 'Purging (aorist participle) our sins, he sat (aorist)' (Heb. 1:3).
- 'By his blood he entered (aorist)…obtaining (aorist participle) eternal redemption' (Heb. 9:12).
- 'Offering (aorist participle) one sacrifice for sins forever, he sat (aorist) at the right hand of God' (Heb. 10:12).

Translations put the atonement one historical step before the session (having atoned, he sat). However, the aorist participles are not necessarily prior to the controlling aorists. He 'sat down at the right hand of the Majesty', and *by so doing*, 'by himself purged our sins' (NKJV). He completed the act of purging our sins *when* he sat.

The earthly-universal/heavenly-limited dichotomy is rejected. The earthly atonement culminates in the once-for-all heavenly act.[37] Universalists need to say that Christ entered heaven and sat down at the right hand for the sake of all people. They need to find universality in the Melchizedekian priesthood in Psalm 110. There is priestly universality in Psalm 110, but it is not salvational. The Psalm evokes the attitude of the warrior priests of Moses' day, who, with swords strapped to their sides, protected the tabernacle from all that would defile.

Thring). There is no need to have a bizarre debate whether the blood shed at the Cross reentered Christ's risen body or what glorified blood is like, nor is there a need to react against that debate by having only a metaphorical 'entrance' in Heb. 9:12 that occurred at the Cross.

[37] Hugh Martin, *The Atonement* (1870; reprint, Edinburgh: Banner of Truth, 2013), 75.

Conclusion

Much has not been covered. If Christ died for all people, am I supposed to believe that he died for Judas, whom, even prior to the Cross, Jesus called 'the son of destruction' (John 17:12)? If God's love is so extensive, why does he not *elect* all (as per Karl Barth's universalism. At least he was being consistent)?[38] What should be said to Arminius' argument that Christ cannot judge all if he did not die for all?[39] Can it be said to an unbeliever that 'Christ died for you'?[40]

The question is, though, 'Why not both?' First, the limited atonement texts have been shown to imply an 'only'. Christ died *only* for the elect. Hence, limited and unlimited atonement are mutually exclusive. Secondly, when viewed through the lens of the analogy of Scripture, universal atonement is feebly founded and must give way to the profuse and clear teaching of limited atonement. The assertion that universal atonement has the exegetical high ground is audacious. It only has any exegetical ground by exploiting the ambiguity of a handful of texts. Thirdly, universality robs the Cross and Christ's righteousness of their power and fails to treat seriously the truth that Christ is our High Priest who presented His blood in the heavenly tabernacle.

The reason that unlimited atonement is attractive is found less in Scripture and more in natural theology. It relies on innate knowledge (or hope) of God's universal love and a theology of glory, reckoning the depths of God's love by the number of heads atoned for. It just feels so right to say, 'God loves you and Christ died for you'.

The real glory of God's love is not its alleged universality. With that 'love', apparently, he feels kindly about everybody and provides a sort of atonement for them that makes it look like he tried to help. However, that 'love' is actually unable and unwilling to save all. A good deal of the 'loved' are assigned to hell. This universal 'love' is also oddly ambivalent about the fallen angels, for whom he offers no help at all.

---

[38] See R. B. Kuiper, *For Whom Did Christ Die? A Study of the Divine Design of the Atonement* (Grand Rapids, MI: Eerdmans, 1959), 44–61.

[39] Arminius, *Works*, 3:323. Why did Adam die, then, and why do all die in Adam (Rom. 5:12)?

[40] Peter Barnes concluded it is inadvisable since it is not said in Scripture.

Rather, God loves those whom he has freely chosen according to the mystery of his grace; he pursues them even in their rebellion; he provides for them in Christ's life, righteousness, suffering, death, resurrection, and intercession; and he brings them safely to their everlasting home in his presence. That is powerful love—selective, but effective! 'O sweet exchange! O unsearchable operation! O benefits surpassing all expectation!'[41]

'Why not both?' Limited atonement and unlimited atonement are not paradoxical mysteries to be jointly believed. Neither is Scripture vague about who benefits from Christ's death. Scripture is clear, God is consistent, and the Cross is powerful. Christ has lived for me and died for me. He has presented his blood in the heavenly tabernacle for me. Therefore, he must speak into my life saying, 'You are now justified. Arise to new life.'

[41] 'The Epistle of Mathetes to Diognetus,' in *The Apostolic Fathers with Justin Martyr and Irenaeus, vol. 1, The Ante-Nicene Fathers*, eds Alexander Roberts, James Donaldson, and A. Cleveland Coxe (Buffalo, NY: Christian Literature Company, 1885), 28.

Thirteen

Covenant, Church, and Baptism

Mark Jones

Introduction

God is a relational Being, who, out of his goodness, freely decides to reveal himself to his creatures, not only before, but also after Adam's transgression. With sovereign authority he speaks words of life and promise to his creatures, both before and after the entrance of sin and death. But he also threatens and curses. No creature can escape either a blessing or a curse from God. God may be for you or against you. If he is for you, everything is well. Conversely, if he is against you, then all is not well unless there is a change in that status. The 'covenant' concept in the Bible helps us to understand the all-important question: 'Is God for you or is he against you?' Indeed, the picture one gets from reading Early Modern Reformed theologians is that all true theology is anchored in and built upon God's covenants.

Christians know that the difference in God's attitude towards his creatures depends on whether one is united to Jesus Christ by faith or whether one finds oneself 'separated from Christ, alienated from the commonwealth of Israel and strangers to the covenants of promise, having no hope and without God in the world' (Eph. 2:12).[1] In Ephesians 2:12 Paul brings together various different biblical-theological themes in the Scriptures. Writing to Gentile Christians, Paul reminds his readers of their perilous condition before they came to be incorporated into Christ by faith. These Gentiles had several particular problems as those outside of God's saving purposes, including being 'alienated from the commonwealth of Israel' (2:12; cf. Rom. 9:4–5). To be alienated from God (Eph. 4:18) is to be alienated from Israel, since the Messiah is from Israel. This Messiah of Israel—Jesus of Nazareth—

[1] Unless otherwise noted, biblical quotations in this chapter are from the ESV.

is 'a light for the nations, that [Yahweh's] salvation may reach to the end of the earth' (Isa. 49:6).

The 'commonwealth' signifies a group of people under a specific government and head. So the Gentiles were separated from God's people who possessed the 'covenants of promise.' These ancient covenants made to Abraham (Gen. 15:7–21), Isaac (Gen. 26:2–5), Jacob (Gen. 28:13–15), Israel (Exod. 24:1–8), and David (2 Sam. 7), for example, were promises that would ultimately find their 'yes' and 'amen' in Christ (2 Cor. 1:20).

Paul celebrates that fact that these Gentiles are now in Christ (Eph. 2:13) and share equally in the same promises that were made to Jews who also put their faith in God's Messiah. God's people, from the very beginning, constitute 'one body' (Eph. 2:16) who belong to the 'household of God' (Eph. 2:19). Far from the silly idea that the church has replaced Israel, Reformed theologians have argued that the church is made up of Israelites, with Gentiles now being engrafted into the Israel of God (Rom. 9:6; 11:11–36). Reformed 'covenant theology' helps us to make sense of these realities where the doctrine of the church and salvation come into the closest proximity.

Various questions have been vigorously debated over the course of ecclesiastical history. Since the time of the Reformation, Anabaptists questioned whether infants of believers should be publicly incorporated into the church through baptism. Baptist divines in England valued much in the Westminster Confession of Faith (1647) and adopted the majority of its teachings in their own Second London Confession (1689), which had been earlier published in London (1677). In comparing 'Westminster' with 'London,' one finds that there are some changes made by the Baptists in almost every chapter, some of which were quite minor. But perhaps the most significant changes occur in the revisions to Chapter 26 ('Of the Church') and Chapters 28 ('Of the Sacraments' vs. 'Of Baptism and the Lord's Supper') and 29 ('Of Baptism'). Do infants of believing parents (or, a believing parent) belong in the visible church or not? If so, on what grounds should they be baptised? The answer to those questions, and others related to that topic, depends not only on one's understanding of the doctrine of the covenant, but also on one's view of the church, salvation, and hermeneutics. This chapter looks at the Reformed doctrine of the covenant, which has been an integral theological concept since the Reformation and especially in the Post-Reformation eras where the doctrine of the covenant was highly developed in a way to structure salvation history. Coupled with this is a discussion of the basic nature of the church and also a discussion of infant baptism as understood by a number of Reformed divines from the Early Modern Reformed era.

The Covenant of Grace

Reformed orthodox theologians have generally had a basically-agreed-upon understanding and definition of a covenant. So whether John Ball, who calls it a 'mutual compact' between God and man,[2] or Zacharias Ursinus, who calls it a 'mutual contract' between two parties,[3] the basic idea of a covenant involves an agreement between two or more parties, which explains why most of the Reformed understood the arrangement between God and Adam as a covenant.[4] With that said, that does not mean there are not certain details in the various covenants in Scripture which show some degree of diversity in how we understand each particular covenant. For example, John Owen notes that 'the word is used in great variety, and what is intended by it must be learned from the subject matter treated of.'[5] Reformed divines knew full well that 'covenant' has a more pregnant meaning in the new covenant compared to the covenant of works made with Adam.

---

[2] John Ball, *A Treatise of the Covenant of Grace...* (London, 1645), 6.

[3] Zacharias Ursinus, *The Commentary of Dr. Zacharias Ursinus on the Heidelberg Catechism,* trans. G. W. Williard (Columbus, Ohio: Scott, 1852), 97. In full, Ursinus defines a covenant as: 'a mutual contract, or agreement between two parties, in which the one party binds itself to the other to accomplish something upon certain conditions, giving or receiving something, which is accompanied with certain signs and symbols, for the purpose of ratifying in the most solemn manner the contract entered into, and for the sake of confirming it, that the engagement may be kept inviolate.'

[4] Richard Muller's essay, ''Either Expressly Set Down...or by Good and Necessary Consequence': Exegesis and Formulation in the Annotations and the Confession,' addresses the exegetical sophistication behind the covenant of works in the writings of the seventeenth-century British divines. Richard Muller and Rowland S. Ward, ed., *Scripture and Worship: Biblical Interpretation and the Directory for Public Worship* (Phillipsburg, N.J.: P&R, 2007), 59–82.

[5] Owen, *Exposition of Hebrews,* in *The Works of John Owen, D.D. 24 vols.* (Edinburgh: Johnstone & Hunter, 1850– 1855), 19:81.

Because the 'distance between God and the creature is so great,' the only way we can have a relationship with God to our advantage is through God's 'voluntary condescension…which he has been pleased to express by way of covenant' (WCF 7.1). The covenant, understood as an agreement, has certain ends. Owen says these ends lead to man serving God as God wishes in order to be blessed by him and enjoy him forever.[6]

In a fine exegetical commentary on Hebrews, a Westminster divine, William Gouge (1575–1653), explains a covenant by using Aristotelian fourfold causation. Thus a covenant may be understood in terms of the efficient, material, formal, and final causes.[7]

1. The principal efficient is God. For none can bind the Creator to a creature but God himself: and that of his own mere pleasure and good will. But the Creator has power to bind his creature to him: and that in what duty he pleases: to which duty the creature is bound readily to yield itself: and that as a creature and servant of God: but more especially as a confederate: as one of those that are in covenant with God.

   The procuring cause is God's pleasure and good will, Eph. 1:11; Luke 12:32; Matt. 11:26. For there is nothing out of God to move him. He is every way perfect and complete in himself. He needs nothing that any creature can do: neither can a creature do any thing that may move him to this or that, further then he in his own good pleasure sees suitable.

   Besides, though there might be something without God to move him, that something cannot be in a creature: because the creature itself is of God: and whatsoever it has, it has from God: and all the ability that is in it to any good, is from God.

2. *The matter* [i.e., material cause] of a divine covenant consists in the things that are covenanted. There are of two sorts.

One on God's part: which is the good promised.

[6] Owen, *Exposition of Psalm CXXX*, in *The Works of John Owen*, 6:470–71.

[7] William Gouge, *A Learned and Very Useful Commentary on the Whole Epistle to the Hebrews Wherein Every Word and Particle in the Original Is Explained* (London, 1655), 251.

The other on man's part: which is the duty engaged: and that in way of gratitude.

3. *The formal cause* consists in the mutual binding of the persons covenanting one to the other. A covenant is a bond, Ezek. 20:37. Herein it is like a vow and oath, which are strong bonds, Num. 30:3. The bond on God's part is most sure, arising from himself, Eph. 1:11. On man's part it is enjoined to him and imposed on him, Gen. 17:7–9.
4. *The ends* [i.e., final cause] of a covenant are of two sorts. Supreme and subordinate.
    1. The supreme end is God's glory. This is the supreme end of all things: and the best end that can be. Now wisdom teaches men to aim at the best end. God being wisdom itself, must needs aim at the best: which, because his glory is, he aims at it. As he swore by himself: because he had no greater to swear by (Heb. 6:13ff.), so he aims at his own glory, because he has no higher nor better end to aim at. At this he aimed in his external decree, Rom. 9:22–23; Eph. 1:6. At this he aimed in creating the world (Prov. 16:4) and in his providence, Isa. 45:7. So likewise in entering into covenant with man. Herein is set out the glory of his sovereignty, by engaging man to what he pleases: and of his wisdom, by ordering matters so, as man's falling, of blessing arising from his own fault, namely from breach of covenant. So likewise of his truth, in performing covenant on his own part: of his justice in dealing with man according to his covenant: of his free grace, in doing what he does on his good pleasure, and of his goodness, in covenanting that which is for man's good.
    2. The subordinate end is man's happiness, compromised under this word, life. This is the end of all God's covenants with man, Rom. 10:5; Gen. 2:9; Mal. 2:5; Ezek. 16:6–8; John 3:16.[8]

[8] William Gouge, *A Learned and Very Useful Commentary on the Whole Epistle to the Hebrews Wherein Every Word and Particle in the Original Is Explained* (London, 1655), 251–252. Robert Harris (1581–1658), a member of the Westminster Assembly, uses the same

By using Aristotelian categories, Gouge is able to offer a sort of 'mini' divinity in terms of the covenant concept. In fact, what becomes clear is the interconnectedness between understanding the covenant in Scripture and other related loci, such as the doctrine of God. The covenant arises from God's goodness, reveals God's goodness, and thus necessarily glorifies God in terms of the supreme end of all things. In other words, God has used the doctrine of the covenant as the means by which he will not only save man and make him happy (i.e., subordinate end, as a subspecies of the final cause), but also the means by which God will be glorified. For this to happen, the material cause, involving both obligations from God and man, as well as the formal cause, whereby there is a bond between man and God, are required. Readers will have to decide for themselves whether Gouge's method brings clarity and order to our understanding of the covenant concept. But it seems to me this method of theology, whether one agrees with it or not, gives us appropriate categories for understanding the nature, purposes, and ends of a covenant.

The term 'the covenant of grace' is distinctly associated with the Reformed theological tradition, in the main because of the truths and theology associated with it. Beginning with the Swiss reformers in Zurich and Geneva, the doctrine of the covenant of grace was formulated in a manner that gave a unifying structure to redemptive history. Because salvation is found exclusively in Jesus Christ, whether for Adam, Paul, Augustine, or Calvin, Reformed theologians have spoken of the covenant of grace as substantially the same for all believers in all ages but they have also been careful to note, with a sensitivity to the unfolding character of revelation, that there are several administrations in which God's covenantal purposes were made clearer to his people. As Ursinus says, 'This covenant is one in substance, but two-fold in circumstances.'[9]

Adam received the first promise (*protoevangelium*) in Genesis 3:15, and this promise of victory culminates in Christ's death, resurrection,

---

sorts of distinctions to describe the covenant of works. *A Brief Discourse of Mans Estate in the First and Second Adam* (London, 1653), 2–3.

[9] Zacharias Ursinus, *The Commentary of Dr. Zacharias Ursinus on the Heidelberg Catechism*, 98.

ascension, and enthronement as the rightful Son of God who has been made both Lord and King of the universe.

The Westminster divines explicitly refer to God's redemptive covenant as a 'Covenant of Grace; whereby he freely offers unto sinners life and salvation by Jesus Christ, requiring of them faith in him that they may be saved…' (WCF 7.3). They speak of a redemptive-historical contrast between two dispensations (i.e., 'times'): the time of the law and the time of the gospel (WCF 7.3). This covenant of grace represents the heart and soul of a Reformed understanding of salvation history. Salvation is from the Lord, but while we can refer to the covenant of grace as a 'one-sided covenant' (*foedus monopleuron*), since it originates from God and depends on Christ's mediatorial work, we can also speak of the covenant of grace as a 'two-sided covenant' (*foedus dipleuron*).[10] As the Confession makes clear, in this covenant God requires faith in Christ for salvation. This refers to the conditionality of the covenant. Ball thus brings out the one-sidedness and the two-sidedness of the covenant of grace: 'The Covenant of Grace is that free and gracious Covenant which God of his mere mercy in Jesus Christ made with man a miserable and wretched sinner, promising unto him pardon of sin and eternal happiness, if he will return from his iniquity, embrace mercy reached forth, by faith unfeigned, and walk before God in sincere, faithful and willing obedience, as becomes such a creature lifted up into such enjoyment, and partaker of such precious promises.'[11] The Reformed distinguished between 'impetration' and 'application.' The former has in view the work of Christ whereas the latter has in the view the application of Christ's work, which terminates upon the Spirit, though the application is never divorced—since it cannot be—from the 'applying work' of the Father and the Son.

The covenant of grace begins in Genesis 3:15. God's redemption is rooted in this promise of victory whereby the seed of the woman

[10] Ursinus says the old and new covenants (both administrations of the covenant of grace) are the same insofar as the conditions remain the same: 'In each covenant, God requires from men faith and obedience…The new covenant, therefore, agrees with the old in that which relates to the principal conditions, both on the part of God, and on the part of man.' *The Commentary of Dr. Zacharias Ursinus on the Heidelberg Catechism*, 99. This point brings together the one-sidedness and two-sidedness of the covenant of grace. We may also speak of 'unilateral' and 'bilateral' aspects of the covenant.

[11] Ball, *Treatise of the Covenant of Grace*, 14–15.

crushes the serpent's head. According to Owen, all true postlapsarian theology is rooted in the protoevangelium, which summarises the gospel.[12] But while the gospel is rooted in this promise, the clarity of God's work will be illuminated by successive stages of revelation.

Genesis 3:15 was not without some exegetical difficulties. Reformed divines were aware of the Papist corruption of this text whereby they understand the 'woman' to be Mary who bruises the serpent's head. But Ball says, 'If the Virgin Mary may be said to bruise the Serpent's head, because Christ was borne of her, by the same reason we may say, she was crucified and died for us.'[13] Francis Roberts offers perhaps the most detailed exegetical analysis of Genesis 3:15 from the English Reformed. Against Rome, he brings up their deliberate textual emendation: In both the Vulgate and the Queen Mary Psalter (1553), they render the Hebrew *hu* ('he') as if it were *hee* ('she'), resulting in the reading '*ipsa conteret caput tuum*' ('she shall bruise thy head'). In fact, Roberts adds, 'for the better countenancing of this corrupt translation, they have by the perfidiousness of Guy Fabricius corrupted the Hebrew text in the Interlinear Bible printed at Antwerp...But our learned Divines [Rivetus, Calvin, and Gomarus] justly condemn this notorious Corrupting of the Text.'[14] All of this is to point out that not only did the Reformed positively set forth the doctrine of the covenant of grace by looking at the relevant biblical data, but they had to engage their opponents and counter their claims. This is to say, the defence of truth often requires an attack against falsehood. When it came to polemics with Rome, the Reformed were not lacking enthusiasm for polemical engagement.

While most Reformed theologians who discoursed on the Noahic covenant viewed at as an administration of the covenant of grace, there were some who were conspicuous by their silence on its redemptive features. The fuller revelation of God's saving purposes was revealed to Abraham. The Latin word *dispensatio* (administration; dispensation;

---

[12] 'Omnis autem veri nominis theologia postlapsaria ejusdem generis est. Variis revelationum gradibus objective tantum aliquoties innovata.' Owen, *Theologoumena,* in *Works,* 17:134 (2.1.2).

[13] Ball, *Treatise of the Covenant of Grace,* 38.

[14] Roberts, *The Mysterie and Marrow of the Bible: viz. God's Covenants with Man* (London, 1657), 194.

economy) and Greek term *oikonomia* was frequently used to discuss the economy of salvation as it unfolded over time. These 'phases' in history had unique elements and the biblical-theological considerations that arose from a careful study of each covenant in its context was a feature of Reformed treatments on the covenant. The idea of a bland systematising based upon a few proof-texts is really more a hallmark of twentieth-century versions of covenant theology than what we find in the works of divines such as Cocceius, Witsius, Ball, Owen, etc.

This covenant proved to be crucial for the Reformed not only in terms of God's saving purposes for humanity, but also for God's placement of children in his covenant. God's will and purposes towards humanity, in the time of Abraham, are highlighted by Owen: 'such an exposition of God's will and of the mysteries of grace, and so illustrious, is given in this explanation of postlapsarian theology [i.e., revelation], that there has hardly been a more abundant attestation of the economy of the one revelation, until He [i.e., Christ] came in whom everything was laid down.'[15] To Abraham, God reiterates Genesis 3:15 in terms of the promised seed. Thus Owen adds: 'the promise of the Seed being given in advance, who is the foundation of all grace, God gracefully promises that He will graciously and immutably be unto him an indulging, sanctifying, justifying and saving God, who, in turn, demands from him faith and a new obedience.'[16] If we consider the content of the Abrahamic covenant, particularly concerning the requirements of faith and obedience on Abraham's part, there is no substantial difference from the requirements of the new covenant. Therefore when Owen asks in his Greater Catechism (Q. 13), 'What is this new covenant?', he answers: 'The gracious, free, immutable promise of God, made unto all his elect fallen in Adam, to give them Jesus Christ, and in him mercy, pardon, grace, and glory, with a re-stipulation of faith from them unto

[15] 'Tanta autem voluntatis divinae et mysteriorum gratiae expositio, tamque illustris, ea explanatione theologiae postlapsariae edita est, ut proventum uberiorem unius revelationis οκονομία, donec ille veniret, cui omnia errant reposita, vix obtinuerit.' Owen, *Theologoumena,* in *Works,* 17:265 (4.1.12).

[16] 'Praemissa Seminis promissione, omnis gratiae fundamento, Deus gratiose promittit se ei in semine illo, Deum parcentem, sanctificantem, justificantem, servantem gratuitò et immutabiliter fore, fidem atque novam obedientiam abs eo vicissim postulans.' *Theologoumena,* in *Works,* 17:266 (4.1.13).

this promise, and new obedience.'[17] This is not hard to prove since in the New Testament the Apostle Paul uses Abraham as an example of justifying faith (Rom. 4).

In this covenant, God gives Abraham a sign of circumcision, which Paul says was '…a seal of the righteousness that he had by faith while he was still uncircumcised…' (Rom. 4:11). This means the sign of circumcision represented God's righteousness, not Abraham's faith. In the Abrahamic covenant, God brings Abraham's seed (e.g., Ishmael, Isaac) into covenant as they receive the same seal (i.e., circumcision) that Abraham received. Unless the sign meant something altogether different for Isaac than Abraham, we must assume that it was a seal to Isaac of God's covenant righteousness. Isaac's faith would need to embrace this covenant sign if he was to remain a faithful Israelite. Circumcising his offspring was an act of obedience by Abraham in response to the terms of the covenant of grace made with him.[18]

So, returning to the 'one-sided' versus 'two-sided' understanding of the covenant, even though God freely promised spiritual and temporal blessings to Abraham, and while the Bible is clear that Abraham was freely justified by grace through faith in Christ, the condition was nonetheless met by Abraham who believed, and it was counted to him as righteousness (Rom. 4:3). Ball says that although Abraham was justified by faith alone, with no other grace co-working with it, his faith did not 'lie dead in him as a dormant and idle quality.'[19] Saving faith is 'lively and operative, attended with every other grace of the Spirit.'[20] Hence the same faith that embraced God's promise (Gen. 15:6) is the

---

[17] John Owen, *Greater Catechism,* in *Works,* 1:482.

[18] Owen argues that the Abrahamic covenant bestows privileges upon the children of believers so that in the covenant of grace children would always belong to the visible church. 'Et quintò, communicatio privilegiorum foederis et ecclesiae, cum *semine infantili* (quod postquam modo peculiari Deo curae esse coeperat, ecclesia nunquam absolute defecit) conceditur, Gen. 17:7.' *Theologoumena,* in *Works,* 17:266 (4.1.13). And Goodwin argued that Abraham's Gentile servants and their children would have been circumcised 'as fore-running pledges and types that both we and our children, who are Gentiles and strangers, [would be] engrafted into this covenant.' *Of Election,* in *Works,* 9:483.

[19] Ball, *Treatise of the Covenant of Grace,* 73.

[20] Ball, *Treatise of the Covenant of Grace,* 73.

same faith that enabled Abraham to walk in obedience to God by being willing to offer up Isaac (Gen. 22).

Goodwin makes the point that God's declaration to Abraham that he himself is Abraham's 'exceeding great reward' (Gen. 15:1) is 'the deepest and most comprehensive expression of love, that God ever made unto any man; and Abraham takes the advantage of this, and improves it.'[21] As Eve is the mother of all the living, Abraham is the father of all who believe. He is the one of whom Christ himself says to the Jews, 'Your father Abraham rejoiced that he would see my day. He saw it and was glad' (John 8:56).

God continues to make further revelations of his purposes for his people, as well as giving clearer light concerning the person and work of Christ, to Moses, David, Isaiah, etc. In their prophetic capacity they instruct the people of God in their infancy. The final dispensation of the covenant of grace is the new covenant. The new covenant is sealed by the blood of Christ. An explosion of revelation takes place in the new covenant because the Son of God is incarnate and, as the great Prophet of God, who only speaks the words of the Father, he has the peculiar dignity of bringing the church to maturity. As Owen says, 'That which before lay hid in promises, in many things obscure, the principal mysteries of it being a secret hid in God himself, was now brought to light; and that covenant which had invisibly, in the way of a promise, put forth its efficacy under types and shadows, was now solemnly sealed, ratified, and confirmed, in the death and resurrection of Christ.'[22]

The new covenant is a biblical covenant, like the old covenant. As such, there is a distinction to be made between the covenant of grace and the new covenant. The covenant of grace is a theological tool used by Reformed theologians to describe God's redemptive purposes towards his people throughout the Old and New Testaments. As such, it has a certain flexibility in terms of how it is defined by various theologians. The covenant of grace in the Old Testament has a promissory character, but because the new covenant is confirmed and sealed by the blood of Christ, the covenant of grace in the New Testament is no

[21] Goodwin, *Of Election, in Works,* 9:428.

[22] John Owen, *Exposition of Hebrews,* in *Works,* 23:64.

longer promissory, but fulfilled. Promise and fulfillment are both aspects of the covenant of grace.

Because of this distinction between a 'theological covenant' versus a 'biblical covenant,' one will find that Reformed theologians did not always emphasise the differences between the old and new covenants in the same way. Some, such as Owen and Charnock, had a stronger redemptive-historical law-gospel contrast than others. By 'law-gospel' I mean in terms of the various administrations of the covenant of grace, especially when the old covenant at Sinai is contrasted with the new covenant.[23]

The Church

Reformed covenant theology brings together a host of doctrines, such as the doctrines of salvation, God, Christ, man, and the church. Regarding the latter, it may come as a surprise to some today to hear the church began with Adam and Eve, not just before the Fall but also after. Working with the 'militant' versus 'triumphant' church distinction, the *Synopsis Purioris Theologiae* (Synopsis of a Purer Theology) says that the militant church is divided 'first, into the Church of the Old and the New Testament.'[24] Many Reformed divines held to the idea of a universal visible church as the goal of ecclesiology. This was God's intention in the Garden with Adam. Adam and Eve were to populate the earth with children of God as God's temple extended to include worldwide dominion. The people of God would have been one: a worshipping community of the faithful who called upon the name of the Lord. Yet, even with the entrance of sin, God's purpose for a world of worshippers

[23] Indeed, on the Continent, a somewhat unique understanding of covenant theology, with a slightly different redemptive-historical law-gospel contrast, emerged in the theology of Johannes Cocceius and his doctrine of 'abrogations.' This doctrine seems to combine elements from both the covenants of works and grace. Willem Van Asselt sums up Cocceius's position: 'Briefly stated, this doctrine depicts five stages (*gradus*) through which God leads humanity to eternal life, and in which the consequences of the violation of the covenant of works through sin are gradually nullified.' Willem J. van Asselt, *The Federal Theology of Johannes Cocceius (1603–1669)* [Studies in the History of Christian Thought 100] (Brill, Leiden etc. 2001), 271–83.

[24] Henk van den Belt et al, *Synopsis Purioris Theologiae / Synopsis of a Purer Theology*, Volume 2, Disputations 24–42 (Leiden: Brill, 2016), 571.

did not change. Rather, it would be realised through the second Adam, Jesus, who is God's (and the world's) prophet, priest, and king. He would be the king of a new people who worship God.

The church (*ekklesia*) denotes a gathered assembly or congregation, which is the basic idea behind the Old Testament word (*qahal*). Naturally, the context in which 'church' is used must determine its precise meaning. Generally, the church refers to God's people, who are believers in the Messiah, though we must also include the elect angels in God's household. If the covenant of grace begins in Genesis 3:15, with the first promise of a conquering seed from the woman, then Adam and Eve possessed enough revelation to worship God in the 'name' of the Messiah. The church refers to those who outwardly profess Christ, which has been called the visible church. The outward or visible church is made up of believers in terms of their profession, but that does not mean there are not those who are spurious believers who will ultimately, whether in this life or at the final judgement, be revealed for who they really are. Hence the visible-invisible distinction, which Maccovius says 'is not a distinction of a genus into two species but a verbal distinction. For in so far as the Church has marks from which it can be known, in so far it is called visible. But as far as the elect are present in this Church, known by God alone, in so far it is invisible.'[25] Likewise, the *Synopsis Purioris Theologiae* says, 'This visible Church is strictly speaking not different from the invisible Church, but it is only considered in a different way: the former as 'coming about,' the latter as 'having come about'…For that invisible Church…is gathered and formed within the visible Church. The invisible Church is inherent in and contained by the visible One.'[26] This distinction has a long pedigree in the church, especially in Augustine's work, *De Baptismo contra Donatistas*.[27]

---

[25] *Scholastic Discourse: Johannes Maccovius (1588–1644) on Theological and Philosophical Distinctions and Rules*. Translated by Willem van Asselt, Michael D. Bell, Gert van den Brink, and Rein Ferwerda (Apeldoorn: Instituut voor Reformatieonderzoek, 2009), 253. Maccovius adds, 'Regarding its form, i.e. faith, the Church is invisible; in respect of its matter, i.e. the people, the Church is visible' (p. 257).

[26] *Synopsis Purioris Theologiae*, Volume 2, p. 577.

[27] See John Norman Davidson Kelly, *Early Christian Doctrines*, 3rd ed. (London: Continuum, 2007), 191–203, 412–417.

Thus from the time of Adam it was necessary that he should be one who has a faith in the Messiah and worshipped God accordingly. Speaking of the Old Testament church, Owen states that all believers have faith in Christ, 'and to deny it, is to renounce both the Old Testament and the New.'[28] He adds: 'From the giving of that promise the faith of the whole church was fixed on him whom God would send in our nature, to redeem and save them.'[29] So the object of faith has been Christ for all who are part of God's gathered people, but the nature of covenant theology also considers the progress of revelation. According to Goodwin, in the Old Testament, 'The Church of God was an infant, and was to grow up by degrees…for such, I say, was the ceremonial law…And then came David and the prophets, and led them up further; but the Church was not grown to man's estate till Christ came.'[30] The maturity of the church was a slow progression, anchored by God's covenant promises, that would see the formal introduction of Gentiles after the death and resurrection of Christ, in fulfillment of the covenant promises made to 'the servant' (Isa. 49:1–12).

Not to be missed is the fact that God's covenant promises to his people provide the foundation for the existence of a body of believers who put their faith in God's provision for them and so live in obedience to God. What was true for Adam, Abraham, and David is still true for God's people today. Without God's covenant there is no church because there is no promise and fulfillment concerning the person and work of Christ. How can one deny that a person who puts their faith in Christ, whether before the incarnation (promise) or after (fulfillment), is not part of the body of Christ?

The Nicene Creed speaks of 'one holy catholic and apostolic church.' The Christian view of the church highlights the catholicity of the church in all ages, not just as a phenomenon that occurred after the death of the last Apostle. Following Augustine, Reformed theologians took the catholic church to include those before, during, and after Christ; they included the church in glory and the church on earth: One

[28] Owen, *Works*, 1:100.

[29] Owen, *Works*, 1:101.

[30] *The Works of Thomas Goodwin*. 12 vols. Edited by Thomas Smith (Edinburgh: James Nichol, 1861–1866. Reprint, Grand Rapids: Reformation Heritage Books, 2006), 1:202.

Lord, one body, one church.[31] Thus the church has existed from the time of Adam, even if somewhat concealed and obscure. As Turretin says, 'In the first interval of the first world from Adam to Noah, the church began in Adam and his family. Hence the faith of Abel is celebrated (Heb. 11:4), and the piety of Seth and Enosh, in whose times 'the name of the Lord began to be invoked' (Gen. 4:26), undoubtedly by public and solemn service.'[32] Enoch and his posterity continued the church till Noah and from Noah to Shem, up until the time of Abraham. Turretin adds, 'With him God willed to make a covenant in a more illustrious manner and thus he preserved the church in his family, which was increased wonderfully in Egypt, until it grew into a most populous nation, which he gathered together into the form of a republic, to which he gave his statues and laws and which should subsist in that polity until Christ, although with various changes.' [33]

As the covenant of grace unfolds, the church comes to an increasing maturity. They go hand-in-hand. The continued revelation of God's purposes in Christ are not in the hopeful expectation of a church one day, but rather to guide the people of God over the ages until the consummation.

Covenant Children

The place of the children of believers in the new covenant has been a source of great debate in the Christian church, especially since the time of the Reformation and the seventeenth century in England. Reformed covenant theology has been adamant that God has not excommunicated the seed of believers from the church in the new covenant. The make–up of the church since the time of the Apostles includes people of all ages, races, genders, languages, backgrounds, etc. The Reformed position claims that the church is not an assembly for adults only. But there is a significant branch of Reformed orthodoxy that also believes that faith is required for baptism. This will require some explanation.

---

[31] We can also understand the 'one holy catholic' church as the church of the New Testament whereby believers are now 'scattered' all over the world and there is no longer a distinction between Jew and Gentile.

[32] Francis Turretin, *Institutes of Elenctic Theology*. 3 vols. Edited by James T. Dennison Jr. Translated by George Musgrave Giger (Phillipsburg, N.J.: P&R, 1992), XVIII.viii.6.

[33] Turretin, *Institutes*, XVIII.viii.6.

Geerhardus Vos raises the question about what, in general, is the Reformed view concerning the meaning of infant baptism. In his answer he makes a number of contentions, one of which is particularly germane to our discussion now, namely, that 'according to the judgement of charity, salvation is ascribed to these children and they are regarded as elect, as their parents are regarded when they make profession of faith, and continue to be as long as they in fact do not give evidence to the contrary.'[34] He takes this to be the generally held Reformed view.

Baptism really establishes in a public, visible, manner, a covenant relationship since it is a naming ceremony. Witsius, agreeing with Forbes, argues that baptism 'is a seal not so much of the secret purpose of God as of the revealed covenant of grace.'[35] Since all supernatural theology is relational and hence covenantal, the baptism of covenant members brings with it promises and responsibilities, blessings and curses, all from a gracious God. What benefits from the covenant of grace does baptism confer upon elect infants who have a right to baptism? Witsius says that the blessings sealed by baptism include chiefly the following: 'In the first place, General communion with Christ, and with His mystical body; and, consequently, a right to the enjoyment of all its attendant advantages. With this view we are said to be 'baptised into Christ,' (Rom. 6:3; Gal. 3:17)…This communion with Christ, without doubt, implies that the baptised infant may be regarded as given by the Father—as redeemed by Christ—as, at least, so far reconciled to God through Christ that its sin can never be imputed to it for punishment.'[36] To this Witsius adds the washing away of sin, including its guilt (answering to justification) and its filth (answering to

---

[34] *Reformed Dogmatics*. R. B. Gaffin Jr., Ed. & Trans. Vol. 5. (Bellingham: Lexham Press) 5:174). It appears Vos was relying on the historical analysis of Herman Witsius when the quotes used by Vos are considered. Herman Bavinck also discusses this issue but his analysis of Reformed views on the matter is poor. See Herman Bavinck, *Saved by Grace: The Holy Spirit's Work in Calling and Regeneration*. Translated by Nelson D. Kloosterman (Grand Rapids: RHB, 2008), 80–94.

[35] William Marshall, *Popery in the full Corn, the Ear, and the Blade; or, the Doctrine of Baptism in the Popish, Episcopalian, and Congregational Churches: with a Defence of the Calvinistic or Presbyterian View. To which is subjoined ... an Essay on the Efficacy of Baptism of H. Witsius* (Edinburgh: Paton and Ritchie, 1852), 307–08. The original work is: Herman Witsius, *Disquisitio modesta et placida de efficacia et utilitate baptismi in electis foederatorum parentum infantibus* (Utrecht, 1693), see xxiv–lv.

[36] William Marshall, *An Essay on the Efficacy of Baptism of H. Witsius*, 309.

sanctification). Thus, regeneration is necessary for these benefits to be applied. Moreover, baptism also signifies a 'happy deliverance from all the miseries of this life, and a blessed victory over the hardships of the world,' through our resurrection from the dead.[37] According to Witsius, the Reformed are all of one mind on this point, namely, the meaning of baptism.

Yet he also speaks of the debate concerning the efficacy of baptism: 'But with regard to the place of regeneration there is greater difficulty. On this part of the subject, I find four distinct opinions among theologians. Some think that regeneration takes place at different periods of time—it may be before, it may be at, or it may be after baptism. Others place it uniformly before baptism. Others teach that infants are baptised unto future regeneration, being incapable of it at the time. Indeed, many contend that God usually confers regeneration upon infants in the very act and moment of baptism.'[38] The language of 'baptismal regeneration' is highly ambiguous and requires a thorough investigation into its precise meaning since the Early Modern Reformed were far too sophisticated to leave their readers assuming this meant a Papist understanding of baptism.[39] The view that we will consider, which I believe is probably the majority view of the Early Modern Reformed, is the opinion that we are to believe that the children of believers are to be baptised because they possess spiritual life.

Children of believers are baptised because they are covenant members. For paedobaptists, this is hardly in dispute. However, more controversial, especially today, is the contention that fellowship with Christ and his body technically occurs before baptism. Accordingly, if our children do not possess fellowship with Christ and the church, they are therefore pagans, without Christ and without hope, and should not be baptised. Witsius says there is no 'middle condition,'

---

[37] Marshall, *An Essay on the Efficacy of Baptism of H. Witsius,* 310.

[38] Marshall, *An Essay on the Efficacy of Baptism of H. Witsius,* 313.

[39] Thus John Davenant: 'Nor do I know any one of our Divines who would pronounce that the regeneration which exists in the creation of qualities (which we call sanctification – the Papal writer's formal justification) is produced at the very moment of Baptism.' *Baptismal Regeneration and the Final Perseverance of the Saints.* A letter to Dr Samuel Ward. Translated from the Latin by the Rev. J. Allport (London: William Macintosh, 1864), 10.

since those who are not 'in Christ' must belong to Satan.[40] To put this more starkly: we either view our children as children of God (i.e., of the covenant) or as children of the devil. If, then, our covenant children have communion with Christ and the church before baptism then they also therefore have remission of sin, which, according to Witsius, 'is the first thing that flows from the enjoyment of the covenant of grace.'[41] Many, if not most, Reformed divines spoke of the 'root' or 'seed' of faith being present in elect infants.

Thomas Manton noted that elect infants 'in general have *jus ad rem*, a right to heaven; but there is no *jus in re*, no actual right, but by faith…As they are called rational before they had use of reason, so we have found that infants may, must,…have a principle of faith, from when they may be said to be believers.'[42] He then explains how this is possible. In his view, they do not have actual faith which 'begins in knowledge and ends in affiance. It remains therefore that they have the seed of faith, or some principle of grace conveyed into their souls by the hidden operation of the Spirit of God, which gives them an interest in Christ.'[43] He notes how different expressions are used by the orthodox: the habit of faith, principle of faith, inclination of faith, etc. Because salvation is of the Lord, infants are enabled by 'passive reception' (so William Ames[44]) to be united to Christ, which means the habit of faith is 'not altogether without act, though it be such an act as is proper to their age.'[45]

Now, the issue is not whether God has the power to grant the grace of regeneration to infants before baptism.[46] Rather, according to

---

[40] Marshall, *An Essay on the Efficacy of Baptism of H. Witsius*, 311.

[41] Marshall, *An Essay on the Efficacy of Baptism of H. Witsius*, 312.

[42] *Sermons Upon Hebrews XI*, in *The Complete Works of Thomas Manton*. 22 vols. (London: James Nisbet, 1870–1875), 86.

[43] Manton, *Sermons Upon Hebrews XI, in Works*, 14:86.

[44] 'Passive reception' was used by Ames, but also other Reformed divines to speak of the Spirit's regenerating work, which was antecedent to the act of faith. See William Ames, *Medulla SS. Theologiae, Ex Sacris literis, earumque, interpretibus, extracta, & methodice disposita* (Amsterdam: Robertum Allotum, 1627). See also John Flavel, *The method of grace…* (London: M. White, 1681).

[45] Manton, *Sermons Upon Hebrews XI, in Works*, 14:86–87.

[46] As Turretin says, 'As to regeneration, however, why should infants not be capable of regeneration as they are of sin (unless we say that guilt has more power than grace)? And as they are rational…what hinder them from being called holy and believers by

Witsius, we are to believe that this is God's ordinary manner of working among elect infants. Thus, says Witsius, 'since God may, from their very birth, receive elect infants into the fellowship of His covenant, may unite them to Christ…there seems no reason why He should not regenerate them at the same time.'[47] Whether the 'root' and 'seed' of conversion is antecedent to baptism or tied to it was a source of debate among Reformed divines. After quoting Cornelius Burgess's position on this, where he connects regeneration 'with that ordinance as a *sine qua non*,' he claims that Burgess's opinion 'is not admitted by the Reformed divines whom he himself quotes.'[48] In Witsius's view, 'The well-known opinion of these divines is, That the efficacy of baptism consists not in producing regeneration, but in sealing a regeneration already produced.'[49] So Witsius quotes many Reformed divines on this to prove his point. For example, Beza says, 'I have little difficulty in concluding on the ground of the divine promise, that they are ingrafted into Christ from their birth.'[50] The judgement of charity is therefore based upon the 'ground of the divine promise.' So, the promise is applied, in terms of our judgement of the child, in a manner whereby we assume them to have been engrafted into Christ and thus his body.

But even the application of the judgement of charity was somewhat disputed. For example, a debate took place at the Westminster Assembly between Thomas Goodwin, Lazarus Seaman, Stephen Marshall, and Richard Vines concerning the meaning of 'holy' in 1 Corinthians 7:14.[51] Goodwin claims that the holiness possessed by children of believers is a holiness whereby they have the Holy Ghost. Seaman believed this removed the 'common & ordinary ground of baptising of infants & layes a new ground.'[52] Goodwin denies that he is arguing

the Holy Spirit given to them, although they cannot as yet exert an act of faith?' *Institutes*, XIX.xx.6.

[47] Marshall, *An Essay on the Efficacy of Baptism of H. Witsius*, 317.

[48] Marshall, *An Essay on the Efficacy of Baptism of H. Witsius*, 319.

[49] Marshall, *An Essay on the Efficacy of Baptism of H. Witsius*, 319.

[50] Marshall, *An Essay on the Efficacy of Baptism of H. Witsius*, 319.

[51] In Goodwin's work on Election he gives an extended exegetical treatment of 1 Corinthians 7:14 that yields many significant observations concerning how he views the children of believers. See *Works*, 9:439–473.

[52] *The Minutes and Papers of the Westminster Assembly 1643–1652*, ed. Chad Van Dixhoorn. 5 vols. (Oxford: Oxford University Press, 2012), 3:206.

they are all actually saved, 'but we are to judge them soe.' Goodwin is not denying that there are some who are not elect (e.g., Esau). He is not actually judging the infallible reality of their eternal state (as if he had insight into the decree of God), but how he is to judge the infants of believers. When it comes to each child, Goodwin feels that he must judge they are saved, even if it may be the case that they are not ultimately elect, which is something only God infallibly knows. Marshall does not think he is bound to judge of each infant that they possess real holiness, but only 'federal' holiness. But Goodwin responded that there are not two kinds of holiness: 'If you [i.e., Marshall] make it any other holynesse, then baptisme is a seale of some other holynesse than the holynesse of salvation.' In Marshall's view, the holiness Goodwin attributes to infants necessarily and infallibly saves them. But Goodwin says, 'The terminus of a mans judgement is to be the Infants saving or salvation, but I am not to have an Infallible judgement of it, but such a Judgement as answers the promise...'[53]

In his work on election, Goodwin discusses his problem with the language of 'the judgement of charity.' He disagrees with the phrase if it is understood as a mere 'it may be': 'But when the Apostle here calls us to judge believing parents' children holy, it is a further thing than an *it may be*...The apostle, you see, says of such children, 'they are holy,' which is more than *it may be*.'[54] Rather than a 'mere' judgement of charity, Goodwin opts for the language, 'a judgement of faith' to be joined with the charitable judgement: 'We give up our judgements to what God promises of them, and declares about them...till we see the contrary.'[55] This judgement of faith is less than an infallible judgement, which only God possesses, but it is more than 'mere hopefulness.'

[53] *The Minutes and Papers of the Westminster Assembly*, 3:207. Manton makes this point concerning the judgment of charity in relation to the fact that many grow up and renounce the faith: 'I answer, in this case we do not speak universally, but indefinitely; we do not say that all infants do believe in Christ, but infants – and in the judgment of charity we presume it of all infants, that die in their infancy. We must leave God to the liberty of his counsels...only we say this in the general, that we have more cause to hope well of all the children of believing parents. Why? Because the grace of election runs and flows most kindly in the channel of the covenant...' *Sermons Upon Hebrews XI*, in *Works*, 14:87.

[54] Goodwin, *Works*, 9:465.

[55] Goodwin, *Works*, 9:466.

Importantly, Goodwin distinguishes between an 'indefinite proposition' and a 'universal proposition,' which goes back to Aristotle. An indefinite proposition comes close to a universal proposition, but is not synonymous with it: 'An indefinite proposition is less than an universal, for it intends some, not all, yet not naming or defining those *some* in particular, we cannot discern them from the rest.'[56] Since he cannot, as God does, distinguish the elect from the reprobate, the title of 'holy' given to children by God is something Goodwin attributes to all, though it is an indefinite proposition. In other words, naming it as such allows Goodwin to extend the judgement of charity and faith to all covenant children while recognising not all will necessarily persevere to the end.

Many of the Reformed held that we are to baptise holy people, that is, those who have the Spirit of Christ. The sign answers to that which is signified. Or, to put it more provocatively: a large strain of Reformed divines held to believers-only baptism, even if the believer was not able to put forth acts of faith. So the *Synopsis Purioris Theologiae* says in Disputation 44.29,

> Efficaciam ergo baptismi non alligamus ad momentum illud, quo aqua externa corpus tingitur, sed in omnibus baptizandis fidem & resipiscencentiam cum Scriptura praerequirimus, saltem secundum charitatis judicium: idque tam in infantibus foederatis, in quibus ex vi divinae benedictionis & foederis Euangelici, semem & Spiritum fidei ac resipiscentiae statuendum esse, contendimus; quam in adultis, in quibus actualis fidei & resipiscentiae professio est necessaria.[57]

---

[56] Goodwin, *Works*, 9:466. Universal propositions are those whose subject is determined by a universal quantifier (e.g., *all*, or *none*; all covenant children are elect) whereas indefinite propositions are those with a universal subject in which there is no number specified (e.g., covenant children are holy). Theophilus Gale affirms the universal proposition, but takes issue with the indefinite proposition: 'The Aristoteleans add, though without reason, a fourth sort of Propositions, which they call Indefinite, consisting of an Universal Subject, without any note of Quantitie. But their mistake herein is obvious: for if an Universal subject be found without restriction and limitation, it must be taken Universally. Whence the first proposition, *Man is learned*, is false; because al men are not so: but the second, Virtue is beautiful, is true, yet not indefinite, but Universal; because al Virtue is so.' *The Court of the Gentiles. Part IV. Of Reformed Philosophie* (London, A. Maxwell & R. Roberts, 1677), 7–8.

[57] Johannes Polyander a Kerckhoven, *Synopsis purioris theologiae* (Lugdunum: Bat-

> We do not therefore join the efficacy of baptism to that moment in which the body is wet with external water; but in all to be baptised, we, along with the Scripture, pre-require faith and repentance, only according to the judgement of charity: and this both in covenant children, in whom we do contend that, from the virtue of divine blessing and the evangelical covenant, the seed and Spirit of faith and repentance should be stated to be; as well as in adults, in whom the actual profession of faith and repentance is necessary.

One must not forget this was a statement by arguably the greatest theological faculty (Leiden, naturally) of its time. The synopsis was a handbook or compendium of theology. It carries significant weight in so far as it reflects not simply an individual opinion but an institutional affirmation of theological truth.

In a similar manner, Ursinus says to be born in the church is to have a profession of faith: 'Actual faith is required in adults, and an inclination to faith in infants…infants born of believing parents have faith as to inclination.'[58] Turretin agrees that the act is not present yet in the infants of believers, but that does not mean that, like reason, faith is not present at all: 'Each (i.e., faith and reason) is in them in the first act, not in the second; in the sowing, not in the harvest; in the root, not in the fruit; in the internal power of the Spirit, not in the external demonstration of work.'[59]

The Reformed belief that salvation is of the Lord nowhere finds more suitable persons to demonstrate this than covenant children. The Westminster Public Directory for Worship call the children of believers 'Christians' and so we baptise them because they are Christians. If, as present-day antipaedobaptists argue, faith is required for baptism, many, though not all, of the Reformed, historically speaking, would agree and answer that we are to judge that the habit of faith is present in covenant children, according to our judgement of charity based upon the promise of God (Gen. 17:7). Baptism is not a sign of a child's faith, nor is it a sign of any adult's faith.[60] Rather, baptism is a sign

---

avorum, 1642), 609.

[58] *The Commentary of Dr. Zacharias Ursinus on the Heidelberg Catechism*, 370.

[59] *Institutes*, XIX.xx.18.

[60] Strictly speaking, we cannot know whether faith be supernatural or natural. We ex-

that children and adults must look to, and embrace by faith until they die—or else the baptism becomes a curse instead of a blessing. Circumcision was not a sign of faith, but a sign that faith embraced or looked to because it represented God's saving righteousness (cf. Rom. 4:11). Baptism represents Christ (Gal. 3:27), in whom our faith must rest. In the case of Isaac, he received a sign that his father, Abraham, received after he believed. This does not make sense unless it is based upon three mutually inter-related factors: the covenant promise; the nature of the church; and the seed of faith.[61] Circumcision was not to mean one thing to Abraham, who believed (Gen. 15:6), and another thing to Isaac. The same is true for baptism: it represents to all who have been baptised the same thing, Christ and his saving work.

Conclusion

God's basic commitment to this world has not fundamentally changed, even from the time of Adam's innocence. Adam's children, if he had not sinned, would have been believers. They would have belonged to the church, the worshipping community of those who are children of God. When God institutes his covenant of grace after the Fall, he does not alter his purposes dramatically. Rather, in and through Jesus Christ, he deals by way of a covenant (again) in so far as he establishes his church, which includes not just adults but also children and infants. Often paedobaptists have argued based upon the continuity of the Old and New Testaments.[62] But God is returning us to a better 'Eden.' One day, the

ercise a judgment of charity even in the case of adults.

[61] The sanctification of Christ proved to be an important argument for the Reformed as to why we should not doubt the holiness and regeneration of covenant children. Thomas Goodwin, for example, gives a fairly representative position on this matter: 'Christ himself, who sanctified our nature, to the end that we might be sanctified (John 17:19, Heb. 2:11), representatively sanctified every age of man he went through, as well as those ages or years of man's life he fell short of. Now therefore he was sanctified in the womb, to sanctify some infants in the womb.' *Of the Holy Ghost*, in *Works*, 6:86.

[62] B.B. Warfield, 'The argument in a nutshell is simply this: God established his Church in the days of Abraham and put children into it. They must remain there until He puts them out. He has nowhere put them out. They are still then members of His church and as such entitled to its ordinances. Among these ordinances is baptism, which standing in similar place in the New Dispensation to circumcision in the Old, is like it to be given to children.' *The Works of Benjamin B. Warfield*. 10 vols. (New York: Oxford University

world will have Jesus, not Adam, as the king, where he will reign with his people. Thus the continuity is not just with God's purposes in the Old Testament in terms of the Abrahamic covenant, but also in terms of God's original intention for mankind. Grace does not obliterate nature, but restores and perfects it.

Thomas Goodwin, among others, makes this point. He argues that God, 'in his ways of grace since the fall, uses as much as possibly may stand with grace, his old institutions given to man in innocency, and takes them all in for to subserve grace, and keeps unto them.'[63] Goodwin claims that 'holiness was thus by generation conveyed by virtue of a natural necessary covenant; but now, though out of a covenant too—'I will be the God of thee and thy seed,'—yet out of a free covenant with his elect, not as a due to the father [Adam] by the law of nature, by which it was a due that if he begat he should beget his kind; but as a mere grant of grace now.'[64] Similarly, Herman Bavinck makes that in the covenant of grace Christ has replaced Adam in order to restore humanity, 'that not just a few separate individuals are saved but that in the elect-under-Christ the organism of humanity and of the world itself is saved...For that reason the covenant of grace does not leap from individual to individual but perpetuates itself organically and historically...It is never made with a solitary individual but always also with his or her descendants.'[65]

This illustrates for the Reformed that to take the Anabaptist view that the infants of believers are pagans, and thus no longer part of the covenant community, is to introduce a radical disjuncture into the manner in which God has worked from the very beginning. Against the Reformed, the manner of God's working changes; the church changes; the covenant promises change.

Press, 1927–32; Reprint, Grand Rapids: Baker, 1981), 9:408.

[63] Goodwin, *Works*, 9:475.

[64] Goodwin, *Works*, 9:478.

[65] Herman Bavinck, *Reformed Dogmatics*. 4 vols. Translated by John Vriend. Edited by John Bolt (Grand Rapids: Baker, 2006), 3:231.

Fourteen

Common Grace in John Calvin and Later Calvinist Theologians

Geoffrey Thomas

Over a decade ago I spent a Saturday morning in Sydney with Peter Barnes whose articles and books I had read and enjoyed. This was a very happy occasion for me. 'What a nice bloke!' was my judgement as we parted, and I wished it was not a 23-hour flight that separated us. A love for God and his word, and a commitment to historic confessional Christianity are joined in Peter to a listening ear and an observing eye concerning the culture in which we preachers bear our witness. In a recent issue of the *Banner of Truth* magazine Peter has a typical helpful article on 'Teaching Children Hard Things' in which he points out that 'television exposes them to the most inappropriate and damaging programs from an early age, *Married at First Sight* and *The All New Monty* ought to attract zero ratings among adults.'[1] Peter also properly knows what is going on in God's world. His books such as *A Handful of Pebbles: Theological Liberalism and the Church*, and *Both Sides Now: Ecclesiastes and the Human Condition*, and his booklet titled *Abortion* are all very readable, real page-turners. That is their supreme attraction after their content. So, I considered this most familiar (maybe over-familiar) subject of 'Common Grace' to be one suitable for me in making my contribution to this festschrift honouring a greatly esteemed and worthy servant of the Lord of creation and of his church.

The phrase 'common grace' cannot be said to owe its origin to the Geneva reformer John Calvin. There is a rare work of Dr. H. Kuiper, *Calvin on Common Grace*; I was privileged to read Cornelius Van Til's own personal copy of it. Kuiper notes that he found only four passages

[1] Peter Barnes, 'Teaching Children Hard Things,' *Banner of Truth Magazine*, no. 679 (2020): 7.

in Calvin's works in which the adjective 'common' is used along with the noun 'grace' and in two of these the Reformer is writing of saving grace.[2] The Dutch-American theologian, Louis Berkhof, following Kuiper was to note that within later Reformed theology, the phrase *gratia communis* became widely accepted to describe the concept that God displays a gracious disposition and activity towards all humanity, not just believers. In contrast, *gratia particularis* refers specifically to God's grace extended uniquely to those individuals whom the Father has given to the Son for salvation, preservation, and glorification—a number beyond counting, likened in Scripture to grains of sand on the seashore. Over time, however, the exact meaning of the term *communis* was interpreted in various ways. Within Dutch theological circles, it became common to regard *communis* as essentially synonymous with 'general,' leading to the popular use of 'general grace' (*algemeene genade*). Yet, strictly speaking, the term emphasises not merely that grace is general, but rather that it is shared or communal—common to all who bear God's image, particularly to those living within the sphere of gospel influence.[3] Berkhof goes on to note:

> In general it may be said that, when we speak of 'common grace,' we have in mind, either (a) *those general operations of the Holy Spirit whereby He, without renewing the heart, exercises such a moral influence on man through His general or special revelation, that sin is restrained, order is maintained in social life, and civil righteousness is promoted*; or, (b) *those general blessings, such as rain and sunshine, food and drink, clothing and shelter, which God imparts to all men indiscriminately where and in what measure it seems good to Him.*[4]

Common Grace in John Calvin

John Calvin is the recognised father of Reformed theology and so any words of his on common grace create a special interest. Herman Bavinck pointed out that Calvin was the first man to overcome the unwarranted dualism between nature and grace, something that is endemic to the system of Roman Catholicism. He was the first theologian to make a

---

[2] H. Kuiper, *Calvin on Common Grace* (Grand Rapids, MI: Smither, 1928), 177–178.

[3] Louis Berkhof, *Systematic Theology* (1941; repr., Edinburgh, UK: Banner of Truth Trust, 1994), 434.

[4] Berkhof, *Systematic Theology*, 436.

clear distinction between general grace and saving grace, between the operations of the Spirit of God which are universally common to mankind at large and the justifying and sanctifying work of the same Spirit that is limited to God's elect.[5]

Calvin seems to have distinguished three kinds of common grace:

1. There is a grace which is common to all creatures in this fallen world which gives them all life and relationships and usefulness in the creation, a *universal, common grace*.
2. Then Calvin also recognised a grace which is common to all human beings in distinction from the rest of God's creatures in the humbler creation. This is an attitude of God's goodness which pertains to men made in the image and likeness of God. These are set in families and they benefit from an earlier grace even going back to our first parents before the Fall, a *general common grace* to mankind.
3. Finally Calvin acknowledges a grace which is particular and limited to those who live in the covenant sphere, members of the new covenant in its widest significance. This grace extends to all the elect, *covenant common grace*.

1. Universal Common Grace

Calvin draws a distinction between the grace which God grants to all his creatures and the grace which he bestows upon the human race of men and women made in his image and likeness. He opens up John 1:4, 'In [the Word] was life, and the life was the light of men.' He distinguishes between the grace of Christ which extends to the whole world in general and that which is bestowed on mankind. John follows verse 4 with the observation that the Word was 'the true Light which gives light to every man coming into the world' (v.9).[6] While all things retain the life which they have received through the agency of the Son of God, mankind is especially adorned with enlightenment, that is, the singular gift of thinking, a consciousness of the past and of the future,

[5] Herman Bavinck, *De Algemeene Genade: Rede bij de overdracht van het rectoraat aan de theologische school te Kampen op 6 December 1894* (Kampen, NL: Zalsman, 1894), 16–30.
[6] Unless otherwise noted, biblical quotations in this chapter are from the NKJV.

conscience, speech and the things of the law written on their hearts. That singular gift is mankind's alone.

Calvin himself clarifies this sustaining grace in vivid terms:

> [T]he Word of God was not only the fount of life to all creatures so that those which had not yet existed began to be, but that his life-giving power makes them remain in their state. For did not his continued inspiration quicken the world, whatsoever flourishes would without doubt immediately decay or be reduced to nothing. In short, what Paul ascribes to God, that in him we have our being and we move and live (Acts 17:28), John declares to be accomplished by the blessing of the Word. It is God, therefore, who gives us life; but he does so by the eternal Word.[7]

Thus, Calvin emphasises that the eternal Word is not merely the initiator of life but its continual sustainer, preserving creation from immediate decay and upholding humanity with special dignity and purpose. The reformer teaches that mankind is above all other creatures a specimen of God's glory, replenished with infinite miracles. The Spirit of God preserves whatsoever he has created, but men and women are adorned with a singular gift by God in that they have reason and understanding.

In what, then, does the universal common grace consist, of which all the humbler creation are recipients? In the most general sense it refers to the gracious attitude of God to all his creation and creatures. It involves his promise not to destroy the earth again with a flood, and his preservation of his creatures; he satisfies the desires of every living thing, he maintains the ozone layers, and his wise laws govern and uphold all living things so that all sin-cursed creatures benefit, whether they are animate or inanimate, or whatever degree of intelligence they may have, whether a vegetable or a sheep dog, they are recipients of a divine grace in respect to profiting from the blessing of divine preservation and nurture.

Calvin wrote, 'Read Demosthenes or Cicero, read Plato, Aristotle, or any other of that class: you will, I admit, feel wonderfully allured,

[7] John Calvin, *The Gospel According to St John*, 1–10. trans. T. H. L. Parker, eds. David W. Torrance and Thomas F. Torrance (Carlisle, UK: Paternoster Press, 1995), 11.

pleased, moved, enchanted; but turn from them to the reading of the Sacred Volume, and whether you will or not, it will so affect you, so pierce your heart, so work its way into your very marrow, that, in comparison of the impression so produced, that of orators and philosophers will almost disappear; making it manifest that in the Sacred Volume there is a truth divine, a something which makes it immeasurably superior to all the gifts and graces attainable by man.'[8]

2. *General Common Grace*

Calvin frequently assures us that there is a divine grace which touches mankind in general and every individual member of the human race in particular. For example, he comments on John 1:1, 'In the beginning was the Word' as follows, 'In this prologue he declares Christ's eternal divinity to teach us that he is the eternal God, manifest in the flesh. His object is to show that the restoration of mankind had to be accomplished by the Son of God, because by his power all things were created and he alone breathes life and energy into all creatures, so that they remain *in statu quo* and because in man himself he has given unique proof of his power and grace and even after Adam's fall and failure has never ceased to show liberality and kindness to his descendants.'[9]

Calvin assures us in just so many words that God is kind to all men and women and that every single member of the human race participates to some extent in God's goodness and grace: 'there is no man to whom some awareness of the eternal light does not penetrate.'[10] Such observations are found frequently in Calvin's commentaries (note especially his comments on Romans 1:21; I Timothy 4:10, 6:17; Isaiah 60:19, 20; Daniel 4:35).

All men, Calvin taught, must consider it a matter of grace that God has made them men rather than animals. To be a human being means to be adorned with the lustre of God's image and this is reason enough why all men should feel indebted to God (*cf.* his comments on Genesis 9:6). In full harmony with this view Calvin asserts that this present life

---

[8] John Calvin, *Institutes of the Christian Religion,* trans. Henry Beveridge (Edinburgh, UK: The Calvin Translation Society, 1845), 1:99. *Institutes* 1.8:1

[9] Calvin, *The Gospel According to St John,* 7.

[10] Calvin, *The Gospel According to St John,* 15.

is a gift of God's kindness and a testimony of his inestimably grace. Accordingly, Calvin takes it that we must consider all those things which tend to support our present life as tokens of God's goodness towards mankind as divine benefits which are gifts of grace. It is an evidence of God's paternal favour towards men that he causes the sun to rise and shine on the evil and the good (I Timothy 4:3). It is kindness on the part of God and an evidence of paternal love that he protects the life of men and women. He is exceedingly kind towards mankind in that he does not supply us merely with 'garrison fare' that is the bare necessity for staying alive, but he also sees to it that we are provided with various joys (Genesis 3:17; Psalm 104:14).

According to Calvin one of the most illustrious proofs of the fact that God bestows grace on mankind in general is to be found in the light of the intelligence with which he adorns human beings. The fall of man has indeed impaired and corrupted the light of reason with which men and women were originally endowed, but it has not been altogether destroyed. Reason is still one of the essential properties of our nature. Calvin says that it is repugnant to the Word of God to charge the intellect of fallen man with all-exclusive total and perpetual blindness. Although men often stumble and fall in their search after truth, and though the capacity to research is biased in everyone, and many refuse to be enlightened by the gospel and the glory of Christ, yet we must maintain that there is also implanted in the human mind a delight in whatsoever is true and a desire to investigate the same. Calvin himself explains:

> There is, therefore, now in the human mind, discernment to this extent that is naturally influenced by the love of the truth, the neglect of which in the lower animals is a proof of their gross and irrational nature. Still it is true that this love of truth fails before it reaches the goal forthwith falling away into vanity. As the human mind is unable, from dullness, to pursue the right path of investigation, and, after various wanderings, stumbling every now and then like one groping in darkness, at length gets completely bewildered, so its whole procedure proves how unfit it is to search the truth and to find it. Then it labours under another grievous defect in that it frequently fails to discern what the knowledge is which it should study to acquire. Hence, under the influence of a vain curiosity it torments itself with superfluous and useless discussions, either not advertising at all to the things necessary to be known, or casting only a cursory and contemp-

> tuous glance at them. At all events, it scarcely ever studies them in sober earnestness. Profane writers are constantly complaining of this perverse procedure and almost all of them are found pursuing it. Hence Solomon, throughout the book of Ecclesiastes, after enumerating all the studies in which men think they attain the highest wisdom, pronounces them vain and frivolous.[11]

With relation to the matters of this present life men and women are endowed with prudence for regulating their lives and for cultivating the various arts and sciences. Everyone realises that human society must be regulated by precepts and people can understand the principles of these regulations while not acknowledging that the foundation for them all is found in the law of God. Again, every individual manifests some creativity to one degree or another because each one of us is made in the image of the Creator himself. The excellent achievements of many heathen artists, composers, authors, and architects indicate that mankind's skills display the gifts of the one whose image they bear, though that image is distorted by the fall and their own sin. None who are not regenerate create to the glory of God.

With regard to the stuff of triune majesty, the glorious person of Jesus Christ and the gospel of grace the reason of the people of this age is limited. They see the mystery of redemption through a glass darkly. They can speak with authority on nuclear fusion, and the genetic code and DNA and molecular biology but they do not grasp the gospel of Jesus Christ, in fact it is foolishness to them. Apart from the sovereign illumination of the Holy Spirit which is the saving blessing known by all the elect of God, human beings without new birth cannot penetrate into the things of the kingdom of God. But that does not mean that the natural man has no knowledge whatsoever concerning God or how he should live. On the contrary, all men and women have a conscience and a *sensus deitatus* which accounts for the world-wide religious propensity evidenced by mankind. This sense of deity is as it were the seed of religion. Every member of mankind has some knowledge of the true and living God and of his obligations to serve that God, but he clamps down on that witness in his rebellion against his Creator. The natural man will not have this God to rule over him. Calvin sometimes calls

[11] Calvin, *Institutes,* 1:315. *Institutes* II.2.12.

this knowledge the 'light of nature' since he considered it to be naturally engraved on the minds of all people. The Genevan reformer also takes it that the light of nature manifests itself in the human conscience which gives them some grasp of the rule of life, so that none can protest to God in the great day, 'but Lord we did not know!' 'Did not I give you a conscience? Was not my glory and Godhood manifest in creation by day and night throughout your life? Did I not give you the insight to distinguish between what was erroneous and what was true, between what was honourable and what was base?' That knowledge has left all without excuse, but it was never enough, nor intended to be enough, to become saving knowledge. All mankind knows more than it practices.

Calvin also declares that the works of God present to mankind a picture of the divine perfections to the extent that mankind is thereby invited and allured to acquire the knowledge of God, and by that acquisition to gain true and complete happiness or blessedness. In other words, Calvin believed that the revelation of God in his works was to a gracious end, that is, the revelation has been given so that it might be a means of drawing sinners of all kinds and needs to himself.

The reformer also had much to say concerning the grace of God as manifest in the ethical life of the men and women who inhabit our planet, especially so in that phase of human life in which the will is more to the fore rather than the intellect. Though Calvin understands the teaching of Scripture to be that the will is subject to sin's dominion, he at the same time believes that sin is curbed in mankind by restraining grace. It does not purge man's nature or deliver him from the lordship of sin. Man still does what sin tells him to do, 'Do not believe in Christ! Do not repent! Do not prepare to meet your God!' and so on . . . but there is this grace which acts like a bridle and curbs the perverseness of mankind's fallen nature. Flagrant cruelties are restrained; the human race is not wiped out. 'Thus, for the good and safety of his people God overrules all the creatures, even the devil himself, whom, we see, did not dare to attempt anything against Job without specifically God's permission and command.'[12]

Again, Calvin would have us regard it as a token of God's goodness when the Lord indulgently spares men and by holding final

[12] Calvin, *Institutes,* 1:257. *Institutes* I.17.7.

judgement in suspense God invites and commands them to repent (*cf.* Daniel 9:13; Luke 13:2; 2 Peter 3:9). The Genevan reformer even insists that there is an element of kindness in the punishments that God inflicts on mankind. He declares that all punishments are like spurs to rouse the inert who hesitate to repent, and all the miseries which we endure are a profitable invitation to repentance.

So how is it that men and women who refuse to put their trust in the Son of God can yet do many good things? Calvin answers that 'the surest and easiest answer to the objection is, that those are not common endowments of nature, but special gifts of God, which he distributes in divers forms, and, in a definite measure, to men otherwise profane.'[13]

3. *Grace to Certain Groups, Classes and Individuals*

In numerous places Calvin affirms that God displays special favour toward specific individuals by endowing them with distinct and remarkable talents—talents that are not universally distributed. Among these exceptional abilities, Calvin includes skill in artistic perception, clarity of speech, logical reasoning, bravery, creativity, strategic prowess in military matters, and leadership capacity. According to the Genevan reformer, these outstanding qualities reflect a selective yet non-saving expression of God's grace, distinguishing some people from others in society. However admirable, these gifts do not necessarily indicate the presence of saving grace. For Calvin, true saving grace produces distinctive spiritual fruits—genuine trust in the Lord Jesus Christ, joyful obedience to God's commandments, willing self-denial, cross-bearing, active discipleship, sincere worship through presenting oneself as a living sacrifice, and a life devoted zealously to good works. Thus, the sanctifying work of the Spirit, transforming the heart and soul, belongs exclusively to God's elect, even though God graciously bestows many impressive yet non-redemptive gifts upon others.

Calvin directly addresses this distinction, asking rhetorically: '[W]hat concourse the Spirit can have with the ungodly, who are altogether alienated from God? For what is said as to the Spirit dwelling in believers only, is to be understood of the Spirit of holiness, by which

---

[13] Calvin, *Institutes,* 1:340. *Institutes* II.3.4.

we are consecrated to God as temples. Notwithstanding of this, He fills, moves, and invigorates all things by the virtue of the Spirit, and that according to the peculiar nature which each class of beings has received by the Law of Creation.'[14]Calvin makes clear that although the Spirit of holiness uniquely indwells believers, there remains a general divine influence in sustaining and enriching human capabilities even among unbelievers.

This principle is further illuminated in Calvin's commentary on John 1:5, where he explains the condition of human nature after the Fall:

> The light given to men in the beginning must not be assessed by their present state since in this marred and degenerate nature their light has been turned to darkness. And yet the Evangelist denies that the light of reason is completely put out; for in the darkling gloom of the human mind there still shines some sparks of that brightness. The reader will now understand that there are two ideas in this sentence. He says that men are now very different from that sound nature with which they were endowed in the beginning: their minds, which should have been radiant in every part, are sunk in the shades of unhappy blindness. And so, in this corruption of nature, the glory of Christ is as it were darkened over. But on the other hand, the Evangelist maintains that in the midst of the darkness some remnants yet exist which show in some degree Christ's divine power. The Evangelist shows, therefore, that man's mind is quite blinded, so that it may fairly be regarded as overwhelmed with darkness. He could have used a milder word and said that the light was 'dim', or 'gloomy', but he wanted to express most clearly how wretched is our natural condition since the fall of the first man. His statement that the light shines in the darkness is not at all meant as praise of corrupt nature but rather to deprive ignorance of any excuse.[15]

In light of the Geneva reformer's insights here, it becomes clear that while these natural abilities, talents, and virtues observed even among unbelievers genuinely originate from Christ's gracious influence, Calvin carefully distinguishes these general graces from saving grace. Human reason, though corrupted by sin, still retains traces of divine illumination, leaving mankind without excuse, yet falling

[14] Calvin, *Institutes,* 1:318–319. *Institutes* II.2.16.

[15] Calvin, *The Gospel According to St John,* 11–12.

decisively short of enabling individuals to enter the kingdom of God apart from special, saving faith. Calvin thus maintains a critical distinction: natural gifts, however admirable, remain fundamentally inferior to the saving grace that alone reconciles sinners to God and grants them eternal life.

4. Covenant Common Grace

John Calvin acknowledges a grace which is common both to God's elect and to all those who live in the covenant sphere and are members of the covenant sphere, that is those who are members of the covenant of grace taken in its widest significance. He identifies their status and experience as the fruit of the grace of the covenant, the overflow of the grace of adoption, the consequences of the common graces of election in all their rich promiscuity to all who are touched by them in family, congregation and community. Family members can reject the saving grace of Christ, church-attenders can sit under an awakening ministry but defy it and remain asleep. A community can know the fear of God at a time of a great awakening while remaining indifferent to the gospel message itself. Calvin justifies the teaching by appealing to the peculiar love and favour the Lord bestowed upon the ancient covenant people, upon Abraham and his seed, not here considering the whole of mankind in general. He speaks of the Jews thus, 'That people, therefore, as if they had been the only part of mankind belonging to him, he favoured exclusively with the knowledge of his name, depositing his covenant, as it were, in their bosom, manifesting to them the presence of his divinity, and honouring them with manifest privileges. . . Meanwhile other nations, as if they had had no kind of intercourse with him, he allowed to wander in vanity, not even supplying them with the only means of preventing their destruction, that is the preaching of his word. Israel was thus the Lord's favourite child, the others were aliens.'[16]

There are many other similar passages which refer to the exclusive grace that was poured out on the Jewish nation as a whole, but such grace to the professing people of God was not restricted to Israel. Calvin believed that a certain covenant grace is granted likewise to all

[16] Calvin, *Institutes,* 1:538. *Institutes* II.11.11.

those who in the times of the New Testament dispensation benefit from the influences of the new covenant sphere and its saving grace, to all who are helpfully affected by that grace though remaining unregenerate. For example, in connection with the opening verses of I Corinthians 10, '*For I do not want you to be ignorant of the fact, brothers, that our forefathers were all under the cloud and that they all passed through the sea. They were all baptised into Moses in the cloud and in the sea. They all ate the same spiritual food and drank the same spiritual drink; for they drank from the spiritual rock that accompanied them, and that rock was Christ.*' (vv.1–4). The source of the spiritual benefits the old covenant people enjoyed was the same as that which the Christian church enjoys today, namely the Lord Christ. They were no less the people of God that we are, enjoying the same privileges of the word of God, the presence and protection of the Lord. However, '*they are not all Israel, which are of Israel*' (Romans 9:6). Calvin intimates that it is possible to belong to the people of God in a certain sense and to receive many benefits which are restricted to the sphere of the covenant of grace and yet not to know the eternal saving benefits of the covenant. This was the judgement of many of the old covenant community right up to the fall of Jerusalem in AD 70 and it happens to those under the influences of the new covenant. The Sardis congregation had a name that indicated its members were alive but in fact they were dead (Revelation 3:1). Non-saving covenant grace was given to Judas so much so that not one of the twelve suspected that he was betraying the Lord and stealing from the money bag. His lifestyle was indistinguishable from the other eleven disciples, his praying, his preaching, his miracles as signs of an apostle, his counselling and advice—all were credible and appreciated. He could not have behaved in those ways without what Calvin argued for, namely, covenant common grace. There are branches that really are in the true vine, and yet they bear no fruit (John 15:1–3).

These people, influenced greatly by God's saving grace, but falling short of union with Christ by entrusting themselves to the Saviour alone, are not unrighteous haters of all that is good, but neither have they received Christ as he has perhaps constantly been freely offered to them in the gospel. They are loved by God in that he keeps them respectful of all that they see and hear in the elect and in a special way he has been like a father to them and they are like children to him in the benefits he has given and they have received and they are very appreciative of the blessings of Christian family and friends, Christian morality and influences. They are in the household of God as guests, but not as family. The gifts they display are also displayed in others who are not raised in Christian homes, but because of a saving grace in the land, an earlier grace that goes back to Adam and that revives often throughout church history, there is today a great attractiveness in many homes where God is not acknowledged, and grand intellectual and cultural gifts are displayed in non-Christian men and women. Many of us have been elevated by a school teacher whose knowledge, enthusiasm and humility made a subject come alive and it changed the direction of our lives. How we wish that such persons had also been gripped by the Lord Jesus Christ!

John Calvin leaves no room to believe that such fine unbelievers might in fact be secret disciples of Christ, rather that such graces they display have come from some contact at some level with the Bible and an earlier grace. But such an influence, though the cause of their intelligence and sweetness of character and sympathy towards many Christian ideals; has yet not created repentance towards God and faith in our Lord Jesus Christ. In the *Institutes* (III.22.7) Calvin homes in on Judas and he states that though Judas had apostolic office and charisma he had rejected Jesus Christ as the Lord of his life. And in his commentary on John 13:18, Calvin acknowledges that the excellent gifts Judas possessed differed widely from the saving fruit and status created by the sanctification of the Spirit.

The source of this covenant common grace according to Calvin—whose benefits are received by both the elect and non-elect—is the living God, the fountain of '*whatsoever things are true . . . noble . . . just . . . pure . . . lovely . . . of good report, if there is any virtue and if there is anything praiseworthy*' (Philippians 4:8). The Geneva reformer said, 'we must be persuaded not only that as he once formed the world, so he sustains it by his boundless power, governs it by his wisdom, preserves it by his goodness in particular, rules the human race with justice and judgement, bears with them in mercy, shields them by his protection; but also not a particle of light, or wisdom, or justice, or power, rectitude, or genuine truth, will anywhere be found, which does not flow from him, and which he is not the cause'.[17]

The purpose of God in diffusing non-saving grace is a varied one. God promotes the welfare of mankind in general. And, by this goodness to all mankind, he proves to be the loving guardian of his children. Again, Calvin teaches that God causes the offer of salvation to be held forth to both elect and reprobate men and women in order that the godly may rest more secure and may embrace the grace of God with greater confidence. Also, God in various ways manifests his goodness to men and women at large in order that he my turn them from their sins and allure them to himself.

The paradox found in Calvin's teaching, and evidenced in all who embrace his theology, is focused on his commitment to the Scriptural testimony that God takes no pleasure in the destruction of the wicked but that they all repent—which he commands—while at the same time Calvin submits to that Scriptural testimony of the divine decree of an election of a company of people more than any man can number, a choice of them that necessarily involves the non-choice of others. This is an apparent antinomy but there is no theology whatsoever that can claim that it can harmonise those two truths, and one may not deny one of those truths in order to obtain a concurrence. They both stand on the evidence of revealed truth concerning those apparently conflicting teachings. The God-breathed Holy Scripture itself presents to us what seems to us to be an irreconcilable paradox.

Common Grace in Later Calvinist Theologians

This doctrine of common grace has been thoroughly examined since the time of Calvin, but especially in the last 150 years.

In the theologians of American Presbyterianism

I. Charles Hodge. His three volumes of *Systematic Theology* were the textbook during my three years at Westminster Seminary (1961–1964), and it contains a fairly detailed discussion of the subject. Hodge

[17] Calvin, *Institutes*, 1:52. *Institutes* I.2.1.

defines it as 'that influence of the Spirit which in a greater or lesser measure, is granted to all who hear the truth'.[18] That statement is apt to convey the impression that Hodge would limit the operation of common grace to those who come under some influences of gospel truth, but Hodge goes on to make it clear that he holds to a broader view of common grace. He writes, 'The Bible therefore teaches that the Holy Spirit as the Spirit of truth, of holiness, and of life in all its forms, is present with every human mind, enforcing truth, restraining from evil, exciting to good, and imparting wisdom or strength, when, where, and in what measure seemeth to Him good. In this sphere also He divides 'to every man severally as He will.' (1 Cor. 12:11.) This is what in theology is called common grace.'[19] According to Hodge the influence of the Spirit in 'common grace' is an influence 'distinct from, and accessory to the influence of the truth'.[20]. It is also to be distinguished from the providential efficiency of God which cooperates with all second causes'.[21]

Hodge maintains that the Scriptures make a broad distinction between providential government, and the operation of the Spirit in the moral government of men and women and in carrying forward the great plan of redemption. 'This is the distinction between nature and grace'.[22]

On the one hand Hodge stresses the idea that all people are the recipients of common grace: 'That there is a divine influence of the Spirit to all men, is plain both from Scripture and from experience'.[23] 'As God is everywhere present in the material world, guiding its operations according to the laws of nature; so he is everywhere present with the minds of men, as the Spirit of truth and goodness, operating on them according to the laws of their free moral agency, inkling them to good and restraining them from evil'.[24]

---

[18] Charles Hodge, *Systematic Theology* (1873; repr., Peabody, MA: Hendrickson Publishers, 2011), 2:654.

[19] Hodge, *Systematic Theology*, 2:667.

[20] Hodge, *Systematic Theology*, 2:655.

[21] Hodge, *Systematic Theology*, 2:659.

[22] Hodge, *Systematic Theology*, 2:666.

[23] Hodge, *Systematic Theology*, 2:668.

[24] Hodge, *Systematic Theology*, 2:668.

On the other hand, Hodge also teaches that common grace is sometimes entirely withdrawn from individual men, church and peoples. One thinks of the Nazis in the 1930s and 1940s—in Germany of all cultured places! Hodge has written, 'Such men have a seared conscience. They are reckless and indifferent, and entirely under the control of the evil passions of their nature'.[25] Reading Christopher R. Browning's *Ordinary Men* is a salutary illustration of this truth. It is a remarkable, chilling and meticulously researched study of Reserve Police Battalion 101 of the German Order Police responsible for the slaughter of Jewish people and their deportation to Nazi death camps in Poland in 1942. They were not fanatical Nazis but ordinary middle-aged, working-class men who came from farms, the town bank, butchers' shops or working on the railways to commit these atrocities as eager killers. Words of Hodge are particularly salutary in the light of that, 'The effects of reprobation are depicted in a fearful manner by the apostle in the first chapter of his epistle to the Romans. Not only individuals, but peoples and churches may thus be abandoned by the Spirit of God. Then unbroken spiritual death is the inevitable consequence'.[26]

As to the effects of common grace Hodge declares,

> To the general influence of the Spirit (or to common grace), we owe
>
> i] All the decorum, order, refinement and virtue existing among men.
>
> ii] To the same divine agent is due specifically that general fear of God, and that religious feeling which prevails among men, and which secures for the rites and services of religion in all its form, the decorous or more serious attention which they receive.
>
> iii] The Scriptures refer to this general influence of the Spirit those religious experiences, varied in character and degree, which so often occur where genuine conversion, or regeneration, does not attend or follow . . . In all cases, however, there is in the first place a conviction of the truth . . . in the second place, with this conviction of the truths of religion is connected an experience of their power. They produce an effect to a greater or lesser degree upon the feelings appropriate to their nature, a conviction of sin . . . It is also natural and according to experience, that the promise of the gospel, and the exhibition of the plan of salvation . . . should of-

[25] Hodge, *Systematic Theology*, 2:670.

[26] Hodge, *Systematic Theology*, 2:671.

> ten appear not only as true but as suitable to the condition of the awakened sinner. Hence he receives the word with joy. He believes with a faith founded on the moral evidence of the truth . . . To this class of persons our Saviour refers when he speaks of those who received the word in stony place or among thorns . . . In the third place, the state of mind induced by these common operations of the Spirit, often leads to reformation and to an externally religious life.[27]

Regarding the mode in which God works when he grants the influences of common grace, Hodge does not recognise a direct and immediate operation of the Spirit. It is through the word that these influences have come. Hodge says, 'so far as appears, this common influence of the Spirit is never exercised except through the truth.'[28] And it is surprising that Hodge in that whole section does not speak of common grace as the source of the material blessings which are showered down promiscuously upon all mankind.

II. A.A. Hodge. Charles Hodge's son is in full harmony with his father as regards common grace, even to that last reference. In other words, he also does not state that temporal mercies such as food and drink and clothing and other material benefits are because of God's common grace. He gives this definition: "Common grace' is the restraining and persuading influences of the Holy Spirit acting only through the truth revealed in the gospel, or through the natural moral effect of such truth upon the understanding, conscience and heart. It involves no change of heart, but simply an enhancement of the material powers of the truth, a restraint of the evil passions, and an increase of the natural emotions in view of sin, duty and self interest.'[29] He expressly denies that common grace ever acts immediately, as he says, 'Common grace is only mediated through the truth and it is merely moral, heightening the moral influence natural to the truth, and exciting only the natural powers of the soul, both rational and moral'.[30] It is also worthy of note that A.A. Hodge asserts that the influence of

[27] Hodge, *Systematic Theology*, 2:671–673.

[28] Hodge, *Systematic Theology*, 2:674.

[29] A. A. Hodge, *Outlines of Theology* (1879; repr., London, UK: Banner of Truth, 1972), 449.

[30] Hodge, *Outlines of Theology*, 150.

common grace 'is always more or less consciously resisted, as opposed to the prevailing dispositions of the soul.'[31]

III. B.B. Warfield. Hodge's successor and admirer held to those same basic views on common grace as those of the Hodges senior and junior, and so he wrote nothing specifically on the subject, their having dealt with the doctrine to his total satisfaction. But Warfield's fascination with short horn cattle—so much so that he wrote many articles on the subject and judged them in agricultural shows—and his admiration of the horses bred in Kentucky, were a lively evidence of his personal commitment to the fruit of common grace among his family and neighbours. So Warfield completed a trio of theological studies which became known as the Princeton School of biblical interpretation.

His contemporary, William Shedd, thirty years older than Warfield, taught at Union Seminary, New York, for eleven years and wrote his *Dogmatic Theology* while Warfield was teaching at Princeton. Their views on common grace were identical; Shedd raised this question on one occasion and thus was challenging those who denied common grace: 'Is it inconsistent in God to do any kind and degree of good to a sinner if God has decided not to do the highest kind and degree of good in his power? Shall God do nothing at all that is kind and gracious to a sinful man unless God should first decide to overcome all the opposition that sinners may make to his kindness and grace? Must God make no offer of mercy to a sinner unless he has decided to make him accept it? There never was an age of the world than now when men more need to be reminded that they are resisting the common grace of God, and rejecting his universal offer of mercy in the gospel, and thus in so doing they run the great hazard of God's preterition.'[32]

IV. Caspar Wistar Hodge Jr. and John Murray. Caspar Wistar Hodge Jr. was the grandson of Charles Hodge and professor of Systematics at Princeton from 1921, passing away in February 1937, just one month after the death of J. Gresham Machen. During his tenure, Hodge wrote numerous articles in the *Princeton Theological Review* and influenced many students, including John Murray, who studied under

---

[31] Hodge, *Outlines of Theology*, 150.

[32] William G.T. Shedd, *Calvinism: Pure and Mixed* (1893; repr., Edinburgh, UK: Banner of Truth, 1993), 105.

him. Murray himself taught briefly at Princeton before leaving to join Machen at Westminster Seminary in Philadelphia, where he taught theology for thirty-six years.

When the doctrine of common grace was challenged in America during the 1930s, John Murray wrote a definitive article in the *Westminster Theological Journal* (November 1942), now included in his *Collected Writings*.[33] In that article, Murray famously defined common grace as '*every favour of whatever kind or degree, falling short of salvation, which this undeserving and sin-cursed world enjoys at the hand of God.*'[34]

Daniel Strange helpfully elucidates Murray's perspective by emphasising two primary dimensions of common grace:

> Common grace is 'common' because it is universal and it is 'grace'; because it is undeserved and given by a gracious God. As with other foundational doctrinal loci, the formulation of this doctrine is extremely rich, complex and controversial. I can only highlight some of the relevant points. The exposition of John Murray is seminal. Murray defines common grace as 'every favour of whatever kind or degree, falling short of salvation, which this undeserving and sin-cursed world enjoys at the hand of God.' According to Murray, common grace has both a negative and a positive function. Its negative function is that of divine restraint: a restraint on sin, a restraint on wrath and its execution, and a restraint on the effect of sin. The positive function is that of divine favour, whereby creation receives divine blessing, non-Christians receive divine favour and goodness, 'good' is attributed to non-Christians, non-Christians receive benefits from the presence of the gospel. It is important to note that with all of these functions, under the sovereignty of God, there can be a great deal of differentiation and variegation in terms of the amount of divine restraint and blessing within a particular society or period in history.[35]

The American Presbyterian tradition outlines common grace biblically by highlighting several key emphases: God exercises divine restraint over human sinfulness, preventing moral and societal deterioration;

---

[33] John Murray, *Select Lectures in Systematic Theology*, vol. 2 of *Collected Writings of John Murray* (Edinburgh, UK: Banner of Truth, 1977), 93–123.

[34] Murray, *Select Lectures in Systematic Theology*, 96.

[35] Daniel Strange, *'For Their Rock is not as Our Rock': An Evangelical Theology of Religions* (London, UK: Inter-Varsity Press, 2014), 89.

He mercifully delays the immediate execution of deserved wrath; He moderates the harmful consequences inherent within the curse due to human sin; and finally, He graciously bestows diverse benefits upon humanity, including moral, intellectual, and societal goods, as well as material blessings. These manifestations of common grace demonstrate God's ongoing benevolence toward a fallen world, even though they fall short of redemption and eternal salvation.

In the theologians of the Dutch Reformed churches

I. Herman Bavinck (1854–1921). Since the appearance of the four volumes of his *Reformed Dogmatics*, the three volumes of his lectures on Christian ethics, and other works, particularly his *Christian Worldview* (with its insights into common grace), there is enormous new interest in and appreciation of the theology of Bavinck in the non-Dutch-speaking world. In European theology, at the popular level of the magnificent Calvinistic preaching by C.H. Spurgeon, or in the literature on dogmatics coming from the universities, there was scarcely a reference to common grace in the United Kingdom or in Germany.

Bavinck first broached the subject in his *Catholicity of Christianity and Church* (1888). But that beginning germinated to produce a fuller treatment. This was in his rectorial address at Kampen in December 1894, entitled 'De Gemeene Genade' that was translated into English under the title 'Common Grace' and translated much later by Raymond C. Van Leeuwe. This has been published by the Bavinck Institute and is available online.[36] In this address, as well as in his later article 'Calvin and Common Grace,' Bavinck traced the origin of the doctrine of common grace to the thought of John Calvin.[37]

According to Bavinck, the influences of God's common grace were by no means restricted to the rational and ethical life of man. In his view the sphere of its operation is as wide as the extent of this fallen

---

[36] See Herman Bavinck, 'Common Grace,' trans. Raymond C. Van Leeuwen, *Calvin Theological Journal* 24 (1989): 35–65. https://bavinckinstitute.org/wp-content/uploads/2014/08/Herman-Bavinck-Common-Grace.pdf

[37] cf. Bavinck's *Calvin and Common Grace* in *Calvin and the Reformation* (London, UK: F. H. Revell, 1909), 99–130. His essay first appeared in the 1909 *Princeton Theological Review* and was initially translated by Geerhardus Vos.

world. God, exercising forbearance towards this present evil world by his common grace, sustains the world as a whole as well as every single creature. It is due to common grace that such institutions as the family and the state are maintained, that society is not utterly disorganised, and that sciences and arts still flourish. But it is also owing to common grace that all individual men and women daily receive untold material and spiritual blessings. Common grace on the one hand is not sufficient to banish sin and to annihilate every trace of its blighting effect, but it does curb its destructive power, and even causes those who know not the grace of regeneration to produce many good fruits in the sphere of civil righteousness. Bavinck articulates this comprehensive influence as follows:

> While it is true that the world has been corrupted by sin, it nevertheless remains the work of the Father, the Creator of heaven and earth. Of his own will he maintains it by his covenant, and by his gratia communis he powerfully opposes the destructive might of sin. He fills the hearts of men with nourishment and joy and does not leave himself without a witness among them. He pours out upon them numberless gifts and benefits. Families, races, and peoples he binds together with natural love and affection. He allows societies and states to spring up that the citizens might live in peace and security. Wealth and well-being he grants them that the arts and sciences can prosper. And by his revelation in nature and history he ties their hearts and consciences to the invisible, suprasensible world and awakens in them a sense of worship and virtue. The entirety of the rich life of nature and society exists thanks to God's common grace.[38]

Bavinck goes so far as to declare that there is much in the heathen religions which must be attributed to the operation of common grace. 'However, an operation of God's Spirit and of his common grace is discernible not only in science and art, morality and law, but also in the religions. Calvin rightly spoke of a 'seed of religion,' a 'sense of divinity.' Founders of religion, after all, were not impostors or agents of Satan but men who, being religiously inclined, had to fulfil a mission to their time and people and often exerted a beneficial influence on the life of peoples.'[39]

---

[38] Bavinck, 'Common Grace,' 60.

[39] Herman Bavinck, *Reformed Dogmatics,* ed. John Bolt, trans. John Vriend (Grand Rap-

Touching the question as to whether the widespread proclamation of the word is a gift of common grace, Bavinck does not speak as explicitly as one might wish. In one place he tells us that the reprobate owe it to the goodness and the grace of God that the evangel is preached to them. 'Conversely, the reprobates also receive many blessings, blessings that do not as such arise from the decree of reprobation but from the goodness and grace of God. They receive many natural gifts—life, health, strength, food, drink, good cheer, and so forth—for God does not leave himself without a witness. He endures them with much patience. He has the gospel of his grace proclaimed to them and takes no pleasure in their death.'[40] In another place Bavinck declares that the external call is a restraining, or repressive, grace: 'The call, by law and gospel, restrains sin, diminishes guilt, and stems the corruption and misery of humankind. It is 'repressive grace.''[41] In more than one connection Bavinck asserts that common grace is subservient to saving grace: 'Although special grace is essentially distinct from common grace, it is intimately bound up with it. After all, though the covenant with Noah is called—for the purpose of differentiation—the 'covenant of nature,' it did not flow from God's nature and was not given with the nature of things; it, too, rests on grace, proceeds from God's patience, and grants all natural benefits and blessings out of God's general goodness. It is a covenant of grace in the broad sense. Further, it is the Father who—not apart from the Son but specifically through the Logos and the Spirit—produces all the forces and gifts present in nature and unregenerate humankind. And this Logos and Spirit who dwell and work in all creatures and humans are the same agents who as Christ and the Spirit of Christ acquire and apply all the benefits pertaining to the covenant of grace.'[42]

But he does not say in just so many words that the former is in every respect subordinate to the latter. There is at least one passage in his writings which seems to favour the idea that common grace is not merely subservient to special grace, but also has a significance of its own, apart from its relation to the redeeming work of Christ. 'But why

ids, MI: Baker Academic, 2003), 1:319.

[40] Herman Bavinck, *Reformed Dogmatics*, 2:398.

[41] Herman Bavinck, *Reformed Dogmatics*, 4:38.

[42] Herman Bavinck, *Reformed Dogmatics*, 3:225.

should he continue to preserve such a sinful world by a special action of his grace? Does he squander his gifts? Is he acting purposelessly? Is it not because natural life, in all its forms has value in his eyes in spite of sin's corruption? The love of family and kin, societal and political life, art and science are all in themselves objects of his divine good pleasure. He delights also in these works of his hands. They all together constitute, not in their mode of being but in their essence, the original order that God called into being at creation and that he still preserves and maintains, sin notwithstanding.'[43]

II. Abraham Kuyper (1837–1920) was one of the most extraordinary individuals of his time in an age of extraordinary men. His life overlapped in part with the lives of such leaders as Chalmers, Gladstone, Spurgeon, Hodge, Warfield, Thomas Charles Edwards, D'Augbigne, Dabney, and J. Gresham Machen. Kuyper was a powerful preacher and a fine devotional writer whose works in this sphere have been warmly greeted in the 21st century in their first translation in their entirety into English. Kuyper also founded the Free University of Amsterdam and was an active politician in a Christian political party, serving as a member of parliament from 1874 and as the Dutch Prime Minister from 1901 to 1905. He devoted much of his writing towards developing an understanding of culture from a biblical perspective, and his thought has influenced such men as Hans Rookmaaker, Cornelius Van Til, Francis Schaeffer and Dooyeweerd.

Kuyper's most comprehensive treatise on common grace was published in three volumes, *De Gemeene Gratie,* 1902–1904. The eight key works of his vast literary output are in the process of being translated and published by the Lexham Press in twelve volumes. The first volume of *Common Grace: God's Gifts for a Fallen World* was translated and published in 2016 (672 pages in length). The second companion volume appeared in 2019, a book of similar size (of 91 chapters). The third volume is currently being prepared for publication some time in the early 2020s. In addition to these works there is also his related work *Pro Rege: Living Under Christ's Kingship* which has recently appeared in English in two substantial volumes, the first of which has 554 pages and the second volume 528 pages.

[43] Bavinck, 'Common Grace,' 60.

Kuyper lays it down as an axiom that the grace of God can be distinguished into three kinds: particular grace, covenant grace, and common grace. Of these, only particular grace is saving in the strict sense of the term. In his volumes on *Common Grace*, Kuyper does not explicitly clarify the exact content of covenant grace as distinct from common grace. His teaching on covenant grace, particularly his controversial doctrine of presumptive regeneration tied to infant baptism, remains separate from his exposition here. Nonetheless, he consistently clarifies the relationship between common and particular grace, stating explicitly: 'Common grace thus operates according to fixed rules, in anticipation of Christ, and particular grace caused Christ to make his entrance precisely at the point where common grace reached the intersection with particular grace.'[44] Kuyper further emphasises their essential interdependence by asserting: 'In everything particular grace is reality and seeks reality; in this way it could not have followed its course apart from common grace. For common grace is precisely what maintained and still maintains the reality of things in opposition to curse and death.'[45] Thus, for Kuyper, common grace provides universal preservation, restraining the effects of sin and enabling human culture and society to flourish, while particular grace uniquely achieves salvation and eternal life, always interacting closely with common grace within God's providential ordering of the world.

Abraham Kuyper's doctrine of common grace further teaches that God mercifully restrains human sin and its destructive consequences, thereby preventing the world from descending into complete chaos. After the flood, God chose 'another route' to manage human depravity, namely: 'through the increase of common grace, sin will be restrained with bridle and rein, so that sin will never again…develop into such gruesome, hellish outburst and tyranny.'[46] Yet, common grace does not merely hold back evil; it positively blesses every sphere of human existence and the natural world. Kuyper explains that this grace 'includes far more than simply bringing about civic righteousness, but one of its

[44] Abraham Kuyper, *Common Grace: God's Gifts for a Fallen World*, ed. Jordan J. Ballor, Melvin Flikkema, and Stephen J. Grabill, trans. Nelson D. Kloosterman and Ed M. van der Maas, *Abraham Kuyper Collected Works in Public Theology* (Bellingham, WA: Lexham Press; Acton Institute, 2015), 1:161–162.

[45] Kuyper, *Common Grace*, 1:775.

[46] Kuyper, *Common Grace*, 1:26.

fruits was to transform the earth that once produced thorns and thistles into a beautiful, luxuriant, profitable nature.'[47] Finally, Kuyper grounds common grace explicitly in God's sovereignty and providence, claiming it is 'deduced directly from the sovereignty of the Lord,' and asserting that 'if God is sovereign, then his lordship must extend over all of life,' meaning that even the fallen 'non-Christian world has not been handed over to Satan...God's sovereignty is great and all-dominating in the life of that unbaptised world as well.' In sum, common grace continually restrains evil, sustains the created order, and manifests God's benevolent sovereign rule over a fallen world.'[48] In sum, common grace continually restrains evil, sustains the created order, and reflects God's benevolent sovereign rule over a fallen world.

Regarding the manner in which God exercises common grace, Kuyper firmly denies that it is always mediated through external means. To the question of whether the Word and sacraments are gifts of common grace, Kuyper provides a nuanced answer. While denying that these are inherently common grace, he acknowledges that the Word and sacraments sometimes serve as instruments of common grace alone. Consider those described in Hebrews 6:4–5, who were 'once enlightened, and have tasted of the heavenly gift, and were made partakers of the Holy Ghost, and have tasted the goodness of the word of God and the powers of the age to come.' Kuyper sees God's purpose here as partly restraining sin even in those who remain defiant toward saving grace. In Kuyper's view, though common and particular grace differ essentially, their spheres not only touch but intermingle repeatedly. When particular grace intersects with common grace, the effectiveness of common grace is significantly enhanced. Conversely, common grace serves as the necessary foundation and presupposition of particular grace. The intimate relation between the two arises from their common origin in Christ—common grace flowing from Christ as mediator of mankind before God, and particular grace deriving from Christ as redeemer. Yet Kuyper, at times, appears to connect the operation of common grace directly with Christ's redemptive role.

On whether common grace is entirely subordinate to particular grace, Kuyper is explicit. He insists common grace is not wholly

---

[47] Kuyper, *Common Grace*, 1:584.

[48] Kuyper, *Common Grace*, 1:xxxvi–xxxvii.

subservient to particular grace, arguing instead that it has an independent purpose distinct from salvation. Besides facilitating the redemption of the elect, common grace promotes the glory of God by bringing to fruition the multitude of talents and abilities implanted as seeds in human nature. Thus, common grace has more than temporary value; its fruits endure into eternity. Kuyper articulates this clearly when he writes: 'But the grace shown here extends to the entirety of human life. Most surely the purpose was so that God's church could find a place to set its foot, and also so that the church of the new covenant would gather together believers from all peoples and nations. But its purpose was also so that in a proper sense God the Lord would continue his work in that broad sphere of human life, not unto the saving of souls but no less unto the praise and glory of his great name.'[49] According to Kuyper, common grace not only prepares the stage for particular grace but also independently displays God's sovereignty and goodness. It provides a stable and flourishing environment in which humanity can develop culturally, socially, and morally, thus continually reflecting God's glory beyond its specific role in redemption.

III. Valentine E. Hepp (1879–1950). Dr Hepp followed Bavinck and Kuyper to the chair of Dogmatics at the Free University of Amsterdam. He was one with his predecessors in his understanding of common grace as the action of God's mercy restraining sin and its corrupting effects in an effectually broad manner. Hepp gave the Stone Lectures on *Calvinism and the Philosophy of Nature* at Princeton Seminary in 1930. One striking feature of the book was Hepp's vigorous denunciation of Christians who find millions of years in the history of the earth!

Cornelius Van Til, in his book *Common Grace,* takes Hepp to task for his confidence in the achievements of God's common grace evidenced in the Dutch school for failing to distinguish between man's original nature in Eden and man's fallen nature now. This has allowed Hepp to view man's reason as functioning in some relatively independent manner. Roman Catholics might do that and Arminians also with their doctrine of the free will of man, but such a methodology is out of accord with the foundational concepts of the state of man's

[49] Kuyper, *Common Grace,* 1:107.

fallenness as viewed in reformed theology. Their forthcoming doctrine of common grace could become effectual in making a school of 'less consistent Calvinists.' Van Til holds that one of the most subtle and effective ways that the natural man can suppress the revelation of the true God is by 'proving the existence of God' to himself! Van Til judges that by that means he makes an idol for himself. Worshipping his idol, his god, he seeks to make himself believe that he has done all that may be expected of him.

IV. G.C. Berkouwer (1903–1996). Berkouwer followed Hepp in being appointed to the chair of Dogmatics at the Free University of Amsterdam. Everyone who knew Berkouwer described him as captivating, well-read, influential and cosmopolitan. And everyone also agrees that his thinking underwent a shift during the 1950s, departing from the classic Reformed viewpoint on several issues such as the authority of Scripture and original sin. As for common grace, Berkouwer asserts that 'the natural man retains some knowledge of God and he shows some practice of virtue and outward discipline' and this necessitates common grace.[50] He says, 'Common grace is an imperfect solution, but it does centre our attention on the gracious act of God in protecting man's corrupt and apostate nature from total demonisation. Grace is at work even in fallen man to bend partially back in the right direction those human powers and endowments which, were man left to himself, would be wholly perverted'.[51] The heathen are held morally responsible as they continually come into contact with God's revelation. It is through God's common grace and by an earlier redemptive grace that we observe the natural man not always following his own selfish way, and not invariably allowing hatred to dominate his entire existence. At times and occasions he is drawn to actions that are commended by the law of God. This is because of common grace.

V. William Heyns (1856–1933). Willem Wijnand Heyns was born in the Nertherlands, studied in Kampen and then immigrated to Grand Rapids. He eventually became a student in Calvin Seminary. He served in four congregations of the Christian Reformed Church and in 1902 was appointed to the chair of Practical Theology, and then in 1904 to the

---

[50] G.C. Berkouwer, *General Revelation*. Studies in Dogmatics. (Grand Rapids, MI: Wm. B. Eerdmans, 1955), 184.

[51] Berkouwer, *General Revelation,* 184.

chair of Systematic Theology in Calvin Seminary. He held both those positions until 1926 when he retired, dying seven years later. His view of the covenant influenced not only many ministers and congregations in the Christian Reformed Church but also the Reformed community back in the Netherlands.

Heyns believed that a certain 'covenantal grace' was given to all recipients of baptism enabling them to respond to Christian nurture as they grew up, but that this covenantal grace could still be lost because it was common grace not saving grace (*cf.* his *Handboek voor de Catechetiek [Manual for Catechetics]).* Heyns wrote that just as the blessing of common grace accompanied God's covenant with Noah in that man's sin was restrained so as to prevent a second catastrophic worldwide deluge, so the more glorious covenant with Abraham was accompanied by the gift of 'enhanced' common grace bestowed on all covenant children. By this grace man's total inability to do any good is taken away and replaced with an inner disposition whereby the seed of the covenant is made susceptible to receiving spiritual impressions. In other words, Heyns taught that all covenant children (elect and non-elect) possess a certain measure of spiritual life that makes them suitable objects for nurture by the church. Pointing to the statement in the thanksgiving prayer of the Form for Baptism—which the minister prays that the baptised infant may 'increase and grow up' in the Lord Jesus Christ—Heyns concluded that 'there must be some degree of life or seed of life present in the child for it to increase and grow'.[52] This belief brought Heyns very close to Kuyper's view of presumptive regeneration, though Kuyper believed that only elect children possessed this seed.

VI. Klaas Schilder *(1890–1952).* Dr. Schilder was a professor in the Reformed Churches in the Netherlands and later in the Reformed Churches in the Netherlands (liberated). In 1934 he became professor of Systematic Theology (which position he retained until his death) and the following year, 1935, he became the sole editor of the weekly journal *The Reformation.* Schilder's lasting achievement was his trilogy on the sufferings of Christ (the second reading of which has continued

[52] Cornelis Pronk, *A Goodly Heritage: The Secession of 1834 and Its Impact on Reformed Churches in the Netherlands and North America* (Grand Rapids, MI: Reformation Heritage Books, 2019), 421.

to reveal to me new aspects of the trial and crucifixion of our Lord). In 1948 he wrote *Christ and Culture* which is germane for our study. Schilder forcefully resisted the German invasion of the Netherlands and thus had to spend much of the war in hiding. In 1944 his denomination suspended him for being a schismatic and the result of this was itself a schism and the subsequent birth of the Reformed Churches in the Netherlands (liberated), with 216 congregations, 152 ministers, and 77,000 members.

Schilder criticised Kuyper's treatment of common grace, Schilder claiming that culture is not based upon any foundation that believers have in common with non-believers. Culture is rather based on the original mandate given to man by God that he should replenish and subdue the earth. As Van Til has written, 'Thus we are brought back to the idea that man as office-bearer is called upon to glorify God in all he does. If therefore we speak of common grace at all, we should do so in connection with a common curse. There is a restraint both of the full blessing and of the full curse. Keeping both in mind we are truly progressive rather than reactionary. We then think eschatologically and have an open mind for the idea of the catastrophe. The popular notion of common grace as offering a neutral field of operation between Christians and non-Christians Schilder rejects with vigour. It is not on the basis of one divine virtue, his patience, that we must understand culture and history in general, but on the basis of all his attributes'.[53]

While the famous 1924 Synod of the Christian Reformed Church was debating and rejecting Hoeksema's denial of common grace and the free offer of the gospel, Schilder sided for a time with Hoeksema, clashing with the Synod's conclusions concerning the question of whether God had a certain attitude of favour towards the non-elect (Schilder denying this). He sought to differentiate between 'creatures in general', to whom God shows favour and 'men in general' to whom no favour is shown, other than the elect. Schilder leaned towards the supralapsarian position which was also Hoeksema's position, and for a time he believed that the Liberated churches in the Netherlands and Hoeksema's Protestant Reformed Churches in America could enter into ecclesiastical fellowship, but the relationship did not last for long.

---

[53] Cornelius Van Til, *Common Grace* (Philadelphia, PA: Presbyterian and Reformed, 1947), 24.

Schilder ultimately rejected Hoeksema's denying any form of divine favour or kindness to the non-elect.

Van Til parted company with Schilder in the latter's accord with some neutral 'logic' in which the Christian and non-Christian could agree. For Van Til there was in Schilder (as in Kuyper, Bavinck and Hepp) remnants of an abstract way of thinking. So it is that to Cornelius Van Til we must finally turn.

VII. Cornelius Van Til (1895–1987). Dr Van Til was my teacher, and his lectures were the noisiest and most stimulating at Westminster Seminary in the early sixties. His definitive work on this theme that we are considering is his book *Common Grace* which gathers together his essays, articles, booklets and books on the subject. The second edition (2015) has a valuable foreword and annotations by K. Scott Oliphant. Oliphant sees Van Til as seeking a 'third way' to think about common grace problems. While one way has been to deny common grace, another has been to affirm a theory of common grace patterned after the natural theology of Arminianism and the theology of Rome. Van Til resists both of those positions, refusing to deny common grace by squeezing out certain truths of Scripture that don't fit in with man's thinking, but then also refusing to stand on so-called neutral ground defending a kind of Christianity that identifies with those who appeal to biased human reason, man-made institutions and traditions both ancient and also populistic. There can be no commonality with such an approach for then there would be no challenge to the non-Christian in those areas of his life and thinking. Oliphant highlights three main and overriding themes to help us understand the substance of Van Til's arguments:

1. *Fearless anthropomorphism.* God is able to love the people he has chosen and given to his Son to save and glorify, and yet also to have a love for all his creatures and show patience, kindness, and graciousness to them, beseeching them sincerely to be saved, declaring that he takes no pleasure in their destruction. No theory of any man can reconcile these two truths. There is no theology that can reconcile two wills of our heavenly Father that seem apparent antinomies, a secret will and a revealed will—in apparent contradiction. But this theology stands on the foundation of the independent testimony of different Scrip-

tures. This truth is monumentally important to grasp.

2. *Concrete thinking*. This develops the first point. The alternative to concrete biblical thinking is to reason abstractly, to take one truth, e.g. God's unconditional election—'and deduce from it that human history is meaningless because it is predetermined . . . or to conclude that God's unconditional decree negates real, human responsibility.'[54] Van Til says that if we reason concretely about God and his relation to the world we are simply listening to what God has told us in his Word on this matter.
3. *Limiting concepts.* In Christianity is a teaching that requires us to affirm truths and doctrines that cannot be delimited by our laws of thought. They are teachings of Scripture that must be affirmed, though they do not conform to, but rather transcend, standard rules of thought. For example, why does God find fault if he has foreordained whatever comes to pass? And the sole biblical answer to that query is, 'Man, who are you to reply with your words that dare to question your Almighty and Omniscient Creator and Judge?' God speaks right; he will do right. And there is not a single rogue molecule in all of our cosmos, and nothing in heaven or hell that can boast that it lives and moves and has its being outside of God's total control. The earth and its fullness lives and moves and has its being in his hands and outside those hands is nothingness.

Conclusion

Common grace is a twig-and-leaf doctrine, not a trunk-and-branch doctrine of the Christian faith. That is, I put it in the same category as such teachings as those dealing with church government, the millennium, the identity of the man of sin of 2 Thessalonians 2, the origin of the soul of the person, the mode of baptism, psalmody, musical instruments in public worship, and the future of Israel. These are issues which Christians discuss and about which they have strong opinions. Within congregations and denominations these opinions are debated, denomination magazines print the various interpretations and

[54] K. Scott Oliphint, 'Foreword,' in Cornelius Van Til, *Common Grace and The Gospel.* 2nd ed. (Phillipsburg, NJ: P&R Publishing, 2015), xxviii.

understandings, while the peace of the church is maintained and alternative opinions are respected.

Common grace is an intoxicating doctrine. Especially if one has been raised in a wholly negative approach to the creation such as to 'come out and separate oneself from the 'world''. Involvement in the world in those circles is compared to painting the deck chairs on the Titanic—'this world will soon end and Christ will return, so that there is just one message we have for mankind, to repent and believe the gospel'. From that position to be introduced to the 'cultural mandate' and the physicality of the world that God has created in all its glory, and to know the liberty for which Christ has made us free to enjoy his creation—all that is utterly revolutionary. It is powerful evangelistically, as well as helping the Christian ethically in his values and attitudes. The priesthood of all believers, the legitimate vocation of every disciple whether a refuse collector, or running a sewage plant, or being a military man, or a home-keeper, or a preacher, to fulfil their vocations, whatever they may be, to the glory of God is the biblical ideal. It is Christ saying that his people are the salt of the earth and the light of the world. It is Christ informing us that we are in the world but not of it. It is Christ praying to the Father that we be not taken out of the world but kept as salt and light in it. That is the cultural mandate.

Common grace is a dangerous doctrine. It is captivating. It promises relevance and interest apart from the perceived limitations of biblical preaching, pastoring and officers' meetings and dealing with falls and congregational opposition. 'See this exciting world of common grace!', I heard the siren's voice calling. But there is so much in the world in the disciplines of the sciences and the arts, of economics and finance and politics, and there is nothing in the Bible that appears to be directly related to it. Yet there are great principles of morality in the Bible, and the general purpose of all our activities is to glorify and enjoy God in whatever we do. We are to be ready to give a reason for what we believe and hope towards all who inquire and we are to do so meekly and reverently. But there is not a distinctive 'Christian' approach to such matters as knitting, mathematics, carpentry, meteorology, design, dentistry, music, sporting activities, etc. Dr. Herman Dooyeweerd's fascinating approach to the world and everything in it is a stimulating, but rather abstruse Christian philosophy in its gigantic development of sphere sovereignty. Francis Schaeffer's best books are those that expound portions of Scripture and stay closest to its exegesis. His very attempt to address the whole thinking of the world and to listen to the opinions and theories of thinkers was enriching, salutary and exemplary, but his expositions of the gospel of grace have been his most helpful contributions to the church. We are glad to know of Kuyper, Van Til, Dooyeweerd and Schaeffer, as well as the many books that keep appearing that engage with cultural matters, but there is danger in all of that. None is easy reading. They are rarely page turners. The greatest challenge today is to bring the heart of the Christian gospel to bear on the conscience and affections of the world we are living in and to do so freshly, beautifully, with pathos and authority. The demand is that the fertile creativity that produces material on the world and life view should be directed toward what Scripture is all about: the glories and loveliness of the Son of God, the offer of him to be our Saviour, teacher, protector and the Lamb of God, and the need to live credible Christ-like lives with the help Scripture gives us so to live. Those are our priorities.

Dr. Martyn Lloyd-Jones, the former scientist and heart specialist who became an evangelistic preacher, was concerned at the growing emphases on the world and life view in evangelical circles. In 1979, two years before he died, at the British Evangelical Council conference, he addressed this trend and I was there listening to him in a crowded Westminster Chapel. His text was Matthew 22 verse 21, 'Then saith he unto them, Render therefore unto Caesar the things which are Caesar's; and unto God the things that are God's.' His concern was this,

> There is such a thing as common grace, and it is not part of the preaching of the gospel to say that the Christian is to take no interest whatsoever in these various aspects of life. They are all perfectly legitimate . . . But we must not give them an order of importance which they do not merit. We must not be over-preoccupied with them. In their place, it is all right to be talking about politics, if you like, and social matters, and art and culture and drama, but they must not be in the centre. You must not be preoccupied with them. That is one of the dangerous tendencies that I observe . . . More and more evangelicals, as well as others, are putting these things into the centre and everybody is talking about the Christian attitude to politics, or education, or culture, or war, or this and that. This has become central . . . If we do then the impression will be gained that Christianity is nothing but some kind of exceptional or strange philosophical attitude

> towards a number of burning contemporary social questions . . . We are living in a materialistic age. We are living in a sophisticated age. We are living in an age when men and women are experts in all these particular matters. You and I ought to be experts on the things of which they are entirely ignorant . . . The real tragedy of the world today is that it has forgotten the supernatural. It has forgotten God. Man is in the centre – his interest, his questions, his enthusiasms, his obsessions. Man is ever before us and so our task is to proclaim the everlasting and eternal God.[55]

Common grace has become a doctrine as slippery to grasp as a newly caught fish. It started as a plea for appreciative engagement with the physicality of the creation that God has made in order for us to enjoy God in what he designed and made and declared to be good—Look! The heavens are declaring the glory of God, so reach out to it with your body, your eyes and ears and fingertips, your sense of smell and taste. God has designed for us to take delight in all that he has created. Fine! But now the doctrine of common grace has somewhat transmogrified.

Whereas once the hope and glory and joy of the new heaven and earth was that we would see the face of God in Jesus Christ, that the invisible God is going to make himself known to us in Jesus Christ—that anticipation is no long emphasised. Now, since the world and life view is stressed, the eschatological emphasis is on the renewal of creation and not on 'going to heaven when we die.' The climax of redemptive history is now merely our resurrection and the renewal of the earth. Little is made of our hope of standing in the presence of God and beholding the face of God first in heaven and then in the new creation. Where is the heavenly perspective that is so crucial to Christian devotion and discipleship? The psalmist said, 'One *thing* I have desired of the Lord, That will I seek: That I may dwell in the house of the Lord All the days of my life, To behold the beauty of the Lord, And to inquire in His temple.' (Psalm 27:4).

Today, we face significant theological challenges concerning God's benevolence toward the non-elect. There is ongoing debate about the sincerity of God's offer of salvation to all humanity without exception, as well as questions surrounding the authenticity of His

---

[55] D. Martyn Lloyd-Jones, *Unity in the Truth* (Darlington, UK: Evangelical Press, 1991), 191–193.

universal command to repentance. Does not Scripture assure that God genuinely promises salvation to everyone who responds in obedient repentance? Thus, our preaching must earnestly plead with all people, urging them to turn from destruction, confidently assuring them that glory awaits if they respond. Additionally, discussion continues about the genuine yet temporary benefits experienced by non-elect individuals who live within the covenant community, and how exposure to the means of grace affects them. Can revelation sufficiently resolve these tensions? Could it be that the clarity of Scripture's free offer is sometimes overshadowed by our zeal to defend other undeniable doctrinal truths? Unfortunately, this umbrella of common grace, intended to shelter the contemporary Reformed church from heated strife and to nurture warm-hearted dialogue, has begun to leak—and we find ourselves increasingly dampened by its unresolved drips.

Selected Writings of Peter Barnes

The listing of works authored by Peter Barnes below is not exhaustive but illustrates the breadth and consistency of his contribution to Reformed theology over more than four decades. His writings reflect a strong commitment to confessional Reformed principles, addressing theological liberalism, pastoral care, evangelism, cultural critique, and historical theology. Through his prolific output, he has sought to equip the church with resources for faithful, discerning, and hope-filled Christian living.

Books

Barnes, Peter. *Abortion: Open Your Mouth for the Dumb*. Edinburgh: Banner of Truth, 1984.

Barnes, Peter. *The Milk of the Word: An Introduction to the Christian Faith*. Edinburgh: Banner of Truth, 1985.

Barnes, Peter. *Seeing Jesus: The Case Against Pictures of Our Lord Jesus Christ*. Edinburgh: Banner of Truth, 1990.

Barnes, Peter. *The Gospel: Did Paul and Jesus Agree?* Durham, England: Evangelical Press, 1994.

Barnes, Peter. *1, 2, 3 John: Knowing Where We Stand*. Welwyn Commentary Series. Darlington: Evangelical Press, 1998.

Barnes, Peter. *The Loss of a Child*. Lithgow, Australia: Covenanter Press, 2000.

Barnes, Peter. *A Handful of Pebbles: Theological Liberalism and the Church*. Lithgow, Australia: Covenanter Press, 2003.

Barnes, Peter. *Both Sides Now: Ecclesiastes and the Human Condition*. Edinburgh: Banner of Truth, 2004.

Barnes, Peter. *Galatians*. Evangelical Press Study Commentary. Darlington: Evangelical Press, 2006.

Barnes, Peter. *Living in a Halfway House: The Rise of Liberal Evangelicalism in the Presbyterian Church of New South Wales, 1865–1915.* Sydney: Revespress Publications, 2007.

Barnes, Peter. *Theological Controversies in the Presbyterian Church of New South Wales, 1865–1915: The Rise of Liberal Evangelicalism.* Lewiston, NY: Edwin Mellen Press, 2008.

Barnes, Peter. *John Calvin, Man of God's Word: Written and Preached*. Edinburgh: Banner of Truth, 2011.

Barnes, Peter. *Lamp Unto My Feet: How God Has Used His Word Through the Ages*. Revised ed. Ross-shire: Christian Focus Publications, 2014.

Barnes, Peter. *Aneityum: Missionary Methods and the Theology of Mission.* Melbourne: Morning Star Publishing, 2016.

Barnes, Peter. *The Forbidden Grief.* Lansvale, Australia: Tulip Publishing, 2019.

Barnes, Peter. *Athanasius of Alexandria: His Life and Impact.* Ross-shire: Christian Focus Publications, 2019.

Barnes, Peter, and Mohamad Younes. *A Conversation Between a Muslim and a Christian.* Eugene, OR: Wipf & Stock, 2023.

Barnes, Peter. *Pain of a Particular Kind: The Loss of a Child.* Edinburgh: Banner of Truth, 2025.

Contributions to Edited Volumes

Barnes, Peter. "The Process of Church Union in Australia." In *Burning or Bushed: The Presbyterian Church of Australia 40 Years On*, edited by Paul F. Cooper and David A. Burke. Sydney: Eider Books, 2017.

Barnes, Peter. "Scottish and American Approaches to the Westminster Confession of Faith." In *Read in the Light: The 1901 Declaratory Statement of the Presbyterian Church of Australia*, edited by Paul F. Cooper and David A. Burke. Sydney: Eider Books, 2019.

Barnes, Peter. "Peter Cameron: Life, Beliefs and Attitudes." In *Principle & Principal: The Other Side of the Rev Dr Peter Cameron Heresy Trial*, edited by Paul F. Cooper and David A. Burke. Sydney: Eider Books, 2023.

Articles

Barnes, Peter. "Good News Bible: Clear and Accurate?" *The Banner of Truth* no. 233 (February 1983): 28–31.

Barnes, Peter. "Open Your Mouth for the Dumb." *The Banner of Truth* no. 244 (January 1984): 17–20.

Barnes, Peter. "Another Gospel Which Is Not Another." *The Banner of Truth* no. 251 (August/September 1984): 61–63.

Barnes, Peter. "William Barclay: an Appraisal." *The Banner of Truth* no. 268 (January 1986): 23–25.

Barnes, Peter. "Use of Church History in Preaching." *The Banner of Truth* no. 287 (August/September 1987): 46–50.

Barnes, Peter. "Loss of a Child." *The Banner of Truth* no. 292 (January 1988): 16–22.

Barnes, Peter. "Do But Themselves Confound." *The Banner of Truth* no. 308 (May 1989): 8–10, 14.

Barnes, Peter. "Obedience to the State." *The Banner of Truth* no. 402 (March 1997): 27–28.

Barnes, Peter. "How We Look at Life." *The Banner of Truth* no. 403 (April 1997): 28.

Barnes, Peter. "Need for Discernment." *The Banner of Truth* no. 401 (February 1997): 25–26.

Barnes, Peter. "Violent Pornography." *The Banner of Truth* no. 400 (January 1997): 17–18.

Barnes, Peter. "Assurance of Salvation." *The Banner of Truth* no. 406 (July 1997): 20–21.

Barnes, Peter. "God Is Not Mocked." *The Banner of Truth* no. 409 (October 1997): 22.

Barnes, Peter. "Holding Two Truths Together." *The Banner of Truth* no. 411 (December 1997): 22–23.

Barnes, Peter. "Difference Between Being Discerning and Being Judgmental." *The Banner of Truth* no. 412 (January 1998): 20.

Barnes, Peter. "Dr Billy Graham Reviewed." *The Banner of Truth* no. 413 (February 1998): 18.

Barnes, Peter. "Biblical Church Discipline." *The Banner of Truth* no. 414 (March 1998): 18.

Barnes, Peter. "Spotlight on Benny Hinn." *The Banner of Truth* no. 416 (May 1998): 20.

Barnes, Peter. "Modern Lunacy." *The Banner of Truth* no. 417 (June 1998): 25.

Barnes, Peter. "Why Church History Is Important." *The Banner of Truth* no. 418 (July 1998): 26.

Barnes, Peter. "Entertainment in Worship." *The Banner of Truth* no. 419 (August/September 1998): 53.

Barnes, Peter. "Fear of Death." *The Banner of Truth* no. 421 (October 1998): 19.

Barnes, Peter. "Limitations of Knowledge." *The Banner of Truth* no. 422 (November 1998): 27.

Barnes, Peter. "Lessons from Psalm 44." *The Banner of Truth* no. 428 (May 1999): 23.

Barnes, Peter. "Miracles and Benny Hinn." *The Banner of Truth* no. 427 (April 1999): 5.

Barnes, Peter. "Using the Old Testament to Evaluate the Modern Ecumenical Movement." *The Banner of Truth* no. 430 (July 1999): 11.

Barnes, Peter. "Handling Disputes." *The Banner of Truth* no. 433 (October 1999): 5.

Barnes, Peter. "The Free Offer of the Gospel." *Reformed Theological Review* 59, no. 1 (2000), 28–36.

Barnes, Peter. "Poisoning of Truth." *The Banner of Truth* no. 440 (May 2000): 23.

Barnes, Peter. "Two Views of Law." *The Banner of Truth* no. 441 (June 2000): 16.

Barnes, Peter. "Tom Wright and Modern Evangelical Revisions of Justification by Faith." *The Banner of Truth* no. 443 (August/September 2000): 40.

Barnes, Peter. "Sleep." *The Banner of Truth* no. 446 (November 2000): 27.

Barnes, Peter. "Is It Right to Fear God?" *The Banner of Truth* no. 447 (December 2000): 26.

Barnes, Peter. "Modern Education: the Missing Foundation." *The Banner of Truth* no. 450 (March 2001): 24.

Barnes, Peter. "Tolerance: a Fruit of the Spirit?" *The Banner of Truth* no. 454 (July 2001): 25.

Barnes, Peter. "Bible's Use of Sarcasm: Irony and Denunciation." *The Banner of Truth* no. 455 (August/September 2001): 50.

Barnes, Peter. "Time and Eternity." *The Banner of Truth* no. 461 (February 2002): 26.

Barnes, Peter. "Violent Pornography." *The Banner of Truth* no. 462 (March 2002): 17–18.

Barnes, Peter. "Killing and Murder." *The Banner of Truth* no. 463 (April 2002): 19.

Barnes, Peter. "Three Illustrations of Salvation." *The Banner of Truth* no. 465 (June 2002): 22.

Barnes, Peter. "Teaching Children." *The Banner of Truth* no. 466 (July 2002): 23.

Barnes, Peter. "Apostle Paul and the Jews." *The Banner of Truth* no. 467 (August/September 2002): 34.

Barnes, Peter. "Glance at Yancey." *The Banner of Truth* no. 470 (November 2002): 24.

Barnes, Peter. "Seeing God." *The Banner of Truth* no. 479 (August/September 2003): 53–54.

Barnes, Peter. "Christianity and Killing." *The Banner of Truth* no. 482 (November 2003): 21–22.

Barnes, Peter. "Election According to the Foreknowledge of God." *The Banner of Truth* no. 485 (February 2004): 7–12.

Barnes, Peter. "What! Me? A Sinner?" *The Banner of Truth* no. 487 (April 2004): 21–22.

Barnes, Peter. "Leadership and the Fear of God." *The Banner of Truth* no. 493 (October 2004): 12–14.

Barnes, Peter. "Books: Why Be a Reader?" *The Banner of Truth* no. 495 (December 2004): 9–12.

Barnes, Peter. "Looking After the Poor: Biblical Principles." *The Banner of Truth* no. 502 (July 2005): 7–9.

Barnes, Peter. "Truth that Sets Free." *The Banner of Truth* no. 503 (August/September 2005): 37–38.

Barnes, Peter. "Coping with Disappointment." *The Banner of Truth* no. 505 (October 2005): 23–24.

Barnes, Peter. "Freedom to Ethics: How Do I Know What I Should Do?" *The Banner of Truth* no. 509 (February 2006): 18–20.

Barnes, Peter. "Perspective on Current Events: Explaining the Australian Riots." *The Banner of Truth* no. 511 (April 2006): 15–18.

Barnes, Peter. "Lessons from Nature." *The Banner of Truth* no. 520 (January 2007): 27–28.

Barnes, Peter. "Cloning Human Embryos." *The Banner of Truth* no. 521 (February 2007): 16–17.

Barnes, Peter. "Christ as God." *The Banner of Truth* no. 525 (June 2007): 17–18.

Barnes, Peter. "Participating in Public Worship." *The Banner of Truth* no. 526 (July 2007): 19–21.

Barnes, Peter. "Wiles of Satan." *The Banner of Truth* no. 534 (March 2008): 20–21.

Barnes, Peter. "Chapter 7 – Key Doctrines." *The Banner of Truth* no. 538 (July 2008): 39–61.

Barnes, Peter. "Can God Just Forgive?" *The Banner of Truth* no. 539 (August/September 2008): 1–3.

Barnes, Peter. "Poverty and Perversity." *The Banner of Truth* no. 543 (December 2008): 20–22.

Barnes, Peter. "Resurrection: What If It Is Not True? What If It Is?" *The Banner of Truth* no. 546 (March 2009): 6–8.

Barnes, Peter. "Commemorating Darwin." *The Banner of Truth* no. 548 (May 2009): 19–21.

Barnes, Peter. "Missionary God of the Old Testament." *The Banner of Truth* no. 549 (June 2009): 22–24.

Barnes, Peter. "Freedom of Religion and a Bill of Rights." *The Banner of Truth* no. 561 (June 2010): 19–21.

Barnes, Peter. "How the Old and New Testaments Fit Together." *The Banner of Truth* no. 567 (December 2010): 26–29.

Barnes, Peter. "Disasters: Weak Human Beings and a Sovereign God." *The Banner of Truth* no. 572 (May 2011): 1–3.

Barnes, Peter. "Prayer: Some Suggestions." *The Banner of Truth* no. 575 (August/September 2011): 1–3.

Barnes, Peter. "Things We Ought to Know." *The Banner of Truth* no. 580 (January 2012): 14–15.

Barnes, Peter. "What We Cannot Necessarily Know." *The Banner of Truth* no. 581 (February 2012): 18–20.

Barnes, Peter. "Augustine's View of History in His *City of God*." *Reformed Theological Review* 71, no. 2 (2012): 90–108.

Barnes, Peter. "Paradoxes." *The Banner of Truth* no. 583 (April 2012): 26–28.

Barnes, Peter. "Same-Sex Relationships." *The Banner of Truth* no. 587 (August/September 2012): 25–27.

Barnes, Peter. "Pointers to God." *The Banner of Truth* no. 597 (June 2013): 8–11.

Barnes, Peter. "Truth Is Offensive." *The Banner of Truth* no. 595 (April 2013): 27–29.

Barnes, Peter. "Abortion: Kermit Gosnell and the Slide to Infanticide." *The Banner of Truth* no. 599 (August/September 2013): 34–36.

Barnes, Peter. "Hard Head and a Soft Heart." *The Banner of Truth* no. 604 (January 2014): 6–7.

Barnes, Peter. "Evolution: Science and Faith." *The Banner of Truth* no. 606 (March 2014): 2–4.

Barnes, Peter. "Chapter 1 – Eternity and Madness in Our Hearts." *The Banner of Truth* no. 608 (May 2014): 39–53.

Barnes, Peter. "How to Be an Evangelical and Avoid the Whole Counsel of God." *The Banner of Truth* no. 613 (October 2014): 2–3.

Barnes, Peter. "Degradation of Words." *The Banner of Truth* no. 615 (December 2014): 2–3.

Barnes, Peter. "Christianity: A Different Way." *The Banner of Truth* no. 618 (March 2015): 2–3.

Barnes, Peter. "Heroes and Models." *The Banner of Truth* no. 621 (June 2015): 5–7.

Barnes, Peter. "Necessity of the Atonement." *The Banner of Truth* no. 623 (August/September 2015): 4–5.

Barnes, Peter. "Everything Is Intertwined." *The Banner of Truth* no. 625 (October 2015): 2–3.

Barnes, Peter. "The Reformation: What Was It About?" *The Banner of Truth* no. 626 (November 2015): 2–4.

Barnes, Peter. "Right Theology Wrong Text." *The Banner of Truth* no. 628 (January 2016): 10–13.

Barnes, Peter. "Western Morass." *The Banner of Truth* no. 630 (March 2016): 27–28.

Barnes, Peter. "Prayer: Our Barriers and God's Helps." *The Banner of Truth* no. 633 (June 2016): 18–19.

Barnes, Peter. "Evangelising Muslims: Five Points of Entry." *The Banner of Truth* no. 634 (July 2016): 7–15.
Barnes, Peter. "Prayer: Some Suggestions." *The Banner of Truth* no. 637 (October 2016): 4–5.
Barnes, Peter. "The Need for Reminders." *The Banner of Truth* no. 638 (November 2016): 1–3.
Barnes, Peter. "Bonhoeffer: Did Metaxas Get Him Right?" *Reformed Theological Review* 75, no. 3 (2016): 170–188.
Barnes, Peter. "Almost a Christian." *The Banner of Truth* no. 639 (December 2016): 1–3.
Barnes, Peter. "Homosexuality: How Should Christians Respond?" *The Banner of Truth* no. 641 (February 2017): 13–14.
Barnes, Peter. "Seeing Ourselves." *The Banner of Truth* no. 642 (March 2017): 1–3.
Barnes, Peter. "Coping with Disappointment." *The Banner of Truth* no. 644 (May 2017): 20–21.
Barnes, Peter. "Decisions Decisions." *The Banner of Truth* no. 644 (May 2017): 6–7.
Barnes, Peter. "Evangelism: Two Models." *The Banner of Truth* no. 617 (February 2015): 2–4.
Barnes, Peter. "Does God Need Us?" *The Banner of Truth* no. 647 (August/September 2017): 14–15.
Barnes, Peter. "Confidence—the Right Kind." *The Banner of Truth* no. 650 (November 2017): 10–11.
Barnes, Peter. "The Religion of Diversity." *The Banner of Truth* no. 657 (June 2018): 10–11.
Barnes, Peter. "What If Jesus Is Good?" *The Banner of Truth* no. 652 (January 2018): 1–2.
Barnes, Peter. "The Attractiveness of Sin." *The Banner of Truth* no. 662 (November 2018): 4–5.
Barnes, Peter. "Hearing a Sermon." *The Banner of Truth* no. 653 (February 2018): 9–10.
Barnes, Peter. "God's Essential Attribute and Our Greatest Need." *The Banner of Truth* no. 656 (May 2018): 1–2.
Barnes, Peter. "Atheistic Miracles." *The Banner of Truth* no. 664 (January 2019): 4–5.

Barnes, Peter. "When There Is Nowhere Else to Go." *The Banner of Truth* no. 666 (March 2019): 19–20.

Barnes, Peter. "Plagues Throughout History and Some Christian Responses." *Reformed Theological Review* 79, no. 2 (2020): 77–96.

Barnes, Peter. "Warfield: Genesis, Evolution, Race, and Eugenics." *Reformed Theological Review* 80, no. 1 (2021): 76–91.

Contributors

Andrew M. Bain is Vice-Principal and Lecturer in Church History at Queensland Theological College (Brisbane, Australia).

Graham Barnes is Pastor of Walcha Presbyterian Church in Walcha, Australia.

Joel R. Beeke is President and Professor of Systematic Theology and Homiletics at Puritan Reformed Theological Seminary (Grand Rapids, United States), Pastor of the Heritage Netherlands Reformed Congregation in Grand Michigan, Editorial Director of Reformation Heritage Books, President of Inheritance Publishers, and Vice-President of the Dutch Reformed Translation Society.

David A. Burke is Moderator General of the Presbyterian Church of Australia and previously served as Lecturer in Ministry and Practice at Christ College (Sydney, Australia).

Michael A. G. Haykin is the Professor of Church History and Biblical Spirituality and Director of The Andrew Fuller Center for Baptist Studies at the Southern Baptist Theological Seminary (Louisville, United States).

Jared Hood is the Principal and Lecturer of Old Testament and Historical Theology at Presbyterian Theological College (Melbourne, Australia).

Mark Jones is Pastor of Faith Vancouver Church (PCA) in Vancouver, Canada.

Brett Lee-Price is a Lecturer in History and Historical Theology at Emmanuel College Sydney (Sydney, Australia), and a Curator of the Arthur W. Pink Archive.

John McClean is Vice-Principal and Lecturer in Christian Thought at Christ College (Sydney, Australia)

Iain H. Murray is an Author, Historian, Co-Founding Trustee and Editorial Director of the Banner of Truth Trust, and Minister Emeritus of the Presbyterian Church of Australia.

Wesley Redgen is Lecturer of New Testament and Greek at Queensland Theological College (Brisbane, Australia) and Pastor of Brown Plains Presbyterian Church in Brisbane.

R. Todd Stanton is Pastor of St Johns Park Baptist Church in Sydney, Australia, and Editor of *Australian Evangelical*.

Geoffrey Thomas is Pastor Emeritus of Alfred Place Baptist Church in Aberystwyth, United Kingdom.

Carl R. Trueman is Professor of Biblical and Religious Studies at Grove City College (Grove City, United States).

Rowland S. Ward is Lecturer in Church History and Research at the Presbyterian Theological College (Melbourne, Australia).

Noel K. Weeks (1943–2020) was a Senior Lecturer in Ancient History at the University of Sydney and Macquarie University (Sydney, Australia).

Bible Permissions

Index

Scripture Index

Genesis

Exodus

Leviticus

Numbers

Deuteronomy

Joshua

1 Samuel

Psalms

Isaiah

Jeremiah

Acts

Romans

1 Corinthians

2 Corinthians

Galatians

Ephesians

1 John

Revelation